MORE THAN A
MILLION
WORTH

MORE THAN A MILLION WORTH

Pradeep K. Berry

Author's Note 360

Copyright © 2021 Pradeep K. Berry

All rights reserved. No part of this book may be reproduced, stored, or transmitted by any means—whether auditory, graphic, mechanical, or electronic—without written permission of both publisher and author, except in the case of brief excerpts used in critical articles and reviews. Unauthorized reproduction of any part of this work is illegal and is punishable by law.

The characters in this novel are fictitious and any resemblance to real persons, living or dead, is purely coincidental. This is a work of fiction. Characters, institutions and organizations mentioned in this novel are either the product of the author's imagination or, if real, are used fictitiously without any intent to describe actual content.

ISBN: 978-1-951670-39-9 (Paperback)
ISBN: 978-1-951670-40-5 (Digital)

AUTHOR'S NOTE 360

10228 Nicolls Avenue, Corona, Queens, New York 11368

CONTENTS

AUTHOR'S NOTE ix
PREFACE xiii
DEDICATION xxvii

1	My Connie	1
2	True Love and Great Destiny	3
3	Our True and Pure Love	5
4	My Heartfelt Tribute to Connie The Painful and Sad Chapter of My Life	6
5	Knowledge Theory vs. Practical for Myself	12
6	The Medical Negligence	17
7	Life and Death Episode Message	22
8	The Story of Sati Savitri	39
9	I would also like to share a true story about faith in religion and greed, I read a long time back	40
10	My Loss and Pain for Connie	41
11	Another Painful Chapter for Connie and Pradeep	44
12	To prove this and as part of my tribute to Connie, I would like to share some remarkable quotes, I studied and knew, but now I am taking them from the internet, to put the exact words	49
13	More Quotes by ChanaKya	51
14	My Uncle's Advice	67
15	Beginning of Our Love	69
16	Connie Was My Destiny	80
17	Some Nice Quotes for our Daily Life	82
18	Gandhi Ji—His Messages and His Teachings	84
19	Nelson Mandela	85
20	Swami Vivekananda	86
21	Education and Career of Connie	88
22	My Connie: The Blessed Lady	92
23	Connie's Passion for Reading	93
24	Reading Passion—Her Intellectual Mind and Brain	95
25	Connie's Love for Music and Arts	98
26	Her Exposure to World Travel	100

27	Connie—Her Charm and Beauty	104
28	Connie's Character and Thinking	106
29	Connie's Character: Part Two	108
30	Connie told me 'Make good use of your time	110
31	I want to feel the presence of Connie in one form or another	114
32	Connie is Still with Me	118
33	Her Home was Her Life	123
34	Cleanliness and Housekeeping was in Her Blood	125
35	Her love for the Best Cuisines	129
36	Great Deeds and Ethical Values of Connie	131
37	Our Love Destiny Would Continue—but with Unhappiness for Me	135
38	Connie and Her Devotion to My Professional Help in Many Places	137
39	Sympathy and Empathy—But Pain	141
40	Cruises—Part of her World Travel	143
41	Connie's Character	146
42	The Truth Always Wins	149
43	Realization and Enlightenment of Pain after Connie's Death	156
44	Different Reactions of People on Grief	161
45	I Can See Connie Everywhere	165
46	My Emotions and India	169
47	My Present Life Pain—After Connie	172
48	Connie Was So Efficient In Everything	176
49	Connie was My Destiny— Like A True Episode on the TV program Wanted	178
50	In my Opinion: The following are Very Strong Points	210
51	April 14, 2016, Pradeep Kumar Berry	219
52	My Connie the Life and After My Connie	232
53	My Connie Her Death—My New Experiences	236

CONSPIRACY	239
SYNOPSIS	265
MEDICAL REPORTS	269
REVIEWS	325

Never seek happiness outside yourself.
Life isn't about what happens to us; it's about
how we perceive what happens to us.
Master your past in the present,
or the past will master your future.

—Open Your Mind, Open Your Life: A Little Book of Easter Wisdom by Taro Gold

AUTHOR'S NOTE

IT WAS A VERY SPECIAL GIFT IN my life from heaven to earth, perhaps was sent or was born in Glenview, IL USA in early February 16. She was Miss Constance Ann Fuller, who later became a senior professor of English, Spanish, German, and French in the USA, after her Ph.D., MBA from the University of Michigan, and Undergraduate from the Carlton College in Northfields in Minnesota, USA. Was it a destiny? Created by the supreme lord to have had met a newly migrated Pradeep Berry from Delhi to Frankfurt to Chicago on January 15, 1976, at 5,15 PM and was picked up by my cousin' husband Late Mr. Bhim Hans and was taken to his house in Park Forest, IL USA. Pradeep Berry was served Indian food and a glass of Shivas Regal Scotch by his Cousin Mrs. Bala HansDaughter of my Father' elder sister or granddaughter of my grandfather, late Lala Durga Parshad Berry, a wealthy merchant in Delhi, Amritsar, Punjab and Bombay. He had died on October 27, 1969, after his wife's death on August 17, 1969. Had he been alive, Pradeep Berry would have never ever been allowed to leave Delhi, India to either join the family business or strict to my Chartered Accountant Practice in Darya Ganj, Delhi. It is like a CPA practice. I therefore have high respect, love, memories, and blessings from Miss Constance Ann Fullerbut now Mrs. Constance Ann Berry since our secret love marriage on the afternoon of January 28, 1976, at 4.16 Am in the Chicago Courtroom. It was a wonderful love at first sight on January 24, 1976, at the Gateway to India Restaurant at 1543 North Wells Street Old town Chicago, IL USA. It was just a beautiful song cum gift from the lord when a beautiful young girl and a young boy fell in love immediately after two hours of conversation with her and her friend Miss Whitney Lombard. The rest is a history till June 23, 2021.

In my whole life, I always respected women during my childhood, and teenage years. However, finally, when I met my future wife on the evening of January 24, 1976, at an Indian restaurant in the famous old town in Chicago, IL USA at the Gateway To India Restaurant on 1543 North Wells Street at the last window table of the Indian Restaurant with her student and a friend Miss Whitney Lombard, I knew she would be mine one day. It was a beautiful educated young girl Miss Constance Ann Fuller, A Professor of English literature, Spanish, German, and French in the Chicago University in Chicago, IL USA. It was a wonderful first sight of love—the way we both had a wonderful intellectual conversation about our family, friends, educational background, humanity and kindness towards others, and happiness in helping others. At the same time, we both were very happy with being able to make a happy evening at the Gateway to Restaurant. The Head waiter Siraj Khan and the busboy Thomsas Cheri-an and the hostess Miss Dennise Ferguson went ahead to get them a Check and an Indian Tea on the house was a very gesture for them as a customer. In return Miss Constance ANN Fuller left a 30 percent tip on their check which was shared by Siraj, Thomsas, Dennis, three chefs, and perhaps myself. They also had a very nice beautiful white scarf on their wallets to make a small token to Miss Dennise.

I was absolutely surprised when I saw them going to get their valley parking in a Blue Volkswagen car with IL license plate CP 1614CB. I was absolutely taken by the license plate number: CConstancePPradeep, 16 is her birthday, 14 is my birthday, C is Constance, B is Berry. Oh, my lord please forgive me for any thoughts except for my life with my future wife, if it can be Miss Constance Ann Fuller. Thanks for the wonderful gift my Lord bless our life and happiness if we ever get married to each other. God was very happy and kind and both Miss Fuller and Miss Whitney were in the same table the next day on January, 25, at 6.15 PM for Indian dinner and it was the day we both decided to have a personal meeting at her house at the 1836 Lincoln Park West in old town Chicago near the Lincoln Hotel and it's still there. We both were in love and we decided to have our blood test on January 27, 1976, at the Crawford clinic in Skokie, IL next to the Skokie Memorial Park. I would never, ever have imagined that would be the place I would have to take her ashes in her plot after her Cremation on March 3, 2015, at 11. 30 Tuesday and March 4, 2015 at noon for chapel of peace and her beautiful grants stone on April 10, 2015, with her name, Mrs. Constance Ann Berry. My most precious darling wife for over 43 years with her date of birth and date of death February 28, 2015, where I go regularly till June 15, 2021.

In our Hindu Dharm, women are prayed as goddesses in the temples as Durga Mata, Kali Devi Mata, Bhavani Mata, Amba Mata, Jagdambe Mata, Pravati Mata, Gori Mata, Gayatri Mata, Sita Mata, Laxmi Mata, Saraswati Mata, Vaishno Devi Mata ever since the time immemorial. However, I would like to add that I, Pradeep Berry not only loved my wonderful wife Connie, but worshipped her as my wife, My best friend, my sister, and even my mother. This was also mentioned in the Chanakya 'book Arthashastra in 521 BC by KautilyaChanakya 'second name as can be found on google and Internet. I would like to thanks my readers, Publishers, family, friends, fans, Audience when I had been interviewed by the President of the TV Channels in Atlanta, Georgia, New York, Los Angeles, Los Vegas, India, Hollywood, Bollywood industry in the USA the German Book festival and London Festival in London, United Kingdom, and the USA. The interview of Husband Pradeep Berry has been watched by over millions of people who had written their thanks to the Author of the book in the USA and India until June 16, 2021. Besides the thanks at the Book festival in the Los Angeles, New York book expos, Miami Dade College in Miami, Austin Texas Book festival, Delhi Indian book festival, German, London, Paris, Toronto, Mexico, Denver, Tuscan Arizona, Book fair.

My Connie

www.bookofmyconnie.com

Untold Secrets of My Connie
My first and Last love with Medical Negative and Conspiracy

www.myconnie.com
www.authorpradeepberry.com
www.conniedarling.com
www.ahrunpradeep.com

Pradeep Berry on Google and YouTube.

Written by her husband Pradeep BerryB.COM, Honours, from Shri Ram College of Commerce, Delhi University and a Battalion Sergeant in the NCC and Eagle Scout and Swimming Captain and a senior banking executive and MBA from the elite USA University whose American-born wife Ph.D. MBA Masters and the senior professor Spanish German and French in the USA and USA Army Base in Germany and France, Mrs. Constance Ann Berry.

PREFACE

Hi, ever read a story that put you on the edge of the seat and changed your perspective? Well, here's one such story! It starts on January 15 of 1976 with a young Indian man on a Lufthansa flight Pradeep Berry—a trained accountant—was headed to Chicago from his Native Delhi, During a 5 hour layover at Frankfurt airport, Mr. Berry was already having second thoughts about the transatlantic journey ahead! And he sure wanted to get back home to beloved India, Only there was one problem… He only had $7 left in his pocket—not enough, by any means, to procure an air ticket back to beloved Delhi He consulted the captain of the Lufthansa flight asking whether it was possible to turn back and pay for the flight upon arrival His only move—the captain said—was to proceed to Chicago and then wait 14 days for the return flight So as fate would have it, the young Indian man would land in Chicago. Raised in a very strict atmosphere in India, Pradeep had finished his undergraduate education and chartered accountancy At the time, he was an extremely qualified professional in Delhi, and was offered many senior positions in different parts of India, along with other career opportunities However, a very senior school friend of his, a then professor at an elite US university had come to Delhi and suggested he move to America. So he began to see a possible future there. Now in Chicago, the young man was edgy and homesick desperate to get back to Delhi. He remembers asking a relative who came to pick him up at the Chicago airport if they could arrange for him to go back to India the next day. Not even dinner and scotch—on that very first night in America—would calm his nerves. He could only catch some sleep after midnight and woke up by 5 a.m. feeling panicky, depressed, and helplessly homesick As the popular proverb goes, *the future belongs to him who knows how to wait.*

Within days of living this quagmire, the young Indian man would meet a beautiful young American woman who would change the the course of his life—forever Mr. Berry met Miss Constance Ann Fuller at an Indian restaurant on the historic North Wells Street in Chicago It was love at first sight—straight out of a storybook From the first word go, the couple had a way of relating to each other. It took 60 minutes for Pradeep Berry and Miss 'Connie' to know they were destined for each other And days later on January 28th, 1976, Connie and Berry were happy to legalize their union in Court—despite no family members being present Barely days after he was itching to leave America and get back home to India, Pradeep was now married to an American sweetheart So much for expectations! In Pradeep's own words—Connie brought happiness and a new passion for life to him. Although he had mentioned to her that he still wanted to go back to India, Connie requested that he see some parts of Chicago before he left. She took him to the Museum of Science and Industry, the Art Institute, Northwestern University, the University of Chicago, the Shedd Aquarium, McCormick Place, Michigan Avenue, Lakeshore Drive, and many restaurants around the city. Soon enough, his desire to return to India was distant but live ember! Although he already had a superb education in India, Pradeep was encouraged to pursue an MBA in America. Initially reluctant, it so struck him that education had no end, and that an American MBA would prepare me for more knowledge and advance his career worldwide. And this brings us to a critical phase in this eye-opening story! The coming of age of this young Indian in the land of opportunity! And the start of an enlightened career—over 42 years—that we can all learn from. Pradeep remembers the challenges he had with his first job, with an an employer who withheld his wages for no good reason It took the effort of his partner—Mrs.Constance Berry—threatening to report this employer to the IRS and Labor Department for him to get his full dues. Soon after, Mr. Pradeep realized that he was better off focusing on his field of experience So he took a job in the field of finance, where he had a formidable educational background. Within 3 months, he already had his first promotion…never to look back again! Due to his hard work and commitment—thanks to encouragement from his spouse—Mr. Pradeep's employer paid for his MBA at an elite university. Before long, he was traveling across the country on professional assignments. It doesn't take much effort to appreciate the contrast and gravity in Mr. Pradeep Berry's progression. Upon landing in the States, Pradeep had been itching to get back to India on the round-trip ticket. He only wished to stay 14 days as he waited for the return flight. But meeting his soulmate seemed to change everything. The 14 days became 6 months. Soon enough, he had no intention of going back to India. Connie served as a key pillar of support for Pradeep during these first days, months, and years in America. Although Pradeep was already a smart and motivated young man back in his native India, it took Connie to bring out the best in him—and set him on a path of career and professional success. Soon enough, he had won the respect of his family members back in India. And his source of encouragement—Connie—had become the star of the family. It is thanks to her that Pradeep quickly internalized American culture, learning to dress, interact, and speak in a way that advanced his career.

During the late seventies and early eighties, Pradeep and Connie worked very hard to build their careers. Mr. Berry remembers that on Saturdays, although he didn't need to do any work, he would get up in the morning and work on his reports because he wanted to master his field and advance his career. It appears, in Pradeep's view, certain things helped him grow from a confused young immigrant to an executive senior management consultant in the banking and finance sector. First and foremost, a CULTURE OF READING. From the onset, Pradeep had learned from Connie that reading would stimulate him and turn him into an intelligent person. Mr. Berry says that his spouse's average reading time was four to six hours a day when she was working. When she took early retirement, her average reading was fourteen hours a day. Well, for most people, this would seem like an impossible feat! Pradeep caught this powerful habit and improved his grip in his areas of interest. A few years later, he was writing articles for MBA students from top institutions across the country. He would write professional pieces on commercial lending, mergers, and acquisition. In the course of doing this, Pradeep learned a lot about hostile merges, how to set up companies, how to run companies, and how to leverage businesses. He recalls that thanks to his reading habit, he was able to pass over eighty professional development courses while working for different finance companies and banks, which were instrumental for career development. Mr. Pradeep also lets us know that balance is important. Outside of work-related topics, he would also read on a variety of interests: from ancient Indian civilization, Buddha, Shakespeare, the Bible, the Koran, Indian classical music, Mozart, and Broadway shows. This way, he also developed his personality outside of work! The second most important factor that we can learn from Pradeep's inspiring story is THE VALUE OF EXPOSURE Right from whence, he was an immigrant trying to figure out his next step, Pradeep got lucky to be exposed to American culture by his beloved Connie. This would prove to be a precious gift for his career advancement. Pradeep would feel embarrassed when his lover would see him as an individual who was not well cultured. But he later learned that this was for his benefit. Pradeep argues challenges us to take initiative to gain crucial exposure in environments where we wish to excel Throughout his professional career—Pradeep has met many people—including his distant family members, who have refused to adapt to elements of the American culture And this is because they do not take initiative. Rather than spend their time constructively, they do their work half-heartedly. Pradeep shows us that it is nearly impossible to gain progression with this kind of lackluster attitude. In this made-in-America story, we also learn that WORKING HARD AND SMART PAYS Pradeep learned during his career progression that education is a constant, daily habit. That nothing comes easy in life. Although degrees have a finite point of completion, education, systems, and technology keeps on changing whether it is in banking, finance, or computers. For example, in banking, different structures have been developed for different kinds of lending. The author would make a point to learn about all these systems… Because he wanted to be innovative and resourceful. It is this very attitude that allowed me to have a fruitful career in one of the most competitive sectors of the economy. And while it is important to work smart and be innovative, Pradeep's the story shows the value of DOING GOOD. One of his professional assignments took place in Ohio in 1987. In this case, a business owner had defrauded Pradeep's employer—then one of the largest corporations in the finance world. Pradeep was working in senior management. He had sent many junior and middle-management personnel to sort out this particular case but without success. So he resorted to solving it himself. On a visit to the subject business premises, Mr, Pradeep learned that the business owner was in hiding, and he had left strict instructions for his employees not to allow any access to the premises or share any documents.

Bringing in his expertise in crisis management, Pradeep was quickly able to get the business owner out of hiding and sit down with him He was candid with him and let him know that the company was highly disappointed with his elusive tactics, leave alone the fraud. He made it clear that his employer would take severe action that the the business owner would regret for a long time. Within no time, Mr. Pradeep was able to turn this situation around. Seeing that Pradeep meant every word he said, the business owner agreed to pay his dues—although he had to sell all his assets (including personal ones) to do this. He even had to sell his car and house. Within a full year, Pradeep's employer had been paid the sum owed which was a lot of money! But the business owner was stuck between a rock and a hard place. So Pradeep chose to do something special—he decided to help this very person.

He decided to refinance his home and find him a decent job. This way, a troublesome situation ended up as a win-win for everyone. Mr. Pradeep's employer was very happy with his work! On a personal level, he had also been able to help an American citizen in need. Effectively hitting two birds with the same stone. Pradeep remembers many other situations where he was able to do GOOD while doing an otherwise tough job. He used these same tactics in difficult situations working in Michigan, Austin, Columbus, California, Seattle, Indiana, Baltimore, New York, New Jersey, Chicago, Denver, Philadelphia, Phoenix, and many other cities.

Starting from NOWHERE and ending up as a highly successful MANAGER in the financial sector, Mr. Pradeep shares his next to—an impossible story as an encouragement to all of us He was encouraged to come forward and share his trials, tribulations, and moments after the loss of his beloved Connie on February 28th 2015.

Mr. Berry has authored two books, My Connie, and The Untold Secret of My Connie to chronicle the diamond of his life—the pillar of his support—Mrs. Constance Berry. Thank you for your kindness and generosity to support dear Dr Mrs. Constance Ann Berry Ph.D. MBA Phil for your kindness and generosity in making my life to be a successful banking consultant and an author of 4 books's on my life with you and your Life with me for 44 years and still new in my life that I just met Miss Constance Ann Fuller Ph.D. MBA Phil American born girl in Glenview IL USA and A professor of Spanish German french and English education department in USA and Germany and France and Spain Army Base and a true humanitarian for the children of St Jude's hospital, cancer and much other humanity's values and teaching the kids and high school Free as birds to avoid having to go through poverty and a few other things I knew you were going to be a part of your life with a passion to see you and your husband Pradeep get a chance to look over the world and the different causes of humanity in his own life, as he and his brother Arun Berry and sister Pappi or Kiran Revri suffered after Both brother's and sister were raised in unexpectedly like orphans and a few other things, which were very painful in my childhood including my elder brother Arun Berry and sister Pappi Berry.

However, Connie was a great wife for 44 years knew all that when she was going to Delhi India on vacation 9 times noticed all that and had told my late father and grandparents who were trying to get out from the embracing situation and A falsely on Connie's view based upon the American people.

Motivated by MY first AND LAST LOVE, MRS CONSTANCE ANN BERRY, PH.D. FROM HARVARD UNIVERSITY, MBA FROM THE UNIVERSITY OF MICHIGAN AND PHIL FROM CARLTON COLLEGE IN NORTHFIELD, MINNESOTA, USA A PROFESSOR OF SPANISH, English LITERATURE, GERMAN language, French GERMAN in the USA army base IN Germany, FRANCE, SPAIN, AND Mexico.

Later in the UNIVERSITY OF CHICAGO ILLINOIS and The UNIVERSITY of Southern California IN Los Angeles AND Heywood UNIVERSITY in California AND Morton Grove high school district students in Morton Grove and EVANSTON; for 40 years until; Mrs. CONSTANCE ANN BERRY DIED OF MEDICAL complications from medical NEGLIGENCE AND CONSPIRACY by HER biological Brother AND HIS WIFE ON FEBRUARY; 27, 2015 at 11 AM OF FEBRUARY 28 2015 PRADEEP BERRY ON GOOGLE LinkedIn AND

Facebook AND Twitter are in memory of MY CONNIE MY first AND LAST LOVE The BOOKS

1. MY CONNIE
2. Untold SECRETS OF MY CONNIE MY first AND LAST LOVE WITH MEDICAL NEGLIGENCE AND CONSPIRACY

Were happily written BY HER husband PRADEEP BERRY ON AMAZON and BARNES AND NOBLE AND other WEBSITES IN the world.

> Thank you., for your thoughts and prayers, and I reciprocate the same to you and your family. It was wonderful to attend the SRCC Alumni on January 3, 2020, and on February 9, 2020. It was my first time, where as I used to attend the Harvard university in Massachusetts with my wonderful Connie, university of Michigan and Carlton college in the USA for my wife. On my note, Alumni of Kellogg Graduate school of management, where Connie and I met late, Mr. Arun Jaitley when he was a communication the minister during Vajpayee' time, when dr Dipak Jain took over the dean of Kellogg graduate school of management from dr Donald Jacobs, Our current principal, Dr. Kaur met Dr. Jain, who too lives in Evanston, Illinois USA. He was also the dean in an NSED in France, where Connie was the professor of American literature, Spanish and German in the Army base and in Germany too.
>
> Now I am writing books for my life and my wife Connie and the humanitarian crisis and depression and suffering from the darkness in our lives and happiness?????? Need your blessings from our wonderful friends…
>
> Sincerely, Pradeep Berry

I also met My chartered Accountant buddies in Delhi India this time, they all were in Shri Ram college, Darshan Kumar who now has a mega store in Kamla Nagar extremely bright and had gone to Nigeria and now opened a wonderful mall Megam?? Moti lal Jotwani, Ramesh Khanna (apparently died last year??) Sudhir Singhla, sorry to see him suffering from cancer in Bengali Market Life and death are?????? On the morning of January 15th of 1976, a young Indian man boarded a

Lufthansa flight headed to Chicago across the Atlantic. This young man—Pradeep Berry—was a highly trained chartered accountant who had toyed with the idea of moving to America on the suggestion of a former classmate who worked as a professor there. But immediately the plane left the Delhi airport on its way to a 5-hour layover in Frankfurt, Germany, Pradeep had second thoughts. All of a sudden, he felt that it had been a terrible idea to leave his motherland India for a distant foreign land. By the time the plane hit the airport runway at the Frankfurt stopover, Pradeep had already made up his mind… He was going back to India! But there was one problem, He only had 7 dollars in his back pocket—not enough to buy an air ticket back to India. So as the universe would have it—Pradeep landed at the Chicago airport hours later, Promising himself to be back in India on the return ticket two weeks later. What Pradeep Berry didn't know is that hidden out of sight, around the corner was a beautiful story that would change the rest of his life. A few days later while hanging out in the city before his return trip home, the young immigrant met Miss Constance Ann Fuller at an Indian restaurant on the historic North Wells Street in Chicago. She was a beautiful and intelligent lady and told him that she had finished her education from Carleton College and the University of Michigan. She was currently teaching while pursuing another Master's degree in Spanish and French. It was love at first sight. He shared his background and let her know that he was set to fly back to India after a couple of days. But Miss Constance suggested that he explore Chicago and learn about the American culture before going back. At least that way he could have some real benefit from his visit to America. She took him to the Museum of Science and Industry, the Art Institute, Northwestern University, the University of Chicago, the Shedd Aquarium, McCormick Place, Michigan Avenue, Lakeshore Drive, and many restaurants around the city. Soon enough, the itch to go back to Delhi had faded and Pradeep was convinced to stay a lot longer and pursue an MBA in America. Pradeep recalls how that first hour when he met Miss Constance was a miracle, a golden minute that would lead to forty-two years of a happy life. As this story is all about! It was evident to this pair that they were soulmates—destined for each other.

    The chemistry was instant! Barely weeks after Pradeep arrived in Chicago, the couple legalized their union in a Chicago court on January 28th of 1976. Pradeep remembers—fondly—how meeting Connie changed his sorrow, sadness, and homesickness. And how it contributed to priceless happiness to his life! Pradeep would learn how Connie loved classic songs from singers such as Frank Sinatra, the Beatles, Elvis, Abba, Christmas music, Mozart, many symphonies. She had two gramophones and old records of singers like Cliff Richard, Tony Christie, and Ray

Charles. And he became extremely fond of all this, gaining a keen interest as well. He came to love Broadway plays and the couple attended many shows together. Connie was also an art enthusiast collecting many artistic pieces for their house. She kept decorative art objects for the house, kitchen, study room, and bedroom. She also collected several historical paintings. She took Pradeep to see many art and cultural shows, expanding his knowledge and outlook! Pradeep's wife and soulmate—Mrs. Constance Berry—would also expose him to a world of travel, planning cruises and trips within and outside the United States. He reckons that without her—he probably would never have traveled the world for leisure. The pair traveled to India seven times, exploring many beautiful places such as the Palace on Wheels, Taj Mahal, Jaipur, Kashmir, and Khujuraho. They say that a successful marriage requires falling in love many times over, always with the same person… Well, Pradeep's union with Connie was the epitome of this! Through the years, they picked and shared many interests, learned from each other, and supported each other through life's challenges. One thing that we can clearly learn from this beautiful story is to make good use of time.

During the late seventies and early eighties, Connie and Pradeep worked extremely hard to build their careers. Connie had completed a master's in Spanish and French, studied at top colleges in Mexico and Spain, and taught these languages to the children of US military members in bases located across Germany, England and Spain for 5 years. She later taught in California before later moving to her hometown of Chicago, where she met Pradeep. While married to Pradeep, Connie would obtain a Ph.D. and further her academic career, eventually becoming a highly esteemed professor.

On his part, Pradeep took an MBA to further his already shining credentials as a chartered accountant—thanks to Connie's steadfast encouragement. He started work in the United States and climbed up the ladder in the financial sector. Pradeep shares how Connie instilled the habit of making good use of his time. On Saturdays, although it was not mandatory to work, he would wake up in the morning and focus on increasing his knowledge.

Connie would read for hours on end—each day—on various topics of interest! This intellectual culture would be very instrumental to the couple's career growth and fulfillment. Another major important aspect that viewers can learn from this the lovely story is the element of support! Pradeep truly believes that his success and career advancement were only because of Connie. She introduced him to American work culture, even going as far as to help with grooming that was right for the professional setting. Connie's support was not only work-related but also extended to Pradeep's personal life! He remembers one instance when traveling to Palm Springs in California.

The roads were very curvy in a mountainous region and Pradeep was feeling a bit on edge regarding driving. It only took a few words from Connie to get him to relax and build his confidence back. This kind of support would encourage him to become a very confident driver, and overflowed to every other area of his life.

Pradeep and Connie learned several philosophies from leading thinkers, leaders, and authors such as Swami Vivekananda and integrated them into their daily life. Yes—it takes a lot of courage and intent to achieve 42 years of a happy, priceless marriage! All of us—young or old—can learn a lot from this. Mr. Pradeep recommends that you have a bond of love, care, and respect for each other in your marriage. As well as full trust and honesty. And to plant your relations as we give water to the plants. These—and other crucial lessons about this extraordinary love story are also expressed in Mr. Pradeep's book, My Connie. *In the second part of this story—and a heart-piercing twist of fate a sad chapter rolled a curtain on Pradeep's life on February 20th of 2015.*

He remembers how his darling Connie fell from her bed at home—on this very fateful date He took her to a checkup at the hospital, where she was required to stay for longer despite her results coming out as normal Connie was to be discharged on February 22, 2015, but this would never come to pass. She suffered cardiac arrest and, after six days, and died on February 28, 2015.

Ironically, this was the day when the pair had been scheduled to travel to Sanibel Island. Over the last decade, Connie and Pradeep had hunkered here during winter—an escape from the cold and snow. It was inevitable that this trip be canceled—following negative reports from a hospital.

Selflessly, Connie had suggested that Pradeep go if he wanted But there was no way he could do that. He couldn't even fathom the idea of going to Sanibel without her All he wanted to do now was to stay and be there for his darling Connie.

From an early age, Pradeep had learned that life is a duty and that this duty must be performed with happiness. Only that for Connie—it was beyond a duty It was love from the bottom of his heart and soul! And when love is involved this way—it becomes a purpose Pradeep remembers how Connie's sickness had begun in 2013. This—and the strain it put in her—would be the pivotal changing point in their out-of-a-storybook marriage story. In the face of the challenge, Pradeep was reminded of Lord Buddha's story. One day Lord Buddha—a spiritual leader who lived in ancient India—came across a lady who was praying to get back her dead son.

Buddha told the woman that if she could get him a bag of rice from a house where there had been no tragedy for five years, he could bring back her son. After going from house to house day and night, the lady was unable to find a household that was free of tragedy. This way, Lord Buddha made her realize the suffering of everyone on this planet. Mr. Pradeep had a great understanding of death and spirituality. But despite knowing that we have no control over death, he was not ready for Connie's demise… Furthermore, they had positively shared that they would live to old age. Connie had a history of longevity and good genes in the family, with many of her relatives living to the ages of 90. Furthermore, she emphasized Good health throughout the marriage, She was careful about the diet, swam regularly, golfed, walked, and engaged in a lot of household and outdoor activities. Pradeep remembers how Connie kept her brain in shape by reading for hours on end. She even served as the president of his building association for twenty-five years and had traveled extensively over the years. Despite all this, the cruel hand of death had taken his beloved so mercilessly! Leaving him in severe pain… Like a fish without water, or an animal being slaughtered—in his own words.

Although many people told him that it would take six months to one year to overcome this painful and shaking trauma, Mr. Pradeep has had it much worse—all a sign of his true love for Connie. Pradeep's pain is made worse by the fact that—he believes—there was medical negligence in taking care of his wife in her hour of need. Mr. Pradeep strongly feels that CPR was delayed and later only performed when he ferociously complained. And that he learned from medical records that Connie was denied her Power of Attorney. He is also troubled by the fact that when his beloved Connie had a Cardiac arrest, she held his hand and wanted to say something. And it bothers him that he didn't know what she wanted to say. This terrible—following more than 4 decades of a happy marriage and companionship—is understandably excruciating. But in yet another lesson that we can all benefit from—Pradeep Berry shows incredible resilience and courage in the face of devastating loss.

Sharing with the world his true love for Connie, and all the immortal moments that they shared. Pradeep has authored 13 books,

- Author, "The Mysterious Death of My American Wife" (2021)
- Author, "Deepest Love Between an Indian Husband and American Wife, Ended on Medical Negligence and Conspiracy" (2021)
- Author, "The Death of American Wife in America" (2021)
- Author, "Well Planned Medical Negligence and Conspiracy" (2021)
- Co-Author, "My Shobha" (2021)

- Author, "The Medical Conspiracy Behind My Wife's Demise" (2020)
- Author, "My Connie Was My Life, Mu Wonderful American Wife: Our True and Pure Love" (2020)
- Co-Author, "My First and Love Last: My Shobha" (2020)
- Author, "The Medical Negligence and Conspiracy: The Demise of My Wife" (2019)
- Author, "The True Story Behind My Wife's Death: My Connie" (2019)
- Author, "My Connie: The Untold Story of My First and Last Love" (2018)
- Author, "The Untold Secret of My Connie, My First and Last Love: Medical Negligence and Conspiracy" (2018)
- Author, "My Connie" (2017)

My Connie,
Untold Secrets of My Connie My First and Last Love With Medical Negligence and Conspiracy
The Medical Negligence and Conspiracy that Led to Demise of my Wife Connie,
And finally **More Than a Million Worth**
All in honor of Connie and her memory.

My biological brother, Arun Berry is going through the loss of Shobha, his wife Mrs. Shobha Berry who died on November 8, 2018, with whom he has been married for 46 years. My biological sister Mrs. Kiran Revri too died on December 20, 2019 whose mother Mrs. Kanta Berry or Kanta mummy was my and Arun Berry'second mother who died in November after the birth of her mother Mrs. Kanta Berry or Kanta mummy when Mrs. Kiran Revri was only one hour old and, we three had to face our third mother, Mrs. Uma Berry, who was very keen to have her children and we three were brought up by our grandparents Lala Durga Parshad Berry and Shri Ishwar Dass Mehra, who took Care of my sister Rita Berry or Kiran Revri. Lala Durga Parshad Berry took care of both Arun Berry and Pradeep Berry during our childhood I have been flying back to Delhi to spend time with Arun and his family in Delhi.

My sister Pappi Berry or Kiran Revri who was married to Mr. Surinder Revri of Alliance furniture died on December 20, 2019. Her mother was The second mother of Arun Berry and Pradeep Berry. After the Death of Arun and Pradeep Berry mother, her sister married my father and she died after 5 years and sister

Pappi Berry was born. Father third wife and she would not Care for the three of us and wanted her children and took our inheritance and housing. It is okay now. She did what was in her mind and it was our fate and in return, I got my Connie my first and last love Mrs. Constance Ann Fuller Ph.D. MBA Phil American born girl in Glenview IL USA and a chartered accountant from the Institute of Chartered Accountants in India and A.B.Com honors from Shri Ram College of Commerce Delhi University India left Delhi to Frankfurt to Chicago, Illinois USA on January 15, 1976, and met Miss Constance Ann Fuller Ph.D. from Harvard business school and Phil from Carton college in Northfield Minnesota and MBA from the University of Michigan and A professor of Spanish German french and English education in University of Chicago, Illinois USA met Pradeep Berry on January 24 1976 and A love on sight was so much more than a love which landed in Chicago Illinois USA Court without any relationship of miss Constance Ann Fuller and Pradeep Berry for the court marriage certificate on January 28, 1976, and this marriage lasted until Mrs. Constance Ann Berry Ph.D. MBA Phil left for heaven unexpectedly on February 27 2015 at 11.10 am of February 28, 2015 in the Evanston hospital in Evanston IL USA, in my opinion due to the medical Negligence and conspiracy by the dismissed doctor and Mrs. Berry's biological brother Michael Fuller and his wife Mrs. Suzanne Fuller whose conscience is an awful Pitt and a cold blood humans loving to the world they visit the church and gives a big show, as how wonderful they are. A family of one thing, Money and money. Perhaps, I would forgive them, but the Supreme Court or the Supreme Lord would not and would like that they pay for their wrongdoings in their own lives and they would pay from their nose.

This book is the 14th book based upon a true story of an amazing Soul. An American born girl in Glenview, Illinois, USA, educated at the University of Michigan, Carlton's college in the USA. A professor of Spanish, German, and French In the USA, Germany, and France. Pradeep Berry a Delhi, India, born Chartered Accountant, MBA From an elite university in the USA and a senior banking executive Is her husband since January 28, 1976, in the USA is still crushed, devastated and grieving for his darling wife Connie and keeping himself busy writing about her life and her great deeds which made him a happy humanitarian partner of his wife who donated to many charities and research. 'This book is the greatest tribute to a wonderful lifetime US-born wife of a Delhi, India, born US Citizen and senior Executive banking consultant in the USA after her unexpected demise by malpractice and medical Negligence and conspiracy. An inspiring story and a motivational speaker has been the most crushed husband while he was seeing his first and last love was dying in front of him in the Evanston hospital in Evanston IL USA on February 27, 2015, at 1.10 AM of February 28, 2015.

Are we truly honest with ourselves? Are we? How many times we evaluate this hidden truth in a day or month or a year or we don't even think about it?? This is a great question, we don't know, neither, we want to know or discuss ourselves or with anyone else, except, we are extremely sick or old or going through a life of our own shadow. Please make a habit of making the game of chess mentioned above very clear by the self-realization that we are what, we don't know or we're not true to ourselves and we must correct it before we leave this earth.

Let's go to the humanitarian mission and humanitarian values to leave behind our names so that this world would remember us. Let's stay away from the crowds and leave behind a legacy of good deeds and humanitarian values.

That is what my wife Mrs. Constance Ann Berry Ph.D. MBA Phil a professor of Spanish, German and French did as she taught for 39 years, suffered from two cancers, looked after her parents and her husband Pradeep Berry and left charities for Education, cancer. Hospitals, research, hospice care, palliative care, schools, animal's, blinds, st Judes hospital are some of the charities after her demise by malpractice and medical Negligence and conspiracy' as mentioned in the book untold secret of my Connie my first and last love with medical Negligence and conspiracy By her husband Pradeep Berry on Amazon and Barnes and Noble and Walmart. www.myconnie.com www.bookofmyconnie.com Pradeep Berry on google and YouTube Don't deprive someone of the hope that may be the only thing that they may have. Miracles happen every day. Don't hurt someone and remember the power of the Supreme Lord who watches us All the time and knows our daily karmas good and bad We can cheat and fool an individual but not The Supreme Court of the Lord We are Born to do great things in this Life and perhaps in the next few lives if we can. The more we all open our minds to other humans and potions to serve humanity's values, opinions and viewpoints the greater is our understanding of others. The more we are curious about how and why things are the way they are, the clearer our minds become much more clear than we can think about. Let your kindness and generosity to the world keep going and going to the whole universe and brings happiness and joy to the humans and animals and the friends and even your enemies.

It was an emotional roller coaster ride in life with a woman, who was born with a disability in Chicago. I knew her father and mother and, after her father died and her mom was looking after her, she suddenly suffered from depression and dementia, but she died on May 20, 2020 and., it was my frustration and shared life of your own is own???

A true but temporary effect of anger for me on her innocence and upsetting day. Now, May 22, 2020, I absolutely cannot be a cruel man to think of a woman who has been born with disabilities and she is now grieving for her mother who died in Honduras and daughter wants to bring her ashes back to Chicago to be placed next to her father. Thanks for getting back to my thoughts about her feelings and I decided to make her a happy person as I would not have a negative comment about her like May 20, 2020. It's a new enlightenment for me and I ask forgiveness from her and my god and god to bless me with a better more passionate person for her and for humanitarian happiness and life for others. Today, May 20, 2020, I absolutely realized that your blood is your own, no matter how much you care for a nonblood friend. The realization came when a Lady of 49 years, who has been staying with me since, February 18, 2020, and her reaction was so different on May 20, 2020, when her mother died in Honduras and, knowing the shock of her mother's death, she's going to have sympathy from her blood siblings and her family, getting no more support from me, and wants to be her own family and siblings. However, I have been a great support to her and she is not getting any comfort from me. She considered me her best friend and family, but May 20, 2020, her happiness is gone, which I consider being a great loss for her and attitude of not getting a peace of mind is towards her own family and not thinking about me and now, I would have to think about myself as a widower, after the death of my Darling wife Mrs. Constance Berry Ph.D., MBA, Phil a professor of Spanish, French, and German was a great wife for 43 years and her death caused me the most crushed and unhappy life with a void in my life.

Humanity has no end to the life and happiness for humanity to itself and to be spread for the world to know you are doing, but do your duty and be a silent partner.

> *Humanity is a great silent society to help others and not for advertisers to show you are doing let it be a silent auction or an unknown number. A sincere man feels for the troubles and tribulations of others and tries his level best to alleviate their sufferings. He is very sympathetic, soft-hearted, and also generous. He is always reliable, quite frank, honest, and true. He is free from crookedness, hypocrisy, cheating, and double-dealing. People place implicit faith in his words.*
>
> Pradeep Berry

DEDICATION

June 16, 2020, I went to 1543, North Wells Street, old town Chicago to visit and pay my tributes and love to my late wife, Mrs. Constance Ann Berry Ph.D. MBA and Phil met me on January 24, 1976, at 5. 45 PM at the Indian restaurant, Gateway to India at the above address. We both met and our love was our first and last love to marry her on the 28, January? 1976. She was miss Constance Ann Fuller Ph.D., MBA, Phil a Professor of Spanish and German, and French. It was a great love on sight that lasted 43 years until she died on February 27, 2015, at 1. 10 AM on the morning of February 28, 1976. It was a wonderful gift of God to me and my family to have a great peaceful relationship with my wife Connie Berry, who was behind my success in life, career, humanity, and happiness throughout our life. Thanks to my wife for this gift to humanity and to survive in my life… There was a new renter in the 1543 North Wells, Old Town, Chicago, IL, USA and he showed me his apartment, where I lived with three chefs and it was a very difficult emotional experience on June 16, 2020. Pradeep Berry signed a book for his help to show me his apartment where I lived. Later, I went to 1836, West Lincoln Park West in the old town, Chicago, IL USA, where Connie was living and I went to meet her and we were very close to coming to our life partner and we immediately got married after 4 days till she died on February 27, 2015, on the morning of February 28, 2015.

Seeing the same apartment where I stayed in Chicago after I moved to the USA and meeting the future wife, Miss Constance Ann Fuller? The future Mrs. Constance AN Berry Ph.D., MBA, Phil. Thanks Connie. More Than a Million Worth is a wonderful gift to humanity written by her husband Pradeep Berry Author of six books.

We have to bear in mind that we are all debtors to the world and the world does not owe us anything. It is a great privilege for all of us to be allowed to do anything for the world. In helping the world we help ourselves. A sincere man feels for the troubles and tribulations of others and tries his level best to alleviate their sufferings. He is very sympathetic, soft-hearted, and also generous. He is always reliable, quite frank, honest, and true. Heisfreefromcrookedness,

hypocrisy, cheating, and double-dealing. People place implicit faith in his words. (Swami Sivananda) Connie was the perfect person for admitting her or her family and her husband's faults and to humanity and to admit the facts of life and death in a positive way to improve her own happiness and unhappiness and suffering with her different faces of life and her emotions. Thanks to my wonderful wife Connie?? A More Than a Million Worth.

1
Introduction

My Connie

"My Connie,"—truly, an extremely rare, priceless, precious destiny and a special gift from God to me—we were *"two bodies with one soul."* Before starting this biography of our true love, I have to give my highest tribute to my Connie and how she became an immortal love for me, a love that will, perhaps, be immortal for us both. I write this book to share my love and to give maximum credit to Connie for this love, for destiny, and evergreen lifelong love. This book, with valuable messages about the nature of love, is a creation of the love and hope, and faith we shared. Imagining this destiny and love is the only comfort I have left. I had never realized how life can be changed by love, and through my devotion to fulfilling Connie's desires, I am sure God would fulfill my wish and hers. Perhaps it is a difficult test of life, an exam we had to face to pass again with a Gold Medal in our next love. In this book, I examine how destiny and love and have shaped the course of my life.

Hauntingly Disturbing Pain Every Moment It is extremely important to mention that Connie's demise is the most painful and is in my mind every moment of my day and night. Even before sleeping, when I dream, and when I get up, pain and thoughts are wandering in my brain. I feel like I am dreaming, but then I wake up, and I start to think so much and face reality and my life. I can emphasize that Connie's love is in my mind every minute of the day, except when I am sleeping. However, the moment I am up, my pain is extreme. In addition to thinking about her, I am still avoiding reality and don't want to believe at all that Connie, my darling has left me. I then go through the pain and it upsets my mind, body, and soul. I don't know what to do and how to cope up. I start looking at her pictures and videos and her computer, chair, walker, and whatnot. I can't think if I am getting peace of mind or more pain. But then I try to compromise by praying at her pictures and touching her chair, her computer, and walker. That gives me some peace mixed with pain, and the lights in her study room are a small solace. It still looks as I am on a business trip and would be with her on Friday. I was dreaming that she is no more, which took my pain to the extreme. That time I was totally in a world of thoughts, specifically, how intelligent, intercultural, and intellectual she was. I have never met a wife like that. I have compared too many of my family and friends, but I can't find anyone like her. I then suffer from extreme unbearable pain. I go into deep thoughts and stops whatever it is I am doing for a short time or even for a long time. I then have to force myself to concentrate on the things I was doing or was planning to do. This much distraction is due to our love, but the love we had for each other. After that, I want to be alone and be isolated. I read one quote, "Life asked death, why people love me but hate you? Death responded, because you are a beautiful life, and I'm a painful truth." Yes, it is the most painful, unexpected, and unbelievable thing. I've always wondered why God didn't grant one thing and didn't hear my prayers. Is God so cruel to his followers that He doesn't listen to my prayers and my friend's prayers? These things are still rattling in my mind, and it is so painful, specifically when you love someone so much.

2

True Love and Great Destiny

TRUE AND PURE LOVE OF ANYONE—WHETHER THAT person is your significant other, mother, father, or whomever—is a double-edged sword that brings pain and joy. If, on one hand, you were never gifted with that love, you would not feel as much pain when the loved one passes. However, if you have been blessed with deep love, the downside is that the pain is so much deeper after they are gone. According to Khalil Gibran, the Lebanese author, life and death are one "even as the river and the sea are one." Gibran also writes that "Like seeds dreaming beneath the snow, your heart dreams of spring." He says to trust in your dreams, for in them is hidden the gate to eternity. I also turn to the holy words of Lord Krishna, as recorded in the *Gita,* a Hindu religious text that is used in courts of law. In this book, when Arjun was grieving over the death of his son Abhimanyu, Lord Krishna told him, "Why grieve? What son? Whose son? It was a mortal relationship and with death, mortal relationships break for good." "Soul has already taken a new birth," "Do your duty by killing your enemy brothers who betrayed you and killed your son, otherwise they will kill you and your four brothers." This true episode is one of the most popular and powerful in Indian history as recounted in the Sanskrit epic history, Mahabharata. The story of the Mahabharata can be found in texts, films, and internet searches. Further, many American and Indian stage actors have played this episode on the stage all over the world.

Speaking of the fleeting nature of life, Lord Buddha wrote that, "Our body is given by our parents and nourished by food; therefore, it will be destroyed one day." This quote comes from one of the books on Lord Buddha that I read in school. A quote in India, "Sadanaamparmatamakahai," which means "God always exists, but there is no relation with anyone before birth and after death," speaks to the fact that our existence is temporary. However, despite this knowledge, it is not always possible to realize this pain we experience when a loved one leaves us, vanishing in an instant. The knowledge provides no solace and it is extremely painful when losing a loved one. The degree of pain we each feel depends upon the love or the closeness of our relation, and we may feel more pain for the loss of some loved ones than we do for other friends and acquaintances. It depends upon the depth of love that we feel, and with that love, we may hope that it will become easier to cope with our loss, although that may not be true. Rather, as time passes, the pain gets worse and we withdraw from our former desires to travel, to dine out, and to do other great things that we used to do with our lost ones and leaves us wanting to live an extremely simple life. "Thinking of you much at this difficult time. What we know is not much. What we do not know is immense."—Pierre Simon Laplace, mathematician, statistician, physicist, and astronomer.

> "One or the Other" One or the other must leave. One or the other must stay. One or the other must grieve. This is forever the way. This is the vow that is sworn Faithful till death do us. Braving what has to be borne Hiding the ache in the heart One whomsoever adored, first will be summoned away This is the will of the Lord. One or the other must stay.
>
> Edgar Guest

Yes, these are great words and philosophies about the loss of loved ones, and may not hold universal truth—or be true for everyone; however, it doesn't provide me with any comfort, solace, or peace of mind. The loss I feel has vanished all of the comforts I once took in spiritual and religious learning and left me with unbearable pain that will last during my lifetime as I withdraw from the world we explored together. Our relationship was and still is extremely strong, built on true love, attachment, and devotion to one another. The death of one half becomes a living death for the other half.

3

Our True and Pure Love

Now I will talk about my most precious love and the friendship I had for my darling wife of over thirty-nine and a half years, Mrs. Constance "Connie" Ann Berry, Constance A. Fuller. We both not only loved but worshipped one other for our pure and true love. I can say with great pride, that we were true *"two bodies and one soul."* Our love was a special gift granted by the Supreme Lord. That kind of love is, in my opinion, extremely rare, and results from a unique destiny. I am reminded of a book I read, I don't remember the name but it's a wonderful song and poem of love. The pain of losing that love rattles me to the bone, while at the same time, I cannot believe the whole happiness and the world are over for my other half.

4

My Heartfelt Tribute to Connie The Painful and Sad Chapter of My Life

THE SAD CHAPTER OF MY LIFE AND the trauma I went through began when Darling Connie fell from her bed at home on February 20, 2015, and was taken for a check-up to the hospital. Although the results were normal, the hospital kept her for two days for observation. Connie was to be discharged on February 22, 2015. However, this never came to pass and she died in February, 28, 2015. The 28th was the date when we were to travel back home from the trip we had planned to Sanibel Island, where we had been going for the last ten years to be away from the cold and snow of late winter in Evanston. We canceled the trip in November 2014 after the negative report from Mayo Clinic that placed her on palliative care, meaning that her cancer had spread in her airways and there was no certain cure. Connie was so considerate; she said, "I hope you're not disappointed that we can't go." She stated, "If you want to go, you can go." I replied, "No way. I would never go without you anywhere. I cannot even think about that. I will be with you no matter how much cold or snow I have to suffer." I was taking full care of her with great happiness. The message, "Do your duty. Life is a duty and you must perform your duty with happiness" came to my mind. "If you cannot perform your duty, sit outside the church, temple, or road and ask for alms (money).

I believed this message about duty all my life, but it pained me to think of staying in Evanston as my duty, as it was not my duty but necessary for my wife. It was my love and care from heart and soul, and for the first time, I rejected this message of my childhood. I may or may not pass this message of duty onto others, particularly the young generation, however, for Connie it became a hurtful message. I asked myself: What duty, which duty, whose duty, why is the word duty in the dictionary? Duty may be bothersome, but not when love is involved, then it becomes a true purpose.

My purpose was to save my beloved Connie from demise, but I lost that battle and it bothers me. I asked God: "Why did I lose that battle." I was serving her like we serve God, and why didn't God see that devotion, knowing that it was loved with devotion. We both had the most important thing: we were one loving couple and extremely happy with each other and hoping that the supreme Lord would watch our true love and would grant us our one wish and not separate us. Again, we were begging the supreme Lord to extend our love and Connie's life. We knew God was always watching our love and sincere devotion and we asked for any forgiveness. There was a time when Connie acted as a mother to me as well as my wife. Now, when Connie was sick, especially from April 2013 onwards, my devotion, love, and pain, was beyond reach and I asked God one thing only: "My supreme Lord, please grant Connie a long life, take some of my karma and give it to Connie by curing her and extending her life. Evaluating our deeds, we realized that we both did good deeds and perhaps our few mistakes were mitigated by good ones. In balance, it seemed that the good was enough to ask God for Connie's health and life in return. I begged as a mother asks for her child. Lord says "I would help you, my child," as seen in the churches. What happened to that child? The answer is very clear for us all.

I have great knowledge of spirituality, death, and birth. These are things over which we have no control, especially death. In spite of this, I was not ready for Connie's demise. She had told me her family had a history of long life and good genes, living up to the ages of ninety-two to ninety-five. She was very positive and had tremendous good health throughout our marriage. She was intelligent and active. She said she would live a long time as she had been swimming regularly for years, golfing, walking, doing all the household work, cooking, shopping, teaching, and driving. In addition, she spent hours reading, was well versed in computer technology, served as the president of our building association for twenty-five years, had knowledge of building laws, watched all the best movies, traveled extensively, pursued higher education, and lived a healthy life. She was extremely careful about our diets. I too also believed and knew she would be given that inheritance of long life. However, I was not sure about my longevity, as my birth mother died at age twenty-six after leaving my elder brother and me at age eleven months and two months respectively. My younger aunty—my mother's sister—was forced to marry my father, to avoid bringing a stepmother into our family. She was married to my father for five years and died at the age of twenty-five, two hours after giving birth to my sister. After her loss, my father married his third wife from another family—our stepmother, who separated us from my father and had two boys by him. She is still alive at age eighty-eight, but my father died at age eighty on November 14, 2003. My paternal grandparents died at eighty-one. My maternal grandmother died at age fifty-six and my maternal grandfather at ninety-three. However, I was quite convinced with Connie's positive approach that I believed we would live until we're ninety.

I mentioned my childhood pain as Connie is not with me, and that brought back the pain of my childhood to some degree, but Connie's loss is more painful than childhood pain. Perhaps, as part of my tribute to Connie, I am writing about this chapter of my life. Otherwise, I would not have written too much pain about my life and my brother's life when we were young in India. As described above, after the loss of our two mothers, our father was controlled by my stepmother. It is hard to believe, but it happened to us and we were raised by both our grandparents. After the demise of my paternal grandparents, my father and stepmother, two of my uncles' wives started treating us badly and started asking me in particular to do so much household work. They would set me to counting thousands and thousands of huge delivery boxes from fifty to eighty trucks and then tell me to open and count the inventory every morning at 4 a.m. After that, I would eat breakfast, take lunch for my uncle when he was in the hospital, study, and go to school. I went to college and finished my Chartered Accountancy—a high powered post-graduate degree. During this time, I would take dinner to my elder uncle in the hospital, studying and sleeping there like a nurse. These paternal aunties would give us food, but after a while we felt that they were obliging us rather than caring for us, although all our living expenses were met by the family business. This situation greatly bothered my father's elder brother. But he was at a loss on how to help us; to fight with four to one was a losing battle. After his marriage, my elder brother was asked by my aunts to take his separate kitchen apart from the rest of the family, although he and his wife lived in our family mansion. I started eating with him, as my brother asked me not to eat with our aunts and uncles anymore. It was a little shock to my aunties when they realized that they had done something wrong and they felt guilt for their behavior towards us. My brother insisted that I not eat with them as he was hurt by their actions. My aunties were telling me that they did not separate me from the family, but I did what my brother told me. Although the electricity and water bill was paid from the business expenses and we were staying in one of our big mansions with no cost to us, the family did not show us generosity. Later, these aunties tried to insist that we pay for our electricity and water bill, but my father's elder brother intervened and insisted that there was no way he would allow us to pay anything. I want to tell a true story about witnessing my grandfather's grief with the death of his son, my uncle, who was only thirty-two years old. When my Grandfather Berry came to the cremation and saw my Grandfather Mehra, realized that he had not understood the pain of Grandfather Mehra for the loss of my mothers, his two daughters. Grandfather Berry broke down and apologized sincerely and from his heart, saying that now he knew what it was to lose a child and felt deeply for Grandfather Mehra's losses as well. This touched me deeply as a child, and I look back at that moment sometimes when I think of my Connie. Her loss brings my childhood suffering back to me. All of these forgotten things come back to haunt me. I am still willing to forgive and forget again, but the pain of Connie's loss is killing me. As powerful as that moment was, it is lost in my pain for Connie. Four months later, Prime Minister Pandit Nehru died from the shock of China's conflict over the Dalai Lama in 1963. When he died, I was in my uncle's room and my grandmother was lying on the floor, weeping. In reality, though, she didn't weep from the shock of Nehru's death, but from the death of her son. I was also weeping for Nehru who I had met many times and regarded very highly. I truly grieved for him. My grandmother told me, "Pipo, why don't you go and attend Nehru's last rites?" I told her that it would be too difficult for me because of the security that would make getting across the city almost impossible. She told me that I should go to see if it would heal me. I realized that I wanted to go, and immediately I thought that maybe I should wear my Eagle Scout uniform. I also had my Boy Scout bicycle, and I went to get it. Right away, I started pedaling. I crossed all of the roads, crossed police lines and no one stopped me they started saluting me because Boy Scouting was very renowned at the time. I was able to get close to Nehru's body, and I saw his funeral. I was both happy and sad, and when I returned home, my grandmother was pleased that I had gone to see Nehru's cremation. It was healing for her to know that even Nehru, a powerful man, could die unexpectedly as her son had. I wanted to give this speech at an Eagle Scout ceremony for my nephew, but I will share it here now instead. After that function, Connie told me she would no longer attend functions for my B family in Chicago. That day, July 14, 2012, I forced Connie to come with me to a graduation ceremony for my cousin's daughter in Orland Park despite Connie's determination to avoid that part of the family. Connie was not feeling well because she had just finished her chemotherapy, but she was such a good person that she accompanied me so that I would not have to go alone. We were both welcomed like a king, and there is no doubt that my cousin and my uncle were very happy to see us. After that, everybody came to us and they were very nice, but after greeting us, they only comingled with other Indians. V.B. took our pictures, but later on, a 100% change came because Indians remain Indians and they showed us that they did not want to associate with my American wife. V.B. had no choice but to call some American guests, as his daughter went to school with Americans and the kids and their parents had been invited. My cousin played loud music and tried to show off, which looked shallow. We could not socialize over the sound of the music. We wound up sitting with a nice American couple, trying to talk, but we all began to feel angry that we had been placed off in the corner. Connie was offended and left the party early, leaving me. My uncle was the only one who was bothered that she and I left early, and no one ever called to check if we were okay and asked why we left the party early. To this day, nobody called me to check how I am or ask why I left early. Even my family who was born and raised in this country have never thanked me or called me.

During her sickness, I had many job offers for senior positions, but I refused these. For the last forty years, I have wondered why, and I think the reason is that I wanted to leave the painful atmosphere of my family home. Now I am convinced that it was my destiny to have Connie as my wife. I am happy that I forgot my Indian career and would take Connie as my destiny over wealth and a great career in all my future lives.

Only I can feel my loss, no matter what family, friends, and outsiders trying to tell me; no matter what they say in sympathy or to provide me comfort and take me out of my loss. It has no effect on me, on my loss, and the sorrow of my daily existence. I only want one thing—Connie. Later, I will discuss the trauma we went through, the pain and suffering of her illness, and the events of her last eight days in the hospital. I can never forget those events nor can I forgive her doctors. There were more positive than negative in my life due to our love, and I am writing my experience of grief. I do not want to offend anyone. I know many people have gone through the same loss, but I am concentrating on my pain. My friends and relatives know my trauma and pain, but cannot understand what I have gone through and I still going through today, on March 27, 2016. I am not ready to follow anyone's advice or to try to forget the past. I want to bear this loss alone, grieve alone, cope alone, and find some temporary ray of light, although darkness will always be in my heart and soul. I am trying to stay healthy, keeping myself busy working on legal cases and housework. I feel that the cleanliness of our home is important, as Connie was a perfectionist and always kept a spotless home. I have written a separate section about the importance of her housekeeping.

I am working all the time to get justice for Connie's early demise, which, in my opinion, was the result of her doctor's negligence. Everyone tells me that even if I get justice (which may take years or even not happen because doctors are politically powerful), what will I gain? Connie cannot come back. I don't want to listen to that. I have lost my one love. I am very well aware that people die suddenly, but I am angry—angry that God did not listen to my prayers and devotion. The one thing I wanted was for Connie to get better, no matter how much I had to sacrifice or how much hardship I had to bear.

I lost that battle and I feel angry with my Lord—why did God not see our devotion to each other and give her an extended life so that we can have our end together? I am not a cruel person, but it has taken my happiness away and left me with pain, and made me withdraw from the world. I no longer do the things I did with Connie. Now, my life is limited to traveling to India to visit my brother. I don't have much of social life. I make business calls and run errands. Some people I speak to analyze our love, but some do not. I am not asking for any sympathy, but I do respect what people tell me. I get some happiness from my brother, his family, and my grandnieces in India, and some good friends in the US, but darkness follows every moment in my heart and soul.

5

Knowledge Theory vs. Practical for Myself

AT SOME POINT, WE MUST COME TO the following realization of death: everyone has to die—man is born alone and will die alone. Does death become destiny or destiny become death? Everyone has their faith in this dynamic puzzle and some try to cope with the imminence of death early in life, while some choose not to think of it depending upon their *love*. When we lose a loved one, we all think that if the perceived cause of death would not have happened, perhaps death could have been avoided. Few examples, if he or she would not have traveled, had not driven, had not gone out in the night or attended a wild party with heavy drinking and driving, had not ridden in a car without a seat belt, hadn't gone boating in the night, perhaps death could have been avoided. Yes, we all realize that death will come, but when it does we are filled with regret. That is the first reaction of someone about death. However, our old sculptor Vedanta says—*death or destiny*. This comes from our ancient beliefs that I learned when I was sixteen years old. Was it destiny that Connie's death came, or was it due to negligence? Some people commit suicide, some shoot others and then kill themselves. Alcohol and accidents, car and motorcycle accidents all take lives. Connie and I always remembered one incident that happened thirty-five years ago. I was driving on Edens Expressway with Connie around midnight while coming back from Oak Park, IL, after a party. We both saw a big man in his 40s speeding on his motorcycle. Connie and I were surprised by his speed. Connie told me, "I do not understand how some people are so daring and take their life into their own hands. Look at him, he might be going over 100 miles an hour."

Connie and I discussed how bold this person was to drive at such a high speed. Connie said, "I am surprised that he is taking such a risk, and without a helmet." She mentioned that she worried about him slipping on the wet road as it was raining and that we should pray that nothing will happen. A few minutes later, we saw him coming towards us, going south in the northbound lane. He crashed into the wall and died on impact. Cell phones were not available in 1983, so we went to look for a phone booth. But before we had gone far, three police cars arrived on the scene. Would you call this his destiny or the result of his lack of common sense? Connie always told me to drive defensively and with full concentration and to avoid driving at night, especially when we went to parties and functions. She was always careful to make sure that we just had one small drink. I had the habit of drinking three or four scotch and sodas, whereas Connie never liked me drinking that much. She would only have one drink and had good control over her habits. I don't know how she put up with me at that time, and I asked for her forgiveness for my childish habits. Although I didn't see it at the time, now I know I was wrong. I regret it and think about her love, the care and concern for me which she had from the first time we met. I even think of that time, that place, and our expressions and happiness. I see that moment in my thoughts and have gone to see that place many times and stay there for hours thinking. The place is there today—the windows, stairs, neighborhood, and street are still as they were, except for minor changes on the side roads. The street names and roads are still the same, and the place where I lived when we met is there. We walked together on those streets for safety. She had to put up with my childish habits although it made her angry. I realized her advice was right and wanted to cut back on drinking. God helped me one day in 1989, and I decided I would try not to drink the next day, which was a Saturday when I would not have to go to the office. I had a wonderful meal and a lovely sleep. Since then, I have never touched even wine or beer. My relatives and friends were shocked and begged me not to be a saint and to have just one drink, but I made my decision not to. A few times when we were flying first class, I was tempted to have a few drinks, but I decided not to start alcohol again. That was my final decision that I have lived with until today, August 16, 2016. When we used to drink, I had the habit of continuing to buy liquor wherever there were great sales. Connie asked me why I would stock up on liquor, which takes up space in our home. Once I quit, Connie was amazed until her death by my determination. My brother and friends were also amazed. Why drive in the dark when you can drive in the sunshine? During snowstorms, drive in the morning when you can see more clearly. It has been over fifteen years since we found out that the motorcyclist in the horrible crash was not drunk, but driving and speeding for fun. Connie and I discussed that accident with many of our friends, and they all agreed that he must have been stupid and brainless. Our Vedanta would say it was his fault and that if he did not drive carelessly, he would not have died. After Connie's demise, even if someone gives me millions of dollars, I will not drive on the highway for more than a few miles.

Our life was most wonderful from our marriage throughout the forty-three years we had together. Every moment of those years is on my fingertips and running in my head all day like a movie, and it is painful. I must write that our love was so special that her death crushed me forever. This is because of our love. I cannot help repeating many parts of our love. Now her death moves around in my mind all the time, and I openly write and admit that I do not like to deal with anyone, nor do I like to be social as every moment Connie comes into my brain, my mind, and my soul. I always keep with me her pictures from throughout her life, in my pocket, my jacket, and on my phone. I also wear some of her unisex chains and watches. I do not want to give away many of her things, nor do I want to sell them no matter how much someone offers me in cash. Our love and sadness during her last few months from 2013-2014 were worse, and February 2015 was like death for me when my Connie died. I cannot ever forget our forty-three years of marriage, and I can say that every moment is like a photographic memory for me. Six years ago, Connie and I attended lots of parties and I loved driving at night, drinking, dancing, and going all over the city. In India, and perhaps in other old civilizations, people think that when death has to occur, it takes the person to that place where death is to occur. To some degree, I believe this because I have seen many instances of this in my life. I would give a few examples to demonstrate.

The story involves a friend of my Uncle Belh and his wife, my English aunty. Their marriage is more proof that love is blind. My uncle, Dr. P.N. Belh, was a world-renowned dermatologist who studied and practiced in the UK and US before eventually returning to live in India permanently with my aunt. He traveled the world for conferences and served as a visiting professor in numerous institutions. My auntie's parents would visit her and my uncle in India frequently.

In the early 1920s, a young Indian Muslim boy, Rashid, left India for the UK at the age of six. Eventually, he was befriended by my aunt's parents who raised him like a son. Rashid remained a bachelor his whole life and lived with my aunt's family. In time, Rashid became the Surgeon General in the UK where he met a young PN Belh at a hospital and decided to give the young student a chance. Uncle Belh eventually got a medical internship from Rashid, and they became friends. In 1971, after the death of Mrs. Behl's father, my aunt, her mother, and Rashid came to India for a six-month visit. This was Rashid's return to India after eighty years of living in the UK. At the end of their stay in Delhi, my aunt's mother and Rashid planned to leave for their return to the UK on a Sunday night, however, Rashid chose to stay two extra days for work. My aunt's mother, Violet, flew back alone, but upon her arrival at home, she got a call that Rashid had passed early Monday morning. His body was immediately buried, according to Muslim tradition. Violet returned to Delhi and tried to take Rashid's body back to the UK for interment, but to no avail. For the next several years, my aunt's mother continued to travel between the UK and India to visit her daughter and family. Many years after Rashid's death in 1976, my aunt called me to say that her mother was coming to visit me and Constance in the US. A day later, my aunt and uncle called again to say that Violet had passed away in Delhi. She was cremated and buried next to Rashid in Delhi. Was it her destiny to die in India in the same way her adopted son had or did this just come to pass by chance? Another story that happened in my family was the tragic death of my cousin, Dr. Behl's son Anil. We were very close growing up, and he was a gem of a person. I taught him Hindi when we were young, and we became great friends, as close as brothers. I was like a father of sorts to his little sister, Vinita. He was studying for his M.D. and was dating a girl, Neera, who was like a sister to me. Anil was crazy for Neera, and they were very close. What happened was that Anil went to England for four months with his family, and while there, Mrs. Behl had a car accident and was very seriously injured. Dr. Rashid and Violet called Dr. Behl and told him many times to come to see Marge, but he did not go because he was devoted to his work. At that time, Anil Behl was away from Neera for two years, and I used to talk to her every day to see if I had any news about Anil. Finally, Dr. Behl called Mrs. Behl and Anil and threatened to disown him if he did not return to Delhi. Anil started studying his M.D. in Gwalior, and was again away from Neera. Neera sacrificed for all these years, and finally, they got married. I was already in the States at this point, and had not been here long when I got a call from my family telling me that Anil was killed in a car crash. I sent a telegram to Dr. and Mrs. Behl and Neera, who had a one-year-old daughter, Natasha. When I went to India, Anil was gone but seeing Dr. Behl for the first time brought new life to us both because we had been mourning his passing. Later, Dr. Behl adopted an orphan, Shushil and they loved him very much. He had no job as an adult, so Dr. Behl set him up as a businessman, and then later on Shushil got married and Vinita was very nice to him. Later on, they had to work through difficulties, but they resolved those with my help and now everything is okay. At her wedding in August 2003, which Connie and I were able to attend, Natasha was able to include the memory of her father and grandfather, and she paid tribute to them, to me, and Connie.

While some people's deaths seem predestined, other people fall asleep and simply never wake up in the morning. People get heart attacks while driving, while in the house, while in an ambulance, and die. Some get saved. Who or what should we believe and why? Do we justify the reason for a loved one's death for our solace as God's decision? Or do we place blame on a series of events and decisions to explain why the person went to that place of death? Would they be alive if they had not gone there? I think no one knows the answer, and if someone says he knows, perhaps, he is justifying death to himself and others. However, even those who believe that life and death are in the hands of God and fate will still question whether a loved one might have lived on if particular events had never come to pass.

6

The Medical Negligence

How do we explain death as God's choice or destiny if there was clear negligence by the medical doctors? In our case, I argued for two years that Connie's doctors caused the problem, and I needed to let other specialists examine her case. When doctors are overconfident, they think they know best and ignore the intuition of their patients and families. Connie's doctors discouraged us from going to Mayo Clinic for a second opinion, asking us what the doctors at Mayo would do when the doctors here in Chicago were already doing everything to diagnose her illness. How can we justify this kind of hubris from doctors? We trust doctors to save our lives, placing them next to God. Doctors have the power to play with our lives, and even those with good intentions may promote a new drug or play into the plans of pharmaceutical companies to make money. In this equation, some people gain, some lose, some live, and some die. A good physician will always refer a patient to a specialist when asked or when realizing that he or she cannot handle the case or may have misjudged an initial diagnosis. An overconfident doctor who feels that he can handle every case is a dangerous doctor. Rather than admitting that they need help, these doctors fear embarrassment. To bolster their egos, they may risk a patient's life.

I may be naive, but I believe that three or four instances of this sort of medical negligence cost me the last ten or twenty years of life I expected to share with my Connie. It would have been easy for the medical profession to prevent her early death as some wrong treatments were given to Connie by overconfident doctors pursuing the wrong diagnosis. She went from pursuing a route back to health to palliative care after Mayo Clinic detected what her two doctors had missed. God did not want her to retreat to palliative care but rather wanted her to continue to fight on. Otherwise, a third doctor who took over her case after Mayo Clinic would not have given us hope, he would have told us that her end was near. Instead, he was full of hope and ready to pursue a new treatment plan. He was prepared to correct the mistakes of past doctors but was never given the chance to help her heal as the hospital's terrible mistake finally cost Connie her life.

About a month ago, I started looking at the medical documents for myself, especially from February 20-28, 2015. The night of the 27th, at 1:10 a.m., my Connie left for heaven, but I immediately went to hell. Many people from different parts of the world have told me for the last forty-two years that heaven and hell are right in our lives. No special heaven or hell is waiting after death. But most people say that the beloved is in heaven, in peace. I never used to discuss this subject, however, I have seen people who are suffering and living in hell, whether they are ill, crippled, suffering from tragedy, or going from wealth to poverty. Some people go from a grand lifestyle to begging for alms, lose a high-powered job and are unable to find work, or find themselves working for minimum wage. I have seen this happen to many people. Is that hell? Then where is the real place for hell? What happens to the soul and body, and where does the soul go? In India, the body has to be cremated, and in many countries, the dead are cremated and interred in the ground. Connie never did anything bad, but she was in hell. Yes, she got sick and later became extremely sick due to the negligence of her doctors. I went to every doctor's appointment with Connie, and she was not given proper care. In my opinion, there were many errors, and some of her medical records were falsified. I was in the hospital with her twenty-four hours a day for eight days. On the 22nd of February, at At 6 p.m., Connie was fine, and at 6:15 p.m., she had a salad. At 6:30 p.m., she had a cardiac arrest. That was the most dangerous thing, and CPR was not performed for one hour. That was the beginning of the end, her death warrant. You could see that the nurses and doctors did not want to perform CPR until I aggressively demanded it. This delay was the beginning of her death.

On the 27th of February, I was gone for less than two hours, and, in my opinion, the doctor we had dismissed as her doctor had no business coming into her room. He caused her tubes to be taken out without my permission, and he had no business even being in the room. I believe that he chose to let Connie die to protect himself from the ramifications of his neglect, rather than admit he had botched her treatment. Upon my return, the doctors and nurses did not acknowledge that I had power of attorney. And while I was forced into hostile arguments with them, they were eight people against one.

They told me that they did not care for my wishes, as they had to respect her wishes. It was all made up, as Connie was crippled and not able to speak or write anything due to the tubes in her mouth and on her hands. I was unable to fight them, and I stayed and talked to Connie after her tubes were out, and she desired to live and come home. So much went on, and no one was helping Connie. In my opinion, the doctors falsified the reports and the document where, according to them, Constance signed her DNR order. That document is not in her medical records, and even today, August, 16, 2016, the hospital has never been able to produce the document.

Mr. (name withheld),

Thanks for your kind message, and you must have received the medical records and discussed the entire story. I want to add that Constance fell from the home bedroom in the morning of the 20th, the day she was to have chemotherapy. An ambulance was called for precaution, and they took her to North Shore Health Care in Evanston. She was kept for a night for urinary tract infections and was to be released the next day as her tests were okay. I saw the DNR code and Constance and I told Dr. X and Dr. Y on the phone to change to full code DR to save her from any cardiac arrest or problems. Both Dr. X and Dr. Y came to the room in front of me and the nurses, and assured us that they have changed the code and Constance will be saved by all means and that's what Constance and I wanted. We were assured and Constance was to be released on the 22nd or 23rd of February 2015. She ate some salad around 6:25 in the evening in front of her caretaker, me, and a nurse. Soon, she felt some sort of breath problem and got a cardiac arrest. I called a nurse and other staff came and requested the doctors to perform CPR, but the doctors refused as the DNR wasn't changed. I shouted like a tiger for them to do the CPR. My tiger's voice and shouting scared them and they did the CPR, but eight to nine minutes were wasted, and most likely that was the first step for her death. They were clear that the tubes would be out on Tuesday, March 2, 2015. I had to make the decision to take her home with palliative care or take her to Holy Family Hospital after they make a small hole in the neck and later rehabilitation. The hole would be closed after she is absolutely fine. They were sure it would work but do I have to go through all that. I told them yes and would take a great gamble, and Constance told me by my writing notes and body language and I was prepared to take her to the Holy Family Hospital. The second reason for her death was again Dr. XB, who had given the case to Dr.MN who was no longer her doctor and had no business hanging around that room and area. In my opinion, he achieved what he wanted—death. He had no business to persuade palliative care and the same nurses who were telling me that I have to make a decision by March 2 and the same with the palliative care doctors reassuring me that they would respect what I want. Constance and I wanted anything to avoid demise. XB wanted death and therefore, when I was gone for two hours to North Brook on Friday, February 27, 2015, XB and his cronies told me when I got back at 1.30 p.m. that they are going to take out the tubes against my will and against Constance's wishes which I have. She marked that I should decide as she wants to live to beautify her home. XB did not listen and said that Constance told him to take the tube out. Absolutely lies. She hated XB after MCR gave us a negative and palliative care report. We both had been blaming XB and never wanted to see his face. Tubes were taken without our permission around 3:00 p.m and Constance was talking to me until 4:30 p.m. but the palliative care doctor came to tell me that Constance may not survive as we promised that we would shift her to the palliative care unit, and after few days, the doctor said, "Mr. Berry, you can take her home with our team and she might live one to even ten years as she is doing well." However, no care was given after 4:30 p.m., Friday. Weekend fun. Everyone was gone and no one came until I was yelling, screaming, and shouting. I have thirty-two minutes worth of videos and a six-minute video from my wireless phone. One can see Constance was suffering, I was shouting and nurses were walking around but no one came. It was after I made fifty phone calls from my wireless phone, and later at the hospital when finally Constance died at 12:50. I was holding my urine for nine hours and it was only at 9 p.m. when two Indian nurses came and put oxygen mask and morphine injection which extended Constance's life from 9 p.m. when the hospice and palliative care nurse came at 7 p.m., and didn't do anything and declared dying at 9 p.m. but the Indian nurses extended Constance's life close to four hours and at 12. Thirty-five minutes after holding my urine for nine hours, I went to the bathroom and was confident that Constance would live and God listened to my prayers, but God didn't give me what I wanted as Constance died at 12:50 after I saw her taking her last breath. What a trauma I went through, and this whole thing is stronger than the medical records. I would like to be a prosecutor to speak in court and to the judge. I am ready to give my testimony in front of XB and the other doctors and nurses. I have to get the malpractice case active and do whatever I can, even going to see an attorney general or the president of the US. I would not have the guts to write to you and in the courts. If I wasn't genuine, I would not have the nerve or guts to do all that I do unless I am right.

Thanks.

7

Life and Death Episode Message

I WRITE ABOUT THIS EPISODE IN THE HOPE that others may be enlightened from reading about our tragedy. I hope that it may save lives for others to read our saga. *Don't trust your doctor blindly, and if needed, get a second opinion.* In four days, MCR was able to diagnose Connie's condition, which her hospital (HH) should have been able to detect long before had they conducted the same tests that MCR ran. Connie and I were both still optimistic that she would have many years left in this life. In my opinion, her two doctors at HH ruined her case with two years of negligence that finally resulted in her death. What difference did her death make to those doctors? They are still working, although they do not seek all options to heal their patients, which is the noble cause of good doctors. As patients, we trust our doctors almost as we trust God when we are ill. Do Connie's doctors think of this bond of trust? In my opinion, they do not. They should have been open to referring her case for a second opinion, but their egos and overconfidence kept them from referring her case even when I specifically requested a second opinion. Connie and I were both convinced that those doctors ruined her life, ultimately causing her early demise. After going to MCR, Connie told me many times that the doctors at HH first ruined her life, now they were taking her life. She told me this many times, which was the most painful thing for me to hear. As long as I live, I will suffer that pain and regret.

Connie was right to say that those doctors had ruined her life and eventually took what should have been a much longer life. When the specialist at HH agreed to take her case after MCR's diagnosis, he was extremely disappointed with the way his colleagues' had handled her case. He asked me who was on the team for her earlier treatments, and we gave him the names of her doctors. He was angry that her case had not been handed to him two years before as he had worked cases like hers as his specialty for thirty years. The specialist ordered more tests and put her on a three-month course of chemotherapy, with plans to run different tests after the chemotherapy was complete. Connie went through two chemotherapy treatments in December 2014 and January 2015. On February 20, while getting ready to go for her third treatment, she fell at home. She was taken in an ambulance to the hospital, HH, for a checkup, and was told that she would be ready for discharge the following day, the 21st. While the nurse was checking Connie, I saw that her chart read DNR. Connie and I told her doctors that this was no longer her wish, and the doctors assured us that they would immediately change her chart to ensure she received all possible life-sustaining care should something happen.

On February 22, while waiting to be discharged, Connie was feeling okay/ but not very hungry. She ate a little salad and five minutes later began to feel short of breath. She suffered a cardiac arrest. Nurses and doctors arrived immediately but refused to perform CPR as the code on her chart had not been changed from DNR to DR. I lost my temper and was like a tiger fighting for Connie, telling them the two on-call doctors witnessed her desire to change the DNR code and threatening to take them to court if they did not perform CPR immediately. Eight minutes elapsed between Connie's cardiac arrest and the start of CPR, eight long minutes that ultimately cost Connie her life. Had the doctors at HH done their duty and changed the code per Connie's instruction, and had the nurses and doctors present on the 22nd performed CPR immediately, I believe that Connie would still be with me today and for many years in the future.

Connie was put on a ventilator after her cardiac arrest. The tubes were to be removed on March 2, 2015, and I had to decide the next step. Although she was unable to speak with the breathing tubes in her mouth, Connie and I communicated through body language and notes that I wrote to ask her questions and get her answers. I would write things down and she would respond "yes" or "no." In this way, I was sure that I knew her wishes and could be her advocate while she was silenced by the ventilator. Tragically, the doctors went behind my back when I left the hospital briefly to attend to the family business. A nurse was with Connie and assured me that she was getting better and I could step out for a short time. While I was gone, several doctors, including her former doctor who had ruined her case and who we had dismissed in October 2014, came into her room. In my opinion, her former primary doctor came to her room from the part of the hospital where he worked to take advantage of my absence and to save his name, his fame, his position, and the annual honor of being named the top head and neck oncologist. I was extremely upset and angry to find him there, and I asked him why he came to Connie's room while I was away. I told him that he had not been her doctor since October and had referred the case to a colleague, a breast and lung oncologist. He did not answer me directly but argued that he had come earlier when I was not in the room along with two other doctors and nurses. He told me that they had to respect Mrs. Berry's wishes, so they had called me back to her room so that they could respect her wishes. I argued with them, telling them that they had all come late that afternoon when I was gone for an hour. That was an extremely dirty, daring, and an unethical thing for them to have done. He had persuaded his medical team to be his 'yes' people, conspiring with him. Now that I had returned to the room, he had his team of doctors and nurses back anything he said because of his high position. I bluntly told them all with anger that they were unethical, amoral doctors who should be ashamed that they broke the oath they took after getting their MDs. Shame on them and shame to their oath. I told them that they all deserved to be punished and that their medical licenses should be revoked forever because they betrayed Connie and me. I told them that Connie, although on a ventilator, communicated through her body language and my notes and told me her wishes. I have those notes with me in my temple of gods, Connie, and some of my departed beloved souls. Mrs. Berry had stated her desire that Pradeep, as her husband, would make the decision and that she was willing to try a tracheostomy. She was ready for that, and so was I. I had told this to many nurses as well as the Director of Social Services and her palliative care doctors.

I know the Director of Social Services, and if the need should arise, I would request that an honorable judge ask her why she was against the procedure Connie and I decided on. She wanted things done her way, and kept an eye on me, watching my movements and the time I spent sleeping in Connie's room. She told me bluntly, like a military order, "Mr. Berry, I do not want to see you in the cardiac unit after 8 p.m. or 8:30 at the latest." She threatened to tell the whole staff that I was to be gone at 8:30 p.m. sharp. I asked many times why she would do such a thing. Who was she to dictate such terms when the other staff and nurses were so encouraging to me, telling me "Mr. Berry, it is so great that you are with your wife at this time of crisis," even offering to let me sleep in an empty room. I thought that was nice, but I told them no thanks, as I wanted to be with my wife. I stayed next to her sitting in a chair or lying down in two chairs, taking a 15-minute nap, or sleeping for an hour or two here and there. I was pretty sure that this director had bad intentions and that some conspiracy was driving her actions. Why else would she have tried to restrict me but not the other spouses? I was angry and blasted her to stop dictating her terms to me, as I did not care who she was. I told her she was not my mother or my relative, and that if she tried to threaten me again, I would report her to the hospital chairman. If she tried to do tricky things to my wife, I would make sure she was arrested for threatening me. She replied in a soft voice that she was worried for my health and about my lack of sleep. I told her to forget all these and tell me what was on her mind, what was her motive? I did not listen to her dictates and stayed with Connie. On the night of the 26th, a nurse told me, "Mr. Berry, we wish we had a dedicated husband like you, as we have not found any husband like you. We have only dated a few playboys who betrayed us for physical relations. They treated us like prostitutes after buying us dinner and drinks. We are looking for nice men who would love us and be honest with us, never cheating on us." I was getting pretty upset and was surprised that these beautiful, attractive nurses and student trainees were so open about their struggle to find a good man. Many men would sincerely love to marry them for their beauty, education, and ambition. But I was in shock and started thinking about how men and women cheat on each other as marriage is a lifelong commitment of honesty and friendship. I always respected women for their great qualities of tolerance and their work as the engine of the family. A man without a good wife is zero in my opinion. My love for Connie and her love for me was the greatest thing I have ever experienced or felt. Every part of her mind and body was truth She had such soft skin and body that holding her hands and kissing her on the cheek or mouth felt so wonderful, and her hands while cooking food or making tea were always shining. Her serving me coffee was the best in the world. I was doing the same for her, serving her excellent tea and cooking anything she wanted. I was willing to do whatever it was to make her the happiest person. I cry when I think of how she used to pack my suits and ties, my iron, my shirts, and other undergarments so that I would look handsome and smart, and she would take pride that Pradeep is her man. I was her man and she was my Connie.

On September 1, 2005, I was confused about whether or not to go to India for two weeks. I was not sure if I wanted to go or stay. I came home at 3 p.m Connie asked me why I didn't go see my family as I had already planned to go and already purchased the tickets. I said, "I cannot leave you as you will be alone for two weeks." She said, "Pradeep, I can come with you, but last-minute tickets are very expensive and we will have separate seats. I don't think it is fair to spend double or triple the money for a two-week trip as after your return we are going on a Norwegian cruise and then Hawaii. I think that would be too much travel for me, and I would not be able to do your packing for the cruise as we are going with the top alumni and professors of the University of Michigan. I think, if you want, you should go and come back in one week, and we will talk on the phone every day." I agreed and found I had no good undergarments. Connie surprised me and told me that she had already gone shopping that morning while I was at work and bought me new undergarments, socks, and new shirts. I was in tears and told her "No, I want to wear them when I am with you. I can buy new ones in India." She had purchased two dozen pairs of special underwear in my size, which were difficult to get due to some ban on imported clothing.

I used only a few and saved them for years. I wore them all except for a new packet that is still unopened in my drawer. It is worth a million dollars to me today, as it reflects her love for me in doing my shopping. The shirts and ties she bought me are sitting in my drawers as I was saving them to use with her on trips to places with different climates. Lastly, she bought me four silk shirts to wear to a special function. She wanted me to wear that shirt, which is very expensive, designer-made, 100% silk, and cost over $100. Connie started getting sick and was hoping that I would wear the shirt to please her. I regret that I was saving it as it was an expensive present, and now that polo shirt is still sitting in my drawer. I see those often and feel regret that I never wore them. Connie never saw me wearing those things. They are sitting in the closet along with cardigans she bought me from Carson's, and two expensive jackets that cost $350 each are sitting with their labels on, along with many other lovely clothes.

Connie died suddenly due to those shameless doctors. She desired to wear them in March when going anywhere—stopping for cake at Benson's Bakery after a doctor's appointment or to get something from Harry and David's, or to get her cheese and chocolates and her favorite frozen yogurt with chocolate from Whole Foods. She would have one every night. One bar is still in my freezer waiting for Connie, but Connie is gone. I thought I could eat that bar of ice cream, but my hands started shaking and I did not want to eat it. My love for Connie has made me think of that bar of frozen yogurt that she was to eat on the night of February 20, 2015, but she was tired and told me that she would eat it the next day. I have written that she fell on the night of the 20th and she never made it back home as she died on February 28, 2015. That frozen yogurt is still in the freezer. All her medical team promised me that they would honor the wishes of Connie and mine. I had told them that our caretaker and I would be there in the hospital 24/7 and that if the need arises, I would book a room in a hotel to take showers or for the caretaker to sleep a few hours. I told them I would be with Connie 24/7, and I did not care if I shaved, showered, or whatnot. I would have my few clothes that I needed, and maybe loose pants to sleep in the chair. I could never think of leaving my wife due to my extreme love for her. The whole hospital staff in the cardiac unit knew and was talking all the time about my love for my wife and my dedication and devotion. They supported me, saying "You never know, your love and devotion may be rewarded and please try everything to see Mrs. Berry get better. Please go for the tracheostomy if you want, we have seen many patients recover from that with rehabilitation and medicine." I was determined to take this course, and so was Connie. But on February 27, 2015, late in the afternoon, as I have stated, in my opinion, the doctors and nurses began their conspiracy. Later, when I got the medical records—anyone can read these and say yes, it is all falsified. I called her caretaker in April 2015, and she got mad and told me, "Pradeep, these are falsified reports as I was there and this is false." I would testify in court that it is all made up as she was the witness right there with me and her name is on the medical records. This betrayal and conspiracy—God help me; I am doing my best to see that these inhumane medical doctors be punished. Today is July 11, 2016, and our wedding anniversary was on the 10th of July. I prayed and prayed and went to donate money to a school for the blind in Delhi and spent two hours with the administrator, some of the staff, and a student. My brother Arun and nephew Ashiem were with me as they drove in Delhi and knew the roads. This is the first time in my life I have ever seen a school for blind students, and they are absolutely very bright—studying for their MBA, JD, government jobs, and going to top colleges and high schools. It was the happiest and most painful experience in my life, and I donated cash in memory of my beloved wife, Constance Berry and they gave me a receipt. This is going to bring some peace to my mind, and I am sure my darling wife Connie was watching me do that noble cause. This is the way I will spend my life until death, and we will meet in our next life. Connie and Pradeep will be together in the next life. We had to make tough choices, including shifting her to the hospital in Mount Prospect for three weeks and then rehabilitation for a month so she could return home. That was the first choice, and the second choice was that once the tubes were out on March 2, 2015, we could take her to the palliative care unit for three days before going home. The palliative care doctors and nurses would then come to the house to take care of Connie, and Mrs. Berry would be fine and live another five or ten or fifteen years as his response had been good. That was her desire—she wanted to go home and she decided that if she had to die, she wanted to die in her own home in the lap of her loving husband, Pradeep. That was exactly what Connie told me.

The doctors took advantage of my absence and told me that Constance told them to take the tubes out and let her die. There was no way this could have happened if I had not left the room for that short time. I would never, ever have allowed her former doctor to enter the room. He had no business coming in as he had ruined her case and had been removed from her care in October 2014. He should never have come to that location that Friday. Connie wasn't even able to talk—we communicated through notes and body language. She told me to make these decisions for her and to do what I thought best for her. As the person is given the power of attorney, it was my decision to do everything possible to save her. Again, I became a tiger and blasted the doctors and nurses. My battle for Connie was eight against one. It was my first loss and all of the palliative care they had promised us was not performed. In spite of my aggressive actions and the phone calls I made, Connie died at 1:10 a.m. on February 28, 2015. I have videos which some nurses gave me, one consisted of thirty-two minutes and another of ten minutes showing how I was fighting to call the doctors, palliative care, and anybody to give her oxygen and treatment, but no one came. The hospital telephones can be seen ringing, with someone saying yes, Mr. Berry, we are sending the nurse, but no one came. At 7 p.m., a nurse finally came but did nothing until 9 p.m., when they declared her dead. Immediately, two nurses came and put the oxygen mask on her and gave her morphine injections, and Connie recovered. I had been holding my bladder since 3 p.m. One friend of mine showed up as my brother from India had called him to say that Connie had died and I was alone. He came at 11 p.m. and I was surprised and he too was surprised to find Connie alive. He stayed and said it truly looks like negligence. We were at peace because Connie seemed fine then. He told me to let him bring his wife to the hospital, but I said no because it was getting late. He insisted. I asked the nurses if I could go to the bathroom, as I had been waiting for nine hours. They said yes. I was a king when I talked to one lady while coming back to Connie's room. She told me nothing would happen to my wife as our devotion to each other was marvelous and rare. I was extremely happy, but I was not truly a king. The moment I entered the room, I saw my friend by the computer with the vitals, and his wife next to Connie's bed telling me, "Pradeep, Pradeep comes, Connie is going, she is going." I was shaken and was broken and was looking at Connie telling her, "Connie, Connie, please do not leave me. Please, Connie, do not give up," asking the nurses to do something, please do something. Her vitals went from sixty to fifty to forty to thirty and finally at ten when I saw her last four breaths. Darling Connie died next to me. I was absolutely gone and wept and wept and fell apart. My friends, along with Connie's caregiver, gave me great support. This episode, on top of her death, was all the more upsetting once I got her medical records. I ask myself, where is humanity? Why is there so much deceit in the medical profession? Perhaps that is why there is so much darkness in the noble medical profession.

Despite this setback, I was still positive that my Connie would live. A great thought came to me: never deprive someone of hope when hope may be all they have left. I thought that miracles happen every day. These messages brought us great comfort. I began to ask God to make Connie normal again by a miracle, the way Jesus brought Lazarus back to life. That prayer was heard, so why couldn't my prayer save my lovely wife? At the same time, I thought of Savitri and Satyavan, a miracle that took place in India 100 years ago. Through Savitri's devotion to God, her husband's life was returned to him. Thinking of these two miracles made me stronger, and I felt ready to fight anything. During her treatment, it was a struggle for Connie to go to doctor's appointments, and even walking too much in the house was difficult as she had to rely on a walker and oxygen. This was not pleasant for us, but being together and seeing each other's faces gave us great happiness.

Ultimately, I saw my darling's last four breaths and was present for her death. Two nurses and a couple of close friends were with me. I could never have imagined her death or the way that HH and the negligence of her doctors killed her. It was one of the most painful, shocking, and uncalled-for things I have ever witnessed. My mind went blank. Connie's body, her face—I have no words for the pain that I felt in my entire being. Could it be true that I would never see her, talk to her, live with her again? I am left alone. I thought of the miracles—was it possible that God might reward me by granting her life again? All those thoughts ran through my mind. Even now as I write on August 20, 2015, every day since her death, these questions and thoughts run through my mind day and night. When I relive that painful episode, it gives me panic attacks. I stayed with Connie's body for five hours, until it was taken to the funeral home for cremation. I will never forget that trauma as long as I live. After two days, I had her cremated and put her ashes in her plot next to her parents.

Doing this was heartbreaking and absolutely broke me. I suffer from that pain and have withdrawn from life. The pain and suffering I am left with are incorporated into my mind and my heart. I must mention that after Connie's demise, I asked Florida Harris if she would be willing to work for me. Her job would be to come at night and sleep in my study room while studying for her master's in nursing. She agreed, and like a sister or family, Florida was very helpful in doing chores and bringing my grocery and food and we would eat together or she would just make something for me. If I was up, she would eat breakfast with me or would leave me sleeping. It worked for over a month until I got the power to stay by myself. At that point, I was working sixteen to eighteen hours a day to handle all the legal formalities and writing the book. It was too much work for me by myself. I had made the decision that I would never ask my family in Chicago, my friends, or anybody to come and help me. I did not even disclose Connie's death until Arun, with anger, informed my sister and family in July 2015 about her death. This book has two parts—happiness and sadness. Sadness has taken over happiness. Sadness is hard to define, and no one can understand that pain but for me. I don't know what I can do while waiting to face the rest of my life, however, I would have to be strong to survive Connie's death. For me, the world is lost. I no longer travel, dine out, go to Broadway shows, read, watch TV or movies, I do not meet any friends, nor do I attend any parties or functions. I want to be alone in a sort of "Robinson Crusoe Economy," where a man lives alone and does everything himself. In ancient times, many scholars and learned people took sanyas, during which they would surrender the world to get enlightenment, peace, and to leave a legacy of learning to the world. Around the world, many generations of people learned from these hermits who withdrew from the world to gain knowledge. In my opinion, today we live in a world in which different generations do not share and pass on knowledge in the same way, and the young ignore the knowledge of their elders. The youth of the 21st century has also contributed to great technological innovations, and the world has gained from it. I believe in applying both ancient and modern knowledge to keep the balance in my life. Connie was also of this view and never criticized any one. We both respected the beliefs of others.

Mahatma Gandhi: I thought of Gandhi, who fought for equal rights during the British Empire. Even though he was a barrister of law, he was not allowed to practice in England. In South Africa, he was thrown from a train by whites, as he was considered dark-skinned under apartheid. That incident shaped him to fight to free India from the British. He was involved in all the Satyagraha, or strikes, and was imprisoned many times. One time, Gandhi was in his jail cell and his fellow inmate told him that he should write a book, which he refused to do. The constant persistent pressure from that inmate led Gandhi to start writing his book, which captured the world market. That book was an autobiography by Gandhi called *My Experiments Living with Truth*. This book has so much wisdom and many good messages for humanity and non-violence. Ben Kingsley acted as Gandhi in the Oscar award-winning Gandhi in 1982. One can see his devotion and the sacrifices he made to free India. Pandit Jawaharlal Lal Nehru, the first Prime Minister of India, Maulana Abdul Kalama Azad and many great leaders were the freedom fighters who supported Gandhi's movement. Gandhi, who is called the Father of the Nation in India, is well respected. I feel upset that his approach to non-violence was not followed for a long time. For the past sixty years, the world has changed and nonviolence looks like it is gone from the dictionary. John F. Kennedy was a great President of the US, along with Abraham Lincoln, Roosevelt, and others who did so much for the US. Dr. Martin Luther King, Jr., Nelson Mandela, and many great leaders did so many great things. King George, the father of her Highness Queen Elizabeth of England, who had a speech problem, finally gave a wonderful speech during wartime. The film based upon this true story, *The King's Speech,* won an Oscar.

These great people were moving around my mind when Connie was in the intensive cardiac unit of the hospital. I was devastated that the delay of these doctors by nine minutes affected Connie's life and later her death. It crushed me and I was absolutely broken and lost my mind. I can never ever forget her condition and her last breaths of death. One cannot imagine what I had to go through because of Connie's death. That death, which I witnessed for the first time in my life was that of my wife. How could someone even think, that I am struggling to save her but she was dying and that ruined my life, my happiness my world, and whatnot? I had forgotten all about my hardships during childhood, all my sacrifices, hard work, education, and, of course, Connie's influence in my life. I was weak in thinking, but kept getting my strength from the knowledge that I had to keep my mind and my brain absolutely focused; otherwise, anything could happen to Connie and of course to me. And then I would worry about her cremation and her wishes for the ashes in her plot, and the chapel of peace. I started praying and again started thinking of many leaders and how they could do such great things. Gandhi was able to say to the British Empire: "It is time you left India." This was a powerful tool, and I was ready when Connie was taken to the cardiac unit, and she was absolutely mentally alert and wanted to speak to me. I was there twenty-four hours watching her like my small daughter and I thought, "She is my wife. God, can I ask if you can grant me one thing, my Connie. Give my Connie back either as a wife, sister, mother, daughter or a small child, but do not take away this second body of mine, and take whatever you want from my karmas or anything. I am willing to do anything to get her back. I just want only one thing, and that is Connie. I am willing to sweep the tables, clean the bathrooms, willing to do any small or big work for humanity, just like we have been doing since we met." Unfortunately, my rhythm was very low. Diminishing theory of lower returns, I decided I need food, clothes, and our beautiful home fully beautifully decorated better than an outside professional by Connie. Connie's death took away all my happiness and desire to go to any restaurants and travelling anywhere, except for a month to see my brother and his family. Even today, I would do whatever God wants me do to do to get

Connie back.. I was sure God was listening to my thoughts, and perhaps watching me at the bedside of Connie. He would definitely grant me my Connie. Another true example of love happened during the Mughal Era of India, one of the kings came during Babar and Human. When Human made eleven round circles around the bed of his dying son as he lay dying, God granted his wish and his son's life was given back. I tried that but due to the position of the bed, I was able to do more than eleven but not in circles. God knows that I was trying round circles, but in the hospital bed, with all the tubes and equipment, it would have caused more damage if I started moving, and in any case, I would have never ever been allowed to do that. It was not my home where I could do what I wanted to, however, my intentions and theory was the same. I was still very hopeful, and that is how I thought of Savitri and Satyavan and other miracles in the world. I was confident that miracles happen every day, and that God would definitely perform miracles as Connie did so much for her parents, for her students, for humanity, for the universities, for the library, for Mexico and the Mexican people by giving free education, teaching, writing, and doing many research papers for them as she was a Spanish teacher and had seen many good and bad things happening there and also in every part of the world. She was fully devoted to humanity, and the idea that what God wants is for me to get access to my door alive and take care of my people—that's what she did for everyone. I was the same way to some extent, but she was the engine in my life for everything. This marriage, our house, household work, laundry, shopping, accounting the household budget, writing checks, shopping, ironing, taking sick and elderly people to the grocery story, helping many neighbors—especially one who was already ninety years old. Connie took her every week or sometimes twice for her shopping, and we were even taking her out 70% of the time for dining out, movies, bringing what she wanted, driving her to her doctor's appointments, cleaning her house, and whatnot. Connie did that for over twelve years. Even when Connie was sick, she took care of her. It stopped when that lady moved and went to an assisted living home in her late nineties.

However, all these thoughts and faith were not granted to me by the Supreme Power. Perhaps there is some sin I must atone for, some slackness somewhere from my current life or past life that was still due, even after my childhood tragedies of losing my biological mother and her younger sister, whose devotion and sacrifice was absolutely unbelievable and painful, as she too sacrificed her great career and had to marry my father to take care of my elder brother and me. How hard it would have been for my second mother, Kanta Mummy, who was a few years younger than my biological mother Shanti Mummy. Both our mothers died. Kanta Mummy died when I was five and a half and my brother six and three months. Kanta mummy died two hours after my sister was born. We brothers remember that death very well, including Kanta Mummy's body, my sister of two hours having her thumb in her mouth, and I was playing with her. I knew and saw each and everything, but don't recall any emotions or being devastated. The true death and tragedy came before and after Connie's death. Her cremation, the interment of her ashes, and her ceremony for two days and after placing the headstone, and then visiting her cemetery more or less two to four times each month. This death and shock is mental agony; it is the most extremely painful thing in my life and will remain that way as long as I live. I know that for sure.

After losing our two mothers another tragedy was waiting for us. My father married Uma Mummy who came from another family. The three of us, my mothers' parents, sisters and brothers wanted Uma Mummy to be part of our family, and more or less adopted her like their daughter. I remember Uma Mummy was nice and, to some degree, loving and had some passion for us and definitely was part of our studies up to fourth or fifth grades. The change came because of all the expenses of the joint family of over 100 members, including my Berry grandfather's four children, grandchildren, and his three brothers who had died and their children, and Berry grandmother's family and their children and grandchildren and outsiders, and so many extended family members were all paid by for by my Berry grandfather. Berry grandfather was very wealthy. Uma mummy was nice as she knew that she has to be to get access to Berry grandfather's money, inheritance and wealth, which was to be divided among Berry' grandfathers' six children. Uma Mummy was nice until she had her two boys, and then her interest towards her three stepchildren began to diminish, until it was just a small part and she never ever paid us a nickel or penny until today. All the wealth was distributed after Berry grandparents were gone when I was twenty-two and had finished my post-graduation and Chartered Accountancy. I should have started working and would have achieved the highest position while getting a big salary, and perhaps we two brothers would have bought a house. I must mention that real estate is extremely expensive in India and especially in Delhi. We still have some of our ancestral houses, although some of them have been sold. I could not even think of buying that as some of them cost millions of US dollars. Uma Mummy had to work and support herself. I think that if we had not lived in our big house or if Berry Grandfather was not there, we would have been with my mother's family and they would have to raise us. My mother had seven sisters and two brothers. During those days, having lots of kids was culturally valued by the rich and wealthy families. Things are different in the last fifty years or more. Later, Uma Mummy absolutely rejected the three of us and never wanted us to be her children. Our further downfall from wealth took us to more or less very limited to life of education, Boy Scouting, sports, clothes, public transportation, and our pocket money was very small until we were in high school and college. We only received our basic necessities. We, two boys, were the first who finished high school, college, and post-graduate studies, and I did another four years of Chartered Accountancy to make our own destiny. However after 1969, after the death of my Berry grandfather, we both were treated with bias. The third mother then played a game of chess and made a big gamble by taking my father to our other big house far away from the main big palace in Old Delhi, in Katra Neel, Chandnichowk. Our house in Katra Neel is now a big tourist attraction. We were residing there and were given the food and basic necessities and some small pocket money until my brother finished his post-graduate studies and got a job. I had one year to finish and four years to complete my Chartered Accountancy, and then my brother started taking care of me as he was told to separate his kitchen from our main kitchen meant for eighteen people, though the house could accommodate over 300 people. But slowly, every other uncle and other Berry family members, my grandfather was supporting left, and we were still there. I used to depend on my brother as doing Chartered Accountancy is one of the toughest degrees, with 3% passing and working an apprenticeship from nine to six with no salary or stipend, as no scholarship was allowed to do this course. After I finished that degree, I was confused about which way to go—start my practice, join the family business, or join the army as I was C certificate and would have been a major after three months of training. I kept on refusing great job offers from banks, foreign institutions, the US embassy in Delhi, Australia, the United Kingdom, and of course anywhere in India. It was a confusing battle and I had no money to travel. I made a great mistake by not looking into my career at that time, but I am extremely happy that all of this happened and I have forgotten those days as God had other plans for me after suffering from my rich family and never receiving my share of the inheritance. I've never even seen a nickel of the millions of dollars that my grandfather left to distribute among my family. My father was a henpecked husband and had two boys from his third wife. It was destiny that they were to get my father's entire portion of the inheritance.

According to the Indian Karta Act, grandchildren have the first right to their grandfathers' property, business, gold, and diamonds. My family did not abide by this law. I came to the US and my uncles and cousins got all of the billions of dollars inheritance that my grandfather Berry left. When I met my Connie, all of that money became valueless to me. I couldn't buy my Connie for all the money on the planet. She was my wife and my Kohinoor diamond. I only wanted her for myself. Now, I am heartbroken, lost, and living an isolated life after the loss of my precious Connie on February 28, 2015. That loss is much more painful than any of my childhood suffering. I do not want that inheritance. Let whoever has the darkness of greed take it and let them pay their dues with compound interest in the next life. Connie's loss is the one which has broken me, and I will always suffer.

I would continue to live a simple life of high thinking, with my outings limited to the health club, the cemetery, and once in a while, just going somewhere by myself. My company is nature: the moon, stars, and sun, and I find happiness in Connie's study room and sleeping with her beautiful pictures in our king—sized bed on my side. I also pray with her pictures and her beautiful table lamp around. Each night, I prepare her bedside table for her with a glass of water and her sandals by the bed. In the morning, I put out her water glasses in her study and in the kitchen, and look at her beautiful pictures hanging in the living room. Our house is a true, great museum of science and art. This is my happiness. I can go to India to see my brother and his family for a few months, but now I am living in the happiest of places, my Connie's house. It is ours, but I call it My Connie's house, her temple or church. This is the way God wanted me to find happiness. I am not happy without her, and I think of her each second, but I have to follow the law of nature and God's order as we are all puppets in his hands and have to do whatever he asks of us. So her house is very soothing for my troubled mind. I have no other choice, I have resources to travel anywhere, but I will not, as Connie's memory would follow me wherever I go as we both traveled extensively in the US and Europe. We never traveled in the Middle East due to the heat and climate, but if I can gain the courage, I might try to see Egypt and Dubai. Time will make that decision.

India holds no fear for me as I am with my brother and his family, and Connie's room with her pictures. All the big rooms are decorated with Connie, so that is very comforting. I also have my grandnieces and two nephews and my niece by marriage, who are very kind to me. My brother, his wife, his two sons, and two granddaughters—my grandnieces which are five and ten and are fun and take away some of the pain I feel for Connie, but Connie is in every part of my body. I will never touch another woman in my life. Never. I will wait as I am sure I will meet Connie in my next life. I am certain this will happen.

Today is April 25, 2016. I went to Connie's grave and cleaned the granite and the grass and a few other things. I generally spend one hour or forty-five minutes when I visit her grave. I could easily spend four hours, and would even not mind going daily. That is my love for Connie. I was thinking what a shame it is to

Connie's memory that her only sibling and his four children and their spouses and grandchildren did not ever come to visit her. I was standing close to Connie's beautiful granite stone where I had these inscribed: "Constance Ann Berry. Best friend and most precious darling wife of 38 years." Suddenly, I wondered why I did not have them write forty years as there were some errors in my troubled mind. I chose the inscription, the granite, the color, and the design of her headstone as I was the only person making those decisions because Connie's brother and his family never came to visit her, even until today. I think it is the most shameful thing a sibling can do to treat his sister so. He and his family are all church—going people. If that is what the church teaches, how can they think of going to church? How does their conscience allow them to go to church, and how does the church allow such people to enter? Connie had one college student, Roberto Ciera. I have a great friend in Mexico, Alfonzo Penna Ciera, who I was thinking of calling. He worked under me along with thirty-six other people when I was the senior management consultant in 1998-1999 in Mount Prospect. Alfonzo came from a rich family, and I used to bring him home to meet Connie. Connie immediately told me that he is from a rich family. Later, he tried to come to the US and wanted me to join him in San Francisco, but I didn't join him. Lovely dogs.

 They are serious and faithful to their master without thinking if he or she is rich, and give unconditional love and eat anything you give. They are faithful to their master even if they have to kill themselves to save their beloved masters. They can judge the character of humans in no time, even from miles away, and stop them coming near you. I wish Connie and I had a dog before she put the evil eye on my Connie. A dog would have torn her apart from this evil from the earth, as great Lord Rama was in creation of God to kill the great scholar, Ravana, king of Sri Lanka, and I might write a note about this in the book. Got on the Internet and read about the Diwali festival in India or Lord Rama and Great Ravana. This true story happened 5000 years ago in India, and you would find out the sacrifice of Rama's half-brothers and how they ran the kingdom of Ayodyapuri until Lord Rama returned from his fourteen years of exile along with his wife Sita and younger brother Laxman. The story is how the younger half-brother looked after the kingdom without sitting on the throne but by touching Rama's wooden sandals until he came back and took his throne. That is what I am doing touching Connie's sandals in the morning and night and placing her water glasses in the kitchen and near her computer and the white glass on her side table in the night. That is the most healing thing for me, that and praying to that noble soul's pictures and sleeping with her framed picture. The picture shows how she was sitting on her chair with a walker in front and another walker with her clothing. That place is a church, a cathedral for me. So on this visit, I was upset that I would ask them to write:

CONSTANCE ANN BERRY, BEST FRIEND & MOST PRECIOUS
DARLING WIFE OF 40 YEARS OF PRADEEP BERRY

I was thinking and thinking and moved around and saw several other stones which had the same color and design as other people's families and they had a beloved son of XYZ—beloved wife and father or husband of XYZ.

Throughout the two years of Connie's illness, she seemed normal in the course of her daily life—reading, writing, working on the computer, keeping our accounts, watching films, discussing things, etc. We were both still happy because being together was nothing but happiness. We were also filled with hope that Connie would live at least another ten to fifteen years as she was an avid reader, and learned that new medicines and treatments are being released. I read the same and was also positive about our prospects.

In ancient Egypt, people mummified the bodies of their dead as a way of coping with the loss of their loved ones. I think it was right for those people to be able to see the body and feel that their loved ones were still with them. I could never have done that with Connie who asked to be cremated. I never thought I, her loving husband, would have to oversee her last rites. Why was this my fate? Connie's pictures and our pictures together fill my house. In this way, my life is a combination of happiness with the memory of our life together and sadness for her loss. While she was ill, my life was dedicated to serving Connie. I brought her tea and juice in the morning after she got up to go to her study with her walker and oxygen. Later, she would make the painful trek to the kitchen for breakfast. Making and serving her the best of breakfast food was my greatest happiness. I felt the same about cooking her dinner, helping her shower, and bringing her a glass of water first thing in the morning and last thing at night. Taking care of her and bringing her to the hospital for appointments and treatments was a mixture of pain and joy. Helping her prepare for these appointments brought both pain and happiness to my heart and soul.

Throughout her illness, Connie was extremely positive although inside she was most unhappy, not knowing if she would ever get better. I used to give her positive feedback, based on my own faith in God and the miracle of Savitri and Satyavan. I was absolutely devoted to Connie and was hoping God would listen to me. However, I lost that battle and was absolutely broken and devastated. After her death, I was only sleeping three to four hours a night and there was lots of work to do. Most important of all was to have her cremated and put her ashes in her plot next to her parents and then putting the stone on her ashes (as per her wishes and the wishes of others). God helped me to do all that, and by my aggressive approach I was able to get the cremation done in two days. I didn't want my darling's body sitting in the funeral home for a long time. She was not a charity case, and I told both the cremation and cemetery people that money was not a problem. I also told them that I wanted the best casket, urns and priest at all the services, including the cremation, the memorial in the chapel of peace, and later at the burial of her ashes in her plot. The same was for the headstone. I was firm and would not compromise anything for money. I provided lunch for the people who came to pay their respect to Connie. I also hired a professional video maker for two days to cover the ceremonies of Connie darling. It was not a pleasant video, but all those sad memories could stay with me to provide me some happiness. While they may give me pain, they also take some pain away. I watch those videos quite often. What I think and how it affects me, I do not know, but I feel that it provides me something. I don't know how much pain and suffering was going on in my heart and soul to be at my wife's funeral, which I never thought I would have to do myself. She was the one I married, and now I had to arrange her funeral services. I am extremely upset about it. I was not ready to lose her and to never again see that great wife who played the role of best wife, best friend, sister, and mother, through different situations in my life. It reminds me what Sahajahhan must have gone through at the loss of his wife MumtaazMahel. After her death, he built the TajMahal in Agra, India; it is an example of love and is one of the seventh wonders of the world. No outsiders can understand my pain, which is in my heart and soul and always haunting me. I know if I start talking about this with relatives and friends all the time, they will not understand my pain and if they say something, I would not listen or follow their advice.

Now I understand what Great Buddha, who was silent for two years after his enlightenment, said upon breaking his silence. Many Gods were worried about his silence and requested that he speak, but he refused. After many requests from all the gods, he broke his silence by saying, "People who understand me know my silence, and if I say something, they would not understand me and think negatively about me. I, therefore, decided to be silent. My message is even if I can change the life of one person out of millions, my purpose is accomplished." How wonderful were those thirty-nine and half years? I pray to God to take away some of my possessions and give my darling Connie back—but I am sure we will be husband and wife in our next lives and this hope gives me strength and I am willing to struggle whatever way I have to *but I want Connie back in my next life.*

8

The Story of Sati Savitri

WOULD ENCOURAGE READERS TO READ THE WHOLE story in the internet or in the book.

9

I would also like to share a true story about faith in religion and greed, I read a long time back

THIS IS A TRUE STORY. THERE WAS once a rich and very generous merchant, who never refused alms to anyone. His neighbor was an evil old lady who would curse everyone asking for alms. A few years ago, some true saints went out asking for alms. The merchant gave them a generous amount of wheat flour, and the saints left happily with their blessings to the merchant. The evil old lady started shouting abuse and curses to both the saints and the merchant. The saints continued, and while they were traveling, a flying eagle dropped a dead rat into their wheat flour. The saints ate the flour and died. People asked their religious leaders, "Who is to be blamed for their deaths, the merchant, the woman, or fate?" The learned religious men replied, "The merchant gave in good faith, so he is above blame. The evil woman is to blame because of her bad tongue and bad intentions. Finally, fate is responsible for their death." I have met some people who were not able to fulfill their daily needs and others who are amassing wealth out of greed. I think this story is right—it is the greed for more and more that is killing the sages.

Lord, you are everywhere, omnipresent, omnipotent, and omniscient. Lord, you are perfect. Your pattern and design of the world are perfect. We accept your orders without question. The rule of Nish Karma, daily duty: do your duties, deeds, and karmas without identification of self with it or its reactions. This is self-realization. We are puppets in the hands of God and we have to perform whatever role he wants us to play. In the kingdom of God, every event and situation is preordained to happen in its proper time. There is a chain of cause and reaction. But God has allotted a function and duty to everyone, and no man, however great he may be, should interfere with the conscience and lifestyle of another man. Therefore, there is so much discontentment, frustration, and crime in the world.

10

My Loss and Pain for Connie

I CAN SAY FOR SURE THERE WAS NO lack in my devotion for Connie throughout our life. However, when Connie was first diagnosed with cancer in 2002 and throughout her illness until her death, the devotion and love for both of us were at their peak. Many of our friends, hospital staff, and neighbors, even strangers knew and wished that they were blessed with that kind of love and devotion. Further, when Mayo Clinic declared palliative care on November 8, 2014, my devotion and prayers to the Lord to make Connie well again were at their peak. Her body was like a God and I prayed over that weak body, her walker, her oxygen, and her clothes and any object which was a favorite of Connie's. I was convinced that God would see my devotion and would give more strength to both of us and that new enlightenment was coming to save her at any cost. I knew miracles happen every day, our good karmas or Connie's best karma would convince God to change the process of palliative care to normal life, and choose to give her ten to fifteen years more to live. That was the only thing I was asking God, and that was what she was asking for as well.

We both shared the good karmas, which were far greater than any small bad karma. We began to feel confident that she would have a full long life. We believed in miracles as we knew of many miracles that had happened. We were sure that she would live another ten to fifteen good years as she had already gone through cancer treatments boldly. Connie would tell me, "God helps those who help themselves." God has the power to do anything, to take and to give life. We were not asking God for immortality. We even knew that someday I might be alone with only God for comfort. I wanted my service to God to save Connie. I decided that I would fight her sickness all by myself, without asking for the help of my friends and relatives. I had read true stories of life in the jungle, of the suffering of animals and people, and how they were granted new life. When these things were coming into my mind, I was growing stronger and better prepared to handle the stress of Connie's struggle. My love and devotion to my precious wife increased immeasurably, and I cherished everything about her, down to her daily routine. I gained confidence that God knew how much love I had for Connie. The saying "If one truly asks God for something with devotion, hard work, and does anything to reach out to him, God is kind to grant that wish," came to my mind. It happened centuries ago during the Mogul era. Hamayun, Babar, and Akbar, the great Mogul kings, asked God for help and they were granted what they wanted. My devotion, perhaps, exceeded theirs. I know medical science and serious illnesses result in the end, but the saying "nobody goes as long as God is protecting them" also has a truth.

There is a true story told by three ladies we met in 2006 and narrated in front of three top medical doctors. The doctors had told these women that they had only a few months to survive. They told them to say their last prayers, as the end was coming. The women went, prayed, and waited. They waited and waited, but still, they lived. It so happened that many years later (sixteen years for one, nineteen years for another, and twelve years for the third), these ladies returned to their doctors for minor illness and asked if they recognized them. These doctors were astonished that their diagnoses had been incorrect. These ladies were childhood friends and neighbors, and my family was in touch with them. I had a few friends who also experienced a similar situation. This gave me new confidence in the ways of life, death, and God. Connie and I were so confident that she would survive. I had one uncle in India who lived with cancer for thirty-three years, and a woman I knew survived cancer for twenty-three years.

These were positive examples that made us stronger. However, Connie used to read the obituary column in the *Chicago Tribune,* and I noticed some die within only a few years of being diagnosed with cancer. These were encouraging and fearful thoughts, but we chose to be positive. I truly did not want anyone to know how ill she was. First, I was very angry with my friends and relatives who had not reached out to us for several years. I took an oath in 2012 that I would not call them or tell them that Connie was not doing well. I would not be open with those friends who were only interested in paying lip service to our friendship. They never once told us that they were with us and we could count on them. I could read the difference between lip service and sincere friendship. I know everyone has problems, but to my mind and Connie's, we had always gone out of the way no matter what. We still called them to inquire after their well-being, their families, etc. Connie was in touch with their sorrows, why did we not get that dedication from them? At that time, I turned to the supreme Lord and said, "It is our battle; please help us, who have such good karma." I was totally in the hands of God, and so was Connie. And yet we lost that battle. Later, at the time of her cardiac arrest, I had another chance to fight the doctors and medical staff like a tiger to protect Connie. It was ten against one. God helped me to fight and to be strong like a boxer, a tiger, like superman or the ambassador of God. But I did not win, instead, I lost the most important battle of my life. I will never forget this lost battle of love and my future.

11

Another Painful Chapter for Connie and Pradeep

BEFORE WRITING, I WANT TO APOLOGIZE FOR mentioning this sensitive issue. Connie's siblings and family did not come for Connie's cremation or any of her funeral services. Connie has only one true sibling, her elder brother, and his family includes his wife, their four grown children and eight grandchildren. They all go to church every Sunday, but they did not come to Connie's funeral. The entire family lives three hours from Chicago, and even her brother's summer home is a three-hour flight from Florida to Chicago. This is an inexcusable shame. When I informed them about my darling Connie's death, these church-going people made their excuses. Her brother and sister-in-law said they couldn't come because of his upcoming knee surgery, which I believe could easily have been postponed so that he could attend her funeral. Even Connie's adult nieces and nephews did not come. This showed me that they do not care for their lovely aunt who truly loved them. They had no compassion for their highly-educated sister and aunt. It is pathetic and shameless for mankind to act this way. In my strong opinion, the main culprit is his smooth wife; a very powerful– a hungry snob who has crossed the limit of her ego. She is arrogant and absolutely convinced that she is of a higher class than anybody else. Yes, she would go where there is a benefit, and her husband, Connie's brother has become most fixed on the *money*. They had a fixation on money no matter where it came from. God's law always rules, as their sons-in-law are mooching them enough. Money is like a snake, it never stays in one place. One day you are rich, and suddenly the money disappears and can put people on the edge. I have so many examples in my fifty years' experience. It would be shameful to them and society if they found out that these church people did not go nor did they send their kids upon hearing of his sister's death. I would not be surprised if the church people would not want to be associated with them. Why do they go to the church? Why? To learn about humanity or to make connections? In my opinion, they go to church to find some widows or widowers to take them into confidence to leave money for them. God will not forgive them, and they would pay a very big painful price for me to see this cold love they had for Connie. This same Connie used to buy cards and wrap Christmas gifts for her family, shopping for them even while traveling the world. Connie used to sew quilts for them and send the children money for their birthdays, Christmas, and other occasions. Over the past twenty-five years, her nieces and nephews lost their love for their aunt Connie. When they were just kids, they had such love for her and always wanted us to visit and bring joy into their lives. We used to go to every function they were in—concerts, graduations, and holidays. Connie invited her family for Thanksgiving and Easter every year. She was exceptionally fond of them all, and they were her only family. From 1976 until 1998, was great fun and joy for all of us. Later, things absolutely changed—greed is a curse of the land.

I must mention that Connie's whole family has always been very nice to me, and was nice even after her death. I am extremely grateful to them for all that. I regret and apologize for recounting this bad episode. One big mistake and years of love and my feelings towards them have changed. However, I would never wish anything bad to them and would like to see them happy and enjoy their life with their kids and grandchildren. Now I am the biggest loser as darling Connie is no longer with me—a terrible loss for me in my life. Perhaps, I am writing this sad family episode to share my loss. I pray to God that one day I can forget the past and forgive them for their behavior.

I would say the same for my extended cousins and their large family, including my real uncle and his family, For three years, they never called to ask how am I doing or how Connie is doing. I was mad at them and did not even inform them that she died. I didn't tell my family of Connie's death until I went to India in May 2015, and even then I waited until June to tell them my sad news. My elder brother, feeling the persistent pressure of his duty as the head of the family, informed my extended family. Since I returned to the US on July 23, 2015, only three people out of nearly seventy came to visit me. As I wrote on August 26, 2015, the rest of the thirty or more extended family members here in Chicago have not called nor stopped by. This episode has made me learn more and more about the world and has made me bitter and angry towards my relatives. I too am angry with my friends of some forty years. It takes years to make friends and develop love with family and friends, but in one second or with one incident, the love is gone forever. However, I find peace by writing Connie's biography, which gives me happiness as well as sadness. I also want to share my own childhood tragedy. My mother, respected Shanti Mehra, was born in 1921 in Lahore and Lyallpur, now in Pakistan after India's independence from British rule, which was achieved on August 15, 1947. She was highly educated and wanted to go into civil service during the British Empire. But can we play with destiny? My maternal grandfather was not wealthy, but he was well off. He was convinced by his close friend, Puran Chand, (whom I never saw but I am still angry at him) that ladies do not go to the UK for jobs and should be married. He suggested a boy of an extremely wealthy merchant in Delhi, India as a possible husband for my mother. My mother was devastated and did not want to marry. She wanted to work and have a great career. I am still very angry and asked why she was forced to marry my father Mr. Ram Prashad Berry, born in 1921. My paternal grandfather was extremely wealthy. Shanti Mummy bore my elder brother Arun and myself before dying tragically young. Arun was twelve months old and I was only two months of age when Shanti Mummy—beautiful and educated—died. I did not see my mother. My family was all at a big loss and thought that as my father was only twenty-seven years old, he would remarry and we two boys would get a stepmother who would neglect and ruin us. My maternal grandparents forced my mother's younger sister Miss Kanta Mehra to marry my father to avoid having a stepmother. Respected Kanta Mehra, who completed her double masters in English and was going for a great career, was devastated and did not want to marry. She had no choice but to marry my father. I am extremely upset with my grandparents and my father for forcing her to marry. We two brothers remember her being a great mother and extremely beautiful and educated. She loved us like her children. But God had other plans. She bore one daughter, my sister, and died after her birth at the young age of twenty-five. Arun was six and a half and I was five and a half when we lost our second mother. We both remember her death and funeral. My father, who was now twenty-seven years old, married his third wife, Mrs. Uma Malhotra, age twenty-seven, who was our stepmother. She played the role my family had feared very well by separating both of us from our father and producing her two boys. That was the end of our great inheritance. We were brought up by our two grandparents and our mothers' younger sisters. Sometimes it bothers me why our paternal grandparents, who owned many properties, houses, and had a fortune, didn't leave a trust or some provision to ensure that we get part of the wealth. As it was, we had only a good education but nothing else.

Arun and I made successful destinies. My paternal grandfather's children had no education, but they did have money, which has been appreciated 100 times. My two half-brothers and other cousins, as well as a living uncle, are getting all the money and giving it to their children. I would have never done this greedy act. I am totally upset and still cannot believe that anyone in the Berry family would do that. They have no compassion, no shame, no guilt, and no sympathy that we had lost our two mothers and suffered, including my father, who became a puppet in my stepmother's hands. They did not give us two brothers a penny. I feel my stepmother must have been a very cruel person. Although I must feel something about my father's death on October 14, 2003, I didn't know whether or not I should have felt sorrow for his loss. We two brothers and two half-brothers performed the last rites for our father. However, Arun and I lost our inheritance and our two half-brothers grabbed all of it. My grandparents were both very charitable and helped many people, but my paternal grandfather's children did not do any charity at all. It is hard to believe that our stepmother did this dirty thing, separating us two smart, intelligent boys, who had many things to offer for our family. My father, too, became like a stepfather and never gave a penny to both of us or to our sister. He changed as a henpecked husband in my stepmother's hands, although he was not able to forget our two beautiful mothers and used to talk to us when he was alone with us.

Greed is ruining humanity everywhere. However, the world continues to exist as there are good people and some of them are really very compassionate. Connie was the most ethical, honest person, and I too was the same, as is Arun. My great uncle, Dr. Behl, advised me about this family war over money and told me, "Son, either fight or forget." He told me to give him my power of attorney and he would get my share as he was very well connected and had a way to get us our share of the inheritance. But Arun and I did not listen to him. According to Indian law, grandchildren have the first right to their grandparent's property and assets. Connie told me to fight so we brothers would not lose our inheritance, especially my brother Arun in India, but we both refused. These days, I forget the strife and do not care anymore. But I want to mention how the The greed of man is a curse on this land. How can greedy people live with their conscience and heart? My stepmother and a few others, who saw something in her, used to tell me, "Pradeep, you are very lucky having Connie as your wife. She allows you to visit India every year." Wives in India would make a huge deal if their husbands go somewhere even for two days.

Only a few of my relatives have ever visited us in the US, while Connie went to India seven times. Each and every one of our family members and friends were highly impressed with her manners. She lived a simple life—she never demanded any special food or any special privileges and accepted whatever was offered to her. It truly highly impressed them. Now, when I think of all these qualities and her special intelligence, I go into the deepest pain of losing my Connie and each and every day of our forty years of marriage, love and care moves in my brain, mind, and heart as if I am watching our lives as a movie. I am storing all these memories in my mind and heart. No matter how I try to explain it, no one will ever understand how I live with my memories. Even a doctor or a psychologist would never figure this out. This is due to the special bond between me and Connie. We had no boundaries, an unbiased love like the smile of a small baby, the soothing effects of the ocean, the early morning voices of the birds, or the beauty of the stars, moon, and sun. Many people told me they knew how lovely and great she was. I would like to tell them that they would not be able to convince me of her greatness. Some feel they have already defined it to me—they could not have known her. Connie was one in ten million. Many times while traveling in cruises or staying in hotels, I asked Connie if I should give a tip or buy a present to the general manager, thinking he or she may not be offended. Connie replied, "No one would say no to a present or money regardless." I found this to be true all my life, except for a very few situations. Connie also told me many times that we should leave a little early to go anywhere as unexpected traffic or other problems could arise. It is better to be there, especially at the airport, early rather than to risk missing the flight. Whether it was traveling or meeting friends at restaurants, punctuality was her theme. I have to some degree forgiven my stepmother since I met Connie, as her love, devotion, charm, external and internal beauty, and my true love and devotion to her made us extremely happy. I considered my darling Connie my wife, friend, sister, and mother too. This may seem very strange to people—that a woman can be my wife, best friend, sister, and mother. She took all my pain on her shoulders and heart and started loving me so much, and I did the same thing with her. My love to her was tremendous. We too were made for each other, and our love was true and pure. In the ancient Indian Vedanta, it is believed that a great wife can play all these womanly roles.

12

To prove this and as part of my tribute to Connie, I would like to share some remarkable quotes, I studied and knew, but now I am taking them from the internet, to put the exact words

THIS QUOTE IS BY CHANAKYA IN 520 BC. "A good wife is one who serves her husband in the morning like a mother does, loves him in the day like a sister does and pleases him like a prostitute in the night." I personally would not use the word prostitute, but Chanakya went into the depth by using this word, and maybe he was right. My world renowned dermatologist uncle told me, "Son, marriage is an art and you have to understand your wife as she is very sensitive, and a husband's love is very important to her, more than anything besides the necessity of life and comfortable living." "A wife surrenders herself to her husband." I have written more on this under my uncle's advice. In our Vedanta, it is written in Sanskrit as:

a. Kaysha: Devotion, career, keeping the house in order. Though, I also believe a husband must contribute more for the house and be the greatest help for his wife. I was very happy doing everything, including cooking, cleaning, and anything to make Connie's life easy. But she did a whole lot too, and we valued each other. She balanced her career, our travels, housework, and learning.

b. Kasrrmeshue: Giving good advice to her husband and to others. I, too, was the same way and we had the best understanding. Value everything equally.
c. Bhojeshue: Means good food for husband and I did the same for her. We both valued everything equally and had no egoistical sense that she is a woman and I am a man. She was everything to me.
d. Shaileshue: Means the love of wife and husband and in whatever forms it takes. In the old times, women and men marry for physical relations.

13

More Quotes by Chanakya

I read Chanakya's books *Arthashastra* and *Chanakyaniti* during high school. Chanakya was an Indian politician and a great strategist who gained great knowledge. He was considered a great politician and one of the best strategic planners in 520 BC.

1. One of Chanakya's wisest aphorisms: **"A man is born alone, dies; and he experiences the good and bad consequences of his karmas, deeds alone, and he goes to hell or the supreme abode."**

Connie and I practiced this message throughout our lives. I am therefore 10,000,250,000% positive that Connie is with the supreme and that gives me some consolation. However, I still live with pain in my heart and soul. I would do my best to reconcile and to survive by doing more good karmas and help humanity, but I will never be able to forget Connie as long as I am alive. She was everything to me. I truly do not want to go to those places we used to go to—shopping, restaurants, and even roads. Everywhere I go, I miss her. It is extremely hard for me to believe that I will never see her again, except maybe in my next life. But I want the exact Connie, with the same face and same external and internal beauty. My faith tells me God will fulfill my request, and this hope makes me strong to do better and better things.

2. **"As a single withered tree, if set aflame, causes a whole forest to burn so does a rascal son destroy a whole family."**

Connie only had one brother. I believe that it was Connie's brother and his wife who destroyed her family with their greed. Her brother and sister-in-law destroyed the whole happiness of their own mother and father, and most importantly, Connie's happiness. Now, when I think of Connie's brother—who is her only sibling—he and his four children and grandchildren were truly proven with this quote. They were nice to us the first five to six years of our marriage, but later we had a relationship of love and hate. Now, after the demise of Connie, none of them came for her last rites and no one sent me condolences. Now, my forty years of good or bad relations with them absolutely vanished. I have no desire to talk or see any of them. Anyone who was not nice to Connie will never be my friend, nor would I like to talk to them or meet them. This is all due to my love for Connie. If she was alive, my bitterness would have been forgiveness, but not anymore. Connie is gone and so are they. Perhaps, they don't care as they only care for money.

3. **"Treat your kid like a darling for the first five years. For the next five years, scold them. By the time they turn sixteen, treat them like a friend. Your grown-up children are your best friends."**

I am convinced that this quote is true. When I was in college and studying my Chartered Accountancy, I was convinced and still am that when your son or daughter is fifteen to sixteen, and especially when they reach eighteen, they become your best friend. I have seen this even at the age of six or seven. I was raised in a very strict atmosphere, and my brother Arun and I were not allowed to disobey our grandfather or any member of our joint family. However, after finishing my undergraduate, Chartered Accountancy, NCC, Eagle Scout, and other things, I was treated as a friend by my family in India. In spite of this, I still object to that friendship as my own Berry family—including my own father and uncles and aunties—saw to it that my brother Arun, my sister Rita Revri, and I never got a penny from our millions of dollars of inheritance. It is bothersome, but after the loss of Connie, I don't want to think of nor need any inheritance. Losing my Connie is the deepest and most hurtful thing now. As far as I am concerned, other than my brother Arun and his family, no other family member of the Berry and Mehra family have a close relationship with me. If I call or meet them, they will go out of their way to meet me with love, hospitality, and would respect me. Bluntly, I have no enemy. I am just extremely angry and devastated that Connie is gone. That loss takes over all of my happiness and joy, and I experienced withdrawal. It would be nice if they came to see me. However, the old love will never come back. I was told an important saying by Mrs. Violet Hopkins, Dr. Behl's mother-in-law. She told me, "Pradeep, you can break a glass bowl either by accident or by falling. You can fix it with glue and it will look the same; however, some marks of the broken bowl will also show. If differences come between friends and relatives, it can come back or not. But even if it comes back for the sake of formality, the true feelings are gone." Now I see parents of young children treat them with love, and especially after eighteen or even after they get married, they are best friends. I especially got hurt, even more than Connie did, when she and I noticed the behavior of her brother. His four kids were young, and we treated them like our own children. We were all very close as Connie's sister-in-law was (and perhaps still is) a wonderful host. But when the children grew up and had their children, her brother—I am sure on the orders of his wife—began to create distance. All of this started some fifteen years ago and it got worse with time. They wanted us to come for a short visit of two days at their house in Wisconsin during summer, at Christmas, and on Thanksgiving. Other than that, they never wanted to come to our home even if they were in Chicago. Our sister-in-law was always the boss, and not even a leaf could move without her permission. Such was her control over her husband, children, and grandchildren. All of this was due to her power over money. Her money ruled her family. Connie told me many times, "Pradeep, when the kids were small, they wanted us to be there for the children. Now, since they have inherited money and their children are grown up, they have dumped us." Her brother, I would say, can only open his mouth and say what his dominating wife says. Even twenty-five years ago, I suggested that we should all go on vacation to India or Europe, or for a cruise, or even for dinner. He used to be very rude and hurtful, telling me, "Pradeep, we are busy for the next ten years." In 1992, Connie went to the UK with her school teachers and friends, and I was happy that she would go. None of the other spouses wanted to go, so I told Connie, "Please do not deprive yourself, go and enjoy yourself." I was very happy, but she was guilty that she went with her friends. I told her, "Don't I go to India for two weeks alone to see my brother and family?" At that time, my father, paternal grandfather, and Dr. and Mrs. Behl were alive, so I was happy to go. This argument convinced Connie to go to the UK for two weeks, and we five husbands of her friends went to the airport to drop them off and pick them up. I used to call Connie twice a day in the UK, or a few times a day when she went with her teacher friends to Cancun, Mexico. Taking Connie to the airport, picking her up, talking to her on the phone, no matter how much it cost, was my true happiness. While writing this, my memory is photographic and I am in pain. My mind is 100% on the movie playing in my head. But that is not happening. Connie is gone. That is very upsetting and painful, but I have to finish her book. So coming back to 1992, Connie asked me to invite her brother and his family out for dinner. This would be a good opportunity for me to feel less alone. Because it was her wish, I called her brother, and he told me that he was in town with her mother, and I asked them to meet me at Hackney's restaurant. Her mother was not too happy that I was coming. She thought I was coming for free food, and bluntly told me, "Pradeep, you would come for free food anytime." I told her, "Let me tell you, if you behave this way I am leaving. I can even pay for your dinner and buy you food for the next ten days. Do not insult me. I only came because Connie told me to. I was invited to the opening of a huge bank for dinner and social networking. I had to say no to the bank and I was even invited especially by the chairman and CEO for dinner as they wanted me to help them shape up their commercial lending department and train the assetbased lending department." I left and met Connie's brother and his wife and mother. I remember asking Connie's brother, "Should we plan a trip together? We will go wherever you want to go." He immediately told me, "Pradeep, we are busy for the next twenty-five years," while laughing and insulting us as they belong to the upper class due to their inheritance. His ego and style of speaking were hurtful, and I decided right away that we would never invite these arrogant people on a trip again. We would never even give them the satisfaction of inviting them. I can assure you that if he had not been her brother, I would have said, "You can go to hell and do not ever ask us to come exchange gifts, and keep your inherited money and kids in the showroom. Goodbye and never dare call us or ask for anything." Who needs these kinds of people whose god is money? I am not ever going to be friends with the whole family who never cared for their lovely sister, my Connie. I do not even have any good or bad wishes for them. They want to be connected with me over Facebook, but I would never want to be their friend. This relationship is over with Connie's death. I know their lovely aunt Connie left them money, and they would grab it. Most people would die for that big amount she left to the four of them. I would say that they are shameful and unethical people. They would grab the money and I'm sure they will not even call to thank me or feel remorse, thanks to their mother who has provided such a dirty foundation. God is watching. I am sure God will not forgive them and they will have to pay for their bad karmas in this life.

4. **"The life of an uneducated man is as useless as the tail of a dog which neither covers its rear end, nor protects it from the bites of insects."**
5. **"A person should not be too honest. Straight trees are cut first and honest people are screwed first."**

Connie and I have both gone through this message. We always followed the same message regardless of the consequences. Although there have been so many painful things we suffered, Connie suffered more. This reminds me of a true episode. In 1984, I visited a huge client of my employer (the largest finance company in the world) in California and took Connie with me. Connie would drop me off in the morning and pick me up in the evening and would go to the library and shopping while waiting for me. This client was one of the largest trailer homemakers in the US and had taken a big loan from my company. I was introduced to the chairman of the board and all the senior management with whom I spent the whole day talking about business, plans, expansion, and all the related things about the loan. Later, they introduced me to their lady accountant. I was highly impressed with her knowledge and grace and thought that she knew the business very well. She was super. During lunch, she asked me if I want to go for lunch and I said yes. She told me that she can't go, so I decided to order food for her, and I paid for that as part of my business expenses.

We were extremely busy as lots of work was to be done, and she closed her office and we both were working while having lunch. She told me her story, which I will never forget. She told me that this huge company was owned by her and her husband. She trusted their employees and her attorney very much. In fact, she adopted that attorney as her son when he was a kid and put him through school, college and law, and treated him as her son. She had a large customer in Mexico and owed the company many millions of dollars in accounts receivables. The customer was in tight cash flow and she gave that account to her adopted attorney and asked all the employees to cooperate as a team. Suddenly, the company was forced into liquidation and she and her husband lost everything. She later found out that her own attorney took all the money from that customer and later bought back the company and made the plant supervisor the president so that now she was reporting to him as an accountant. Her will gave her husband the strength to work as an ordinary worker in their company. She further told me that since they lost the company, she and her husband had never gotten a call from the Rotary and Lions Club, other charitable, arts, and theaters clubs where they used to give charity and host dinners. All their wealthy friends disappeared. She stated that the only people who came forward were the food vendors who brought their trucks to the company to sell breakfast, late snacks, lunch, and dinner to her 1000 employees. Those food vendors bought them a small place to live, gave them food daily, and met all their expenses. All of their rich friends who used to invite them in return for donations were gone, but these vendors helped them to survive. They went from riches to rags and lost their entire world. It was such a heartbreaking thing for me. While agreeing to approve the new loan for the company, I put in a clause stating that we would only lend the company this huge amount again if she was made the Chief Financial Officer, replacing the current one, who knew nothing and was making fifteen times more money than her. I openly stated that unless she is in that position, as she knows all the customers and business better than anybody, we would not grant them a loan. I also stated that the attorney would have to face the penalty for his crime as he cheated on our previous loan. The deal was approved, the crooked attorney went to jail, and we recovered our loan and the new CFO was there, making fifteen times more money and was extremely happy with her new life.

I finished my work early on Friday afternoon to be with Connie who came after checking the hotel. We enjoyed a long drive that day and stayed in California's Orange County for five days. Connie was in tears when she heard this story. I am writing this as a great tribute to darling Connie, who is no longer with me physically, but the whole scene of her picking me up and driving through Palm Springs is with me as a photographic memory. In fact, the whole of our lives and love, our travels and each and every thing for forty years is a movie in my mind and heart twenty-four hours a day. Throughout my career, I dealt with many such episodes. Connie was very supportive and helpful in giving me 100% moral support and sometimes accompanied me on some very hostile borrowers who engage in fraud and do the most unethical things for our worldwide largest finance companies where I was on the senior management team. I was given the most troubled, difficult, large, new, and old borrowers with over 100 million loans to one borrower, Three of them were in Chicago, two in Michigan, two in Columbus, Ohio, three in California, two in Houston, different small and large cities of all over the US. Also, a few jobs were in France and Germany. One of my jobs took place in Columbus, Ohio in 1987. The owner defrauded the lender for whom I was working Many junior and middle-management field examiners went to his office. The owner had run away and was hiding for months, and he had given instructions to his two senior management staff not to allow anyone from the lender, and they were all denied access to his premises. Let me explain that since we were secured lenders, we had the right to enter, even to do a surprise walk-in. However, we had a practice that we should notify our borrowers that it was time for due diligence and ask if it was convenient for them to provide the documents we needed, and we used to send our borrowers a list of our due diligence requirements. Again, it was our courtesy to do so; previously we had relied on surprise. Finally, since I was an expert in crisis management, I was asked to go. I showed up at the borrower's office and presented my business card. They were truly nice and asked me to sit and have coffee. I told them, "You three people did not allow my four juniors in, and now you are reluctant to let me enter and see your books. "They said no way could I review the books, and I told them, "I have the right to do anything, and if you do not let me, I will report to my senior management and we will take strong action against you that you will regret for the rest of your lives. Please know that I am not letting you play this game and let me see whatever I want to see, period. "They told me, "Mr. Berry, you are very strong and determined, but we are helpless as our boss had told us not to allow anyone," I told them to let me talk to your owner and boss as I am not leaving like the others and you better be careful and let me talk to him, and if he has refused to give his number where he is hiding, tell him the senior management person is here and he is determined to be here until the whole thing is discovered. They were panicky and went behind closed doors and talked to the owner, and slowly they told me, "Yes, you can only see a few records but we cannot provide anything else." I was determined and told them that, "I am even going to go through the locked room of your boss, and you better be ready to cooperate with me; otherwise, you would be part of the fraud. If we have to go to court and take orders, you would all be involved in protecting your boss and perhaps you should think of yourself, your wife, and your children as you do not want to be involved in case this is turned over to the FBI once fraud is detected. Now please, you either listen to your boss or me." They both went to a room and came out after twenty minutes and told me, "Mr. Berry, we are going to do anything for you as we do not have the money, salary, and anything. We would lose all, so please, go ahead. Also, do us a favor, we have not been paid for three months and have been working free for him in anticipation that we would be paid all our dues soon." I assured them that we would make sure they got paid, but let me do my work, we can all go for lunch or dinner and have more discussion and talk and be friends, and I am here to save you and your boss, if he cooperates with me. They were happy. I took them for a nice lunch and an exclusive dinner. At dinner time, they told me, "Mr. Berry, It has been over six months since we had dinner, drinks, and desserts. You truly are a gem and we feel that you are going to do good things for us. We are with you as we do not want to go to prison or pay heavy fines as we can't even find other senior positions and would be doomed forever." That was it. The next day, I worked and worked and went to the owner's room and his drawers, and I was thrilled to find a stack of locked files where it was mentioned and signed by the owner describing his scheme of defrauding our lender. There was a conspiracy between the owner and his largest customer and that was the largest US company. I took all those documents and told them that I am going to the Federal Express office as some information is sort of important for me to send to my office overnight. They said, "Mr. Berry, we leave at 6:00 p.m. You go to the Federal Express, which is open until 8:00 p.m., and go to the hotel afterward, and we will see you in the morning. That was one of the best things besides others in my life. Previously, I was also put into those situations and even different kinds. Now, Connie darling comes into the picture, and I told her about it and she was worried about my life and I was as well. I kept flying from Chicago to Columbus for two months—Monday to Friday. Connie was instrumental to sacrifice all that heavy travel of mine and internally, we were both concerned. However, she too was strong and encouraged me by saying that, "This is the US Pradeep, don't think about anything. You have been doing these kinds of hostile situations and you have earned your name in your senior job and that is why they had promoted you to this senior position. and I take pride in you. I am with you, I can accompany you for a few weeks and I even got my vacations, and I can teach during school and college break." She did take a week off and went be with me, staying in the hotel, dinner and all. I told my employer, and they were thrilled. They told me, "Pradeep please take Connie and we would pay everything for her." It was advantageous to both of us, and they knew Pradeep would detect the large fraud. That perhaps was my last Friday, and I was to meet the owner in the office at 9:00 a.m. I did not tell Connie that I was slightly worried about what the owner would do, nor did I disclose this to my employer. God is great all my fear knowing that he is a six feet strong man might try to harm me physically or throw me from the fourth floor. One way or the other he had found out that I know everything. I went to him; Connie was sitting in the restaurant downstairs in case some violent act happens or so. That was the greatest support I had; with Connie downstairs ready to make a 911 call in case anything happens. I went to the owner, and surprisingly, he stood up and shook my hand, and asked me to sit down. He ordered coffee, some bagels, and closed the doors. Only two people behind those big closed doors. I bluntly told him that I knew everything, and perhaps he knew too. He agreed to cooperate with me and said, "Mr. Berry, I do not want to go to prison. Please tell me how you can help me." I politely told him, "Mr. Z, please cooperate with us. Come admit it to us and get the large funds in millions. How are we going to get those funds? You have defrauded us, and you know well that you can go to prison for life. Please ask your customer to help you as they have deep pockets, and they would never like to be seen in the paper or TV that they were part of the whole white-collar crime." He was asking me for mercy. I felt that he was regretting now and was crying that he did all that and was willing to do anything and cooperate. We also needed him as he was an expert in turning millions of dollars' worth of raw material inventory, and work in process inventory into the finished goods and sell and get paid on COD basis. He could start paying our full loan and we do not have to take any write off in our P&L and Financial statements—losses. The owner cooperated with us for six months, and he and his company worked hard while we were funding the payroll and stated paying the IRS part of his liability of loans. In one year, we were paid back the large loan, and the owner had to sell his home, car, and everything for any shortage in our loan. He was practically on the road. We helped him to refinance his home, helped him find a decent job as he was an engineer and expert in his field. I took the initiative to help get his three senior management employees another job. It was one of the wonderful things in my career, and later on I kept doing the same kinds of most difficult situations in my career until September, 2005. Since then, I spent every day with Connie except twelve days each year going to India from September 1-16, 2005, twelve days in 2006, twelve days in 2007, and ten days in 2011. In between all those days, I was with Connie every moment even from India four to six times a day when I left my thing in my profession months, we collected all or loan any call to call the in the morning, The owner who was six-feet tall and strong put all the expenses in expense account position employer if you feel that way, ask your employer to get anything and I would make sure, you all are part of this and, perhaps if Since we had decided that we are coming on such date. Very hostile and extremely bad behavior of the owner of the company in Chicago in 1985. Another challenging but one of the best in 1981 in Chicago truly made my career and so many others how I handled I do not know how after *My Connie*. The worst of course is losing My Connie. The same types of episodes happened in Michigan, Austin, Columbus, California, Seattle, Indiana, Baltimore, New York, New Jersey, Chicago, Denver, Philadelphia, Phoenix and many more cities. I will always remember and wonder how I was able to do all that. Perhaps, I would like to describe all of these as a case study for the coming young blood to gain knowledge in the field of crisis management. These were extremely great challenges that I had gone through, and I am lucky that my employers trusted me to handle the challenges with these banks, finance companies, and equity players. It was a win-win situation for them and for me. I know for sure that there are many other brilliant people with lots of things to teach, but I would also like to add some of my knowledge as a legacy in Connie's memory.

Michigan was special. For three months in 1981, I would travel to Michigan every Monday through Friday to liquidate our borrower or sell the company to avoid any write off on our large loans. Connie was on a two-month vacation from teaching and was busy doing her research in the hotel we were staying while I was working at the office. But we had breakfast, lunch, and dinner together, and went sightseeing on the weekends. These things are important to me as my traveling job had become a joy. The best work travels I had was when I had to go to Germany and France, and I asked Connie to join me so that I wouldn't be lonely. It was in September 1996 for over two weeks. I never felt lonely and was amazingly happy. Let me write, when I think of all these times, I practically start shaking and become absolutely devastated. Each and everything is fresh in my memory—every single day's activities like dining, driving in Germany and France, sightseeing on weekends, and going to the winery. I can write an entire book about our traveling which might have over 600 pages. I will see if God's and Connie's blessings are showered on me. Now, I do not think, I can travel even for a night except to visit my brother and his family in India. How much has changed in my life due to one person, Connie? Many people would never understand this, but I am happy writing for Connie and myself. If someone appreciates my book, I am extremely grateful to them and obliged that they are giving tribute to Connie.

In 8th grade, we learned about the true story of Oh Master Ji (Oh My Teacher. This took place during the early 1940s, and it concerns a Hindu teacher who worked at a small school in a village. This teacher took great pains to teach his Hindu, Muslim, Sikh and all other students with love and compassion. Suddenly, riots broke out between Hindus and Muslims. Villages started burning and there were sectarian killings. At that time, there were many Hindu and Muslim bullies fighting against each other. So it came to pass in this village that conflict began between Hindu and Muslim. One Muslim boy went to the teacher's home and brought his daughter to his own home. Later that day, when the teacher came home and found his small daughter missing, he was devastated. His neighbors, who had seen the boy take the girl, told him where to look for his missing daughter. The teacher, thinking the worst, was extremely upset and took a big knife to kill his Muslim student who took his daughter. On his way to his house, he was sad and asked God, "Why would my student take my daughter? I gave my love to all my students and took lots of pain in teaching every student like they were my own children. Why would he do that to me, what evil did I do to him that he should do such a thing?" All these thoughts were wandering through his mind and the teacher was determined to kill his student. From half a mile away, the teacher saw the boy and started running to kill him. He came across to him with every intention of killing the boy.

Suddenly the Muslim student said, "Oh Master Ji, I have been looking for you. Thank God you are safe as your daughter is with me safe and sound. I brought her to my house like she was my own sister before anybody could harm her. Please come and rest and I would send you and your daughter with ten of my friends for protection." Master Ji was overjoyed that his devotion to teaching all the students paid off, and he apologized from the bottom of his heart for the negative things that had been in his mind. Connie and I have tried to apply this true story throughout our lives. But, now it is bothersome that our selfless, unbiased love and respect for all our relatives and friends did not make them realize our pain in difficult times, especially when Connie was alive. God gave me the power to reciprocate my love for Connie when she became slowly more ill. That power, which came from love, was more than the strength of 150 people. This is all due to our true love towards each other. I also chose not to inform anyone of her illness, and decided to cope with my loss with all of Connie's power. However, each and everything of our forty years is like an ongoing movie that plays in my mind and soul all the time—it is very painful. My relatives and some of my friends did not show me compassion even after her death. Only a handful of people came to give their condolences. I have been extremely angry with them and, perhaps, even with myself. I told my family that if they would come to visit me, I would order food for them. But they never came, and now that more than two months have passed, I don't know how I would react to their presence. I am angry and bitter over Connie's loss. If Connie could only return to me, I would forgive everyone and treat them nicely.

6. **"Whores don't live in the company of poor men, citizens never support a weak company and birds don't build nests on a tree that doesn't bear fruit." Connie and I have been very sensitive about this message throughout our lives and cared for the weaker section and never cared for the fruits or rewards.**

7. "He who is overly attached to his family members experiences fear and sorrow, for the root of all grief is attachment. Thus one should discard attachment to be happy." Yes, it is a good quote like many others, quoted by me many times. However, it is not practical for me at all, and I would perhaps never leave that attachment to my Connie.
8. "O wise man! Give your wealth only to the worthy and never to others. The water of the sea received by the clouds is always sweet."

Connie and I applied this message all our lives. Connie left a generous donation for a charity to her alma maters—Carleton College in Minnesota and the University of Michigan to provide scholarships for needy students, to the Red Cross, American Cancer Society, and to the Mayo Clinic. I have started giving on an annual basis to all of the organizations she favored. This gives me happiness. Connie always followed this message until her end and hopefully I can keep doing the same thing in the future too. I have seen people give great support to many noble causes after the death of a loved one. Hospitals, educational foundations, schools, colleges, churches, temples, and mosques are patronized in honor of the deceased whether that person is a spouse, child, or other loved one. I am sure that these noble gifts heal the loss of those people. I think there is great healing power in giving to charity in the memory of a loved one. Connie and I have never gone against the wisdom of this quote.

9. "Do not put your trust in a bad companion nor even trust an ordinary friend, for if he should get angry with you, he may bring all your secrets to light."

How true it is, and we both went through this in our lives. I have become more careful after Connie's demise. Among my friends and relatives, whom I considered our well-wishers, I see a big gap in their trustworthiness after Connie's loss.

10. "The fragrance of flowers spreads only in the direction of the wind. But the goodness of a person spreads in all directions."

Connie had that quality of goodness, and she did not have to practice. It was in her blood, in her brain and she left marks on many people all over the world. I get so many letters and appreciation from all those people all the time, and they are joy but painful as well. Connie went so suddenly I can't believe she is gone. I have to then see the reality every day, every moment, or wherever I am. In the health club, the grocery store, while reading books, checking the mail, organizing her desk, her chair, in our bed, our shower, our kitchen, our car and everywhere I turn.

11. **"Education is the best friend. An educated person is respected everywhere. Education beats beauty and youth."**

Connie and I tried to live by this message all our lives, and I am extremely grateful for that. We both had great education and kept actively learning to gain knowledge throughout life. Education stops after completing schooling and attaining degrees, but knowledge has no end, and that is why Connie was reading so many newspapers, magazines, and watching intellectual TV programs such as 60 minutes, the news, 20-20, Night Line, Mystery, WGN 11 public programs covering different world events and music, taking intellectual tours with scholars all over the world, listening to lectures, reading books, visiting the library, and watching intellectual movies, rather than wasting time gossiping, holding stupid conversations on shallow topics. She would research such diverse things as new recipes or new medical treatments from the books and internet for our greater knowledge. Although I have, from childhood, had a foundation of seeking knowledge, Connie instilled this even further in me. I will never be able to repay her in my many lives.

12. **"It is better to live under a tree in a jungle inhabited by tigers and elephants, to maintain oneself in such a a place with ripe fruits and spring water, to lie down on grass and to wear the ragged barks of trees than to live amongst one's relations when reduced to poverty."**

Connie and I always followed this great message and to this day, we don't owe anything to anyone, except our bodies, which we owe to our parents. People took lots of things from us, which we gave with happiness. Some borrowed loans and other things, yet today, January 17, 2016, no one has called to return those loans, and now I want to forget the debt. We managed, rather Connie managed, all the budgets and financial planning so that we never depend upon anyone except the supreme body which belongs to God.

13. **"Test a servant while in the discharge of his duty, a relative in difficulty, a friend in adversity, and a wife in misfortune."**

I don't want to insult Connie's family, but her siblings really and truly were the most painful thing in this category, both when she was alive and after her death. Their behaviors were worse than the worst servant, friend, or relative to be tested. Connie and I went through this many times and we tried to forgive them, as difficult as it was. Connie never expected that relatives, friends, and people we helped in any form would ever betray our friendship. Now, I don't know if I have the ability to forgive them for their betrayals. I would rather cut off my relationships with those who were using us and have disappeared from our lives when they got what they wanted, especially when Connie was sick from the middle of 2014 until the end. I am extremely bitter and angry because of their neglect, though perhaps time will heal this deep wound.

14. "If one has a good disposition, what other virtue is needed? If a man has fame, what is the value of other ornamentation?"

How true is it? Connie's internal and external beauty truly did not need any other ornaments or makeup to show the world her true self. Those people who knew her and anyone who came across her in life were amazed at her knowledge and inner beauty. No one I know ever had anything bad to say about Connie, rather they esteemed her as the best of the best. She was gifted with so many inner beauties in education, knowledge, hospitality, housekeeping, traveling, and wherever she leaves a mark. It is the truth, I am not trying to brag or exaggerate her goodness.

15. "The one excellent thing that can be learned from a lion is that whatever a man intends doing should be done by him with a whole-hearted and strenuous effort."

Connie was a lion and she did follow the above message throughout her life. She took on any project—education, housekeeping, hospitality, shopping, bookkeeping, organization, duty toward her family, husband, friends, and neighbors. She did not lack anything.

16. "Foolishness is indeed painful, and verily so is youth, but more painful by far than either is being obliged in another person's house."

Connie reminded me of this message every time I was having a hard time making a decision or if I was faced with a user who sought to take advantage of our soft hearts.

17. **"Do not reveal what you have thought upon doing, but by wise council keep it secret being determined to carry it into execution."**

Connie and I followed this message and practiced it throughout our lives. We never gave up once our minds were set on a course of action. We were firm believers of this message, no matter how difficult or how impossible our course seemed. We never gave up except when I lost my battle to save my Connie.

18. **"The world's biggest power is the youth and beauty of a woman."**

I applied this message to Connie all my life and will continue to do so. She was beautiful both externally and internally. I agree with this message to some extent, but due to lifelong love for Connie, I sometimes don't want to believe the truth of this. Connie was Connie. I cannot find any other person like Connie in my life. We will definitely meet again. It is my faith. There have been movies and stories about rebirth and meetings of couples parted by death. God knows the answer.

19. **"Never make friends with people who are above or below you in status. Such friendships will never give you any happiness."**

Connie and I never thought of this as we sought friendships with people who were like us in education and intellect. We cared nothing for the income of our friends, but only cared that they contributed something to the world. We had some very great and intellectual friends. I don't know if I will meet them again without Connie. Connie was so special and helped forge those friendships. Even if I meet them, my memories will haunt me and our friendship will not be the same as it was.

20. **"The serpent, the king, the tiger, the stinging wasp, the small child, the dog owned by other people, and the fool: these seven ought not to be awakened from sleep."**
21. **"There is no austerity equal to a balanced mind, and there is no happiness equal to contentment; there is no disease like covetousness and no virtue like mercy"**

22. **"As soon as the fear approaches near, attack and destroy it."**

Connie was very successful in this message, except in November, 2014 after the Mayo Clinic. But even then she was still positive. The episode I described above was the most painful thing in our lives. She is gone, and my life has become unbearably painful and I don't know if it will ever end. I do not think it will.

23. **"He who lives in our mind is near though he may actually be far away, but he who is not in our heart is far though he may really be nearby."**
24. **"There is poison in the fang of the serpent, in the mouth of the fly and the sting of a scorpion; but the wicked man is saturated with it."**
25. **God is not present in idols. Your feelings are your god. The soul is your temple.**

14

My Uncle's Advice

MY UNCLE TOLD ME THE QUALITIES OF a wife: "Son, a wife is precious. If we truly do the analysis from an educated and intelligent point of view." How true it is. No wonder Connie is always in my heart and soul, and would remain that way all my life. Now the world is different, and that is why the divorce rate has gone up tremendously among the younger generations; lately even with couples married for decades. I wonder why. I still cannot believe that divorce is healthy for anyone. There is an answer to solve this dilemma. I think marriage is an art, and we have to care for that every day or week as we give water to the plants and to the gardens. Our cell phones and new innovations such as the internet are good for emergency talks and important things. What did we do when we had no cell phone twenty-five years to thirty years ago? What did we do when we had no TV or other gadgets eighty years ago? We had simple lives and high thoughts. It is terrible that a sacred marriage is so easily broken. How can we expect the people of the world to be friends when there are fights between couples or families with kids? Are we progressing or going towards darkness? Gandhi truly stated, "technology would ruin mankind." Now the world is different. Perhaps newly married couples enjoy intimate relations, fun, entertainment, and kids but still end in divorce though. Why? This is not the case with everyone. There are beautiful marriages that last for lifetimes, which I truly love and I give credit to those couples. They have my greatest respect.

In our marriage, it was love. To love and care for each other was the most important thing for us both. I want to mention openly, without offending anyone, that Connie had the same beautiful body until she got too sick for two years and was getting weaker and weaker until she was finding it hard to even walk or do anything. Her two doctors spoiled her body with their mistreatment, and I hope

God takes care of them. As she grew weak, her body became a god for me. I used to touch her feet and worship the same beautiful body like God. I was not praying to God so much as I was praying for her body. It was and still is my most painful memory. I knew I would have to live for her. Her weak body was my God. Perhaps when Buddha left his palace as a child, he saw weak and fragile bodies, death, and other suffering. I was no different. But I did not become Buddha, nor will I ever be. However, I would serve Connie's wishes for charity, education, and for making humanity better.. Although we were from different cultures, I never thought that a wife is secondary to her husband. In my case, Connie was extremely important, and I cared for her as much as she cared for me. Perhaps that is why I am writing this book.

That is why Gandhi said, "I have the highest respect for a woman as she is the incarnation of tolerance." I followed that message all my life. He further stated that "A woman can tolerate most of the things her husband does, including drinking, gambling and cheating on her; although she would be extremely hurt, she finally may forgive him. However, if a husband suspects a woman's character, that is death for her."

As I mentioned before, I had forgotten our bad childhood memories once I met Connie. My happiness was Connie. Now, the tragedy of my childhood is nothing. Connie's death is much more painful and unbearable. This is because of Connie's love, but Connie death is absolutely unbearable. Now, my biggest loss and unhappiness is the demise of Connie. I don't care for all our wealth. I would concentrate on helping humanity, and teaching and following the path of Connie's honesty, loyalty, ethics, charity and selfless work. I followed these same principles but I would do more to get some ray of happiness from her memory. I will never be able to forget her goodness in my life.

Now I feel I understand why the young in India used to consult their elders during a crisis and when faced with problems. The elders had worldly experience which can't be learned in school. The knowledge of seniors comes from facing a life of problems. Perhaps, within my limits, I am getting ready to share what I have learned from my own experiences. I still have to learn more. I can learn from everyone I meet. Education reaches an end point, but knowledge keeps going if you seek it. Knowledge is like an ocean, there is no depth to it. That is what I have always believed.

15

Beginning of Our Love

WHEN I CAME TO THE US FORTY-TWO years ago, it was an extremely difficult decision to make. Back home in India, I had an excellent education, all the comforts of a wealthy family, and the makings of a successful professional career. I did not feel in control of the unknown variables of my life in going to a foreign country, whether for a short or long time. A possible destiny of mine had already failed to come to fruition. I had thought of going to the UK to study Chartered Accountancy from the Institute of Chartered Accountants of England and Wales, but my grandfather, fearing that I would leave India, forbade me to study in England. He wanted our family to stay in India. Some of my friends from college and my Chartered Accountant colleagues left for the US and UK, which made me think that perhaps my future lay in the US. With the encouragement of a friend who was teaching at an elite American university, I began to really consider moving to the US. I eventually decided to go but postponed my move by six months to rethink my decision. Finally, I did it. I took a Lufthansa flight to Chicago with a stop in Frankfurt. I had a five-hour layover in Germany. Those five hours waiting for the flight to Chicago were the most troublesome hours of my life. Once the plane was on the runway, I became extremely homesick and depressed, thinking that I was giving up my brother, my maternal grandfather, my aunts, my friends, and my education to restart everything. I would be like a newborn baby in a new place. I got up from my seat and started calling the hostesses who tried to force me to sit down with my seatbelt on. Their many attempts to force me to sit failed. I was desperate to get down from the aircraft, and eventually, the captain came to me to ask me what the matter was. I told him honestly that I wanted to go back to India and to please let me get off the plane in Frankfurt so that I could take another flight to India. He tried to persuade me it is not possible as the aircraft was on the runway. But my persistent request made him compassionate about my predicament. (I would have been arrested for this behavior in the present day). He asked me to show him the return ticket and told me that I had a restricted ticket, so I must stay in Chicago for fourteen days. He asked me how much money I had, and I said seven dollars. His response was that I would be struck in the Frankfurt airport for a long time with no food, no hotel, and no flight. I told him that I could request any airline to take me to India and upon landing. I would call my brother and he would pay for the ticket. Captain told me it would not happen that way and advised me to go to Chicago, spend fourteen days there, and take a return flight back to India. After landing in Chicago, I asked my relative who came to pick me up whether he could arrange for me to go back to India the next day. He was dumfounded and did not say anything. I stayed with my first cousin that night, and she was surprised by my behavior, but calmed me down with Scotch and dinner. We talked and I finally went to sleep at 12:30 p.m. and got up around 5:00 a.m. with a panic attack, depression, homesickness, and terror at finding myself in some other part of the planet. I started thinking desperately of how I would go back to India.

Later, some friends and cousins came to welcome me thinking I was happy to have arrived in the US. But I was in a depressed world, thinking of going back home. They told me to calm down as homesickness happens to everyone. I was wondering why they were no longer homesick, and why didn't they offer to help me go back to India. After fifteen days, I came to live in my own house in Old Town, Chicago, right across The Second City, to supervise an Indian restaurant. The restaurant was in a four-story building, with the restaurant on the ground floor. Each of the upper three floors consisted of five bedrooms and two baths. It was one of the best-known Indian restaurants in Chicago. I was living in my bedroom, and the three Indian chefs who had the other bedrooms were my companions. I was counting the days that remained for me to return to India as my return ticket was to expire after four months. There was great pressure placed on me to go back to India to establish my professional career, to help run the family business, and to commit to an arranged marriage. This pressure caused me great stress. I was living in a very confused, puzzled state of mind, and I dealing with homesickness. I started meeting many Americans and Indians who became my friends. Late one night, John Candy from Second City came to the restaurant with most of his cast. I did not know anything about him or Second City at the time. Later, they all become my close friends and were a great support to my troubled mind. Each weekend, a good-looking man would come to our beautiful bar for drinks and sit smoking by himself. I did not know who he was. One night, an American teacher who I had hired as a part-time waiter asked me if I knew who he was. I told him no, and he told me he is a famous film critic, Roger Ebert. I introduced myself to him, and he was extremely happy and was full of love and passion for his work. He started coming for long hours to talk to me. He became a good friend of mine and showed me some of his work. He also asked me to come for a movie premiere. The people I met—Roger Ebert, John Candy, and the Second City cast, Don Ross, Andy Shaw, journalists, and politicians like the Honorable John Metcalf—helped to cheer me up and showed me that I had a place in the US. Eventually, I fell out of touch with those friends, and I have not seen them since 1977.

Students of international languages at the University of Chicago also came to the restaurant with their full class. Mr. Douglas Goodman, who was studying Indian languages, became my dearest friend. He started taking me out for my audio recordings to send them to my brother in India. Douglas got married to his college girlfriend, and both of them went to India and visited my brother for four days in our huge ancestral house in Old Delhi. The house is still there, but no one is living there anymore as my family is living in different houses today. I have not seen Douglas since the late 1970s, but I would love to try to find him now. He and his wife would be great friends in my life now, although Connie can never be replaced at any cost. I even get panic attacks and feel greatly depressed from the unhappiness I face by writing this book. I cannot even imagine that Connie is gone. It is absolutely heartbreaking, and I find myself extremely weak in writing this book. I am of two minds, unsure whether or not I should write. But I also feel that I must write this, no matter how difficult it is for me to put the words on the page. I truly want to restart this life, taking me back to where I was forty years ago. That would be the happiest thing—Connie and Pradeep in this life again.

My Connie met me in the next two months, and that absolutely brought me happiness; a new life and passion. We had lots of conversations regarding my plans to go back to India, and she respected my desire to return but suggested I must see some parts of Chicago before I left. She told me to go to the Museum of Art and Science, the Art Institute, Northwestern University, the University of Chicago, the Shedd Aquarium, McCormick Place, Michigan Avenue, Lakeshore Drive, and many restaurants around the city. She also suggested that I enroll at an elite university for another graduate program, this time an MBA, before going back to India. I was reluctant to do so as I already had a superb education from India. Then it struck me that education has no end, and an American MBA would prepare me for more knowledge and advance my career worldwide. I have had the opportunity over the past thirty-nine years to gain more exposure and advancement. Further,

Connie suggested that once I returned to India, I might regret it if I did not take advantage of my chance to know American culture and to experience European culture on my return trip to India as I would have the chance to explore Germany and other countries on my flight back. She suggested that although I was well educated, there is a difference between knowing things and seeing them, meeting people, and exploring. She even told me that I should study foreign languages to advance my career in India. It would also benefit me if I decided to come back to the US after my marriage. She said that it would benefit me in the long run, and accordingly, I can choose my destiny with my future wife to see where we would like to settle for our careers. She told me that she has finished her education at Carleton College and the University of Michigan. She is also teaching and doing another Master's in Spanish and French. Although she already knew the languages well, she was motivated to study further to advance her career. Meeting her took my sorrow, sadness, and homesickness. I was a different person with the most joyful life. I felt a new revival of happiness, and so did she. Now, I knew why so many obstacles, so much unhappiness had kept me from India. It was my great and happy destiny to meet Connie, and begin a new chapter of my life with her. We were two bodies with one soul. That happiness can't be bought at any price on this earth. All of the wealth on the planet could never buy the happiness and the love we had.

My Connie also went through great happiness, but her happiness waned and later she faced the most difficult time due to her sickness, which was made worse in no small part by her one sibling and his extended family. However, the disruption of our happy life by this family episode was minimal compared to her sickness and in my strong opinion, her death came about through medical negligence. The family problems with her brother and his family, although it was painful for Connie and me, were nothing compared to the negligence. It could have been mitigated if the events of February 28, 2015 had not happened. All these things are mentioned in different sections in this biography of my Connie, and they crushed me, leaving me to live in isolation with my unhappiness. Secondly, families have differences that get resolved, and the unresolved differences are not as painful to me as the family was once extremely good to us. I count that as a small issue now that Connie has passed. I am reminded of a true story of Lord Buddha who came across a lady praying to get her dead son back. Buddha told the woman that if she could bring him a bag of rice from a house where there has been no tragedy for five years, he could bring back her son. After going from house to house day and night, she was unable to find a household that was free of tragedy. That is when Buddha made her realize the suffering of everyone on this planet. But even this story does not lessen my pain.

It was a miracle that our first meeting of one hour was the happiest sixty minutes of our married life. That miracle led to forty years of life together, and yet it ended with one of my biggest regrets, a regret that I will have to relive for the rest of my life. I left Connie's hospital room for one hour, sixty minutes, and that cost us both. In my strong opinion, her doctors came in my absence and falsified her medical records, ending Connie's life. I became a lonely person without my Connie. Sixty minutes brought us together for forty years, and after forty years, sixty minutes separated us. I was struggling to make the decision to stay or go, which became a boon, but that was the greatest thing of my life, as I met Connie and immediately we knew we were one. We escaped and got married.

As a young man, I was an extremely qualified professional in Delhi, India, and was offered many senior positions in different parts of India along with other career opportunities. But when a very senior school friend of mine, teaching at an elite university in the US came to Delhi and suggested I go to the US, I began to see a possible future there. It took three months for me to decide if I wanted to go. I decided to go for exposure for two months, with a senior job in the restaurant, food, import, and export business where I was responsible for accounting and cash flow, finance, and running the whole operation with other employees. Although it was not my field, I decided to get some different work experience. I was ready to go back after two months as I was very home sick, but my employer requested that I work a minimum of four to six months, and even that seemed too long. I was about to leave when I met Constance Fuller. It was true love in one meeting, and after dating for a short time, we got married. It was our first love and last one. Constance Fuller became Mrs. Constance Berry. Constance Berry and Pradeep Berry became an exceptionally strong, devoted, true, pure, and loving couple. I would say our marriage was full of fun, love, and care for each other that there were lots of people we met surprised to see that love, wishing that they had the same rhythm with their own spouses. I knew this special marriage would remain that way as long as we lived. "A great wife and a good friend are only for the lucky ones,"-a great quote from Indian culture. I must mention that my first employer did not pay my salary for two months, saying his cash flow was bad, which was not true. Connie spoke with him on my behalf, telling him that no one works for free and he better pay me, otherwise she would report to the IRS and the Labor Department. I was not paid for a week. Connie told him a second time that he had better bring a cashier check with proper tax deductions that same day, or else she would report him to both the departments and Pradeep would quit. I got the check right then and worked another two months with pay.

Connie wanted me to go back to my own professional career and advancement for which I had the offer before coming to the US. I returned to the field of finance, and I was promoted three months after that. I never looked back. My employer paid for my MBA in an elite university, while I was traveling close to fifty percent of the time all over the US. During these two years, Connie sacrificed her life for my work and college, and we had very little time to interact as she was also studying to advance her career. During that time, I noticed that many of my friends and coworkers were having problems with their spouses because they were asked to travel and be apart. Some of those coworkers got divorced, which was an eye-opening experience for me. In spite of our time apart, Connie and I were enjoying our lives, taking nice vacations, and having fun experiences that surpassed those of our friends, co-workers, and clients. I would like to mention a true episode that I experienced. I was extremely depressed when I was leaving for the US as it was something new and I truly did not know if I wanted to go or not. My mind was set on no, but some people told me to go and try out a new thing. I was on a Lufthansa flight from Delhi to Frankfurt with a five hour layover before my flight to Chicago. I got depressed in Frankfurt airport as I had never travelled out of India. The moment they announced the Chicago flight was ready and I sat down, my depression culminated into a panic attack that was so bad that I got up from the seat when the plane was on the runway. A hostess told me to sit but I did not, delaying the flight. I would have been arrested if it happened today. Finally, the captain of the plane came and asked me what was happening, and I told him the truth. He was nice and told me that I am causing trouble, but he asked me to show him my ticket so he could see what could be done. I showed him the ticket, and he explained that it was a restricted ticket for fourteen days and that only after staying fourteen days could I fly back to India. He asked me how much money I had, and I said seven dollars as it was the maximum amount the Indian government allowed due to the lack of foreign currency in India. Now things are very different. The captain told me, "Mr. Berry, I can let you off at the Frankfurt airport, but with seven dollars, you would be stranded and would be in big trouble and would not even have a meal or hotel and you would be suffering.

He advised me to touch down in Chicago and stay there for fourteen days and then come back, as I had the round trip ticket. Those fourteen days became forty years in the US, and now I am delighted that I came and met Connie and progressed in my profession. Without Connie, I would have come back to India after six months, or maybe even earlier. Sometimes destiny brings you to the most unlikely of fates in life. Again, I never expected that I, her husband, would have to oversee her cremation and last rites. I still remember my first meeting with Connie and how she brought a new life to me. I would like to recount a few more true incidents. One: It was in 1994, and I had to travel in the winter to Michigan to evaluate a new large borrower. I did not want to go alone, but the other junior associates working under me were on their Christmas vacations and some were in different parts of the world. I requested that Connie come with me, and she traveled with me and I did a fantastic evaluation. The same kinds of things happened many times in 1981, 1984, 1993, and 1996. She knew how to entertain herself by seeing different sites, exploring shops, and reading on the hotel balcony. She would pick me up for lunch and after my work, and we would go out to dinner. I would work late in the hotel, and she would read her book and watch TV. *Where would I find that diamond?* I did the same for her mother since 1989 after her father died. In 2006, I left my career to devote myself to her and to traveling all over the world. Although we traveled from the early days of our marriage, she wanted to see the world and with five weeks of vacation a year and my own consulting, we could not work and travel as much as she wanted. During the last three years of her treatments, although we traveled some at that time as well, I was 200% with her every moment of her life. It is so painful that she died before her time.

I must mention that our love was unconditional. We immediately knew on our first meeting that we were in love, and there was no need to have a second meeting. We knew that this is a nonstop flight to the world and we can't even think of getting off the plane. Many people have many dates, many meetings, sometimes their families inquire about one another or ask the family's permission before couples decide to marry with a huge wedding. We were successful without fighting the war of these hassles and compromising for family. I am always happy to see those couples who have been married for a lifetime. Our faith and values were that marriage is a lifetime commitment. We were lucky we passed our silver anniversary, but we failed to make it to our gold anniversary because of medical negligence. That negligence was so quick it did not give us time, especially time for me to save my partner. I absolutely failed in my battle. It was a big war, and I fighting alone against so many people. I wish I had a strong army behind me, but I was alone and the other side had too many fighters. One black belter, no matter how well—trained, is going to lose.. Now, after her demise, even a judo or karate expert cannot win if he is attacked by many enemies or betrayed by those he trusts. This is what happened to us. What a shame to humanity. Even animals have some principles. Kings many centuries ago, for example Porus and Alexander, had some principles. However, at the same time, there is an old saying that says never let your enemy go.

I loved it when Porus won many battles against King Alexander and pardoned him. Later, Alexander won and Porus was brought as a prisoner of war to the palace of Alexander. Alexander then asked Porus, "How would you like to be treated?" The brave Porus tells him, "I want to be treated as one king treats another king." During that episode, Alexander's bodyguard wanted to attack Porus. Porus told the guard, "Don't you know how to behave and not to interfere when two kings are talking?" King Alexander was very happy and told Porus that he would give him back all of the weapons and wealth he had taken. Porus again tells him, "It means you are obliging me and then you want me to be obligated to you and always consider that you showed your mercy, and I would have to respect you as my king." Alexander immediately told him "No, Porus, Alexander wants you to be his best friend, and now I want to come and shake hands with you as my dearest friend. I am desperate to have a friendship with an extremely brave man, and I would feel honored that Porus is my dear friend."

This true episode reminds me of many things in our life as we were always the best of friends. We never even thought for a minute that any differences no matter what would come between us as long as we both are alive. We also thought that if something happened to one partner, that other would not only love but worship the one who is gone and wait until the next life to meet again. That is what I am doing with great pain but with hope for this love. I have seen these things in my eighth-grade studies of ancient civilizations and the Vedanta, which is an open book for anyone to read and research, and tells of various true episodes. With the technological advances of the twentieth century, many Indian movies were made as far as one hundred years ago and remain hits today for the older generation. It is said that the new generation now is not taught the principles expressed in such films. As Gandhi-ji stated, "Technology will destroy humanity," and therefore, he was not in favor of too much technology. One can see that we have lots of technology, but the destruction of humanity, greed, love of money, and materialism have taken over with technology. The answer is hidden in the above sentences.

It also reminds me of Julius Cesar and how his close friend, Brutus betrayed him. In Connie's case, in my opinion, medical negligence and betrayal by the doctors during my one-hour absence was a much more serious stabbing to a crippled handicap like Connie after her cardiac arrest. She was fighting for her life, and the medical staff and the hospital were supposed to be the parents of this crippled sick person who could not speak or move as if someone had tied her completely in a small cage. Even a tiger or a lion cannot save himself in that cage. If you think you are brave, go alone or with ten people without any weapons and have hand-to-hand combat. I would call those people brave, and the medical staff was no braver than if attacking a helpless, powerless animal with weapons or guns. I was also attacked behind my back when I was gone for an hour. I would have shown my power if they were brave, and waited to attack me to my face. I would have jumped and attacked them like an animal in wild life. But cowards are cowards and attack from behind. A brave person would always come in front, face-to-face, giving a full challenge—let us see who is powerful. But they were worse than Brutus. Her biological sibling and his family were equal to so many Brutuses, but would be her friends when they wanted something. There is a saying that some people are givers and some are takers. This was the case with Connie and her family. People never ever change. Greed is greed, and as time goes on, it keeps on increasing just as a wild fire always grows. A fire never says, it is enough, let me stop, as I have had enough fire; I am satisfied and want this fire to become cooling rain to help the suffering people in the heat who have no cooling system and are struggling to take shelter. Just as people without air conditioning suffer until some humanitarian gives them a cooling system for their hard work. They are not beggars, nor do they want to beg. But then the old theory of supply and demand comes into play for the whole population during bad economic times. Let's hope, it gets corrected. *As man has made the mess, only man can correct it.* I have to mention again that Connie was extremely adventurous, and ours was the first marriage, and she left behind the most precious memories of happiness in my life. Yes happiness, but perhaps some punishment was also part of the package and that was the last three years of her sickness. Now I do not know if I should be thankful to God or call myself grabbing punishment of my life that she is gone from my life and my hands are asking for mercy to God to grant me one more chance and to give me Connie back. I am absolutely lost. Before coming to the US, we all used to watch both Hollywood and Indian movies with my brothers, school friends from college and chartered accountancy, and my family. Girlfriends were absolutely banned, I would say in that era. Forty years ago, it was the same way, then thirty years ago it was a new way, twenty years ago, the waves were beginning to move fast, fifteen years ago it was moving towards a bronze medal, ten years back it touched silver, and currently it has exceeded gold medal. With hope, we planned to win the Kohinoor diamond. It would have been impossible for me to think of being without Connie, as if I was falling from the top of the Himalayas. Connie would have saved me from falling; now, that is not possible, as we both see each other in our dreams and are desperate souls dying to meet each other. The movie *Who Kaun This* (Who She Was) was based on this theme, and I can only see her in my dreams and simply talk to her soul. We are like two desperate souls. I am reminded of the raga based, melody song *Naina Barse Rim ZIM,* which means "eyes and soul falling to meet each other as desperate souls." What I am going through now is living the same melody and the scenes of that movie. Why does she not come to me? I try to catch her, but she is gone. Has she taken a new birth or is her soul still waiting? My heart is breaking. I confess I realized this is Connie. I am going through that, I am seeing Connie everywhere, but I can't touch her, can't talk to her, but I am seeing her soul coming to me. My heart and soul is making me go and catch her, but in reality I can't get her. Who was she? I am sure it is her soul coming to me, and I am desperate to have her back, but I am upset that I can't even touch her. She was my wife and she is still in my heart and mind, and I keep seeing her but I can't believe that she is gone. I see her soul, her face, and I suffer. This movie can be easily seen on YouTube and I am sure it is on Netflix. It would be listed under international movies or Indian hit movies. Another touching Indian movie from Netflix that I asked Connie to watch with me in the house was *Anupama,* a love story of a husband and wife. The husband has a similar situation to me after the demise of his wife. The movie shows the widowed husband blames his newly born girl as the cause of his wife's death, and he gets absolutely isolated with all his wealth, servants, and business, and loses interest in life. My life has practically the same theme, making me bitter with my family and friends who did not call Connie or me for one year. The same with some of our friends, who for six years, never even bothered to ask, "How is Connie?" They may wonder how many times did I call? Should I blame them or myself? My shock is so deep that I want to blame them without realizing that others may have lots of problems too and they are all justified. Yes, they are; however, I am not even conscious of my fault—never—as my loss has pierced my every minute of thinking about Connie. I would respect all of them but nothing can heal my constant thoughts of my wife.. I don't talk to them or maybe don't want to describe the trauma I faced. Even if my family and friends know or come to know, no one will ever be able to understand a fraction of that trauma. God, please forgive me. Will God be able to evaluate the trauma? But, I have to thank the Lord for not punishing me for my behavior. I surrender and ask for mercy and forgiveness that I am already going through that suffering of losing Connie, and I ask for forgiveness. From our very first meeting, we were happy together without even going out on a date. We wanted to spend more and more time with each other, and were happy to be alone together. We did not try to cultivate hundreds or thousands of friendships just to be happy. We were extremely happy in each other's company. In spite of this, we were very social, going to parties, dancing, eating out, etc., but we were honest and sincere and never let another man or woman come into our life together. All of our life we were pure—we never cheated or hurt each other, and we were never jealous or attracted to another person. We took an oath, to be honest to each other no matter where I had to travel or if one of us had to work late or go to a work party alone. When I was out of town, Connie would drive alone to events and be sure to return by 10:30 p.m. so we could talk before going to bed. We both had to leave early for work the next morning, regardless of how late we stayed up talking the night before.

16

Connie Was My Destiny

Again, I was happy after meeting Connie. Connie was my destiny and my reason for coming to the US. She was the greatest thing in my life and helped me forget all my childhood pain. Now the true pain of losing Connie is much harder than my childhood pain was. I would re-live the pain of my childhood for Connie's presence anytime now, and more realistically, in my next life. We had so much love for each other, and I am living with great pain now and living in hope that we will both meet again. This much faith I have, and the revival of this faith gives me the strength to bear this pain. I know miracles happen, that reincarnations happen. Hope gives life. Never deprive someone of their hope, and ask God to grant their wish. These are great tools and thoughts that wander through my mind at times. It helps to know that God knows all this and will definitely grant this wish in our next lives to be the same couple—"Connie and Pradeep." I would be granted this desire of having Connie even if I have to see hardship mitigating the joy of having Connie. It would be the best thing for both of us, and I am sure of that.

I only had seven dollars when I landed in the US. Neither my father nor the rest of the family has ever paid me a single penny from our inheritance. Connie and I got married. I was extremely happy and started working hard. I was smart and motivated to show her and my family back in India what I was capable of. After three years, once my family knew that I was doing great in the US and that we were comfortable with what we had, Connie and I went back to India together. Things were very different with my family. They had always respected me, but now we were treated as if we were kings. That is why I must mention, "Success and winners are always respected."

"We must play to win no matter what the game is." I do not care for that now, but the loss of Connie is deeper. I would practice many great messages that I have studied and known for years in memory of Connie and for my own peace. I thought of what Jesus said: "Father, forgive them, they know not what they do." It is natural for me to undertake self-examination in order to remember and evaluate my past deeds and to think of the holy preaching of the Bible, Gita, and Quran. Soon, the holy sermons came to my mind.

a. Surrender and accept when you are helpless, but keep the mind and body active.
b. Think of my past deeds to act correctly in the future.
c. I must prepare for mental and physical hardships if I want to survive and do noble things for humanity, including teaching and sharing my knowledge, and learn more for myself.
d. Pray for the self and humanity and the world.
e. Keep busy, occupy my mind, and pray for forgiveness from Connie for anything bad I ever did that hurt her. I ask her blessings and keep doing good things for her sake.
f. Find a purpose in life to do things, which Connie would appreciate.
g. Lead a simple life of high thinking and deprive me of the great pleasures we had—traveling and dining out, etc.
h. I am doing that and perhaps I will not go on cruises or any trips, except to India to see my brother and his family and other members of my family.
i. Lord Krishna had stressed an evenness of mind in all circumstances and situations, skill in action and overcoming the law of opposites, working without attachment and considerations of returns, rewards, and prizes.
j. They told lies and got ahead in life, and here I am telling the truth and stagnating.
k. Adam, in the Bible, said in a similar vein, "Allow your mind to think and say anything it will, only do not identify with it. Allow your body to do what it needs but do not react, everything would happen on its time and accord."
l. Religion is not a business; it is a mission, a great way of life.
m. Manu said, "The whole world is kept in order by punishment, for a guiltless man is hard to find: through fear of punishment, the whole world yields the enjoyments which it owes."

17

Some Nice Quotes for our Daily Life

IT REMINDS ME OF WISE QUOTES FROM my late uncle, Dr. P.N. Behl, "Darts, barbed wire and heated spears, however deep they penetrate the flesh may be extracted, but a cutting speech, which pierces like a javelin to the heart, none can remove—it lies and rankles. Bad language used in anger or otherwise hurts the person. The wound of the dagger heals but the hurt caused by the speech leaves a permanent scar on the heart. Hence, control of the tongue and speech are very important. Never hurt others with your words. I strongly recommend austerity in speech, body, and mind. A man's job is to help one another and not to hurt each other. The latter is an animal instinct and not a human one. A good cheerful word can win the hearts of others, a bad word makes enemies. Similarly, a dirty look can be killing: a cheerful smile is always appreciated. Women can seduce with a winsome look and a sweet word. Self-restraint is very important and essential in all walks of life, restraint in speech is important. If you hurt or abuse somebody with foul words, you hurt him. He becomes an enemy and vows to take revenge. Further, if he returns your foul language, it shall hurt you as well. One can put knives and arrows in somebody's heart no matter how deep it is, but it can be taken away with medical treatment. But a bad deed and a bad word from the mouth rattle and rattle the whole life, and the person sometimes keeps a tendency for revenge." I would slowly try to follow the above great messages.

Further, per Khalil Gibran, in one of his books, he said, "My the soul is my friend who consoles me in the misery and distress of life. He who does not befriend his soul is an enemy of humanity, and he who does not find human guidance within himself will perish desperately. Life emerges from within and derives not from environs. I came to say a word and I shall say it now. But if death prevents in uttering, it will be said by tomorrow, for tomorrow never leaves a secret in the book of eternity.

I came to live in the glory of love and the light of Beauty, which are the reflections of God. I am here living, and the people are unable to exile me from the domain of life for they know. I will live in death. If they pluck my eyes I will hearken to the murmurs of Love and the songs of beauty. I came here to be for all and with all, and I do today in my solitude will be echoed by tomorrow to the people.

What I say now with one heart will be said tomorrow by many hearts." Prayers have a very soothing effect on a troubled mind. But sometimes, that fails, depending upon our love and devotion, and I am going through that pain every moment of my life. My suffering is worse than I ever thought after Connie's demise. I am aware that we all have to go one day, but I am not able to accept that now because of my deep love for Connie.

18

Gandhi Ji–His Messages and His Teachings

Now I think of Mahatma Gandhi, Father of the Nation of India. His sacrifice and fight to get India's independence from British rule succeeded on the 15th of August 1947. He was a barrister by profession and fought for equal rights in India and in South Africa. A small built man can get freedom for all. Why then can't I get peace of mind and the power to bear the loss of Connie? However, this is a personal loss, and I cannot use this example. Gandhi said, "My life is My Message." "Truth always remains forever." "Non-violence." "My uniform experiences have convinced me that there is no other God than Truth." God can never be realized by one who is not pure of heart. Self-purification, therefore, must mean purification in all the walks of life." "But the path of self—purification is hard and steep. To attain perfect purity one has to become absolutely Passionate in thought-free, speech and actions: to rise above the opposing currents of love and hatred, attachment and repulsion."I am bidding farewell to all the readers, for the time being at any rate. I ask them to join with me in prayers to the God of Truth that He may grant me the boon of Ahimsa in mind, word, and deed." "I have nothing new to teach the world, Truth, and non-violence are as old as the hills," By M. K. Gandhi. These are some of his messages that were extracted from his famous book *The Story of my Experiments with Truth,* an excellent book for all readers.

19

Nelson Mandela

President Nelson Mandela was a big follower of M.K. Gandhi, and practiced non-violence and suffered for years in jail. But he forgave everyone, and his truth and sacrifices made him the President of South Africa. He was a world—renowned figure in the history of the world. He mentioned when Gandhi was going back to India, "India gave us Mohandas Karamchand Gandhi, and we returned to India "Mahatma." The same Mahatma became Bapu and Father of the Nation.

In 1982, a great movie, *Gandhi,* was released, where Ben Kingsley played the role of Gandhi. This film and Mr. Kingsley won the Oscars in 1983. It was a wonderful true movie, which helps to elevate the mind and lets you find inner peace. I might watch it again to get more enlightenment, and to reduce some of the pain from losing Connie. How much peace I would get, I am not sure. The great Dr. Luther Martin King, Jr. was also a follower of Gandhi and fought for freedom and practiced non-violence. He, too, left behind a legacy for the world.

20

Swami Vivekananda

Swami Vivekananda attended the first world religious congress in Michigan Avenue, Chicago, Illinois, USA in 1893, and said, "If you forget and forgive, that ends everything." He was the first person in history who said in his opening remarks, "My Dear Brothers and Sisters of America" before his long speech. People were in tears. There is a street in Michigan Avenue—where the world religious congress takes place in a hotel—which has been given the name "Swami Vivekananda Marg." He stressed, "Strength is life, weakness is death." "However long this life is, do something different so that the world can remember you, otherwise, what is the difference between you and the trees and stones. They also live, die, and decay." These messages are from one of his books. Marg is a Hindi word which means *showing the right directions to youngsters, to students, to men and ladies which direction to go in sorrows, to help people for humanity, to show new rays of hope when stressed, to show away to go in the path where they can realize their bad deeds, to show new ways of living to the criminals who are ready to remorse their crimes, and to show a new way to all the purpose of life leading them to become good citizens and mankind.*

I suggest that readers do further research on Swami Vivekananda. These messages are great and were very meaningful to me when I was young and helped others, but it does not provide any comfort to me now that I have lost Connie. I hope I find some ray of hope and that is *reincarnation.* It is my true and solid faith that if there is any supreme power, he could listen to our love. This hope allows me to have some peace once in a while. Further, if I have done any good karma, the Supreme Lord will fulfill my desire in my next life. Also, my pain will be heard by the lord for sure, and that great hope is a power in my life now.

In memory of Connie, I want to share some thoughts on the great poet Tulsidas—we had to study his work in sixth grade. Tulsidas' poems can be read on the internet or in books. I remember the great Tulsidas as one of the most learned poets and scholars of the sixteenth century. He was too obsessed with his wife and her absence was like his death. One night she had to go see her sick parents. Tulsidas was not able to stand missing her. He walked through the night in the rain to see her. Since it was late and raining, he used a rope to climb up to her room. His wife was very upset and told him that it was 2:00 a.m. and he was there and foolishly climbed to her window. She told him that he was lucky to be alive; the rope he used was actually a huge python. Perhaps the python was not hungry and was enjoying the rain; otherwise, he would have attacked and killed Tulsidas. She then told him to devote his obsession to God so that he can learn and become something in the world. That was his enlightenment, and he surrendered to God and wrote many chapters on spirituality and education which are known throughout the world in the Sanskrit language and have great meaning for soothing the mind.

21

Education and Career of Connie

CONNIE WENT TO ONE OF THE BEST high schools and to Carleton College in Minnesota, one of the finest liberal arts colleges in the US for her undergraduate degree. She later transferred to the University of Michigan, another top college. After graduating, she taught junior and senior high school for a few years. Later, to advance her career, she took her master's in Spanish and French. She studied at the top colleges in Mexico and Spain, and then taught Spanish and French to the children at US military bases in Germany, England, and Spain for five years, and then in California. Later, she moved back to her hometown, Chicago. That is how I met her, and she became the true love of my life. Connie exposed me to American culture, dressing and polishing me to advance my career, though I equally had one of the best educations As such, we both had professional careers, but that didn't interfere with our love and understanding, even though I was traveling all over the US, but was home for the weekend and sometimes more. We were in touch four or five times a day over the phone while traveling apart. Our Friday through Sunday night, we were always together, and depending upon the reports I was writing, I was in my Chicago office for weeks and home each night. It was a great life combined with our professional senior positions. Connie taught for thirty-four years and took early retirement, but continued substitute teaching to keep her teaching license, and she was in great demand for Spanish and French. She got offers for full-time teaching positions with different school districts but she turned those down. I told her to forget work and to enjoy life and travel with me and have fun. She enjoyed teaching and had very close teacher friends whom I used to meet and with whom we had wonderful times. I give great respect to my wife as a teacher who did her duty.

Also, in honor of Connie's character and memories, I would like to mention some quotes I learned from my uncle Dr. P.N. Behl. Wisdom leads to freedom, Education to Character, Culture to perfection, Humanism to joyous living In a sense, human beings sometimes are crueler than the animals, when greed comes. Our thoughts wander in all the directions And many are the ways of Man, The Cartwright hopes for accidents, And the physician for the cripple And the priest for the rich patron The blacksmith seeks day after day The customers endowed with gold Our thoughts all run towards profit For the sake of spirit, of mind Let go all these wondering thoughts.

Character: Man is what his character is. A man of good character makes his life good, while a man with a bad character usually ruins his life and mankind. Character means goodness of heart, tenacity, truth, living by your words, discipline, respect for others and elders and for the weaker sections of the society, respect for the teachers and wise. A man without character is considered to be worse than a beast. People with weak character are usually feeble, meek, and easily changeable.

After retiring, Connie would go for weekly lunch with her teacher friends, and I was very happy. I also used to go with them as it was like a close family. Although she kept substitute teaching, she had more time to travel with me when I was traveling, and that made my life absolutely great. I combined working and traveling to have great fun.

I remember her going many places with me and her company gave me comfort. The most important time that I needed her was when I had to go to Germany in 1996 for two weeks and then to France for another two weeks. We went to California, Dallas, Michigan, and many small towns. I think it was a great help that she was able to travel with me so that I would not be lonely. I would have never dreamt that loneliness was tolerable, but her demise has crushed me, as I will never see her except in my mind. All the thirty-nine and half years of memories are painful. They are:

1. Daily diary with beautiful handwritten notes of things we did.
2. Household notes of bills in folders.
3. Receipts of cash and credit cards.
4. Names of all the vendors and suppliers with phone and telephone numbers
5. Day services such as painting, carpet cleaning, car service, and other utility stuff was done with notes of how much was paid.
6. Her different drawers of clothing with lists of the contents.

7. Her drawers of important documents.
8. Her makeup kits, with date, expiry, and all other details.
9. Our pictures of traveling with notes of when and where it happened, and sometimes names of friends written at the back.
10. Her letters from my family, her family, and our friends.
11. Important certificates and pictures for the future, just in case.
12. Years and years of our marriage anniversary, birthday and Valentine's Day cards.
13. Separate books for household inventory, with the date of purchase and prices.
14. She would read different designs for ladies and men and accordingly would order new clothes for her and me.
15. Appraisal values of our paintings and actual cost.
16. Medical reports and all the payments.
17. Medical reports and medical history for both of us.
18. Our business and pleasure trips.
19. Old canceled checks for future references.
20. Folders of her parents' pictures and their important documents for any future reference.
21. Folders of her grandparents and their pictures and letters.
22. Most important wedding cards from friends and relatives in special decorative plates.
23. Keep special napkins for different occasions.
24. Keep different greeting cards for different occasions.
25. Special thank you notes and special great quality diaries for different purposes and to write notes with her absolutely beautiful handwriting.
26. Variety of coasters, table mats, table cloths, special candles and silver, plates, and glasses etc. for different occasions.
27. Her beautiful writing for forty years, well organized; perfection in all aspects is one of the most painful things besides losing her.
28. All the brochures, itinerary of all the cruises to Crotona, Italy, Ireland, Norway, Budapest to Amsterdam, the Caribbean, Alaska, Spain, London, France, Germany, seven times to India, Palace on Wheels in India, Jaipur and Agra twice by air and car. Khajoraho, Bombay and our stay in Hotel Ambassador, Sun and Sand. Germany a second time, Berlin, France, Vienna, Switzerland, and fifty to sixty more. All are individually organized and are in the files, intact in separate folders in her big cabinets.

I was just curious and cleaned some of the files on August, 14 at 12:30 a.m., and was very upset to see how smart she was, and now all that fun we had is now over with her demise. I see all those and get upset. I think and look, and put them back nicely in the cabinets. I do not want to throw them away nor do I want to give them to any foundation or library. It has our diplomas where we were studying culture and food along with history of the places we visited. The last day, all the people in the group had to prepare and present on the stage. If you have done your homework and answer or write those in the one to two-hour exam, you are honored with the diploma. I do not think those diplomas have much credit, but at least it will get you into the door for some position if you have a postgraduate degree. It is a very tricky diploma. We never ever even tried to do anything with it. However, it's a nice thing to show to our friends. Now, Connie is gone. It's a monument for me, for my own happiness or sadness. I am going to keep them.

29. I found ten books of the world's best cuisines and recipes that Connie had been reading in the papers and magazines and nicely cut and paste in the books. I am sure restaurants, libraries, and educational institutions would be delighted to have them. I am sure they are like antiques. I would see what I would do with them. I would decide. Connie also started doing volunteer work in Wilmette library for two to four hours every Wednesday even when she was sick. She took that work very seriously even when I told her not to go when she was sick, but she said no and continued to volunteer. Later, I started dropping her off and spending time reading and buying books for donations too. Everything we did was wonderful as she was my obsession and was my love.

22

My Connie: The Blessed Lady

CONNIE WAS HIGHLY INTELLIGENT AND AN INTELLECTUAL, and I am only going to mention a very few of her philosophies, otherwise I would have to write another book with all her beliefs she applied in her life.

Connie always had Irish Blessings in her book as a book marker. "May the road rise to meet you. May the wind be always at your back. May the sun shine warm upon your face, the rain fall soft upon your fields. Until we meet again, may God hold you in the hollow of his hand." These are some of the quotes from St. Francis de Sales in her bookmarks: "Make yourself familiar with the angels and behold them frequently in spirit; for without being seen, they are present with you." "God grant me the serenity to accept the things I cannot change, the courage to change the things I can and the wisdom to know the difference."—Salesian Missions.

"Remember your debts of gratitude," "Live in a way that leaves no regrets." "Everything people say or do is ultimately noted in the belief that those actions will lead them to happiness." "Your dream is possible." "Never seek happiness outside yourself." "Seek to understand your mistakes so that you may never repeat them. "These are a few quotations from *Open Your Mind, Open Your Life* by Taro Gold.

23

Connie's Passion for Reading

CONNIE WAS A GREAT READER. SHE USED to read the *Wall Street Journal, Chicago Tribune, Barons,* and the *New York Times*. Additionally, she used to read a minimum of sixteen magazines and health journals from elite universities, and used to give me important health care topics to read. I, too, was a great reader, mostly of the business sections of all the newspapers. I also read articles about professional development, articles on different topics and writing, and I also found time to read articles on health care. I have always been fond of reading true story books, whereas she used to read both fiction and nonfiction books. She reads philosophy books and other nonfiction genres. She would read *Consumer Reports, Chicago* magazine, and at least ten other different magazines to get the most popular news and best rated appliances, cars, TVs, and anything related to the home. Also, she would let others know the same. It was a great humanitarian cause. She loved exploring different cuisines and restaurants, attending Broadway plays, symphonies, and other things. She loved these cultural events and made me see all those with her. Now, I would have a very simple and plain life with all the withdrawal symptoms of my grief. The more I think, the more I want to write on each topic of her life.

I am convinced that I will never find another diamond like her in my life. I hope and pray that God grants me, Connie, as a wife in my next life. I have a strong feeling that we will both meet in our next lives. This belief is the only thing that gives me happiness, as I have lived an upsetting life due to the loss of Connie. After her loss, I began to read those articles that she had suggested that I was not originally too interested in. After reading them, I wanted to read the same articles many times over. Her awareness, intelligence, and common sense were beyond approach, and she was super smart and busy all day long. I am blessed to have such a gem in my life, and no one else can ever replace her, nor do I ever want to replace her. She was absolutely amazing and beautiful in my forty years of life and was always writing and building her knowledge of different topics. Connie was a super reader. Her average daily time spent reading was ten to fifteen hours a day when she took early retirement, and before that, she read five to six hours each day.

Connie used to read many intellectual books; she must have read over 8,000 books during our marriage. She was very fond of the authors Susan Vreeland, Elizabeth Phillips, Jane Robinson, the comedy of Woody Allen, Shakespeare, Ruth Rendell, Tom Wolfe, and Jon Krakauer to name a few. Besides that, Connie also loved all cookbooks, health-related books about symptoms and their causes, and different recipes of world cuisines. She loved to read *Time* magazine, *Consumer Reports*, travel books for destinations around the world, and world history. Connie loved cutting recipes and trying them for me and her friends, listening to old classical records, watching Oscar-winning movies, European movies, and listening to different music genres including Elvis, the Beatles, the Bee Gees, Frank Sinatra, Mozart, and hundreds more. As I mentioned, we saw practically all the Broadway shows including Joseph and the Amazing Technicolor Dreamcoat, Mama Mia, Miss Saigon, Elephant Man, Frank Sinatra, Irish songs and plays and I would have to write 200 pages to write all of these down. This time, when I am writing, I have pain in my heart and soul, feeling that Connie was truly one in a million and this diamond has left me totally alone. I am going to miss all that, depriving myself of the world, including plays and Mozart, which was my passion with her. I was just reading about Turkey and its ancient heritage where King Alexander and Cleopatra visited. I would be totally depressed and would get a panic attack if I ever decided to go alone or with any family member. I can't even think of going. The only thing I like now is to go to the health club, do important household work, and staying home. I think I can go see my real elder brother and his family and my grandnieces in Delhi, India, That is all. I now have realized that every author has written books in memory of someone, showing that authors write about their loved ones and that is wonderful, otherwise, without this content, such a book is not perfect.

24

Reading Passion – Her Intellectual Mind and Brain

I WAS THINKING ABOUT CONNIE'S READING HABITS AND her interest in diversified magazines and knowledge the other day. Our whole family, including the entire Berry family, consists of about 200 people, three generations of my grandfather's sisters and brother's families included. Some of them, about fifty to sixty have settled in the US, and some of them are smart—some are computer engineers, and some of them have graduate degrees. There are about 100 people on my mother's side. Overall, if we consider a population of 300-400 people, including some of her friends, I can prove it statistically, that out of the whole population, Connie was the most intelligent person of all and the most well-read too. I don't think anyone amongst the group can compete with her as far as intellect in every subject goes. The people I am talking about are very successful in their businesses and are intelligent. One of them is a medical doctor. I can even compare Connie with her, and she is a medical doctor who studied in America, and her husband is also a doctor. I don't know why people think medical doctors are like gods, but this is the way they think, and this is the way they are. I think these doctors may be very good in their own field, but do not know any subject other than medicine. In my opinion and my experience of forty-three years with Connie, I spoke to my family members who are medical practitioners one day and found that they don't read anything other than their medical books. I don't think they know anything about the world, or about ancient civilizations, or about the histories of different countries. Their knowledge is just limited to the medical field.

I would say that Connie was a gold medalist in her knowledge. Business people, like doctors, are very good at what they do, but know nothing else. So it all boils down to the intellectual level of a person—what can they discuss, or what do they know about diverse topics? I feel that an intellectual person should be able to discuss world languages and cultures. Connie knew every state in India, their languages, food ways, and cultures. At the same time, she was familiar with most world cultures. For example, she knew how different countries in Europe such as Ireland, France, Denmark, Germany, Norway, Italy, and Spain progressed, and what they did, whether they were Communists or Democrats. This kind of vast knowledge, I don't think I have ever seen before or will ever see again in my lifetime. When I think about it, I realize that Connie was brilliant. In this particular area, she exceeded me a million times. She even knew the history of India; however, she, like me, sometimes questioned whether the Mahabharata or the Ramayana really happened. Some Indians believe that the histories recounted in these epics truly occurred, but some are skeptical. Some are confused, but most Indians, including me, believe that those events really occurred. So when we have a question about these things, such as yesterday when I was watching Ramleela in Delhi, we ask ourselves what we believe. Most of my fellow moviegoers believe in the story of Ramleela, but some people don't believe in it—they said it was a show and considered it to be mythology. So if I have my doubts, I don't think we should single out anyone else. Having said all that, Connie would put across her point in a brief moment and be done. Those who speak less and read more are often more intelligent than those who speak often and don't read. I mentioned this before and I am repeating it now: listening is golden. Connie's intelligence was internal and external. I was very lucky to have Connie in my life. Her loss has rattled me and I don't have any peace of mind even eight months after her death. People want to see me become normal again, but I feel that it will take me years to overcome my grief. The only happiness I get is from meeting new people. The people I met when I went to collect her medical reports were much better to me than anyone else, even better than my friends. Our real estate agent, who I spoke to for a couple of hours recently, showed great compassion, and it was a mental stimulation for me. I am seeking out this kind of environment.

I just want to say this about Connie's reading—her knowledge was immense. I want to give you one more example. I did not know that while she was reading about twenty magazines, she was also giving a copy of that to our neighbor because she was a widow and could not afford to pay for the subscription as she looked after her family. Since Connie was already a member of those magazines, she subscribed to the magazines for our neighbor. The other day when I was talking to her, she told me that she knew I was going to India and like always, would get her a gift from there. She asked me not to get anything from India, but instead subscribe her to the magazines that Connie would read. I was very happy to hear that. I had not known about this selfless charity of Connie's. I will continue her legacy of helping people. This gives me immense happiness, but at the same time, it makes me sad. I was not sure that I would actually travel to India until I got on the plane on October 20, 2015. On the night of the nineteenth, having only had two hours of sleep, I packed all of my papers into a briefcase and carry-on bag. I will now have to spend hours in Delhi sorting these papers and making copies. I will leave these documents in Delhi and take copies back to the US. Connie knew about all the documents, and dealing with them makes me very tense. Connie always helped me to organize my documents when I traveled. That was her greatness; she was the whole world to me. I would definitely mention this about her reading. I have said this before, that she must have read somewhere between fifty to seventy thousand books in her lifetime. She could read very fast, and she would always find time in the night to read. She would carry books with her on the plane; she would take them with her wherever she would go. Sometimes I would get sick of her reading! I couldn't believe she read so much, and she wouldn't even talk to me. So she would tell me that there was nothing to talk about. She would then put the book down, only to start reading again after a while. I would get irritated, and then she would get irritated and she would ask me why I couldn't pick up a novel and read. I would tell her that I liked to read the business section of the local papers and the *Wall Street Journal*. She would tell me that I needed to develop a habit of reading other things, like novels. She would say that instead of depending on her to explain why world events like wars took place, I should read it on my own. Although I knew these things, I wanted to refresh my knowledge. Once Connie read something, she never forgot it. That was the difference between us. I want to reiterate that of all the people in my entire extended family, she was the most intelligent of them all.

25

Connie's Love for Music and Arts

Connie loved old classical songs from many musicians, such as Frank Sinatra, the Beatles, Elvis, Abba, and Mozart. She also loved Christmas music and many symphony and plays. She used to have two gramophones and seventy to eighty year-old records of singers like Cliff Richard, Tony Christie, and Ray Charles. I, too, was extremely fond of all that and our shared interest was a plus. I loved Broadway plays and so did she. Of all the plays we attended, we never left early. We saw many plays, including Mama Mia, Miss Saigon, Elephant Man, Joseph and the Amazing Technicolor Dreamcoat, and Elton John's plays. Regarding the arts, Connie used to collect many artistic pieces for the house. She had special baskets for different places, like for her newspapers, magazines, small decorative art objects for the house, kitchen, study room, and bedroom. She also collected several historical paintings. She took me to see many art and cultural shows. She was a member of the Museum of Art and Science and donated money to TV Channel 11, which is supported by the public and provides absolutely great programs. Channel 11 breaths of air music, history, Christmas programs, and symphony shows.

Connie was curious about the subjects covered by different magazines and TV channels. She would read reviews and ratings of the channels and shows and knew which shows were popular and had good ratings. She also knew which program was going to end and when it will end, when a new show was coming along, and the ratings of films in theaters. She would watch awards shows like the Oscar and Emmys, and the country music awards. She enjoyed programs like Night Line and 20-20.

Connie also loved to travel to cities with important artistic events. Connie took me to Santa Fe, New Mexico, in September 1993 and I loved it. She knew that during September, craftsmen come from all over the world. She enjoyed shopping for herself and me in Santa Fe. I still have all those objects in my possession. Connie also took me to Austin and Dallas, Texas for different cultural shows. She took me to a very exclusive furniture store in Florida in 2002 to get new furniture and to Wisconsin for different handmade watches. We went to Germany and to a German market in Milwaukee to purchase nutcrackers. Connie had season tickets to the North Lake club for stage plays, Marriot stage plays, and we often went to Las Vegas, where we must have watched over seventy beautiful plays. We saw Mama Mia! twice—in Chicago and Las Vegas. We also saw Jersey Boys twice at different places. Each city has its own cast while the show is the same.

26

Her Exposure to World Travel

CONNIE EXPOSED ME TO WORLD TRAVEL, WHICH I truly enjoyed. She used to study and plan the best of cruises and other trips. I am extremely grateful and obligated to her for the beautiful cruises and other trips we shared both in the US and in some of the most exclusive places in the world. Without her, I would not have traveled the world for pleasure. She often told me that I didn't take any initiative to plan anything other than trips to India. She came to India with me seven times, and made me travel to the most beautiful places in India, including the Palace on Wheels. It was a treat, and I would recommend this trip to everyone. It is a princely trip designed for kings during the British Empire. The Palace on Wheels runs from October through May, and in the first week of January. We went in 1995, and the Palace on Wheels is one of the best and finest trips in India. My readers can find more information on the internet if they would like to take this trip, which goes from Delhi to Rajasthan. Connie was amazingly happy during our trip, and she mentioned it for the rest of her life. Writing about this is difficult as my mind is 100% on Connie darling who is in my soul. I'm always thinking about her death, the medical negligence, seeing her dying, and thinking that I am dreaming that she is gone. I am thinking of her cemetery. The most painful thing is her ashes under the green grass on which I have to stand to touch her beautiful granite stone. That kills me even if I am not there. I am 7,000 miles away from Evanston and from her grave in Memorial Park Cemetery in Skokie, Illinois. When I think of Connie, the green grass that has ashes kills me. Under that grass is my Connie, *her* body is under that grass and I am walking over that beautiful and intelligent Connie. Although her body in that casket was put in with the help of four professionals, I was truly to be part of that. Body and casket were together hiding Connie darling inside. How can I do such a thing and burn my Connie darling in that? How do I know she is dead? It's very much possible that she was alive and weeping, crying, saying, "Pradeep, why do you put me inside and please let me get out from this covered thing as I am suffering from suffocation." Like in the small tube of the MRI, I am sorry to do this sin. I recall a true episode of one of the most painful things I ever did. My first cousin, the son of my father's brother A.P. Berry, and who we used to call Kallo, some called him Kallo Babu when he turned twenty—five. We all lived in our big mansion in Katra Neel Chandni Chow in Old Delhi. When I came to the US, Connie must have been waiting for me and I know with 100% certainty that Connie was my destiny. Maybe God sent us on Earth so that I had to meet and marry her. Maybe both of us had some past relationships which were incomplete, and God gave us a chance to be together again for forty-two years. The Palace on Wheels is a very ancient place and it's an attraction for foreign tourists, mostly American citizens who are crazy to visit and wish they could see India.

We traveled to the Taj Mahal, to Jaipur, Kashmir, Khujuraho and other places in India in her seven trips. I also traveled frequently throughout the US for my professional career, and if Connie was on vacation, she used to accompany me. I was very happy and had a ball while I was working. Sometimes I would work long hours and she was very capable of exploring and finding the best places by herself. Later, she would talk about her adventures and would take me to see all that she discovered. If I had been alone, I would not have done anything. All these truly made me curious to explore more about travel and shopping. All these experiences made us compulsive shoppers for clothes and gifts, and we had a great collection of the best pens, picture frames, shoes, clothes, and many more items for the house and for our family and friends. We were very social for a while, and later, we both were so happy that we didn't care if we were alone or not. We used to have few evenings every week when we would go out for dinner and for visiting or inviting over friends and family, but we preferred being by ourselves to share our love and company. We talked of different things, sharing our knowledge and reading, and spent our time together writing, dining out, shopping, traveling, driving together, and going to the health club and small gatherings of friends. We were inseparable and used to feel lonely without each other. I think it was a great time and love, and even if we were sitting in the same room doing different things, as long as we could see each other, we were happy. I know that sometimes this kind of love is very painful because spouses who feel this way cannot go on if something happens to one of them, but we had no control. As we traveled together, we saw practically half of the most important parts of the world, in addition to our travels all over the US. We saw Broadway and Las Vegas shows and symphonies in different parts of the world, including Vienna. Dining out in the best restaurants to experience new cuisines was a powerful part of our lives. Connie wanted the best, but was financially conservative at the same time. She took me to Spain in 1987 for two weeks. We went on an Alaskan cruise in 1988 and visited Alaska a second time in 1989. We went on a Caribbean cruise in 1989. We also went to New Orleans in 1989 and spent time in the French Quarter. We went to New Mexico in 1990. We also took many mini-vacations over long weekends, traveling to Santa Fe and even to England. We took Michigan University Alumni trips to Tuscany, Ireland, Denmark, and Norway.

One of our greatest memories, especially for Connie, was my sense of humor and laughing when our friends of thirty years started calling me doctor. Because of them, a cruise ship of 1400 people truly believed I was a medical doctor. The older ladies in the cruise, in particular, spread the word that Dr. Berry was on board and not be afraid to climb a historic building. I told them not to worry, to breathe deeply and climb slowly, and they complimented me as the best medical doctor. Other senior ladies told me they loved sweets and asked if they were harmful. I didn't want a lawsuit, and I had to improvise. I asked, "Are you diabetic?" and when they said no, I told them to keep eating and not to worry. They stuffed themselves with sweets, and I began to worry that if anything happened to them, I would be in trouble. But God is good and I started getting letters from many people who were cured by Ayurveda medicine and yoga. I decided that I would never do that again, and we started to no longer travel with our friends except to Spain. Connie and I decided to focus on each other and began to drop the friends who were not close to us. Now they want me to join back in that group of friends, thinking that will help what I am going through without Connie. Later, we took trips with Vantage Cruise, a two week trip in Norway and another river cruise for seventeen days from Budapest to Amsterdam. We took a Christmas tree cruise for twelve days in England during the winter, and we went to the French Rivera, Germany, France, and seven times to India. I went home almost every year for two weeks to see my brother in India. But from 2011 until 2015, I did not even think of going back to India due to her health. I did not even think of leaving her for one day when she was sick. I left my high-powered senior position in 2006 to be with her, and I have no regrets at all. Rather, I was happy that I could serve her and that gave me the greatest satisfaction, but I could not bear the pain of losing her. She wanted to go to Australia, New Zealand, and China, but some way or another, we could not go. I will regret this all my life. We went to Door County three times and many other beautiful places in Wisconsin like Lake Geneva and Crystal Lake; each city in California, including Palm Springs, where she found the standing table she had been looking for two years. She was a perfectionist. We also want to all the cities in Texas and North Carolina and Nevada, especially Las Vegas. Living in Chicago, we saw all of the Broadway shows that came to the city. Later, from 2005 to 2014, we went to Sanibel Island for five weeks and also to Marco Island, staying for three weeks at the Hilton Marco Island Resort to escape the cold weather and snow of Evanston, IL. It was nothing but fun, love, and billions of dollars worth of our happiness, which money cannot buy at any cost. Connie was very conservative and not concerned with high society. She never wanted to impress the world, as she was very modest and not a showy person. She enjoyed meeting interesting and intelligent people. We both shared the same rhythm, and respected every human being, whether educated or not, as we both have always been down to earth all our lives. Now I have lost that momentum and will not enjoy the same life without her. Many family members and friends tell me that life keeps on going, but there is a big stop for me; seeing the way our life together was.

27

Connie–Her Charm and Beauty

CONNIE WAS CHARMING, ETHICAL, HONEST, GIVING, FAITHFUL, and extremely intelligent and a great reader, in addition to being an incarnation of tolerance and strong will. She was exceptionally beautiful, both externally and internally and from every angle, and a wonderful wife and best friend. In addition, to being well-rounded and bright in every aspect, she was the darling of my family and friends. Whoever met her became her fan and friend, and accordingly, become our friends too. Connie was born in Glenview, a very affluent suburb in Chicago. She loved her parents, and was very faithful and always offered help at any time. She used to invite them to our house every week. I also enjoyed having them, and we were all very fond of Indian food, which we both used to cook for them. In their old age, Connie took care of them. I, too, was involved in helping Connie care for them. Her father got sick first and we were there every moment to help and support him, including taking him to doctors' appointments and trips to the hospital. We were there when he died in December 1989. We asked her mother to stay with us after his death, but she refused. Let me make it clear, her mother was crazy and after becoming a widow, her life revolved around her four grandkids from her only son. She wanted to stay with them, but they refused to have her and she kept on trying but in vain. I think it was a pathetic and dirty thing for Connie's brother to deprive his mother of her old age. Their behavior was the same towards his father, who was sick of them, and his wife (my mother-in-law) for her obsession with the grandkids. We brought her mother to live in our house for months when she was sick, otherwise, she was living in her own house. Later, Connie's brother and his family took their mother to Wisconsin, a three-hour drive from our home, and put her in a nursing home against her will. They feared that Connie's mom may not leave all her money to him.

Connie had told her brother that they were welcome to see their mother's will, that their mother had left an equal share for them both. Despite this, her brother and sister-in-law did not trust us. "Greed of Man is A Curse of The Land." The rules of greed sometimes rule the world; I feel like animals are better than human beings. Animals will kill their prey only when they are hungry, whereas man keeps on exploiting and killing out of greed, even when he has enough and has satisfied his hunger.

We used to visit her mother every month, sometimes twice a month, and stay in a hotel for two nights and take her out for lunch. We have this satisfaction and happiness, knowing that we made her old age and her last fifteen years of life extremely happy, even after her husband's death. We both were instrumental in arranging her cremation and service in the chapel of peace, and in putting her ashes in her plot, next to her husband. Connie was extremely upset after the loss of her parents and did much charitable work, which gave her happiness. It is extremely important for me to mention that Connie and I would have brought her mother back from the nursing home if Connie was not suffering from a rare skin disease, pityriasisrubrapilaris (PRP), in 1999 and 2000, and that the disease was more painful than her fight with cancer except in 2014 and 2015 when she suffered from her spreading cancer. Connie was extremely hurt that her siblings and their kids were not nice to Connie's mother who sacrificed her life and money for them. I am not trying to write bad things about her siblings and family, but we were both upset, and it was a tragic thing for me to see my wife's agony during this time. I would mention more painful episodes in "Another Painful Chapter for Connie and Pradeep."

28

Connie's Character and Thinking

There is no end to the greatness of Connie's thinking and her character. She was loyal and honest, never lied and always forgave, gave without taking, had great work ethic and maintained our household without asking me for help. She never depended on anyone but always found a way to cope on her own. She was very brave and bold. If someone was in error, she would tell him to his face and make him realize his mistake. Connie did not care if someone was wealthy, and would be friendly with all intelligent people. She did not run after wealth or social power; that was not in her blood or mine. We cared for what people were and not what they had.

I give my tribute to Connie by quoting the following messages from Swami Vivekananda. Swami Vivekananda quoted the following messages. These sometimes give me strength, but still, they do not heal my pain.

1. "Have faith that you are all brave lads, born to do great things. Let not the barks of puppies frighten you; no, not even the thunderbolts of heaven, but stand up and work."
2. "Your country requires heroes; be heroes. Stand firm like a rock. Truth always triumphs. A country wants is a new electric fire to stir up a fresh vigor in the national veins. Be brave."
3. "Trust not the so-called rich; they are more dead than alive. The hope lies in you—in the meek, the lowly, but the faithful. Have faith in the Lord. Give me a genuine man; I do not care for anybody to help you. Is not the Lord infinitely greater than all human help? Be holy—trust in the Lord, depend on Him always and you are on the right track; nothing can prevail against you."

4. "Faith, faith, faith in ourselves, faith in God, this is the secret of greatness. If you have faith in three hundred and thirty millions of your mythological gods, and in all the gods which foreigners have introduced into your midst, and still have no faith in yourselves, there is no salvation for you. Have faith in yourselves and stand upon that faith and be strong."
5. "All truth is eternal. Truth is nobody's property; no race, no individual can lay exclusive claim to it. Truth is the nature of all souls. Who can lay special claim to it."
6. "Look upon every man, woman, and everyone as God. You cannot help anyone, you can only serve. Serve the children of the Lord Himself, if you have the privilege. If the Lord grants that you can help any one of His children, blessed you are." We both applied these messages throughout our lives, and I will continue doing so for the sake of Connie. My message to all my readers: Please have a bond of love, care, respect each other, have full trust and honesty, plant your relations as we give water to the plants. Connie and I did all that. Without Connie I am suffering like a fish without water, the pain an animal feels when slaughtered, or the pain of human beings and animals that are killed by others. Gandhi was right when he started his movement of nonviolence, fighting never brings peace. Living by the code of an eye for an eye would destroy the world. Please try to understand how sensitive the relation between a woman and her husband is when they are married. The majority of wives only want love, care, respect, security, a faithful caring husband, comfortable living, and a nice family who cares for her. Wives can sacrifice many luxuries and material things in return for their husband's love, but they must have that love. Yes, there are exceptions, but in my opinion, the first one holds. Husband and wife must admit and say to each other these three words: *I love you.*

29

Connie's Character: Part Two

I WANT TO WRITE MORE REGARDING CONNIE'S CHARACTER. I think I can tell you we were made for each other. I was raised in an environment with very strong values and with an emphasis on character building. Our grandparents were very strict about focusing on studies, sports, and other activities like Boy Scouts and the National Cadet Corps (NCC). I was extremely good in Boy Scouts; I was the NCC battalion sergeant and had a lot of other extracurricular qualifications. We were given the strongest foundation possible to build our character. That also meant not having any relationships or attachments to the opposite gender. The priority was to get educated first, and all other things could happen after one was well settled in life. In reality, because we were brought up this way, we never really even thought of having any female friends. It wasn't like today where it is very common for people to have boyfriends or girlfriends where they might or might not marry each other. In any case, that was a different era.

Connie was also brought up in exactly the same way. Her focus was only on her education and her research. She was keen only on her studies and she was not interested in parties or meeting men. She was very happy with her close-knit family and girlfriends. Her mother was very strict, and Connie herself had a moral code that meant she was not interested in those parties that involved drinking and dancing. In addition to her education and her intellectual nature, we found this to be a common aspect between us. I think this is one of the contributing factors behind our getting together. Ordinarily, I would have gone back to India for an arranged marriage, as there were a lot of proposals from rich families which had come my way. Perhaps God wanted me not to go as I was destined to meet this girl Connie who was beautiful both from the outside and from within. Connie liked to say that I was her first boyfriend and she was my first girlfriend, although we really started out as only friends.

To this day I don't know how I gained the confidence to talk to a woman because if you are from India, talking to a woman is the most fearful and dangerous thing. Of course, after I came to America and met ladies in my corporate life, I developed the courage and faith to form friendships with women. The reason is that in America, men and women have been raised in a different environment, they have been brought up full of confidence right from their childhood. I remember when I first came to this country, one of my colleagues, who was working under me, told me, "Pradeep, let me tell you one thing, in this country children are given the maximum freedom." I was astonished to hear that because in our era, even though we were given freedom, we were also watched like hawks. We were always kept track of—our activities, where we went, etc. I noticed a big difference in our cultures. If you talk to people over here you notice how confident they are, irrespective of their age, because they have been brought up in such an environment. I'm not trying to criticize or hurt anybody's feelings; I'm just sharing my own experience and knowledge without offending anybody. When I go to the health club or to shops or even in my professional life, women talk to me as if we have known each other for years. There is a lot of joking around and our conversations are full of fun. I have not seen that kind of atmosphere with Indian ladies, whether they are married or otherwise. They tend to be very reserved, so I think it is a big cultural difference which I find very interesting. Once again, it is not a reflection of these cultural ways of communicating. I have traveled all over the world, and whether it was in America or Europe, I find that outside of India, people are friendlier and more open with strangers. It is not as if people in India are not like that they are very wonderful and hospitable, but there is some kind of a rhythm missing. I find that sometimes even young Indians are reluctant to talk. Even in America, I've met many Indian college students at school, often they don't even say hello. At times, if I ask them if they are from India—to which they mumble yes and claim that they need to get back to their work. This has happened several times, and to some degree, it has upset me, but then I decided that this is a cultural difference, but that is not the answer. A simple smile and a little hello are always good.

30

Connie told me "Make good use of your time

During the late 70s and early 80s, both of us were working very hard to build our careers. On Saturdays, although it was not mandatory for me to do any work, I would get up in the morning and work on my reports because I wanted to increase my knowledge and I wanted to advance my career. I used to put in that extra effort, I used to give 200% instead of 100%, and Connie would do the same. The only difference between the two of us was that while working, I would turn on an Indian program called Chitrahaar. I used to watch that program from 8 o'clock to 9 o'clock while I worked. Connie would let me watch it, and not say anything. She was very selfless; she probably thought that since I enjoyed it, she should not interfere. Those were very interesting days for both of us. One day in 1979, my uncle, Dr. Behl, came to our home when I was watching Chitrahaar. He turned it off, and said to me, "Why on earth are you wasting your time watching this useless program? I know that you are working from 8:00 am to 9:00 pm, but instead of this junk Chitrahaar, why don't you watch some financial programs, so that you can do both, just like I do. I listen to some lectures while writing my book, this way, you teach yourself." His British wife told him, "Pran, leave him alone, let him enjoy his program." He replied to her, "Listen, Marge, you don't know, this is about his career. He is my favorite nephew and I love him very much like my son. I want him to shine and I want Connie to be proud of him. So he should stop watching Chitrahaar." Turning to me he said, "Pradeep, forget about this lousy program and concentrate on your work." I enjoyed watching it for one hour and I thought at that time that my uncle was being very tough on me.

Later, at the age of fifty-five, I realized what he was trying to say then. Now I don't enjoy those kinds of programs anymore. From 1984 to 1985, I got into the habit of watching Indian movies. Connie was initially happy that I was enjoying watching the movies. Later on, when she saw that the habit was increasing, after about one year, she told me, "You waste your time watching movies which have no theme, girls are dancing and boys are running. These are not intellectual movies. If you really want to watch interesting movies, watch movies based on true stories which make sense. Those movies have some sort of intellectual ending. You are not learning anything from Indian movies, it is the same plot: a hero fights with 100 people, the hero can do anything, then a villain comes, then they have a flight, the villain hits and hurts the hero, and finally hero meets heroine. The actresses are gorgeous. I love their dresses and sarees, but they are lip-syncing the songs; dancing unlike the actresses in a ballet or Broadway show or stage play where they are properly trained to sing. These Indian actresses no doubt are beautiful, but the background dancers are not so beautiful because they want to show the contrast between the background dancers and heroines. Our American movies are not like that." I used to watch a lot of American movies when I was in India, we never missed American movies. After coming to the US, maybe because I was homesick and was away from my family, I started watching all the Indian movies which we used to watch in the theaters in India. That habit persisted for a year or two. Connie told me, "If you use the time you spend watching movies to reading your reports, business documents, the New York Times, the Wall Street Journal, or even novels, you will get knowledge." I said, "I don't like to read any novels, they are useless fiction. I like reading the autobiographies of people like Nelson Mandela, John F. Kennedy, Mahatma Gandhi, Dr. Rajendra Prasadin, Mark Twain, US Presidents, and people who did research in different fields, medicine, and other books, but mostly I preferred reading business books relating to my profession. She said, "Read whatever you want, but keep the habit, because it will give you a hobby, it will keep you occupied and it will stimulate you and you will become an intelligent person." Her average reading time was four to six hours a day when she was working. When she took early retirement, her average reading was fourteen-fifteen hours a day. She used to read magazines, books, newspapers and very selective and intellectual books and articles. I used to read during the days that I was working, but after I took time off, I started writing articles for MBA students and for many institutions. I would write on my passion, my subject area, which is commercial lending, merger, and acquisition. People used to ask me questions on the internet and ask my advice on how to solve them. There were questions from all sorts of people about banking, internet banking, and the commercial loans sector. There would be questions about hostile mergers, how to buy companies, how to run a company, how to start a company, how to leverage it, and many other things including improving sales. I used to write because I really had lots of knowledge; this knowledge did not come because I am a special man of God but because I worked hard for it. I went to an elite university in the US for my MBA; I passed over eighty professional development courses while working for different large finance companies and large banks, which were mandatory to be promoted and to build knowledge. Without bragging, I can talk and about any subject or topic, whether it is about my career, spirituality, ancient Indian civilization, Buddha, Shakespeare, the Bible, the Koran, Indian classical music, Mozart, or Broadway shows. Thus, I developed my personality a lot and all the credit goes to Connie. If Connie was not there and if she had not helped me, I would not have changed myself. I started feeling embarrassed that Connie may see me as the same person who was not well cultured, well developed. Thus, I ended up outshining both of us.

I don't mean to offend anyone in my lifetime, but I see certain people in my own family, there are about fifty of them, who don't do anything on weekends, and who don't read or research papers. The only thing they do is gossip and waste their time all day. I am surprised that some of them are born in the US but they have not adopted any elements of American culture. Their knowledge is limited to their job. Some of them, even though they were born in the US, were fired ten to fifteen times, despite their qualifications. I wonder why that happened; I think it was because they were doing their job half-heartedly from nine to five, and not doing much to enhance their career. For the last ten to fifteen years, they have been begging me to find them a job. Often I helped them to find one, only to learn that they were fired because they did not know the subject.

Nothing is easy in life. The only thing that pays is hard and smart work, and innovation. Education is a constant daily habit. Degrees have finite points of completion, but education and systems and technology keep on changing, whether it is in banking, finance, or computers. For example, in banking, different structures have been developed for different kinds of lending. I know all these new systems because I am interested in learning. This is all because I want to be proud of myself, and I was also doing it for my wife so that she could say I am also an intellectual person. That was the reason why, when we were going on different trips all over the world, I used to interact with people more than she would. She was sort of quiet. When the final exam at the end of the trip came, Connie answered the questions. She answered because I was not well prepared. She did a fantastic job, so she used to tell me, "You should also take some initiative." Then I would stand in front of 100-200 people and talk about the subject area. I worked very hard for that. These incidents I am narrating would not have happened unless Connie was there. That is why I feel that Connie was special, and I will never find Connie again, except in my next birth. I am praying every day that I get Connie again in my life. This is very important to me; I am willing to sacrifice anything for that. As I have repeatedly mentioned, her loss has been the most painful thing in my life and no one else will ever understand what I am going through. Our love was one out of million people. When I say this, I want to ask for forgiveness, because people will think I am talking nonsense. They will say that their love was also the same. I agree that their love was maybe the same, but I don't know their stories. Our love was great because we were known as "Connie and Pradeep" everywhere. At least 50,000 people must have told us over the last forty years, including friends, family, and colleagues, that we were too attached, and that God would bless us. Many people used to tell us that both of us were special.

31

I want to feel the presence of Connie in one form or another

My love for Connie was very deep and pure. We had the greatest love for each other. I sometimes feel guilty or selfish about my grief, but I have seen many tragedies. Those tragedies also affected me very badly; regardless on whom the tragedy had befallen. I always thought about these tragedies. Why did they take place and why do such things happen? After the death of Connie, I don't want to think of all those tragedies. All those tragedies are mitigated by Connie's death. I don't want to remember them. How has Connie's death changed my way of thinking? I don't want to say it is selfish, but you really only understand the grief when it happens to you, when someone very close, like a special wife who meant the world to you, passes away. Connie and I were inseparable. I don't think I should feel guilty about it. Even if I feel guilty about it, I don't want someone pointing it out because it is solely my point of view.

God forgive me for what I want to say, but if something happens to someone unless it is someone who I really truly care about, I would not feel sad or sorry. Connie's death has made me really bitter and angry, so perhaps I will not care deeply for the grief of others. I will probably only feel sorry for their pain. The new realization in my life is that there is a difference between feeling sorry for someone and truly feeling their pain. I know that we all have to die. If someone is older than me, and my relatives, if something happens to them, I do not know how I would react. Even if I go to their funeral or their last rites, I am not going to say a whole lot of things. I will stand quietly in the corner thinking about it, and maybe at that time, my tragedy will be with me. I will be there as a bystander without any emotions. The reason behind this is that so many people who I thought were close to me did not care during my three years of pain, so I will not feel for them. Even if someone is very close to me, yes I will feel sorrow, but nothing more.

Nobody will be able to match my love and the depth of the feelings I had for Connie. What I'm writing is very difficult to put down on paper, but this is how I feel. Some people will hate me, some people will think it's good that I'm being honest, yet others will think I'm correct and will say that I was very much in love. Some people will think I'm selfish and that I have a one-track mind, but I'm not really going to worry about them. If someone says something to me after reading this, my only response will be to say that I'm sorry. No one can compare my loss with any other person's. Connie was very special to me and will remain so.

On September 29, 2015, I went to visit her at the cemetery. I used to go there two or three times a week and I decided to go again. I think I was there for thirty to forty-five minutes. Whenever I go there, I have noted that I get some peace of mind. Maybe what I feel is not a peace of mind exactly, but is just a shadow of letting go of the grief for some time. I feel that I am with her when I go there. The pain inside is deeper since I had never expected that I will have to live to see this situation. She was alive six months ago, with no inkling that she was going to die so soon, and today she is no more. It was just yesterday that I used to take her to the hospital and doctors. I remember how we used to sit together and chat and suddenly in one second, everything is gone. Going to the cemetery makes me feel that. I think that mentally, I'm ready to live near her headstone. People will think that I've gone mad but I'm not crazy. I have seen how people used to live with dead people in some parts of the world where I have traveled, such as Egypt. I think if I had a choice, and they allowed me (which I think is next to impossible), I would live in a small house near her. Even if that life would be very hard for me, I would still take it. I have never had that experience, nor will I ever have it. It might look like the most stupid thing to do, but every individual has a different way of expressing grief. Many people don't think like I do about this subject. I want to write every single thing which is coming from the core of my heart that I have already conveyed. I have thought many times, and have shared this with my brother and everybody when I went to India and spent two months there with my family. When I think of going back to India for a month to have a change of scene and get some work done, I will see how I feel. When I leave the house for an extended period, the things I used to do with her like preparing her meals during the day, praying in her room and to her picture, and at her cemetery will haunt me now. I will feel that her soul is still around. I know that her soul is in peace but my mind is not at peace. So I think it is going to be very difficult for me. In India, the girls really weep and cry when they are leaving their parents' home after marriage because they will be missing their family. Similarly, I weep whenever I have to go anywhere. The girls cry for maybe one day, but I am grief-stricken whenever I go out of the house for more than a few hours, except when I go to the store or health club when I know I'm coming back home shortly. If I have to go anywhere for an extended period, or if my relatives come to visit me and I go out with them, at least I will be in the US, so the gravity of the pain will be a little less, but I will still be thinking about her. However, if I go overseas, then the gravity of the pain will be a million times stronger as my mind will be at home. After I reach my destination, maybe I will handle it for a few days, but after that, I will get restless and return home. So many times I think that I should go for one week or a couple of weeks, but then I realize that it is not a short journey; it takes a lot of time to reach India. It is not always easy to go for a week or ten days. It was a different time when we were working, and Connie and I would both go or I would go alone to India, but I would never be gone more than two weeks, including travel. Later on, I cut it down further to twelve days including travel because then I knew that I was responsible for my work and for Connie. Now there are no responsibilities. I have left my senior position, I am not working anymore, and Connie is no more. The attachment to home has caught me in a different way and it is very difficult to get out.

I don't think my grief will lessen; rather it will become worse as time passes. Many people told me that it would take me six months to one year to overcome this, but I feel it is going to take much longer than that. It is a sign of my love for Connie. I don't know what Connie must have gone through when she was sick with that cardiac arrest, and how she was holding my hand and she wanted to say something, but could not speak. I don't know what she wanted to say and that bothers me. This would not have happened if she had passed away in the house, without any mistakes done by the doctors. I would have been very affected, no doubt about it, but the trauma I saw, the medical negligence by the doctors, the way they delayed their response to her cardiac arrest and the three weeks I spent fighting with them, that trauma is worse than anybody can go through. I pray to God that no one should go through it. I am very upset about it and I just cannot believe it happened in the US. Things like these happen; some people say it was destiny, some say her time on earth was finished, but I don't buy that. I used to believe that when the time comes, you pass away. I refuse to accept this kind of death which comes after so much suffering and negligence by doctors, so I now say that the end time is in our hands.

I think I am being naive, but my love for Connie is still there. I'm being very honest. Some people will appreciate this, some people will say I am stupid, yet others will say that they realize it was true love. Hopefully, they will learn something from this. This is how I feel, and I think I am going to put it in the heading 'realizations of my pain and the pain of others.' The only way I keep myself very happy is by talking to people I meet. They listen to me, especially young ladies over here, and they get touched by my story. Then I casually ask them if they want to tell me about themselves if they are comfortable enough to do so. I think that they are very honest and once they trust me, they share their stories. They say that they wish they had a marriage like ours. They wish their husbands were like me, and say that they are still searching for the kind of love Connie and I shared. I think that in that respect, I am extremely lucky. Many people in stores and restaurants, who don't know me, have told me that I am lucky. When I make phone calls to various companies and talk to various people, I have observed that ninety-nine percent of people are touched by my story. Maybe two percent of people say that I should get on with my life, but I don't think I want to hear that. I think I need sympathy all the time for this incident. I know that whenever you ask for sympathy, you show your weak points, but I don't care now. I am going to write what I feel. I think that when you read something written from the core of the heart without worrying about what people will think, it becomes a gem of a book. That is how true stories are written, and so many movies are made about real-life incidents. I ask that people listen to me, and I hope that they will understand my emotions at this time. It is 5 a.m. and I am now going to sleep.

In the past, I would wake up at this time and go to the health club. Yesterday, I was awake until 7:30 a.m. writing, but I didn't have to worry because it was a weekend. But tomorrow is a working day and I know I have to do a lot of work. Even then, I could not help writing her biography because I want to get it published as soon as possible. One day, when this book is published, I will go back to my original routine of sleeping by midnight and waking up by 9:00 am. My main priority right now is to keep talking to the attorneys; I am ready to go to the highest court of law. I will not leave any stone unturned in my efforts, the rest I leave it up to God. I beg Connie to give me the power to succeed for her. I pray that I can find some attorney who will take my case and that we win the case, then I will be somewhat happy and Connie will be happy. That is why I am determined to go through with it. People ask me what is the point in pursuing the case, and I tell them it is for my satisfaction. This is the way I feel about the trade-off of my love with other tragedies.

32

Connie is Still with Me

For the last eight months, I have noticed that Connie has gone away; however, while I am at my house seeing her pictures, I feel as if Connie is still with me and talking to me. Yes, it's a good feeling, but more than that it's a very sad and upsetting feeling, too, and that is stronger than the good feelings. The other thing I have noticed is that for the last four months, from July 2015 onwards, when I turn on the lights if I wake up in the middle of the night, I feel as if Connie will get disturbed by the lights as my first thought is that she is asleep. I then feel shock and realize the truth, and that is a double-edged sword and like an arrow in my heart. It takes me more than an hour to go back to sleep, and again in the morning, the same arrow strikes; one can see better in the morning as the house is empty. I leave the lights on in her office until 8:30 in the evening and at 8:30 in the morning, automatic lights come on until 10:30 a.m. as then turn off at 10:30 in the morning when there is enough natural light. These days, of course, my sleeping hours are extended well beyond the usual 1:00 a.m. I go to sleep at 4:30 or 5:00 a.m., and even on occasion as late as 8:00 a.m. That was when I had written an email to some legal advisors as they are already at work at 8:30 a.m. When I was working, I was in the office by 7 o'clock, and at other times, I was at airports by 5:00 a.m. or at the pool by that time of the day. This shows how life has changed. There are people I know who are older than me, and who maintain certain daily habits. They get up at 4 o'clock and go for a walk and then go on to work at 8:00 a.m. Although this is not a universal fact as daily routines and waking hours change from person to person. Not everybody is the same, people are different. However, I am only relating my experience. The other day at 6:30 a.m., I was preparing to sleep and when I went over to my balcony, I saw people walking dogs on the sidewalk. It was bright and early and people were going to work, and that reminded me of my earlier life back in college and mostly with Connie. We both used to get up at 6:30 a.m. and Connie would leave by 7:40 a.m. and I would leave at 7:45 a.m. or sometimes earlier. Since I had to travel in my great profession, I used to take my car or take a train depending on where I was going, or perhaps at 5:00—6:30 a.m., my limousine was waiting for me for the airport. Later when Connie took early retirement after teaching for thirty-six years, and doing volunteer work at the library, she kept the same schedule until 2006. I also left my career to be with Connie for traveling, enjoying life, going to her medical appointments, dining out, shopping and other things. We were together all day and night. Yes, I used to visit India for two weeks every year, and my last trip was on November 6 through November 20, 2011 for twelve days. My next trip was on May 17, 2015 after her demise and when my world was over. It was the same for Connie too. Time changes, the economy changes, and nobody can predict nature and its changes. Morning is followed by night and that in turn leads to morning the next day. Nobody can control rain and snow, or sunshine. So these days I feel as if Connie is around. I can feel the vibrations, and these days, the vibrations are increasing in intensity. I feel sometimes that I should wake Connie up as she is getting late for work. When I realize she isn't there anymore, I still tell myself that perhaps she's in the bathroom or maybe she is in her room watching TV and reading her books. But when I am lying down, I suddenly realize, "What am I thinking? Connie is gone, she's no more!" It takes me twenty minutes to one hour to digest this and it is the most painful experience one can go through. So these are the experiences I am going through right now. I am in Delhi today, and last night I woke up unsure as to where I was—at my house or elsewhere. I thought later that I was sleeping at home. I eventually realized that I was In India, and it was so surprising for me that I dreamt of Connie thinking I was at home. I think it will take me a certain number of days to understand that I am in Delhi. But my mind is somewhat happy to be in Delhi. I am happy to be with my nephews, grandnieces, and my brother, but other than them I have no desire to meet anybody else or to do anything else. I'm slightly tired right now, but I'm going out with my brother and nephew to the market to get some snacks or go somewhere for a couple of hours. I might go to the health club, but other than that I am in no mood to meet or be friends with anybody or to attend parties and gatherings. These are all sad occasions for me. People tell me, it's ok, Pradeep, it is your grieving period. I'm not sure how long the grieving period is going to last. Perhaps it will last forever and will become part of my life as long as I am alive. It is possible that this is why I am so keen to arrange things in such a way that after I am gone, my house, art, furniture, rugs, and other expensive collections are taken care of. It often worries me as to what will happen to all of those things. People tell me to look after my health instead of worrying about all these material things. But they don't understand that I am not talking about material things, but Connie's soul or blood is in every single one of those items, which have been collected over the years. So it's not just about the material possessions, and I am not crazy not to want to sell them and get money in return. These have Connie's life and soul in them, how could I possibly ever get rid of them. So this is the tremendous hardship that I am facing and it is worse than anything else I've ever experienced before. I have faced many other tragedies, but I have forgotten about them or at least tried to. I will never be able to forget Connie's loss. I believe there are two kinds of losses. One is related to money and property, and there are disputes over them, leading to lawsuits and overall ill-feeling over money. But I am not talking about money. Money is nothing to me now; it is just a way to live. It is just a way to maintain myself and my lifestyle of simple living and high thinking. I am content that way. Even if I suddenly get millions and millions of dollars, they are not going to bring back my happiness or Connie. If there was some kind of means, and I know it is impossible, whereby if you donate all your money somewhere and get your loved ones back, I would get Connie back. There are countries where you can donate money and get into schools and colleges. This is mainly for the private institutions, not necessarily for the good institutions. There are good places in India, and of course, America has got one of the best educational systems in the world. So there are a lot of vocational courses where you can get a degree but you have to donate a lot of money. But it is not possible that I can donate money and get Connie back, because if it was possible I would have given away all of my money. I was watching the Ram Lila which is an episode from Indian history and my brother and his daughter-inlaw we're discussing it with me. They mentioned that the characters in it have the ability to curse others and take their lives back. I wish I could find some of those people so that Connie might come back. They said it was not possible as they had done a lot of sacrifices for a very long time to achieve that ability. I agreed that their sacrifices were more than mine. Although as I have said in other chapters about the story of Savitri and Satyavan, if they could do it, why can't I? The answer was given to me by my brother's daughter-in-law. She said those people were different at that time, they had special powers because they had never done anything wrong in their lives. She said I must have good karma but it is possible that without necessarily intending to, I may have done something wrong. I agreed with her, perhaps I lied and other times I did not listen to Connie. There were occasions when I did not follow her advice, if not giving her a tough time. She used to ask me to develop new things, as she was very interested in my progress in life. Maybe I have sinned, but it is true that she tolerated a lot of things from me. I don't know the answer. Only God knows the answer, but it is also true that there is nobody who can bring Connie back. And that is very painful. I just marked that I should keep talking about this chapter for as long as I can, but at the same time more is not always good. "More is not always better," Connie said to me. I know there is a lot of repetition in my story, but it's all right to repeat things, especially as people will get reminded of things once they read again. Also, I don't use words like "my wife" or "her" which sounds impersonal. That is why I use her name, Connie, again and again. Perhaps it is not the best way to write, but for me it is the best way. Those other words don't carry the same weight as the name Connie, at least for me. I don't expect that everybody will like my writing or that I will be a bestseller or that this will be the best book in the world. I am only writing and expressing myself and hoping that even if only one person can understand my pain, I will be very happy. I won't say there is only one because many people have already requested a copy of the book. In fact, most of the people who are asking for a copy are unknown to me. There are people from technical support, or computer technicians, or customer service representatives for different airlines, and some of them are employees of call centers where I used to call for my banking needs, or companies like Visa, Citibank, or Bank of America. They listen to me as I have to tell them honestly that Mrs. Berry is no longer here. The other day I spoke to this person from *Consumer Report* magazine for almost an hour and half! He was almost in tears, and he gave me a prize for the subscription. I promised him that I would begin reading all the magazines that Connie used to subscribe to, which are very instrumental in building knowledge. There is another book called *Health and Nutrition* as well as another to do with wellness and health. There is another magazine called *Men's Health*. There are magazines to do with women's health and nutrition, and I don't want anything to do with the magazine for women, as I don't want any other woman in my life, but maybe I will subscribe to the others as it'll give me happiness when I read them. This is a new experience for me. I will also give away some of the other magazines that others have requested as I will never turn down any request that has anything to do with Connie, except, of course, a request for some of her personal possessions like her jackets. The other day she wore a jacket and asked me how she looked. That picture makes me cry and I have had it framed, it shows Connie laughing. That was true love. I remember she'd gotten a brand new jacket and she was very weak. She always worried whether she looked nice or looked bad. She really looked very pretty and kept looking at me. That picture goes through my heart like a sword or arrow and makes me break down. So before I came to India, I carried that picture with me, a small one in my pocket and my briefcase. I am going to keep looking at that picture; it has become the most important part of my life. People will think I am talking about emotions, mental issues, I don't care, but I know I am still able to do many constructive things, especially relating to Connie. These are not just emotions but are facts of my life. The other day, I had gone to the store to return some things I had thought we would enjoy. As per their policy, they took them back, but the man asked why I was returning them. When I explained, the man was really touched and went out of his way to help me. The other thing was that on the 19th of October, 2015, before departing from the US, I went to the cemetery. I had decided on the flowers that I intended to buy. I went into the store and told the young man what I needed. I showed him Connie's picture and he was really bothered by the story. He complimented Connie saying she was beautiful and refused to charge me for the flowers. He said that out of two different colors, one flower would be from the store in Connie's memory. The young man said that because I was a regular customer, the store wanted to give me something as a token of appreciation for the memory of my wife. It was only $6.50, and I took the two different flowers. I went to the cemetery and it was very dark. I took pictures and sought Connie's blessings so that I could go to India in the morning. I slept for barely two hours, and now I am here in Delhi. I hope the day will come that I will be in my own house back in the US. I'm really confused because if I stay there, I am very unhappy, and if I'm here in Delhi, there is some happiness but some sadness as well. So I am living in those four parts of the world, with happiness mixed together with sadness. I have no idea when it'll get better, but I have to take it one day at a time. One day at a time.

33

Her Home was Her Life

To Connie, it was very important that her house be decorated with the best of things. Her taste, I believe, was much better than that of any professional. She was very selective in choosing the right items and matching things—furniture, decorative items, paintings, carpets, kitchen and bathroom appliances, floor, tiles, and millions of other things. We got much praise and many compliments for her decor, the cleanliness of our house and quality of our home. Friends used to wait for an invitation to come to our house to see the soothing atmosphere and great food. We were extremely happy for our hospitality. She was extremely organized, and would keep lists of everything. She kept the carpets and windows clean, and kept a careful schedule of what to clean and when. I have to say, our house has always been absolutely neat and clean. Perfection, quality, cleanness, changing styles on certain things were in her blood. I have not seen anyone like that nor will I ever. I remember when she renovated her kitchen with granite stone and tiles in 2006, it took both of us over two months before she chose her matching materials and fixtures. Later, she hired the best company to put tiles on the floor, granite stone on the kitchen counter, tiles on walls, appliances in the sink, and the kitchen. Friends gave her many compliments on the renovation. She invited all of our neighbors and friends for drinks and snacks. They all said that our house was the best house they have ever seen. These were all our American friends. We received the same complimentary remarks from thirty Indian families when they came to visit. In addition, they asked us to invite them back again and again. The same thing is applicable for her furniture, tables, lamps, chairs, and other things. A few years ago, she wanted a walk-in shower and hired the best company and the best materials. It took one month to finish, and we had to live with just one bathroom. After that, she replaced the air conditioners and other appliances which, perhaps, I would never have replaced. I was extremely helpful and happy for her that she got the best. Since she was my life, I was getting the greatest happiness to see that she is happy. Serving her, making her happy and healthy, and not depriving her of anything, was the only happiness I was enjoying. It gave me the most powerful motivation to deal with the world and all human beings. My happiness was teaching the new generation and sharing my knowledge. Guiding new professionals was a great time, and I was extremely happy as Connie was with me, either at home or out together. I am not going to enjoy all that now. I will explain why that is in her "demise chapter." However, I would like to teach and share my knowledge, education, and the experiences of our life, which might take away my loss and pain for my happy days. Later, I am lost again. Temporary happiness and sadness are going to be my life from now on. I have seen the suffering of spouses married for a long time after the death of one or after divorce. How intense that pain is, I now know more. I am suffering from that pain and from withdrawal symptoms, which are incorporated into my mind and my heart. This book is a little happiness, but the sadness is much more with me. I don't know what I can do, and I am waiting for what life I will have to face. I would live to fulfill Connie's wishes, which is still painful as I can't see her. In ancient Egypt, mummies are a great example of how people dealt with the loss of their loved ones. I think it was right for those people, at least they could still see the body, which might have given them a feeling that their loved ones are still with them. I don't know if I could have done that or not, as she wanted to be cremated. I never thought that her husband and her love would have to go through the pain of handling her cremation and other things. How much pain and suffering I went through, I just don't know, and would like to know why I had to experience that. Her pictures and our pictures in their many frames around the house are my life, and the paintings on the wall in our house. My life is a combination of happiness and sadness, and I cannot choose which emotion I should feel. I will have to go through my whole life to find the answer, if I am meant to find that answer. Now, my pain and withdrawal symptoms are incorporated in my mind and heart.

34

Cleanliness and Housekeeping was in Her Blood

While talking about Connie, I must say how neat and clean she was in the house. She kept our house like a museum. She used to take a keen interest in the house. Her collection was just unique. Sometimes it used to take her years before she could make a decision about the fabric she wanted, the kind of covers to use, the kind of kitchen design she wanted, the kind of granite she wanted to use, etc. She was very selective in the house. I would say that her taste, her thinking, the way she used to perceive things, was many times better than any interior decorator. She was very particular about cleanliness in the house. She could not tolerate dust in the house.

She was very particular about the laundry so she would change bed sheets every couple of days. She was so efficient and organized that cleanliness was ingrained in her. No matter what time it was, whether night or day, she would take a shower and change her clothes. She would wash laundry every two days, including my clothes. She was very particular that I wear a shirt for only one day, and she would say, "No! It is more than enough!" Sometimes I used to argue, "No, I just wore it for one day, I can use it for one more day!" She would say, "No! Look at the collar at the back! You have a professional job; people notice the small things like your collar." I would say, "I don't think so because I wear a three-piece suit." She would say, "You are not going to compromise. It is better that you buy, or I will buy for you, ten or one dozen white t-shirts and shirts. You will not wear them for more than one day." Then I would ask her, "Is it not too much work for you to do the laundry?" She would say, "I can handle it, it's not that difficult. Doing laundry in the house is very simple. You just have to put it in the laundry room and then you have enough time. I just do two loads every other day. It makes no difference."

She was very organized; she would iron my shirts, t-shirts, socks, and handkerchiefs. I think these things show how dedicated she was to me, and she would make such an effort to see that her husband looked great all the time in his professional job. She used to feel very proud about me. I used to get a lot of compliments from my office, especially when I was working for Heller. They would say, "Mr. Berry, we see you as the most fashionable person in our whole organization. How do you do that?" I would say, "Well, my wife Connie is very particular about my suit, and what kind of tie, scarf, and pen matches it." He would say, "Well, she has made you a model. I think you should be in the model industry." So, I would say, "Well, it's not like that, but I really like being well dressed." I got many awards as the best dressed person of the year. I dressed like that from childhood, wearing three-piece suits, so I carried on that legacy.

When I think about it now, I realize how much energy she spent caring for me and how much pain she had to bear. God bless her! I don't think I could have done all that with so much affection. Sometimes I would be upset that she would even polish my shoes. I used to feel like a criminal that my wife was polishing my shoes. I did not polish my shoes as I thought that it's just dusting. Here, = shoes don't get dirty. But she would say, "No, I think the first thing people notice is shoes, and a well-dressed person is always liked. You have so much intelligence and personality. Being well dressed will be like the icing on the cake." I think that attitude really put a sparkle in me. I used to take pride in it. Regarding her clothing, she would rather buy two clothing pieces that were expensive and pretty, rather than buying several cheap ones. She always emphasized, "Pradeep, I think it is better to buy good quality and buy less. Whenever you buy, buy the best quality because they will last longer and look good." We had friends who held good positions, and they would wear polyester shirts and cheap suits and ties. She used to be surprised that they could thrive in the corporate sector. Eventually, she could not tolerate it any longer and she told them, "I hope you won't mind my saying this, but I think in your profession when you are holding a good position, you should not wear those polyester shirts and polyester jackets. I think you should try to learn how to dress up in a professional way. This is not a blue-collar job." Also, I remember once in a year, when we did inventory accounts, we would be delighted that we wouldn't have to wear a suit. We could wear casual clothes. Mostly people used to come in jeans. She told me, "Jeans are unprofessional."

She never allowed me to wear a pair of jeans. So, she was very particular even for casual clothing. She bought me so many different kinds of pants and shirts. I think I must have over 100 shirts, and they are sitting with me. Some I never wore, and some I wore maybe a couple of times. I am never going to give away those shirts because those are big memories and they are great gifts from my dear wife. I think I can go on writing about clothing. I have lovely pairs of socks by Nautica and Pierre Cardin.

She was very classy, and I think all the Italian ties she bought were lovely. She used to buy at least one or two ties for me every month. Whenever she would go out, she would buy something for me. She would never ask me to pay for anything. I used to tell her, "Well, you are spending so much money." She used to say, "No, it is my love for you." I used to reciprocate that. I used to travel, wherever I would go, sometimes I used to go to India, and I would bring a lot of things. She was so considerate. She would say, "No, I think I want to pay." I would say, "That is not right. You spend so much money on me and when I want to give it to you, you want to pay." She would say, "No this is the way I am. I generally feel bad." I would say, "No, please in the future, don't ever say to me that you have to pay me because this is my love for you. The way you love me, I love you." So, she would say, "I will accept it but don't buy too much. If I ask you to buy one sweater or two bracelets you get so many!" She was very fond of silver. So, she would say, "Ok, you can buy me one necklace and one bracelet." I would buy maybe ten bracelets and ten different kinds of necklaces for her. So, she would say, "You know what, you don't know the difference between one or two or ten! When I tell you to bring one or two, you always like to bring so much. What a collection I have!" So, I would say, "Just keep it. Or give it to your friends, or give it to your nieces." She would say, "I think next time when we go, we will try to return them." Just as she was very considerate about my money, she was also conservative. She would use coupons and save money. About our house, she used to say, "I would rather travel all over the world and be house poor." That's how we started enjoying life, and we went all over the world on different cruises. I can name hundreds of them. We went with University of Michigan, with Carleton, with different alumni and with professors. It was all intellectual, and there were lectures, studies, and sightseeing. The cruises gave a lot of intellectual input in every area of our life. This is one of the great qualities which she would combine in her house. She used to combine housekeeping together with my clothing.

These were some of the qualities she had. I am going to write in more detail about many episodes and stories where she used to excel. We went to Ireland and she said, "You have to dance this Irish dance because it is a cultural activity. Irish culture will ask you to wear these green clothes and the girl will ask you to dance with her." She was not jealous that some young girl would dance with me because it was a part of the Irish culture. She was very happy to see me dancing. She took pride that her husband was dancing and he could dance in the Irish style.

I want to mention these things. I want to continue writing so that we can leave a legacy about how much we love her, and how much love she could give you. I always consider my wife Connie as not only my wife, but also my best friend, sister, and mother. I think in Indian culture, in 500 BC, Chanakya wrote about the same four qualities of women and how they can play these different roles. It is also written in Sanskrit, in our Vedanta, that a woman has four qualities which I already mentioned. There were times when her love was like a mother, and her advice was like a sister and friend. As a wife, she was a great companion. These kinds of qualities, I would say are very rare. I am lucky that I had this opportunity. It was my destiny. There were a lot of girls that my family had chosen as prospects for me, and if I had gone back, perhaps I would have been married to one of them and I would never have seen Connie again. I lived all these years because Connie was with me, and now after her demise, everything is over. This is most painful, and I pray to God that He can take anything from me, but He should give my wife back, give my Connie back. I really hope that in our next life we will be together again as husband and wife. I would say, if there is any power, if there is a miracle, we keep on taking new life every time and we are always husband and wife, and enjoy the same kind of life. If that happens, I am going to get over my anger. After a few years, we will meet again. This is a great hope. You should never deprive someone of their hope because hope maybe the only thing they have.

35

Her love for the Best Cuisines

CONNIE WAS EXTREMELY SELECTIVE ABOUT THE FOOD we ate. She liked to cook and eat the highest quality food including vegetables, fruits, meat, fish and desserts, and wine, both at home and in the restaurants. She was an amazing cook, and made different varieties of food and homemade desserts which I would never be able to get in my life without her. They were fresh, not fat, and absolutely healthy and organic. She was the engine for taking me out to the best restaurants for excellent food. Her selection was extremely great and she didn't care about the prices, although she was very conservative in many ways and knew how to save for old age and rainy days. Cutting coupons to save money was her great hobby. Her passion for reading about new restaurants and recipes and trying different food from all over the world was unique. I enjoyed all of that a whole lot. At the same time, she looked after the house—shopping, cleaning, doing laundry, and taking care of my professional clothing and accessories, including ironing clothes. This was a gift of God to me. At the same time, her choice of casual and traveling clothing was another unforgettable gift of my life. She truly loved me to do all that for me. I had never before been blessed with that kind of love, except my elder brother who took care of me when I was in India. I would have to write a whole new book on every subject that I am writing about to cover each of her qualities. I also helped her with everything, as she was busy and we both were partners in cooking and shopping. It was due to my love for her, that I learned excellent cooking and shopping, with her or alone. When I came to the US in January 1976, I didn't know anything about cooking except how to make tea. It took lots of self-teaching, and I can say that now I am an excellent cook. Now, I doubt I would cook as I have lost interest in food due to her absence.

Morels are one of the finest foods in the world. They are very expensive, even as dried mushrooms. India is one of the world's most important producers of morels. Even in India, they are considered a delicacy, and during my grandfather's time, they would be served at every marriage and major function. Guests expected to be served morels, and a host who couldn't afford them would have to apologize. I may ask my niece, Mona, to bring some for me when she visits, and I am sure she knows how to use morels to prepare vegetable dishes and rice pulao. I used to bring some for Connie, and she also used to buy them from Whole Foods or Spice House in Evanston. Another healthy delicacy that we loved was saffron rice. Saffron rice was a favorite dish of ours, and saffron, like morels, is a rare delicacy.

36

Great Deeds and Ethical Values of Connie

Connie Darling did so many great deeds of karma. That includes, but is not limited to, charity for different organizations, schools, colleges, low income families, hospitals, the Red Cross, the Salvation Army, the USA Olympics, and foundations for children and for education. She was instrumental in looking after her parents, besides taking them to doctors 'appointments, to buy groceries, cooking for them, and bringing them to our home for dinner. After the death of Connie's father on December 20, 1989, we both insisted her mother come and stay with us permanently. We would have been very happy to look after her. But her mother refused, hoping to be near her grandchildren, whom she adored and got the biggest joy from while sacrificing many things. In reality, she cared and loved them much more than Connie Darling and Pradeep. It bothered us. It was painful and we felt betrayed. However, we both decided that if that gives her happiness, let it be. We used to do whatever she wanted us to do whenever she asked. Many times, she behaved badly with us, taking the side of Connie's brother's family and being nasty to us. We tolerated that for her happiness. Later, Connie darling told her mother, "Mom, you better be nice to Pradeep because when you are old, Pradeep and Connie would come to rescue you as he has been brought up to always respect elderly people. "Connie's mother still had one hobby, and that was her grandchildren. Right from the beginning, when Connie came into my life, it was a mind-blowing experience for me. Connie told me that her mother is extreme, and I didn't understand this, because my elder brother and I were brought up by our grandparents and I came from a joint family system. Connie was so right. After Connie's father died, her son and grandkids didn't want to do anything with her. Her son told me many times

Connie was in tears after I told her. She told me, "He has so much money that he and his family does not have to worry for generations, but our own mother and father, who did everything for him, haven't a penny." I, too, was extremely hurt, and perhaps told him something jokingly, as they were in our home for Thanksgiving. Later, again, he told me the same thing. It holds absolutely true. He did not spend a penny for his father or his mother, not even for their funerals. He has all the wealth for his family, their spouses and grandchildren, and even for his three sons-in-law whom he and his wife shower with money so that they can have full control over them as they are so possessive of their kids and grandkids. Money buys everything for them. It would never ever have worked for Connie and Pradeep. Connie and I made the decision that we would do anything to make her mother's old age happy. It truly happened. Connie and I were instrumental in looking after her mother. It was great to serve the elderly. True love should be selfless and we should sacrifice to see others happy. I have seen many examples of these kinds of sacrifices. During our lives, when Connie and I met, it was true love in the first meeting. We both wanted to be together and hopefully marry. Connie frankly asked me if I had some other person in the US or India as arranged marriages were common in India. I said that my parents and family have selected many girls and their families for me to marry. However, I didn't know if I had that desire. She told me, "I don't want you to regret anything later and I am willing to sacrifice my love if you have someone waiting for you in India." She also stated that she would then never marry anyone except me. I immediately told her the same thing. I would only marry Connie. It breaks my heart and upsets me that I am writing this after forty years. Where is my Connie? Where did she go? Why I am left alone and when will I meet her? I will forgive everyone in my life and start all over if Connie comes, which I know is naive thinking, but I want to think for my happiness. In her absence, I am reminded of the cruelty of Connie's brother and his family towards their mother. I remember very well that Connie's father always told me and Connie to take care of his wife if something happened to him. He also told me, "Pradeep, my son and his wife have so much money that they can buy or do anything." Her son too admitted to me that "Pradeep, my kids are well set, and they don't have to worry for anything in their lives, including my grandchildren." He was pretty sincere and honest. I truly admired him and told him; I am very happy for you all. Connie's brother told me to tell his mom to make her own friends, as neither he nor his kids have time to spend with her, as he has built a mansion on the lake to enjoy and wants to travel the world and have their own life of fun. Connie was extremely hurt for years about this and so was I. Let me make it clear that it's a very unique family, and I have not seen any other American people behaving this way. American people, I know, in general are helpful and full of compassion. I tried to forget all that and started to give Connie the maximum of support and love to help her overcome her troubled mind. Further, I would have never ever written this if Connie was alive. Her demise has brought to light many hidden painful episodes. Now, all these things are new wounds in my life. Connie used to bring her mother to our home to stay for months. I was very happy to see that Connie was happy, and Connie's happiness was my happiness, and it gave me the joy to see them both happy. Most of the crimes in the world have many reasons, however, in my opinion, the majority of them are due to money. Greed, property, love, and jealousy are pretty common.

Connie and I were extremely upset when her own brother, who hadn't cared for his parents, suddenly decided to take his own mother, against her will, to a nursing home rather than his own big home. Their own home and the nursing home were three hours away from our home and their mother's home. There are plenty of nursing homes near our home. The motive was kidnapping her for money. Mother was not keen, and her son and his wife played on her weakness—her grandchildren. Connie and I knew their motives. Connie got a rare skin disease in September 1998, and it was difficult to diagnose. It was PRP, and that restricted Connie's ability to bring back her mother. She wanted to come back to her own house, however, her son and his wife were determined that their mother lives in the nursing home so that they would have a hold on her money and be able to ensure that she did not give anything more to Connie. They wanted to get everything she had so that Connie would get little of her share. Money is a disease, and it absolutely proved true. Connie had told him that Mom is leaving an equal share for her and for him after she dies, and that he was welcome to verify that from the will and from the bank. Greed is a curse on this land. Her brother and his wife didn't want to believe what Connie told them so they planned to keep her mother under their control so that mother may not give more money to Connie. How wrong and dirty they were.

Connie was the most ethical, honest, selfless, charitable, giving person that I have ever met. I truly mean this. I might have lacked somewhere, but Connie was perfect. She was looking after her mother without expecting anything in return. She used to buy her what she needed and spend money on her. Connie told me that her parents put her through school and college and that is enough. I am extremely grateful to them for spending money for my education. Further, due to them, I can make my own living. It is absolutely amazing and true that she never ever took a penny from her parents. Instead, she worked part-time jobs to pay for her Master's Degree and other education. I was new in the US, and was surprised to see that. In

India, we were used to asking for everything from our parents or grandparents. It was a new wave for me, and it took me few years to know and learn about it. I am now the same kind of a person, who is a giver and don't expect anything from others nor I would take anything from anyone. In the past, many people wanted to give me a token, but I couldn't accept it. I am sure God is going to take an extremely powerful revenge on Connie's family, as they are not human beings, but have animal instincts.

37

Our Love Destiny Would Continue — but with Unhappiness for Me

OUR LIFE WAS A TRUE STORY OF pure love. It was wonderful to feel, and vibrant to enjoy each moment even while we both worked on highly professional senior positions. Everything looks different now. She is gone, and I am lost. I will not go to the places where we went; it will haunt me like Dracula, making me even go through more pain and suffering. I wonder if I would find an answer to my loss. In memory of Connie, I might start humanitarian acts and teaching undergraduate and MBA students and professionals in the field of commercial financing, mergers and acquisitions, buyouts, crisis management, and, if needed, spirituality or world economy.

Sharing knowledge is the best way for me to survive for Connie, and she always loved to share her knowledge with others. I will always seek her blessings and forgiveness for any mistakes I made. Her life was to live for me, and mine was to live for her. I am thankful that, with a broken heart, I was able to do her cremation in two days and enter her ashes in her plot next to her parents. My happiness and unhappiness were a necessary combination. I wanted the best cremation done in two days to cut my pain as she was special and God kept me alive to do that. It tears me up to think of what would have happened otherwise. She was very special and not a charity case. Peace comes and pain starts after seeing and praying to her. For thirty-nine and a half years, our life was ingrained in the house. It is full of her memory, our pictures going to different places, her cemetery, and the maintenance of her best-designed house, with very selective furniture, the kitchen, the bathroom and carpets, and other selections of these thirty-nine years. Living here is a double-edged sword; however, these are my lifelong possessions. I am sure we will meet again in our next lives. And currently, though physically she is not with me, spiritually she is here and still guiding me.

While she was going through medical care, I left my high-powered income and professional career and truly enjoyed every moment with her, including taking her to the doctors, shopping with her, and other things. Serving her was a great joy. Although I was very upset about her health and for the last two years it was painful for both of us, still sitting and looking at her and the satisfaction of being with her was happiness enough and I was devoted to her. I was extremely hopeful that Connie darling would be alive for another ten to fifteen years and I always used to worry about her and pray to God to keep me alive to take care of her. I never thought she would go so quickly, and I was shattered and practically broken down and I didn't think I could survive my loss. But I prayed to God to keep me alive to do her cremation and chapel of peace ceremony and to bury her ashes on her plot next to her parents. I told the funeral home and crematorium that I wanted the best of everything for her last rites and that I would not compromise with the cost and the quality. It has given me happiness as well as lots of pain, which I will experience as long as I am alive. Each and every moment, Connie is in my mind, and my heart is broken when I think of the last few months. I start shaking and lose all my happiness. I don't think I will be at peace anytime. I have no desire to remarry or have a great social life. I get both peace and sadness at our house. Even when I am visiting my family in India, my peace of mind is not there. My brother and his family give me all their love, but Connie still remains in my mind, body, and soul, and I don't enjoy anything. Yes, my brother and his family, and my two grandnieces are keeping me happy, but inside, I think of Connie, too. Now I realize why people enjoy their grandchildren. Still, I have seen many relatives and friends who were missing their spouses and not gaining much happiness from their grandkids. To each his own?

Some people immediately go for a second or third marriage after the death of their spouse. It is an individual choice, depending upon the love they shared and other factors, and there is no universal law governing the choice to remarry or not. In my case, I took the demise of Connie extremely hard, and I have known for years that true love happens only one time in life. This is the way I feel, and I don't expect everyone to agree with me. I am not perfect, and I think of many things I should have done but could not do for her due to circumstances. At the same time, we did so much that others can't even imagine or think of it.

38

Connie and Her Devotion to My Professional Help in Many Places

The experience of traveling was her great gift to me. Her exposure to American culture and the development of my personality was an absolutely precious gift for my career and advancement. Connie bought so many things for me to make sure that I always looked great. She never, ever lied, cheated, or hurt anyone. She did so many selfless things to help me and to help others. If I start writing all the other things she did, I would have to write another book. In reality, there is no end to her good karma and deeds.

My mind is absolutely blank and I can't wait to write that Connie darling was extremely exciting and fun. I have never ever seen such a great person. She was a wonderful human being and super bright and beautiful. I too did good karma. That would justify as to why I am upset that God didn't save her when there was hope that she would live and do more in the world. Why didn't God save her from death?

I truly believe that my success and advancement were only because of Connie. I am absolutely certain of that. Last night around 3:00 a.m., on July 29, I was just sharing the childhood lie of my elder brother and me. Immediately, I realized that had I not gone to the US, even with my advanced education and joining my family's booming business as my father's elder brother had offered and desperately needed me to join with a 25% share. At the beginning of 1975, after the death of our eighty-five-year-old employee, the 25% share that my grandfather had given him because of his devotion and intelligence, despite his lack of higher education, became available. I was told that he was a six-year-old kid when he was hired by my grandfather to work with him in the business, as he had no one to feed him. Later, he was trained and absolutely was the engine and the right hand of our business. My uncles were neither educated nor bright, and that's why my grandfather gave him a 25% share. That is how I was offered the opportunity to take his spot. My father didn't encourage me, saying, "Son, you are exceptionally bright and should go for your own career." The truth was he wanted that share to be given to my half-brother. I refused as many variables were uncertain. How would my father and his young brother treat me? Then I decided to go to the US. Had Connie darling not met me, I would have been back to India and everyone would have been badmouthing me and what not. I am sure I would have been a failure and had so many hassles in my life, though getting a great job was not difficult, but Connie was my destiny. I am sure I would have been extremely unhappy in India without her. Thanks to Connie for my success and destiny, and I know that we were meant to be husband and wife, a special reward and gift of God.

I would like to write about an incident that occurred when Connie and I were traveling towards Palm Springs and we came across the most powerful sight you can imagine. We were driving in the mountains and the roads were very curvy, and I asked Connie, "Do you think there is any problem in driving? Do you think people take that many chances in driving?" She was familiar with the surroundings so she told me, "Oh no! I don't think you have to worry about it because it is pretty safe and it is not like in underdeveloped countries where people worry about driving. It is just this time of the year, unfortunately, you are not finding too many cars, so don't worry! Just relax! And also if you are uncomfortable, then I can drive and you can just watch." But I told her, "No, let me gain some confidence." So it took us about two hours and then we finally reached Orange County. That was one of my most difficult driving experiences in the United States on the mountains. When I came back, I said, "Oh my God! That was a piece of cake!" And Connie told me, "I told you that!" I think the reason I am mentioning this incident, is to point out how Connie helped me to gain confidence about driving, about every aspect of it, and how to control the car. When we came back from where we stayed, I was really ready to drive anywhere, especially in California and San Diego. So this is worth mentioning how much Connie helped me in every aspect of life.

One time, my friend Palli, who lived in New York, invited me to visit him at his house (which is now owned by the Clintons). I was forty miles away, and was scared to drive there at 8:00 p.m. for dinner. Connie, who was in Chicago, asked me to please not go, as I was driving a rental Lincoln, and New York can be dangerous if you get lost. I thought I had good directions, but I didn't arrive until 9:15 p.m., and they were waiting for me with ten dishes on the table. I could hardly eat as I was worried about the return trip. I was such an idiot on this occasion. I did not have the telephone number or the address for the hotel I was going to stay in. I was lost for hours and drove until 2:00 a.m., and I was convinced that I would never reach the hotel. The only choice I had was to call my friend at two in the morning to come to rescue me, but then I worried that he would think me an ignorant fool if I called him for help. Palli was extremely rich because of his inheritance from India and his large, wealthy family, but he respected me because I had no inheritance and the best education. I have not talked to Palli since Connie died. He used to call once or twice a week to check on me and Connie. Perhaps I should fly to New Jersey and surprise him with a call asking him to meet me at the airport. He would never let me stay in a hotel but would have me stay in his house. He was a childhood friend of Arun Berry, and thus also my friend. I have thousands of friends all over the world that loved Connie and respect her, but I do not want to have to tell the whole story about her illness and the negligence that led to her death. I would get so very upset to have to tell all of my friends. That is why I am happier living in isolation for now.

We were trying to find different places to go, and Connie told me, "You know, the best way is to call the hotel people or let me get the magazine." She was very good at reading and finding out directions. So we stayed for two weeks in Palm Springs, Orange County, and San Diego and we enjoyed every single part of it and also a couple of other places. So I must say Connie had a super-intelligent brain. Later on, we went to Carlsbad, which Connie knew and had read about. We made many trips like that. I am just sharing her experience, and after that, she also told me, "Next time, next year, we should go to Santa Fe." Let me tell everybody that Santa Fe is one of the most charming places. It is the third-largest place on the earth as far as art and crafts are concerned. Number one is considered either France or New York. Even if New York is number one, then France is second and then Santa Fe. In Santa Fe, people and artists come from all over the world. I was amazed at the art I saw in Santa Fe, New Mexico!

The other great experience she gave me was taking me to the French Quarter and that was really magnificent. We stayed in the French Quarter, and the food and the culture there are totally different. We really had a ball, and she showed me everything because she was very adventurous. I must say that I was not adventurous whereas Connie was very adventurous, and as a result of that, I was able to enjoy many new experiences because of her adventurous spirit. A similar incident happened later when I was working in San Antonio, Texas and my employers told me, "Pradeep, do you want to come back or do you want to stay there?" So I said, "Well, I don't know." To which they offered, "If you want, you can have Connie fly over and just put it on the expense report." So I called Connie and she flew over. I picked her up and we stayed there for one week and it was a ball! I was working and she would drop me at the office, pick me up for lunch, and then she would go and do her shopping. In the evening we would go back to the hotel, I would work for half an hour or an hour on my report. Then we would go and have fun. Again, in the night, when we would come back, she would watch TV and I would do my reports. So this way I think Connie was a great contributor in traveling with me so that I was not lonely. Connie told me, "Pradeep, having the best quality clothes, shoes, suits, ties, jackets, matching clothes that show you to be a well-dressed person is extremely important, especially in the US for people working in a professional career." I knew all of that, however, she taught me much more. Connie and I were absolutely involved in gaining knowledge and sharing with the world. According to Chinese and Indian philosophy, it is a sin to not share knowledge. It is our primary duty to share knowledge with those who want to learn; otherwise you waste your time and theirs. People who think they know everything are the most ignorant. Connie and I have come across many of them, and they only want to gossip and tell useless lies that they are overqualified for jobs and try to fool other people. They do not realize that others are smart and they have made a fool of themselves with their bragging and lies. Such people are left without respect and with only handful of family and friends, often depending on their parents. These circumstances can ruin marriages. A wife wants her husband to no longer be a mama's boy, and mothers should make their sons realize that their wives come first and mothers second. Some mothers provoke discord, telling their sons that they are henpecked, and these small things may break a marriage. No wife can tolerate a husband who ignores her and is always with his family. Why did he marry her? It would have been better to have stayed a bachelor and live with his parents and lead a miserable, lonely life looking for a wife. Even then, only a desperate woman would marry such a man, and that too would be according to her conditions and might be a marriage without love. I could write an entire book on this chapter based on mine and Connie's research. With our work and travels, we never thought of publishing, especially when Connie began to fall ill and we decided that youth and time would ebb like time and tides. I am glad we did, and the results are this: My Connie died unexpectedly on February 28, 2015. No more travel and dining out for me, and I will have to go on living in pain, although I may make jokes and pretend to be happy when I am with someone. Sometimes I am extremely happy, especially when I am having an intelligent conversation with intelligent people. I like to talk to everyone, regardless of their education or wealth. I love people and animals, and I respect every human being as part of the planet. I am not so great myself that I have to decide about people. I must have many faults, and I want to teach everyone from my faults and weaknesses.

39

Sympathy and Empathy—But Pain

I WOULD LIKE TO ADD IN MY MEMORIES that I am really trying to understand the pain of some of the people I have met in my professional life who have gone through more tragedy than one can imagine. Though even at that time I understood how much pain there was, after the demise of my darling wife Connie, I can really understand the gravity of the pain that they went through. I will give an example that I must narrate. I think it was sometime in 1983. I had flown to Charleston, Virginia for some work. Actually, I flew on Sunday night because of Connie. She had gone with her students to show them the political system in this country. In those days, she was teaching Spanish, French, and political science. She had to leave on Friday and was supposed to come back on Monday. They were to visit the White House among other places. Since I was not doing anything, I left on Sunday afternoon. My clients, the borrowers, were the second-largest trucking company in the United States. They were desperate to get a loan at that time as the trucking industry was deregulated. This company was struggling in their business although they were very wealthy. To expand their business, it was important for them to show certain credits in their financial statements. When I reached there, the borrowers picked me up and took me out for dinner, and then I stayed in the hotel. The next day, one of the senior partners took me to his house and treated me to dinner. Now here is the real story that I wish to share: On Wednesday, as I remember, one of the main owners, who was extremely wealthy, took me to his house. He said, "Mr. Berry, I want you to have dinner with me and then maybe you can sleep in my house." It is very rare that a borrower, who is not known to me, will take me to his house. I think he must have liked me very much—my professional approach, my conduct, and my behavior. He was highly impressed. He said, "Mr. Berry, let's go out tonight and I will show you something." It was pitch dark when he took me to a place and he stopped his Audi car. Then he got out of the car, and he said, "Mr. Berry, please walk with me to this place." As I walked, he said, "You know, this place where I have brought you, is where my young son, who was twenty-four years old, was killed in an accident. As a result of that I have really lost everything. I cannot function because of this tragedy. My son was going to take over my business. All my hopes are gone. My daughter, though she's working, is not capable. She is not highly educated. My younger son has no desire to do anything except to become a truck driver. I have bought him a truck costing $250,000." We were chatting in the night and he said to me, "I don't know, Mr. Berry, somehow or the other I feel that you should join me. I will pay you double the salary or three times the salary you earn now plus I will pay for your wife's salary and I will buy you a house and I will give you 30% to 40% stock in my company. Finally, I will give this company to you as I cannot work anymore because of my son's tragedy." He was practically begging me, really requesting me to accept, and said, "Please listen to my pain and please move to Charleston, and I can assure you that you will be very happy and because of you I will get a new life." I felt very sorry for him and I was confused. It was a good offer but at the same time I thought of Connie's career, of the repercussions of leaving Evanston, her parents, and everything else, so I declined the offer.

It continued to bother me that this person had gone through such tragedy. I've been trying to contact him, and I found out later that he closed his company due to his shock and grief, and then he sold it and just disappeared. For the past twenty-five years, I have been looking for him, but I cannot find him and I have no idea where he is. If he is alive or if he's out there, I would love to go and share his tragedy and my tragedy.

Now I understand what he was going through at that time. It is something you understand when it happens to you. This is what I want to add. I have many other stories that I will mention related to pain. When some other person is in pain, that pain does not seem too deep to you as an outsider, but when the same thing happens to you, you realize how painful it is. I will never forget this realization which relates to me and is affecting me deeply.

40

Cruises – Part of her World Travel

CRUISE TRIPS WITH CONNIE: ONCE AGAIN, I want to say that Connie was instrumental in putting this love for travel in my blood. I went on many cruise trips with Connie, as she was very adventurous. She took me along and gave me the opportunity to go to different parts of the world. She used to take interest in reading about which cruises are available from the University of Michigan, which is supposed to have some of the best cruises. Recently, I heard Carleton has also started offering cruises. We also made some trips which were not cruises, for example we went to the Black Mountains in Germany and France. We also made trips related to my business. During one of our trips to the Rhine, Connie had a desire to go and take another trip which was from France, which would go through many countries, all the way up to Amsterdam. From Amsterdam, it would go further to Switzerland, from there to one more country where you would rest overnight in a hotel and return to the US the next morning by flight. They also provided the option of adding extra stops if you wished as we did in Norway. We flew with them and since we were part of the Advantage group, we stayed four days in Bergen. It was such a wonderful thing and a beautiful country. Connie and I stayed in the hotel with about thirty people. On the final day when we had to depart from Bergen back to Norway in a ship, ninety-eight more people joined us.

All these trips that I have mentioned above were not the kind of trips ordinary people make. The people that came on these trips with us were interested in learning and they were intellectual people. These trips are not just ordinary trips, and there would be many lectures given at each stop by different professors speaking about different topics. For example, on one trip, they spoke about different lakes. They would explain how the dams on the lakes were constructed, how the water is controlled in the Daniel and Rayan Rivers, and how they have to match and control the water. It is a magnificent thing to see how the York men have controlled the water system. In addition to these lectures, there would also be beautiful sightseeing excursions in small boats which carry 120 or 130 passengers only. The tourists on these trips were intellectual people from the sponsoring universities who graduated in different years and were mostly seniors. There were no kids on these cruises and only very bright people and professors. There were doctors, professors, banking and finance professionals, and teachers. We would share common tables during breakfast. We would sit with different people for every meal so we could have stimulating conversations with various people. Sightseeing would also be done with different groups. In the buses, the drivers, coaches, and guides would guide us and they would tell us the history of the places we visited. As a result of that, we learned so much about the country and its history. We would also visit different schools and colleges, meet the professors there, and listen to them speak. Finally, there would be a small exam which we had to pass. I don't mean to say that they would give you grades so you could get a degree but it meant a whole lot because nobody wanted to fail those exams. So we really had to study for the exam! Cultural activities would also be included in the program, for example, we would have to dance according to a particular culture. When we were in Ireland, it was part of their custom that girls as young as seventeen to nineteen years old, would ask the guests to dance with them. I was sort of embarrassed, when one girl just grabbed me and said, "Come man, we have to dance!" So I had to dance with her for half an hour in the Irish way. Connie was watching me, but she didn't feel jealous. She didn't think, "Oh my God! My husband is dancing with a young girl!" It was acceptable to her because Connie had a lot of faith in my character, and I also had a lot of faith in her character. However, it is not very popular in Irish, German, or French culture for men to ask ladies who are not their wives to dance with them, so when we had to dance in France it was mandatory for me to dance with Connie, and we were very well dressed for the occasion. I knew the different kinds of dance steps to some degree, but Connie taught me lot of different steps. She also told me, "Pradeep, you should take some dancing classes," which I did. So look at how many cultural things she exposed me to, and how she cultivated in me a love for dancing and experiencing different cultures. This, I would say, added to the experience for me. I think with so much experience now. I can talk about it in schools and colleges for hours! I can explain different points of the cultures I've been exposed in. How Irish, German, English, Norwegian and American cultures are different. This world is really a magnificent place if you know where to go; however, there are people who will just go in the buses and they don't get that same experience because they are not educated, and they don't have professors and coaches to guide them in the trip.

I recently got mail from Carleton College announcing that they are taking a trip to the Rhine and Switzerland. We have already been on this trip, although they are covering slightly different cities this time. I would love to go with Connie if she was alive. We would never have thought twice about it and we would just have made the reservations. The trip will start in November, but I don't think I want to go because I know I will be depressed. I also received a brochure from the Carleton Alumni Association about a cruise that is going to Sri Lanka for nineteen days. I thought that in case I'm already in India, I can take a flight to Sri Lanka and join them there. I'm not going to go on my own accord without approval from Carleton. Carleton would love to take me because it is not really a business but also based on feelings for their former students. Connie's connection with Carleton will give me the power to say that Connie is with me and she would be happy that I'm attending a cruise. I know that I will not meet Connie, nor will I be able to meet Connie's batch; however, I'm sure there will be a younger batch of people. I will feel like there is some sort of a bond in our conversations during lunch, dinner, or other times. I will have some sort of a background, a great tool and power to talk about Carleton, and why I came to the cruise. Then I can talk about my wife Constance Berry, how she was part of Carleton, and my memories of her. Since people are so compassionate, they will definitely respect me for this. They will give me moral support and they will say, "Oh Pradeep! I think you should do this more and it's a good tribute to your wife Connie and it will be the greatest thing you can do!" So they might encourage me to travel more, otherwise, I will be sitting in the same big hole.

Connie went to Harvard and she went to top universities in Mexico and in Spain. She finished her MBA in Spanish in both Spain and Germany. Both of us were there when she was teaching. I had gotten myself transferred there since we had offices all over the world. So we were together, and I would say in my married life of forty years that she accompanied me for travel on an average 30% of the time. My company used to pay, so they made my life very easy.

41

Connie's Character

Regarding Connie's character, I think I can tell you we were made for each other. I was raised in an environment with very strong values and with an emphasis on character building. Our grandparents were very strict about focusing on studies, sports and other activities like Scouts, and NCC. I was extremely good in Boy Scouts, was the NCC battalion sergeant and had a lot of extracurricular qualifications. We were given the strongest foundation possible to build our character. That also meant not having any relationships or attachments with the opposite gender. The priority was to get educated first and all other things could happen after one was well settled in life. In reality, because we were brought up in this way, we never really even thought of having any female friends. It wasn't unlike today where it is very common for people to have boyfriends or girlfriends where they might or might not marry each other. In any case that was a different era.

Connie was also brought up in exactly the same way. Her focus was only on her education and her research. She was keen only on her studies and she was not interested in parties or meeting men. She was very happy with her close-knit family and girlfriends only. Her mother was very strict and Connie herself had ethics where she was not interested in these parties, which involved drinking and dancing. In addition to her education and intellectual nature, we found this to be the common aspect between us. I think perhaps this is one of the contributing factors behind our getting together. Ordinarily, I would have gone back to India for a pre-arranged marriage as there were a lot of proposals from rich families which had come my way. Perhaps God wanted me not to go as I was destined to meet this girl Connie was beautiful both from the outside and from within. Connie liked to say I was her first boyfriend and she was my first girlfriend, although we started as only friends.

To this day I don't know how I gained the confidence to talk to a woman because if you are growing up in India, talking to a woman is the most fearful and dangerous thing! Of course, after I came to America and met ladies in my corporate life, I developed the courage and faith to do so. The reason is that in America men and women have been raised in a different environment, they have been brought up full of confidence right from their childhood. I remember when I first came to this country, one of my subordinates, who was working under me, told me, "Pradeep, let me tell you one thing, in this country children are given the maximum freedom." I was astonished to hear that because in our era, even though we were given freedom, we were also being watched like hawks. We were always being kept track of—our activities, where we went etc. So I noticed a big difference in culture. If you talk to people over here you notice how confident they are, irrespective of their age because they have been brought up in such an environment. I'm not trying to criticize or hurt anybody's feelings but I'm just sharing my own experience and knowledge without offending anybody. When I go to the health club or shops or even in my professional life—women talk to me as if we have known each other for years. There is a lot of just joking around and conversations are full of fun. I have not seen that kind of atmosphere with Indian ladies, whether they are married or otherwise. They tend to be very reserved so I think it is a big cultural difference which I find very interesting. Once again, it is not a reflection on anybody whether Indian or otherwise. I have traveled all over the world, whether it is America or Europe, I find that except in India, people are more friendly and passionate. It is not as if people in India are not like that, in fact, they are very wonderful and hospitable but there is definitely some kind of a rhythm missing. I find that sometimes even young Indians are reluctant to talk. Even in America I meet many Indian school and college students—often they don't even say hello. At times if I ask them if they are from India—to which they mumble yes and claim that they need to get back to their work. This has happened several times and to some degree it has upset me, but then I realize this is the way they were raised, so it is unfair to blame them. Connie also told me the same thing.

She used to tell me that when I used to meet some Indian friends it felt as if we were glued to each other like brother and sister. I'd say to her that it may seem like that, but in reality, I felt as if I was imposing on them, as it was I who made an effort to go talk to them whereas they were reluctant.

Our interactions were full of such exchanges because we were of such innocent character. Possibly because of this I told her that we should get married. Connie thought about this for a while but she was not sure. She wanted to know how long I intended to stay in the US or if I'd leave her high and dry. She said to me "Pradeep, you know I like you and care for you and love you. But I don't want the possibility that you may leave me alone and if you do so I will not be able to bear the loss. I think I will go crazy if you leave me and you never know what I can do because I am not one of those who can remarry again. To me marriage is sacred."

She said I should take a few months to think about it. Even when we were about to get married, she asked me ten times if I was really serious. She did not want to be betrayed. She asked me repeatedly if I had any doubt whatsoever or if I was marrying her under some kind of pressure or force then we were better off remaining friends. I remember reassuring her that I would never leave her under any circumstances. I will treasure the memory of Connie in her bridal gown as she said all these things till the day, I am alive. When I think of those days, I really feel hurt and it reminds me what a wonderful gem my Connie was.

42

The Truth Always Wins

The last position I held in an organization was as the head of the Midwest region, General Manager, or you can say Head of the Division for leverage funding. Before that, I had my own consulting firm. When their offer came Connie told me, "Pradeep, I think you are making a big mistake by joining this large company. They are offering a very good package, but you are doing much better in your consulting and already have projects lined up for the next six months to one year. I think that you shouldn't get tempted because it will be very hard for you. Just think about it. Right now, you have your own consulting firm; you travel when needed and then you can come back home. You have a choice whether to go to the office or work from home. You are only looking for benefits. These benefits are mitigated with the fact that your freedom will be compromised. Your consulting allows you to spend more time at home if you don't want to work for a few months. This sort of thing will not be possible once you join." She was totally against me joining, but this company was persuading me and I was confused as it was a difficult decision to make. It was in December 2002, and I remember not being able to sleep for the whole night. Connie was so upset with me in the morning, she said, "I don't think you ever want to listen to me, and you will regret it." I think Connie was right. It was a forty-five-minute drive to the office. We always had two cars, one car Connie would use, and the other car I hardly drove because I was flying most of the time. After that Connie told me, "I think considering the amount of money you spend for parking and maintenance and the fact that you hardly drive, you should get rid of this car. We have one car, and if you are working in the Chicago area, your company allows you to rent a car. You can always rent a car." In my consulting work, it was not mandatory to have a car because they would pay for mileage. But it was just my idea that I wanted to have a car in case Connie drove the other one. But she said, "Where do I go alone? Wherever we go, we both go together!" So finally, I listened to her and sold my car. When I got this job, we had to buy a second car. Connie decided she would pay for the car. Look at her sacrifice! She told me. "It is your duty to buy your own car, but don't worry, you have been very kind to me so I'll buy you a new car." She bought a new car in two days and she would drive her car, which was also brand new. So again, we were stuck with two cars. So on the first day I wore my suit, and drove the new car to reach the office about twenty minutes before time. I was standing in the parking lot and thinking, "Should I go inside or not?" I was just about to leave when suddenly the Vice Chairman, who had hired me, saw me, and said, "Pradeep, what is happening? We are all waiting for you and we have hired ten new young blood MBAs and some graduates. They are all waiting because you are going to be responsible for starting a new division, so please come inside and we are going to welcome you." So I think for a minute, and I felt happiness. In the office I met everybody; they were all excited and happy. They told me, "Now that you are here, we are going to learn from you and we are going to grow." So the first day was totally enjoyable. But on the way back home I thought, "Oh my God! Now I will have to start going back and forth again every day." It meant getting up early! I was used to my own independence earlier and now I had lost my independence, so I went into serious depression in January 2002 that lasted for about six months. Connie told me, "I told you! You might as well quit the job." I talked to my other consulting clients and they told me, "Pradeep, people make this mistake. Don't worry about it. If you want to quit, quit right away and start our projects." I think I should have listened to Connie and started on my projects right away. I was independent, I was getting paid more. If you compare the benefits between working for an organization and selfemployment, they are equal. Overall, even if they were giving the benefit of Medicare, I think with my own practice, I was still ahead. So now, since I was committed, I did not quit. As much as I wanted to, and as much as Connie wanted me to quit, she sacrificed her wants for my decision. I was miserable. Later on, I started liking the job because training all those twenty-three to twenty-four—year-old young people was the only thing that gave me happiness. Looking back, I think maybe God wanted me to train them in three years compared to the ten years it would have taken them otherwise. There was another person working there as a senior but surprisingly he did not know anything. He used to think that he was my boss, and I told him, "Listen, I am not working for you. Rather you are going to be working for me." There was a lot of politics involved, so when I shared this incident to my senior boss, who was the chairman, he told me, "Since I hired you, you are reporting directly to me and all the staff of twenty people will be reporting to you. You are their boss." This man still thought that he is my boss so I was unhappy and I was about to quit. Then they told me that they warned this guy, and told him, "If you don't behave well with Mr. Berry, we will get rid of you immediately." So finally he apologized to me. I am mentioning this because I don't know how political connections work. I left that position in 2005 when Connie became sick. After that, I took an oath that I would not work at all and would dedicate myself to Connie. Now I will recount an incident that shows the dedication of Connie. I had left the job I described above, and I had to find new medical insurance. My old company offered me coverage for eighteen months. I said, "I will take it." I was in a senior position, so they gave me insurance called COBRA, and I had to pay more than what they were paying. I was paying the full cost because the program was very good, so when it ended after eighteen months, I was fiddling around getting quotes from different insurance companies. I found out that there are a lot of loopholes with these policies. Sometimes they can say, "We don't cover you for this, and we don't cover you for that." Medically, I was totally fit, I didn't have a problem, but still, you should take precautions. When these companies have to pay a buck, they are very careful and they can also say, "Oh it was a precondition." That way, they don't have to payout. I had heard that from many people. My insurance company, though, was very clear, and they had sent their policy in writing. But Connie told me, "Listen to me. My insurance from the Education Board System and Illinois Teachers Association is very large. You better take my insurance because my insurance is the best in the country." Of course, they used to subsidize her insurance coverage. She said, "I will pay." It was very expensive; almost double the amount I was paying. I was paying $300 and it was about $750. So I said, "Why to pay $750 when I am not sick." She said, "Listen, you never know. If God wills that you be sick and you have to claim then they will say that you have a pre-existing condition. So don't get involved with all this nonsense, I will pay." So I said, "No, I will pay." So she said, "Listen, I am telling you. If you wanted to pay $350, you pay only that much, the rest I will pay from my own pocket." I declined, but it was greatness on her part, how much she loved me, and how much she cared for me. Otherwise, in this day and time, I have not seen anyone offering that. Since she truly loved me, she paid for part of my insurance for several years. Later on, I think she was not getting the government Medicare. Medicare is a system where everyone has to pay when they are working as Social Security where you pay 50% and the same way with FICA which is also, the same thing, the revenue from the taxes all goes to the government. So we all have to pay, it is the law here. Only if you pay do you get a check, whereas in my case I had to pay for every single thing on my own. I used to get a 1099 form, which is only issued in the US. Other countries don't issue a 1099. They send you a statement showing how much you have earned if you have a foreign account or something like that. So I was getting my 1099, and I filed my taxes very promptly. Connie would tell me, "I don't want you to ever miss any income because by chance if the other company has not sent you the 1099 form then it is your responsibility to pay." I said, "I know that." She said, "Otherwise, if we get caught by the IRS, there will be a lot of trouble, and I don't want to get into trouble." And I know that both of us were ethical so I said, "You don't have to worry about it." One time, one of my clients told me, "Mr. Berry, we are not going to file the 1099 form. As far as we know in Human Resources, we don't report that." I said, "It's not possible, someone must be reporting it because you have to report this as part of your P&L. You are wrong. I will not take any chances. Either you send it because someone might find out electronically, or there will be problems. I want to be honest and I want to sleep well." So we were both ethical and everything was going fine. So the time came when I decided to take my earlier benefits, which is called social security. Connie was paying into the Education Board System where she was not qualified to get Medicare. She was just missing maybe ten credits, and maybe one year of teaching. She had worked very hard at a private institution that was taking care of her social security and Medicare. I made a big mistake which I regret, in my consulting. She used to do a lot of work for me. When I was so overwhelmed with the reports, she used to edit my reports. She used to print them out; she used to make the folders for me. She used to email my borrowers, she used to do a lot of other work, and I should have been paying her some money as a secretary and I would have put it as an expense and I would have saved on my income tax. During this time she would have gotten those credits for her Medicare. She would have been independent to get in a year or year and half of what she did free of cost for me. I wish to God that I would have paid her enough money because it would have helped my taxes and it would have helped her get Medicare. She was so nice, she never even asked me to pay her. Where would you find a rare person like Connie?

It was bothering me today while I was swimming. I thought what a big mistake I made with that great precious diamond. I was very upset, and I said, "I pray to God that Connie will forgive me because she did so much work for free, selfless work, but I did not realize her worth." Later on, when I got the rest of my social security, then she was definitely eligible to go into Medicare. But there was also a problem because there was also a time factor, which we did not expect. The Medicare people told us, "Once you get your benefit, Mrs. Berry will also be entitled to social security and Medicare right away." I have a full record of all those people. But they refused to pay, and I decided to fight, so we fought with the people involved with social security. They said no. They were charging her more premiums, and they would not give her the benefits for another two years. So finally I appealed, I had to fight for the right thing, and Connie told me, "Just forget it." But I said, "No, you have done so much for me, now I'm going to do the same thing for you." So I filed for an appeal, although they say that in the appeal, you generally lose. But I thought if we have done some good karma, we will definitely win. So there were two choices, either we could go for trial in front of the judge, or we could have it over the phone. We just thought that if God is there to help, we will win regardless, whether we go to court or over the phone. So we got a letter that on such and such date, at exactly 11:30 a.m., the judge would call us. Luckily on that date exactly at 11:30 a.m. the telephone rang and the secretary said, "Are you Mr. Berry? Is Mrs. Berry with you on the line?" I said yes. So then the Honorable Judge came on the line and he said, "Mr. Berry, Mrs. Berry, how are you?" We replied, "Honorable Judge, we are fine, how are you doing Sir?" He said, "I am fine. I understand you have been appealing. It has been the most difficult thing, and I think the final verdict was already given to you. I do not know why there is so much confusion, and I don't think I can do anything for you or reverse it for you because the final judgment has already come." I told the Honorable Judge, "If you listen to us for fifteen to twenty minutes, both of us will be very grateful to you." Then I started telling him that we were both very ethical people, we had been paying our taxes for the last forty years, we were good citizens of this country. We always paid our taxes in time; we were not involved in any crime. My wife had been a teacher and professor for thirty-four years. She had gone to the top schools, I had so many degrees. I told the Honorable Judge, "My petition is this. Honorable Judge, we will never tell lies. I have the names and dates of these people." He said, "I got all that in written letters. How do you prove it?" So I said, "Well, I told you under oath, you earlier asked us to take the oath. I said all this under oath. This in itself is a big thing in the US that we are saying this to you on the phone under oath." I said, "I don't think you need a better explanation than that. I have my handwritten note, which I can mail to you or fax it or send a copy, whichever way you want. But it's a little amount, we are not going to lie to you Sir, this is definitely the mistake of this person. She was very rude to us, and she was sort of jealous maybe that Mrs. Berry is making more money in her retirement than she will. She was spiteful because she asked me why she needed Medicare since her income was so much, she could pay any amount of money premium. She had no business to be so rude because she was just doing her job, and we are entitled to our rights. We have paid our taxes; it is not as if the US is paying us for free. It is our money we have contributed into this system. My wife contributed into a different system and she is only getting the pension. But she is not getting any benefits and she is maybe short of one credit of maybe one full year, and I think you should reconsider." The judge listened to all that and said, "Both of you are very ethical people. You people definitely deserve it, and I will have to look into further investigation. I will make calls, and talk to those people. I will give you my answer in the next three or four weeks. Good luck to both of you; it was nice talking to both of you. Let's see what happens." We were still confused, but from the message, I could understand that hopefully, we would receive a positive answer because he mentioned it when ending the phone conversation. We were both convinced that we were going to get a positive reply. With great help from God, in two weeks we got a letter that we had won the case and it was written that whatever extra Mrs. Berry had paid in premium, whatever was not covered, they had to send us a check back. So the amount which we lost, Mrs. Berry got everything back from the hospital and the Medicare system. So this is called the United States of America, this is called karma. So this is why we should be honest because honesty always stays through the life of the person; dishonesty is caught very soon, and people lose their trust. Especially in America, there are two things people don't like: lying and not asking for an apology or showing remorse. If you apologize right away they will forgive you, but this is why this country has an advantage. I'm sure, in every country, this is the way, but it is true especially in this country. Whenever there is a trial and a murderer says, "I am very sorry, I think I made a big mistake, and I apologize to the family members of the people whom I killed and I hope that they will forgive me." If he shows remorse like that, the judge will give him a lesser sentence. If the murderer says, "I am not going to apologize, I am not going to do this, I have done the right thing," then the judge will increase the sentence. I think people who are reading my book and are in the US will not take much interest because they already know, but if someone is in India or another place, I think this will be a great example. I'm sure, even in India, people are very intelligent, and they will know. But still, I think it is important for me to write this incident which is a tribute to my wife; it was because of the beautiful things she did that we got rewards. Unfortunately, despite all these things I'm saying, the truth is that Connie is no longer with me, that is the biggest thing. No matter how much I praise her, it is not going to bring her back. I hope that I become her husband in my next life so that my purpose will be successful. I pray to God all the time, "God, give me Connie, *the* Connie, the only Connie, same beautiful, externally and internally beautiful Connie that should be with me, and in our next life, we should meet when we are very young, as young as in kindergarten." That would be a wonderful thing to happen to us. That we would start as little children, later we would grow up together, and then fall in love, and get married. And if that happens, I think I will be the happiest person. I don't have any other wish like being born into a multi-millionaire family or being born rich. I only want Connie, who would be my sweetheart from a very young age. If that happens, my sorrow, my pain will go away. Today if I hear God telling me, "Pradeep, I grant you, after your death, immediately, when you are reborn and Connie is already there, she may be older to you by a couple of years and you will be able to meet her." I will accept it; however much older she is to me. I will accept if I hear a voice saying that in the next life, she may be older, but she will still be your wife Would you accept it? I would say yes. I don't care if I'm fifteen or sixteen years old and she is thirty years old, even then I will accept it, I love her that much. Miracles do happen, and I'm ready for anything. Even if she meets me like a sister, or she becomes my mother, I would still take it, regardless if she is my wife, sister, or mother. That is why Chanakya quoted that, "A wife can be your wife if she can be your best friend, sister, and mother." The same thing is written in the Vedanta about the duty of the wife. So this is my pain, it doesn't lessen if I go to a support group or read. Connie is on my mind all the time.

43

Realization and Enlightenment of Pain after Connie's Death

"Memories of My Paternal Grandfather"

WANTED TO SHARE ONE MORE THING, AND that is about my paternal grandfather, my father's father. He was a very learned man, very spiritual, very knowledgeable. He had four sons and several grandchildren, and we were, of course, his first grandchildren. We lived together, all seventeen or nineteen of us, in a very big house in Delhi. My grandfather was pretty wealthy; he was supporting everybody and his sons were working in the business too. We were students then and we're just about to finish our education. When my grandmother died, I remember he did not go to the cremation, but he asked his elder son and everybody in the family to just take her away. He managed to say some sort of goodbye. It was clear then that he was very upset, but I still fail to understand why he did not perform the last rites or even attend the cremation. After the cremation, he asked if everything was done properly, which we confirmed. He used to stay alone on the ground floor, while the rest of us stayed on the other four floors of the house. I think we were all ignorant at that time, but he was all by himself in a dark lonely house with many rooms. I remember asking him if I should stay in the same room that my grandmother used to be in, but he declined. He said that he was fine, and he was very knowledgeable adding, "You people have to study, and as a result of that, I don't want to do such things that may ruin your studies." I think I asked him a couple of times, but perhaps I did not mean it very seriously. I doubt if I had thought of the pain he was enduring then because I felt he was very knowledgeable and capable of handling it. He was the one who told us about the inevitability of death, and I felt that such a learned man would cope. However, to my surprise, within no time he started deteriorating rapidly. He had the support of his family, but he was just not himself and despite being surrounded by so many people, he was very lonely inside. I think he especially struggled at night, a time when we are all alone with our thoughts. We never thought it would happen, but quite unbelievably, he also passed away after two months. When I think about it now, I realize he went through a lot of pain before he died. I feel today that he must have suffered terribly, but he never said a word to anybody and bore the pain silently. He did not write a biography or share his feelings with anybody. I am sharing this to tell everybody that one should not be silent and that they should share their pain so that they can let others know that they should be prepared to face this kind of unexpected tragedy. That is why I think I am feeling more pain because although I have seen these kinds of painful moments, I had not imagined how difficult it would be. I thought that I would suffer perhaps 50-60% but not 100%. Now that it is happening to me, I am enduring it with lot of pain, more than 100%.

I saw the same thing happen with another family member who was living in the US together with his children and grandchildren. He was also very close to his wife, and I think close to his grandchildren as well because he was happiest when talking about them. When his wife died, however, he totally turned around and felt very lonely. I don't think he had any great love for his own sons and doubt if he was crazy about even his grandchildren. Additionally, I think there was a dispute about money amongst his children and it gradually became worse as his children wanted to grab his money. As a result of this, there was deep enmity amongst his daughters-in-law. It was around this time that he moved out of the home. Sometimes he was living back in India with his daughters or with some friends in the US, and at other times in a hotel. He used to tell me, Pradeep (he used to call me Pappi) and he used to call me every day and I remember I used to call him at least six times or more a day. I used to call him uncle and made sure I called him irrespective of whether I was working or traveling. He got a new lease on life from me. I don't know what the connection was, but perhaps because we had long relationship, he trusted me. I did a lot of work for him when he was going through this crisis. I settled his accounts; in fact, I even spoke to his children as to why they were misbehaving with him. I spoke to his daughter-in-law and other members of the family, reprimanding them for stealing money from his account. I doubt if that made much of a difference though. I remember a time when I called him at the hotel he was staying in. I spoke with an Indian Gujarati gentleman attending to him. He said to me, "Mr.

Berry, I want to worship you and touch your feet. Why don't you come over here?" When I wondered why I should do that he told me that Uncle thought of me every minute. He told me Uncle used to wait for my call from the moment he got up in the morning. When I called again the next day, the gentleman said, "Why don't you come here, I want to meet you because you are really something; you have the power to heal his wounds."

He told me my uncle looked forward to my call in the morning at 8:30. I used to call him from my office and we would speak for half an hour. I used to call him in the afternoon and the evening as well. I was doing it out of my love and compassion as at that time I was feeling very sorry that he was missing his wife. I had no idea in reality as to how much he was suffering, and because it was twenty years ago, I can only guess. The difference between these two examples and mine is that they were still occupied with their families. Such was not the case in our lives because we had decided not to have that kind of extended family. Thus, in our case, our love was 100% split between Connie and me. We had time for each other only.

Their love could be 50%-40% towards the wife or 70% or 30% towards the children. There was surely a distribution of love between them and their children and grandchildren. His wife was extremely fond of their son too, so much so, that sometimes she used to fight with her husband over them. So I think they suffered so much despite there being a division of love. Sometimes I compare that with my situation and wonder how much suffering there can be if one is 100% devoted to someone as Connie and I were to each other. Even in other cases, if there was a 100% devotion to the other person, it's just not possible. For example, if you travel with your grandchildren, your wife is alone at home. Similarly, if the grandmother leaves her husband alone for months while she is with her grandchildren, there cannot be a 100% devotion to each other. So it is not an apple to apples comparison, but I can see that he still suffered after his wife passed away despite there not being a 100% commitment.

I have seen another case that is somewhat like mine. I have seen a few cases where a husband was married to his wife for about forty years, and when she died, the husband had no regrets whatsoever. He missed his wife as you would expect, but not as much as I thought he would after forty years of marriage. He used to say, "OH Mr. Berry, it is fine you know." He was thinking of making more money, which sickened me, but I suppose different people behave differently.

There was another person who was married who supposedly could not live without his wife. This woman was so sincere to him and I was shocked to death when I found out what happened after she died. Some five or six years later, he went and brought in another bride. He thought he would be happy and look what happened, his bride took all his money and left him on the road!

So these are different variations of life, and everybody goes on with their own thing. I can give you a thousand examples, but that is not the purpose of my biography. Although I saw the pain of many people, their pain is totally irrelevant to me as my biography is meant only for my wife. I would say to some degree, pain is always there of your dear loved ones whether it is your wife or whether it is your children. It is a different kind of pain but it is difficult nevertheless. Some people have overcome the pain of their loss, or perhaps they are just acting. Some manage to keep going. I spoke to one friend of mine who lost his son because he committed suicide, and he did not want to talk to me saying it was a topic he wanted to avoid. I respected his wishes but he called me the next day apologizing about his rude behavior.

He said his son was his darling and shared a little bit of his feelings. Thereafter I was careful not to bring up the topic unless he wanted to talk about it himself. I suppose everybody is different and people handle their grief differently. Some start giving to charity; some marry again, certain people start doing humanitarian work—that's the way it is.

In my case, I don't think I will do anything in a haphazard way. For example, the last couple of days I have kept myself busy writing articles, meeting people about important matters, talking to attorneys, etc. So there are some diversions, but the moment I leave the office, the pain starts right away. The confusion starts, and according to psychologists and psychiatrists, sometimes when you start thinking about one thing, it stops you from thinking about other things. In my case, I do not even want to go to those places where I used to go with Connie. I have written that I have stopped reading the newspaper and stopped watching TV. Whenever I read the name 'Constance Berry' on the magazines we receive, it really truly bothers me. I begin to think perhaps I should start reading them, but I don't think I'm ready right now. I am determined about one thing though, whenever I receive a letter from MCR and other organizations in her name, I will definitely donate some money to the extent possible. Connie passed away at the hospital close to our home. Connie had given good donations to the HH hospital and that is the same hospital where in my opinion, medical negligence took place and she died. I am sure she would not have given a penny. I still get letters from Connie asking for charity. I do not want to give a penny to HH. Reading her name, going through her drawer, going to her room, not finding her in her bedroom washing her clothes is the most painful thing in my life. The other day, I was sitting at my desk looking for certain papers and I found her degrees. I could see how much love she got from her students, how much appreciation she got from the dean, and how many prizes she had won! I knew about these things, but at that time I was not appreciative of their value. Now, all those things are like a monument to her. Last night, I saved all those things in her room and got busy organizing all of them. I sorted out all the degrees and gifts and letters from her students and school authorities. I look through all the tributes that Connie received from her college and the dean, noting how she was highly regarded. When I read these things, I really lose control and wonder: Isn't all the knowledge and education that one has futile? All of us have to go one day, none of us is special. I think the doctors made a mistake with Connie. If the doctors had acted differently, Connie would have still been with me today. The main problem with me is that Connie did not die of natural causes, but her life was snatched away by these doctors.

44

Different Reactions of People on Grief

I HAVE SEEN MANY PAINFUL CIRCUMSTANCES AND THAT is why I want to understand how people who have lost their spouses, who are very important to them, react to their painful situations. This is what I am trying to find out for my own knowledge, but their experiences are not going to help me. People tell me to read books about Buddha, where he asks disciples to get rice from any house that has not seen death. I have read it, and I know all those things. People tell me there is no house where tragedy has not taken place. I know that, but because of my over-attachment and my total pure love for Connie, all my knowledge has vanished. I absolutely don't want to compare events which happen to different people to my own circumstances, but at the same time, I am curious about people who lost their spouses and how they dealt with it.

I know some people dealt with it very positively. I have some friends and relatives who just accepted that now their spouse is gone, they have to carry on. I was really surprised because they were very close to each other. I don't know if these people were really close to their spouses or they pretended to be, sometimes people pretend they are close but they are not really very close. When the wife of one man I know died, I don't think it made much difference in his life. He was very upset, but at the same time, he just carried on without mentioning her to me. We met many times after that as he was my distant relative, but I don't think he ever mentioned her to me. I used to ask him how he felt without his wife, and he used to say, "I'm okay, she had to go, and she had to go." I was surprised that he was regularly going to parties, drinking, and wherever there was a function he would be there. I don't think he was in any pain. Now people challenge me, they say, "How do you know he was not in pain? Maybe he was suffering but did not say anything!" I would probably reply that if the person is suffering, or if that person is in pain, he would not be mixing up with people and acting normal. In my judgment, I did not see any remorse in his life that he lost his wife. So sometimes reaction brings action and action brings reaction. The whole family told me that he had adjusted, and he was not missing his wife much, and that was very surprising to me. I also want to share one more incident. I think it was some time in 2012. We were in Captiva Island, one of the most beautiful islands in the US, south of Fort Myers, Florida. There are two excellent islands, one is called Sanibel and the other is Captiva. The islands are very small, less than ten miles in length, and there are beautiful resorts that preserve some of the natural setting, with beach front views of the Gulf of Mexico. It's just beautiful, and they don't allow any fast food, they don't allow any large buildings, they don't allow any commercial shopping centers. It's a very isolated kind of place for people to relax, and it is mostly a second home for the rich. It's a very rich place, and people who have gone there they really love it. It is one of the world's most important places for collecting sea shells. So people come there from all over the US, and I think it is just beautiful. So we used to go there from 2005 onwards, spending five weeks in Sanibel and then three weeks in Marco Island. On one of our trips, we were both having lunch at a very famous place, and it was very special to Connie. There is a special kind of fish called grouper, which is available only in Florida, especially around Sanibel and Captiva. It is a special delicacy available only in the state. You will not get this grouper fresh anywhere else in the US, just like salmon comes only from Alaska, and we had the best quality grouper when we were there in 1987 and then again in 1989. They catch the fish in the ocean and immediately prepare the fish, which is just out of this world. Similarly, in New Orleans, they have white fish which is absolutely delicious. So going back to our incident in Captiva, there is a restaurant called *The Bubble Boy*, where they make their fish in a brown paper bag, and grill it. It is just magnificent, and perhaps one cannot get that taste anywhere. It is absolutely fresh like fresh coffee in Hawaii.

When we went to the big island, Kona, Hawaii in 2006 and 2007, we visited many Kona coffee and chocolate farms where we got to taste different types of coffee and chocolate. We both bought coffee and dark chocolate of different types, which are only grown in Kona Island, Hawaii. Similarly, Kona has other delicacies which are just super. In India, mangoes are the best in the world during the summer. India also has many different fruits and vegetables which are seasonal. Nature and God have been very kind to India. I think India is the second largest producer of fruits and vegetables in the world. It is the largest producer of potatoes, milk, fiber, jute, cotton, silk, jumbo shrimps, leather hides, iron ore, and basmati rice. The South Indian coffee in India has a completely different gorgeous taste. I know every country has regional differences in climate, food habits, and food. The economist Thomas Malthus mentioned that every fifteen to twenty miles, the language, food and culture of people are absolutely different. Now, since we are living in a global society, the distance probably might have gone up to twenty to thirty miles. If I go thirty miles or forty miles from where we live, people over there have different ways of living. The houses are different and the standard of living is different. If I go 100 miles away, then local lifeways are completely different. I think Malthus was absolutely right when he said that India is a rich country inhabited by the poor. So coming back to this point, we met a person who was sitting by himself in a restaurant in Captiva Island in Florida in 2010. I'm sure he was close to eighty years old, handsome and good-looking. He had maintained himself very well and looked very educated. He was sitting next to us and we kept looking at each other. Finally, I decided to talk to him. He asked us, "Why don't we sit together for lunch?" So Connie and I started talking. When asked where he lived, he stated Spain, but that he came to Captiva every year for three months in a small house for vacation by himself. After I asked him if he has a family, he said that he has two daughters and six grandchildren, and they all live in Spain, and when he meets them he enjoys them. However, more or less he lives alone. I asked him about his wife. He said, "I lost my wife twenty years ago and did not marry again. She was my darling, she was my love, and I would never remarry. I am alone and I am fine." I was very much taken aback. So I said, "Pardon me for asking, but what was your profession?" He looked at me and said, "Do you remember seeing my face in the 50s and 60s?" Then I suddenly remembered that he was one of the most popular journalists who used to cover India, China, and Asia. He was one of the most intellectual journalists and a TV personality, who would announce the world news. He told me he had met Prime Minister Nehru and Dr. Rajendra Prasad. Later, he also met Prime Minister Shastri and many other politicians. He knew everyone. Then I recollected, and said, "Yes! My God! What an accomplishment for you!" Then he said, "No, I don't do anything now. I used to travel extensively and was very happy. But after the loss of my wife, my darling who was my baby, I don't travel so much anymore." I did not have the experience of losing a spouse at that time and hence I couldn't sympathize. Now I am recollecting that incident and imagining what he must have gone through, or maybe even now he must be going through. I think it is one of the examples I want to give.

After Connie and I said goodbye to him, we were still talking about him. He was being looked after well by the young waitresses, who treated him like their father and helped him if he needed something. I don't know whether these kinds of experiences make me strong or weak. I am not going to compare his life with my life, and that is my message to people: we should not compare our situation to others. It is good to compare to get some knowledge, but if you think that you can follow the same principle as another, if you follow a particular person and he is your idol, it does not work. If someone says, "Look at him, take that example," you cannot be that person. The doctors gave me examples of people who worked their way out of grief. I am not ready for that because their pain maybe different, my pain is different. I think people should not compare losses, and when people are grieving, other people should not say a whole lot except to tell them, "Please look after your health, do whatever you want to do, whatever makes you happy." One should not dictate to people how they should lead their life, because one cannot understand the pain others have gone through. I want to let people know this important message: Do not play with somebody's sentiments by giving them false hope. Some people recommend that I read some autobiography or biography of some person. I have read these, and I am still reading them, but it has made no difference to me. That is an indication that our love was unique. I can only say that. Perhaps many people have never had this kind of love, this kind of feeling we had for each other. I don't want to make this a very negative book; I don't want people to feel that I am talking about my pain. I think in this kind of hidden pain, there is a hidden message as well. The hidden message is that one should try to understand the grieving person's mind, a person who was so happy with his wife, who was his first girlfriend, and the last one. People should appreciate what I have been through rather than just telling me, "Oh! This is God and life. Forget about the past, life goes on." I don't want to hear all that. I don't have any other choice than to go on, but I want my own very simple life and I don't want to go anywhere except India because it gives me some happiness to be with my brother, his family, and my grandnieces. After five or six years, I may be able to travel somewhere. Right now, I'm still getting so much mail, so many invitations from Viking, Vantage, University of Michigan, Carleton, and other elite colleges whose sponsored trips we went on. I will not go on these trips, as Connie's memory would make me more depressed and upset and I might have panic attacks when I remember our trips and being together. I would remember how Connie used to be with me every minute, how we used to take the taxi, get out at the airport, and fly by ourselves. When we were with the Michigan University tour, how happy we were! We would be picked up and stay in a hotel, and then go on the cruise or sometimes a land tour or both, depending upon which tour we were taking. I won't go to the places I have been with Connie. I might go to places where I have not gone before, like Turkey, Egypt, Saudi Arabia, or Dubai—places where we wanted to go, but somehow, we could not. People behave according to what they believe, but I hope they will understand the message I am conveying.

45

I Can See Connie Everywhere

I WOULD LIKE TO MENTION THE MANY PRACTICAL things about the sadness I feel. For a long time after Connie's death, her caretakers and other people did the laundry. I didn't do it because I was doing other things. Today, I wanted to change the sheets and wash the few clothes that I have so I was waiting for our helper to come. But since she is not coming until next week, I decided to do it myself. So today, September 20 2015, I started doing laundry. I think it is one of the most emotionally difficult things I did today. It was intolerable, especially when I changed the sheets. The sheets are very clean, and the side on which Connie used to sleep hasn't been touched. It was just very painful for me to have this experience. This is same kind of heartache I feel when I see that she is not in the bedroom, her study room, the living room, the kitchen, and that she no longer shops with me or rides in the car. I remember when we had just met each other forty years ago, she had so much stamina to take care of everything. She was full of energy. She would change the sheets two or three times a week, making beds, doing the cleaning, doing all the laundry, including my clothes, ironing our clothes, and putting them neatly in the cupboard. She was a perfectionist. When she got sick later on, I think in the last two to three years, only then did I do a lot of household chores. I was not a perfectionist like her. I would put my garments here and there and not hang them properly. So many times she would come and she would see the way I had arranged her clothes, and she would say to me, "Is this the way you want to put away my clothes? Haven't you seen how I would do it?" I would tell her these things were not important anymore and that we would have to change our priorities. By then she did not have much energy and was not very argumentative. So remembering such small things are very painful for me. I thought I must write about this experience, and right away I started writing.—It's around two in the morning, and I decided that I have to write this so that I will not forget. I think these kinds of things are the true rhythm of pain. Another thing has just popped up in my mind; maybe I should write another book or change the title of the book to *Living in Pain for 3 Years* or *Living in Pain for 18 months* so that I can describe how suddenly our health can deteriorate. I think the doctors ruined her body. Otherwise, I would have never imagined that she would go downhill so fast.

I avoid going to her shower room with a walk-in shower, which she specially built for herself. In one of our bathrooms, we had a tub, and when she couldn't use it for the last two to three years, she spent a lot of money and got a walk-in shower built for her so that she could enjoy her baths. Sadly, she did not have enough time to enjoy the new shower. I just cannot believe that when she got sick for about eighteen months, she was not capable of taking a shower herself. She was on the oxygen tank, and she would sit on the walker and I would make her comfortable so that she could enter the shower. She was very modest and independent. She would ask me to just pass her the towel and leave the shower. I would later help with the drying after she was done with the shower.

Her legs were swollen, and I used to massage her legs with cream for a few minutes every day. It used to bring tears to my eyes that she was retaining so much water. I thought her doctors were not very concerned, so I reprimanded them. I would tell them that they saw Connie only for a few minutes and they were so busy, but if they were forced to see what she was going through for twenty hours a day, they would realize the damage they had done to her. I said this to the doctors so many times. One of her doctors was very good in the beginning, and when the case went out of control, he was willing to listen to anything and he would not answer back, although I'm sure he didn't like listening to criticism. If he had argued with me then, maybe we would have had more complicated problems. I was ready to fight with him in the court of law. The most important thing for me was Connie, and I had decided that if the doctor said anything or argued with me, I was ready for a battle. I think I did not pursue that more because I did not want to get distracted from paying attention to Connie.

One of the other things I face every day when I go to check my mailbox, or if I am coming in from the front door, is that I imagine I can see her sitting on the balcony with her walker along with her oxygen. I remember how I would bring my car outside, help her into the car, and she would sit with me on one of our numerous trips to the hospital. I know it was the most difficult thing for me and her, but even then it gave me some happiness as well as sadness. I used to feel more sadness, but also feel a little bit of happiness that she was still alive and she was with me and we were together. Even if I had to carry her wheelchair, I would be very happy, and such happiness I had never felt earlier when we were taking trips all over the world. I think this was true love. When we were young and we were having a lot of fun all the time, that was also love. But later in our lives, our love was like worship to God. Just like you surrender yourself and become a saint like you have renounced the world, I had left the whole world, and practically my whole life was to be with Connie. Her weak body had become my place of worship. So instead of praying to God in the temple, I would offer my prayers in form of my devotion to her. Whenever I would see her sitting, sleeping, or uncomfortable, I would pray to God that if there was good karma, to please give her strength and make her better. This is the way I was worshipping her.

Even now, it is very difficult for me to take a shower in her walk-in shower. To avoid that, I go to the health club almost every day. I swim and exercise and then take a shower there. These are the lengths I go to to avoid the pain. I am not saying that this is the reaction of every human being, because although everyone has gone through grief, they may have had some different experience. I am not trying to compare myself to them, nor am I trying to say that I am the only person who has seen suffering, because every individual on this planet has gone through some kind of suffering, and everyone's suffering is different. I consider happiness and unhappiness as sisters, and my philosophy is that a candle has less light and more darkness. With a candle, only a few people can study, but if you move away from the candle there is darkness.

I think it is very difficult and I don't want to be ungrateful to the mighty Lord, but I am certainly in a lot of agonies. I cannot describe this agony. It is very easy for people to say that Connie was sick for a long time and that everyone has to pass away, but I have not only seen her death, I have also seen her suffering. I'm sure many people have seen that. I'm sure there are people who are all alone like me, and there are people who suffered by themselves. I'm not making any comparative statement, nor do I have any statistics, but I think in my life I might have seen very few people who were alone. Even in those cases, they found children, a spouse, friends, and far away relatives to come and help. Some of the widow ladies used to volunteer with Northwestern University. I'm not sick right now, but if I ask faculty there for help, then students there, who have a program that helps seniors who live alone, will surely come and help. I don't want to ask for their help right now because I want to be active. I should keep on moving all the time. The things I am describing right now are very painful, and I don't know how long it will take me to overcome the grief. People who thought they understood my pain do not even understand it 1%. I think it is very hard for me when they say that they are sorry that she is gone. If they had seen the kind of suffering I saw, then perhaps it would have stayed with them for their whole life. This suffering will stay with me until the day I die. Every single incident has stuck in my brain, mind, soul, and heart like a movie.

It may be a good message, or it may be a depressing message for people. I have no idea how readers will perceive it, but at least they will know how to pre-plan and be prepared so that they don't have to go through this. I have seen many people who had no plans, and they suffered in the end. However, there is no guarantee that even if you plan something, things will work according to that plan. Look at Connie; she had planned long-term care, but look at what happened. If I have offended anyone, I want to ask for forgiveness, because this is my personal experience and has no relevance with anyone else.

I remember seeing a box office hit Indian movie during our teenage years, "Woh Kaun Thi" meaning, "Who Was She." It can be easily seen on YouTube even now, and I am sure with Netflix. It is an excellent movie and has super songs. After Connie's demise, I always have been thinking about her and keep her beautiful face everywhere I go: walking, riding in the car, picking up and dropping me at the O'Hare Airport. For most of her life, if she was available to pick me up (and she focused on being available to pick her Pradeep), in spite of my saying, please don't, please don't as it's a four-minute walk from the Am Track when going to my office and back, especially if I was working until late in the evening. Of course, going to the airport was a different love of Connie to meet her husband as quickly as possible, and I was desperate to run from the plane with my carry on—containing my fantastic three-piece professional suits and at least two shirts, ties, undergarments, shaving kits, and what not. There was a great love in that carry-on and how Connie used to pack and empty and then do the laundry and would never allow me to wear anything but Ralph Lauren or Christian Dior shirts and Nautica socks to match each outfit. I was wondering all my life how my wife is like my mother getting me up early, making sure that I dress properly and according to the season of the year. How much love was involved in that, and how she must be thinking of going to Marshall Fields (now Macy's) to buy these things for me. Her clothing, and my ties, suits, and those carry-on suitcases are still with me, and though I may have to spend money to get it fixed, I would especially carry that carry-on along with two of her suitcases. I am talking about the suitcases she bought me thirty years ago. I have preserved them and will continue to preserve them. That is a source of Connie's memories with me. Who she was is now like two desperate lost souls waiting to meet each other. That is what the whole movie and beautiful songs and lyrics are about. I would try to translate the lyrics into the English language and would compose my own songs. If possible, I would work hard and get an album with professional musical instruments and directions, etc. "My Tribute to My Love."

46

My Emotions and India

I MUST MENTION THAT CONNIE DARLING WAS AND would be special all my life. Our first trip to India was in July 1979, three years after our marriage. We were both thrilled to go, and spent seven weeks in India. It was great for us, our family, and friends, and I was finding if I had come to a different planet. We stayed with my brother and every day, from morning 'til night, family and friends used to walk in, as the tradition for visiting was to walk in without calling beforehand. At that time, people in India offered true hospitality. Now, a small percentage of friends and family members call before visiting. I think I prefer that to surprise visits. Nowadays, people have less time to visit due to work and the traffic in India. In Delhi, some families live far away and traffic has become a big problem. I don't want to travel far in the city to see people because of traffic.

Connie and I went to Kashmir, Taj, Jaipur. We went sightseeing in Delhi and saw historic and ancient places. Some of the most beautiful places in Delhi are Chandni Chowk and Connaught Place. The shopping is excellent and lots of fun. You can find handicrafts and things that are exported all over the world. For lunch, we would have picnics or go to the houses of friends and relatives. We went to dinner every night with relatives. We started going to the home of my uncle, Dr. Behl, and my English Aunt Marjorie. I was extremely close to them. Connie and Marjorie became best friends, and after we returned to the US, Uncle Behl and Aunt Marjorie visited us in Evanston, along with their daughter Vanita, who was like a daughter to me. We had lots of good times, and my uncle refused that I take any time off work as he was devoted to his medical profession, writing books, attending conferences at Northwestern University and presenting his thesis, etc., and mixed his trip with vacations. Connie was also working, and we did our best to provide the hospitality.

I learned a great lesson which I have been following until now, except for later when we were getting a comfortable life. Uncle told me, "Son, I want to stay with you, to spend time with both of you and pick up the three years we spent apart, missing each other. While I am here, I would like to contribute to your bills for food, gas, telephone, electricity, etc." I told him that it wasn't necessary as we could easily afford to house them, and I would not take a penny. He said, "If you don't take my offer, I will stay in a hotel." "Son, I can very easily afford to help out, and you are both working people, and unless I contribute, I would rather stay in the hotel and you would have to come and meet me and have lunch or dinner with us." I did not argue, and I told him that he would never ever stay in a hotel when I could house him. I would accept the cost of the phone calls to India as it was three dollars per minute compared to thirty cents now. He agreed, and the consideration he showed me enlightened me. Connie and I did not stay anywhere in India except with my brother and at Dr. Behl's house. I then started getting emotional about India. I wanted to come every year to India for my vacation. Connie also started to join me, however, after four annual vacations, Connie started telling me, "Pradeep, can't you go every two years or eighteen months so we can visit Australia, New Zealand, China, and Egypt, and do few more cruises with the University of Michigan." I never ever said no. We both were confused that it is a long flight to Australia and suggested that we can stop for a week in India, and take a flight from Delhi as it's not that long from Delhi to Australia, China, and Russia. I have to blame myself all my life and regret so much that she truly wanted to see Australia and New Zealand. She, later on, was not ready for China, Egypt, and Turkey, or even India due to the long flights. I only regret missing Australia and New Zealand. I know that those two she was most interested in. I must mention that I had four Indian friends who were professionals, and we had worked together in the same profession and lived in Chicago. Their wives were part of our family. I can say those four friends, their Indian wives, and Connie and Pradeep were absolutely close. All four and their spouses took two trips together and never asked us. Connie and I were very much hurt and they made some big excuses. It hurt us very much. Connie told me, "Pradeep, these four with their Indian wives only want Indians and Indians only. I definitely know that the Indians in my circle always wanted to be Indians in the US. I told my friends and relatives bluntly that you think you are in the US but you do not have a single American friend regardless of how intelligent or educated you are, but you all get together like a big carnival and remain Indians but Indians, Indian food, Indian Songs, Indian dresses, Indian languages and go to India for visits showing how wealthy they are. Indians in India except highly educated would be considered that he or she lives in USA. Indians in India are very polite, to some degree are ignorant about their profession, education just one word. She is or he is from America. People like me who have lived over forty-two years can make out in a second what kind of a person he or she is. I do not mean to insult anyone. The thing is why did they pretend that they are different or have this thinking that we live in America. They kept to themselves, although, at every function and parties, marriages, and in our home we all meet. We decided that it is better for us because we have different tastes, styles, and different approaches to being private. Immediately, we did a self-evaluation and got the answer that we truly do not want to go with anyone but just both of us. Later, many other friends and the same wanted that we should go together but we both decided not. This is a very important point.

We truly wanted to be by ourselves and until Connie's demise we two were together. I did not want or need to see anyone. Not even my own fifty to sixty members of my family, father's sister's children, these four and their wives went with spouses to Australia and New Zealand. They never asked Connie and Pradeep to go with them. The fact is they called and told me and Connie that we must see both the countries. I asked them how come you did not ask us as we would have gone together. I will always regret that Connie was not able to go to Australia and New Zealand. There is no way I would ever even thought of going to these two places. No way as Connie's memory, her love, her passion and our lovely pairs of two parrots, and that two with pure love and inseparable Connie and Pradeep, now it is only Pradeep. Connie is gone. This pain is a sharp edge and there is no treatment, no compensation.

47

My Present Life Pain–After Connie

IT IS SO PAINFUL FOR ME TO think of going anywhere without Connie. Sometimes, I feel I should try to go to a restaurant and travel by myself to see how I feel. Right away, my brain and heart tell me no. This is due to the fact that in our lives, we always went together, except when we were working. I had to travel quite a lot and so did Connie. I have not gone anywhere without Connie in the last ten years. The only exception was that I used to go to India every year for two weeks, which was also difficult. Even then, I would have panic attacks at the thought of leaving Connie for two weeks. Connie used to make the decision that I might as well go. I still did not want to go, because leaving her was difficult. I would go to India, but I would miss her. Again, from the moment when she used to drop me at the airport, it was extremely difficult for me to decide whether I should forget about going to India and come back home to Connie. Connie was strong and used to give me the power to go, otherwise, I would regret leaving her and after a few days, I would be on the phone booking return flights. The decision to go or to stay was difficult. In the end, I would decide to travel, but my mind was always on Connie. I would call her five or six times a day and have long talks with her. Connie used to tell me: either go or don't go, and if you go, I can keep busy with cleaning the drawers and organizing my stuff. This statement, and knowing we would be in touch over the phone for hours, made my yearly trip to India to see my brother and his family possible. It was a struggle then. Now, the same struggle is still there when I leave the house alone. In reality, all these are signs of our love.

Once in a while, I think I wouldn't mind going somewhere, but the thought of going or even taking a flight reminds me of Connie and scares me, makes me upset, and immediately my heart tells me, no, and finally, I don't even think of going. Her unbearable absence stops me from going anywhere. The only place where I can go is to see my elder brother and his family in India. But even that has become upsetting; to leave our home, her chair, her table, her computer, her walker, her oxygen, her study room, and all the rest. Even leaving the car and the garage is hard. How much pain I have to face and will always have to keep facing. Repeating this is not good writing, but it has a soothing yet painful effect on me. I never want to stop saying the same message. If someone in my situation or perhaps someone who has not fallen in love and wants true love, perhaps this book may give them some solace. At that time, you may forgive me that this book was no good but might appreciate the depth of our love. Leaving home to go to India is just unbearable. My mind tells me I should forget going anywhere. Home becomes my favorite place to stay. I had mentioned this earlier, before I diverted completely into painful memories of our traveling together. Thoughts of Connie and her memory shake me. My mind then thinking of the most painful episode I went through, and I start wandering if it is true that Connie is gone? Again, I block my mind and want to believe Connie is in her study. I totally forget that events like her cremation, chapel of peace ceremony, and the interment of her ashes in her plot next to her parents were all performed by me. I wonder how I could have done all of that. Is it true that I was brave enough to do all that? The answer is that my love and God gave me the strength to do all that. My shock and pain were at the deepest love of pain. I had never had gone through that painful episode of losing someone, losing my wife and my world. I was upset and in deep pain, however, I could not bear the pain of knowing that Connie's body is in a funeral home. My wife was not a charity case, and I wanted to have her cremation and burial done immediately. I am again repeating this episode many times. It is due to my constantly thinking about Connie. It is due to the deep love that I have lost. Even after nine months of living in pain and suffering from that, nothing has changed. The saying that time heals pain has no truth; rather, my suffering continues to increase. One common saying is that any incident of some fall, cut or little burn looks like it is fine, but its effect is worse the next day. I am giving one instance, though I have seen many painful events. One of my uncles died at a very young age. My aunt was grieving very hard. Her mother-in-law's sister said to her, "Right now you are surrounded by lots of family members and friends. Once they go to their homes, you will have to bear this loss and pain by yourself." Connie's fall, the ambulance taking her for a check-up at the hospital, staying with the hope of coming back the same day or the next day was painful. But the happiness of coming home on February 22, 2015 was tolerable. However, the evening before her cardiac arrest absolutely shook me totally, and the delay in performing CPR and my fight with her doctors was filled with anger. Her lying on the hospital bed with tubes in her mouth was unbearable, fighting at the time for her tubes was painful for me, and then taking the tubes out without my permission was a criminal act and shook me each minute. Her demise broke me down completely. I don't know how I could handle all that. Later, her cremation and the interment of her ashes in her plot was another trauma. That trauma still haunts me after nine months. At that time of great shock and pain, I had to ensure the best cremation and select the best of caskets and urns along with talking to a priest about the services. My mind was occupied and that pain took a different direction to do many things. After all that, a different kind of pain took over as I began to do the legal work, and so many things occupied my mind and life. This pain definitely came in different waves. I haven't had that experience before. My priorities were to ensure that she had the worlds' best funeral. I know that was done.

I am writing about Connie's demise and the whole episode again and again. It has two reasons: first, my pain, and second, that is how the human brain works and how many new brain cells open up which were not used. God has given us billions and billions of brain cells, but on average, we don't use half of them. I would say, at least for me, new brain cells opened and some of the cells I was using, I now feel that I am no longer using. This is a new segment of my life, and our relationship is making me write all these things. I still have no answer for this, and I doubt if I would ever find that answer.

Today, April 27, 2016, I was coming back on the train at rush hour, when so many people travel to go home from work. I especially wanted to observe the younger generation in their twenties and thirties, some were working, some were students. It was extremely soothing to see them with their smart phones and ear plugs. All of them were busy with their phones, which is happening now in many countries, both developed and underdeveloped. I saw the same in Delhi, too, the two times I have been back since Connie's death. Honestly, it was nice, but it brings me painful memories of Connie. In the 1970s to 1990s, traveling on the train was absolutely different, as most of the middle and senior management people were nicely dressed in suits and ties while reading papers like the *Wall Street Journal, Economic Times,* and *New York Times.* It was a half hour of leisure for them. Offices opened at 8:15 a.m.., and after reaching the office, the senior managers would have the same newspapers in the office. It was mandatory to read those papers to find out about business news and to research market shares, the strategic planning of companies, and the ratings of Fortune 500 companies. All that in it was like a Ph.D. student's workload in addition to the fifty to sixty hours per week that they worked. I did very well. It was a very happy life, working and sometimes spending 80% of my work traveling, staying in top hotels, and living off of the company expenses. I used to think that I was a king and happy as Connie was also a professional and had to leave by 7:15 a.m. to be at colleges and schools where she taught Spanish and French. Punctuality was a must for her. For me, with the amount of traveling I did, if I was a few minutes late that would be mitigated by my work. I used to work sixteen to seventeen hours a day when I traveled, and many of my juniors would say, "Pradeep, it is 5:00 p.m. You are leaving early. Good life. You enjoy your easy independence; no one is there to say anything to you, man. We have to work another hour, you leave early." This was a very sarcastic, planned remark, and it used to make me mad. I used to tell them, "You sit on your rear end the whole day doing nothing and take a two-hour lunch, your productivity is zero and that is why you have to stay long hours. Why don't you work hard from 8:15 to 5:00 and cut your personal phone calls and lunches. I wish I could get rid of you as you are a burden on the payroll and get paid for doing nothing." I hated those sarcastic comments. Later, senior management was informed of this, as they keep track of the efficiency and productivity of their employees, and our Chairman started firing these unproductive employees. He openly told me he wanted the best employees, and five professional development courses were required to stay in that largest worldwide finance company. There was a lot of hard work, but many awards and rewards in return. Our motto was "We are playing to win." That became my theme: I wanted to be a winner at any cost. Connie was a winner, as she was teaching and at that time there was much less political rivalry and jealousy in education. One of the reasons is that the economy was good; unemployment was very low compared to today's 10% unemployment rate. I would say that the rate is worse than that, as many people have stopped working and cannot find a job and unemployment benefits beyond forty-eight weeks are not available. As such, those are not part of the census, and therefore the the figure is distorted.

I would say that when Connie and I were in senior positions at work, this was the best time of our lives. We had no cell phones and no computers until 1988, although we both became experts at computers and smartphones. "Necessity is the mother of invention." That was the life I had with Connie. Now, I feel I am lost in an unknown world without her, but I find her in our sweet home, as she is still with me. All these forgotten things have come to my new eyes and new brain after going through the whole traumatic period that began in April 2013. In 1998, she contracted PRP and her family problems were at their worst. I believe the stress of these things caused her cancer. Her immune system was weak with the stress of PRP and the issues with her brother, causing her to fall ill with stage one breast cancer. I am positive of this, whatever the doctors may say. It was the stress caused by her brother and his wife, along with Connie's mother, that made her sick. The greed and cold blood of Connie's brother and his family is difficult to imagine.

48

Connie Was So Efficient In Everything

CONNIE WAS SO EFFICIENT IN EACH AND every thing, whether at home, grocery shopping, taking care of the laundry, ironing, keeping our clothes properly folded, hanging clothes properly on the hangers in the appropriate closets and drawers. She was also efficient at accounting and keeping inventory of the house, including our clothing, silver, furniture, paintings, crystal, glasses and other kitchen wares, carpets, and each and every thing. She also was very particular about the cleaning of the house, ensuring that the carpets were regularly cleaned, the table polished, the oven and granite counters cleaned. She kept track of our monthly expenses of food with receipts, house assessment, electric bills, telephone and Internet. She also compared television and Internet bills for accuracy. By doing this, she saved us lots of money when the company billed us the wrong amount. She used to cut coupons from every Sunday's newspaper and other papers to save our hard-earned money. I am convinced that due to these habits, she must have saved over $30,000 to $50,000 in forty years. It was not that she was miserly or cheap. She was conservative, and the money she saved was used for other shopping, travel, dining out, or whatever. This habit of hers also made me save money when I did shopping for her, for the house, and myself. Today, I can still do all of these things, but I am heartbroken and don't even shop much nor do I care about money. Her demise has taken away all these qualities. I get lost again and again about these things, and the pain brings back memories of everything. I repeat, and perhaps will keep repeating, all of this about Connie and her qualities. I have taken her demise very hard. I don't think I will see any ray of happiness.

Our karma reminds me of Connie's many great deeds, and mine, too. In March 1993, my Uncle Behl told me that I should come back to India to handle his pharmaceutical companies and four charitable hospitals, provided that Connie agrees. It was absolutely a great opportunity for me; however, I was confused about it, and Connie told me that she can try living six months in India and six months in the USA to look after her mother. Although we were both ready to sacrifice for each other, it was a difficult decision to make. Finally, I went back to the US and was promoted to a very senior position. I hired many employees and they had to be trained, as they had little experience in my field. It was a great challenge, and there were times I regretted passing up my uncle's opportunity. But later it worked out well for over five years. At that time, one employee didn't have the minimum experience of fifteen years, but I trained him well in the most basic work in less than four years. In this way, I was able to help him, his wife, and their children. After three years, he decided to apply for the same kind of a position, but earning few thousand dollars a year more. I advised him not to go and to spend more time to learn from me. But he was sure that he knew everything. I could have given him more money, but I didn't as I had to train him again. He left his position with me for a few thousand dollars more a year, and I told him that he is not training and few thousand dollars might not be worth the experience he would lose. Afterward, he was always in touch with me and Connie. Connie always told me that "Pradeep, you are a very kind man and always willing to help others, that is a good thing. However, I hate to interfere in your feelings, but many people take advantage of your soft touch heart. You have been hurt so many times, so think before you try to do good—these people are users and call when they need your help." I knew Connie was always right and I was still the same. Now, after the demise of Connie, I realized all that and am extremely angry that people, friends, and relatives, have betrayed me. Connie is not there anymore to see how correct and smart she was, and I didn't take her advice seriously. I must admit now that Pradeep is changed, and would not allow anyone to take advantage of my soft heart or the fact that I am always ready to please them. I would never like to see those ungrateful people and users anymore. Connie's demise has shattered me and changed my happiness and to some degree angry man, except my brother and his family and some unknown people. I would always be nice and helpful to outsiders. I spent Christmas and Thanksgiving alone in 2015 for the first time in the forty-two years I have lived in the USA.

49

Connie was My Destiny— Like A True Episode on the TV program Wanted

IN MEMORY OF MY CONNIE DARLING, THERE was an excellent weekly TV show of one hour, Wanted twenty years ago. Connie and I always watched this program. The program was to request the audience to inform the FBI if anyone had seen or had knowledge of these hardcore criminals. The journalist used to ask that even if a viewer had a clue about them, please inform the FBI on the number provided. One of the programs was very touching and absolutely applies to my life too. My entire career and its advancement are due to one person and that is my beautiful wife and friend of forty-three years, My Connie. The program was about a successful business and a wealthy man in his late forties. This man, when he was ten to twelve years old, lost his way and didn't know what to do or how to survive. The same kid was weeping on the TV had been looking for the man who encouraged this kid to remain in the USA and gave him an American gal and one dollar to explore the USA and find his fate in the land of opportunity. The same kid after finding success was looking for the man to meet him and say thanks and to serve him as his father and his family for any help and would do anything for him as he was the person who encouraged him to go to the USA. He was weeping; saying please let me know if you recognized this picture of him. was not a man but a god for his support. Connie was absolutely amazing in my start in the US. She was everything for me and my success. Connie was my best destiny and was instrumental to my success.

The following section includes email messages I have exchanged with friends, family, and organizations.

From the Carleton Alumni Network, Alumni Farewells:
Constance (Fuller) Berry September 4, 2015 at 2:12 a.m.
Pradeep Berry

I don't know where to start and where to end. I can write and write, but it is no ending story of true love. Yes, I am Pradeep Berry, Husband of over 39 years of my most precious, best friend and darling wife, Mrs. Constance Berry (Connie)—Constance Fuller when she graduated in 1959. I had the opportunity to visit with Connie to Carleton, I would say six years ago, during her Alumni. I truly enjoyed and the food and the lectures were great. My Connie demised on February, 28, 2015, which was not expected. I wish, in my opinion, she had listened to me to go to the Mayo Clinic, the best on this planet, which detected her condition in four days on November 8, 2014. However, it was too late. My life has changed since then. I don't know what I am going to do without Connie. She was everything for me. We were two bodies and one soul. I pray to the mighty lord, we meet again in our next lives, as the same loving couple. "CONNIE AND PRADEEP." This hope is giving me the power to live and fulfill the desires of Connie, though physically, she is not with me, but the spiritual way she is with me, and watching over me. I am also writing a biography for Darling Connie and would do my best to bring many parts of our lives, while giving some great quotes from many world scholars and their quotes. I just feel like talking and talking about Connie, which gives me the most power. I could have never imagined I would go through such pain, as I know very well that we all have to go one day. God exists all the time, but human beings and animals have to go. However, when it comes to me, the loss of some special person knowledge vanishes. I am only quoting this only for myself, as each person handles things in their own way. But I have to bear this no ending pain all the time. I pray Connie to give me the power to bear this loss. I can realize the pain of the king who made the seventh wonder of the world "Taj Mahal" in memory of his wife, Mumtaz Mahal, as she had asked him to build a special monument in her memory, "so that the world can remember their love."

Pradeep Berry
—Loving Husband.

"My full efforts for her Justice" This recounts my legal battle for justice after Connie's death. This is the second voice message for honorable Mr. Please fight for the justice. This is the US and not an underdeveloped country where there's no justice and no humanity. If there is no justice for my 43 years of marriage to the most precious super education and priceless American born darling Constance Berry, I would say we should not take pride in the USA. We then are in the same crowd of other countries. USA has an obligation to investigate the case even if these doctors have to be summoned in the law of the court under oath. We need strength and courage to do this to leave a great future for the coming generation and keep the USA on top of the world. Thanks for your help and support in looking into this.

Sincerely,
Pradeep Berry

Dear Pradeep,

I have received and reviewed your legal inquiry. (Name Withheld) Law Offices is honored by your request that we review your potential claim. Sadly, we cannot accept all the cases we are offered and regret that we are unable to represent you in connection with this claim, and cannot take any action on your behalf. This does not mean that we are expressing an opinion that you do not have a viable claim; other lawyers may be very willing to undertake your case. Also, remember that there are one or more statutes of limitations and/or statutes of repose that may apply to your case. This means that if you do not file a lawsuit within the time established by law, your claim will be barred FOREVER regardless of its merit. Therefore, if you wish to pursue your claim, you should contact another attorney without delay to discuss the appropriate time frames and to take IMMEDIATE action to preserve your claims. To locate a lawyer that practices in this specialized area for a second opinion, you should contact the Chicago Bar Association Referral Service.

September 29, 2015
Dear Mr. (Name Withheld)

I had been reading your articles. I am writing for My Darling wife of 40 years—Mrs. Constance Ann Berry, a graduate of Carleton and University of Michigan and Master's in Spanish and French. The most diamonds in my life, died, in my opinion, due to the negligence of Drs. until I took her to MC, and they detected in four days—Palliative Care. I am in deep pain. She was born in Glenview in IL, American—highly intellectual and a great reader and more and more. We were two bodies and one soul. I should finish with the book in a couple of months. Thanks.

Sincerely,
Pradeep Berry

"Many tributes For Connie from Our neighbors"
Dear (Name Withheld)

Thanks for coming to the peace ceremony of my darling wife—Connie of over 40 years. I am absolutely at a great loss without her, and she was the most important part of my life and would remain that way. I miss and miss her all the time ——of day and night. I used to go to India for two weeks every year but didn't go since 2011. I was in a different mood then. Now, I am planning to go to see my brother and his family and other family members this weekend for two months, depending upon how I feel. I have not told any of my relatives in India or over in Chicago about her demise, as I took her death very hard. The only person I told is my real elder brother. I have been busy sorting out many things, how mighty Lord gave me the strength, I don't know. I have to find a way to cope with this never-ending loss. Connie had always thought very highly of you. She went suddenly from my life, leaving me alone. I can't believe or imagine. Thanks for your time and support.

Sincerely,
Pradeep

Dear Pradeep,

Thank you so much for this note. It was an honor to attend the service for Connie; I always had such high esteem for her. From the time I moved into this building, she was a source of good sense, good humor, infinite practicality, and kindness. This building overall would have been a much worse place were it not for her, not only in terms of her leadership for all those years, but also in terms of her radiant goodwill. She was truly what the Biblical phrase calls "salt of the earth." We all were lucky to have her, but you most of all, of course. Never having been married, I can only imagine what you're going through in terms of the loss you feel at every moment. But I do know from having watched friends and family members move through grief that you WILL get through it. Things will become easier, and you'll be able to let go of things gradually. But grief has its own schedule with every single person; there's no timetable. I am very glad you're going to India, and for such a long time. It will truly give you time and space apart to breathe, to be, to consider what life might hold for you in its very different form now. And you'll be with your brother, another thing about which I'm glad. If I may presume to say so, a person can't do all of this alone. We're put here to lean on and help each other; let your family do that. You deserve to be supported right now.

Take this time for yourself. You have spent years devoting your time to Connie, which of course was the best and the right thing to do, but now the caregiver needs some care.

Godspeed,
Pradeep.

I hope that when I see you next, you will be refreshed and will have found a measure of peace. (Name Withheld) From (Name Withheld) I pray that the frustration and anger over the bad memories of Connie's care heal, Pradeep. They will only weigh you down. Connie had such a long, beautiful life, Pradeep. I've forgotten how many cancers she survived and all the suffering she experienced—yet, kept pulling her up. Surely, God was with her cancers and suffering. In each incident, God blessed her with more time—and again more time—and again more time. He prolonged her life, along with your care, far longer than other cancer patients. He could have taken her with first cancer or anyone immediately after that. Instead, He took her after this last cancer. She needed to be at peace. Her struggle was for so long. She didn't want wheelchairs, oxygen and walkers, and seclusion at home, Pradeep. If the doctors failed—and if they lied to you—that is very tragic, Pradeep. What you will do about this, I don't know. However, it will only take away from the time you have remaining to enjoy God's blessings and what Connie left for you. Don't let emotional cancer eat away at you, Pradeep. We'll talk later Pradeep (Name Withheld) (Name Withheld) Thanks for your kind words. Yes, you are right, I didn't want to be social anymore, and wanted every time with Connie. I was happy if someone wanted to come and see Connie and be there for hospitality. Her one friend used to visit every two weeks, I used to serve her cookies, pastry's from Bakery and make a different kinds of milkshakes, etc. All these things gave me happiness. As long as we were together, I was happy. Her two weeks in the hospital, and my anger like a tiger, on 8 doctors, including others, would be remembered by them whole their lives. They were the culprits. I told all of them, when they went behind my back to take her tubes. They are inhuman; I never expected this from you all, two doctors and 4 nurses and shame to you and to your profession and you are ruining the image of doctors, whom we consider next to god to treat sickness and Dracula's behavior. Her tubes were to be taken out on March 2nd and they told me that I had to decide what to do next. I had to decide. They took out the tubes on the 27th without my permission. However, I have lost my Kohinoor Diamond. When I went to India in May 2015 for a little change, I, too, as an American citizen was invited to the USA embassy to celebrate 4the, July. The program was extremely wonderful, but I was thinking of Connie. There were over 1000 USA citizens and their families. Guard of honor, band, food, drinks, singers, dancing, fireworks, rides, and things for the kids. They don't allow anything other than USA citizens. I talked to the USA staff, Indians working there as well as the Food preparing people for the USA citizens in their own kitchen in the USA Embassy. They don't allow any food from outside. Everyone has to pay for the entrance and food. Delhi Police and military security were there. Diplomatic people live like lords and there were USA tourists, students on exchange programs, etc. It was nice but with Connie" absence, I was very depressed and thinking wish she was with me to have thousands and thousands of better times—it would have been gold. I would tell you more about it, when I get back on 23 July. Thanks for your kind words and phrases. Anything you want me to bring? Don't hesitate.

Pradeep

(Name Withheld)

Trust you and your family are doing well. I have been thinking about you for a while, but just didn't write it is hot and I stay mostly in the house in air conditioning. I do go to some places if my brother and his son are going. They offer me to take anywhere, I want to go but I don't think I have a great desire to do much nor do I want to meet anyone, as I used to when Connie was alive. In fact, some of my other family and friends, I don't want to meet I am happy with my brother's family including his two boys, Mona, and the girls. I am waiting to come back to my home, knowing that Connie is not there, but still, her lovely decorative place gives me both happiness and unhappiness. Also going to her cemetery gives me the same. I have practically lost my charm of doing, going, and meeting my friends and relatives here and in Chicago. I am happy meeting people, like you, (Name Withheld) and (Name Withheld) outsiders, like in the funeral home ladies, who helped me for the cremation, and few selective. I don't think I want to see Connie' siblings. I know, they want me to come and see them but I won't. They could not find a time to see Connie. Connie was too upset with their behavior for a very long time but still wanted to see her family. I never ever said no and we used to meet but inside Connie' siblings were insecure that her grown-up kids, don't come close to us, as they were crazy for both of us… I would not say anything to her siblings except hello. However, I don't want to meet as Connie's absence would pain me. Let me know if anything new. Take care

Pradeep

Dear Pradeep,

It would be presumptuous to say I know your pain. Only a person who is experiencing it knows its depth. Yes, it will be difficult for you to return because you had been so very busy at the time Connie died (making arrangements, taking care of business). Then you had (Name Withheld) with you. Next, you had Mona and the girls with you. Then, you went to India. Constant movement. When you return, everything will stand still for you and you will have to be strong. You will have to learn more than ever on your God. You already know that. Pray for direction. Pray for the right people to be presented to you in your life. Prepare first, to feel the grief here all alone. But if you ask God for direction, you will be led to the right people, places and things to help you move forward. Again, Pradeep, I can only say that we are alone in our grief. We can feel alone in a crowd. You will get through this. You will not "get over" it, but you will be able to live a full life with Connie at your side in a different way. You are not giving her up. Give my love to Mona. She is such a lovely lady and such a good mother. Please don't worry about bringing anything back for me, Pradeep. Take care of yourself.

Pradeep,

(Name Withheld) You were and still are such an exceptional husband, Pradeep. Not too many women are given that gift. You, Pradeep, will someday have your own spring—your own Eternity. For now, all you can do is remember Connie in your heart…in your dreams. She is with you. Talk to her as if she were standing next to you. Now she is all-wise, all-knowing; she can read your mind and your heart without you ever speaking words. They know us more than they did when they were with us. Take care, Pradeep. (Name Withheld) Thanks for your kind words and phrases. I renewed Connie's account which perhaps night had canceled as I had no desire to read, watch TV and other magazines and I was still paying for the TV as (Name Withheld) but billed me saying they would put a hold but they charged the whole amount and they are doing the same thing. Consumer Report person was very nice and he renewed Connie and yours and due to the circumstances, he was touched and was charging me and less than the regular prize and upon Connie's wishes he gave great price for you also and now I would get from January and you I think when yours is expired. So you would keep getting it and I would get happy to read on her behalf. (Name Withheld) would still be in the picture and certificate you would have to take, I can tell you, and no matter you say no. I might leave on 20th October, 2015 and, I was thinking of one month or five weeks but then I made the reservation for December 24. This is due to the fact that I am using my miles and they have little inventory but I would keep on checking to come early. Please suggest me, am I going for a long time. Two things, I feel it is long for you to do the things. Secondly, I would be thinking of Connie's house that she is gone and home is alone while I too missing her chairs, her computer, her room, her pictures and her Cemetery where I come quite often. In fact, I am writing this from the Cemetery. India attractions are that I want to see my brother and his family and Grandnieces. However, I can try to come early if I am missing Connie and her rooms and the home atmosphere. How much my life and mind has changed due to Connie? I am writing her biography and want to finish at the earliest. Time would do that. I never thought I would be so much upset and suffer pain for Connie. I never ever do not want to see her family nor do I want any relationship with any of them. Here, I have (Name Withheld) and few in the health club and I just talk to people in the stores when I go for shopping grocery. That is enough

(Name Withheld)

Thanks a lot for your kind words and phrases and I am extremely great full to you for your kindness. Yes, I am truly going through a series of pain and suffering due to my wife of 43 years and I will be not happy with any of my friends and relatives, though it may be a temporary diversion of my mind but after that I would be the same. I don't enjoy anything and stopped eating at the super restaurants and food and travel. I just make a simple food to survive and that is all. I have no desire to travel like we were doing it. I was the happiest person who has now become totally different. I don't buy anymore that God had a different purpose and I ask God what bad I did or she did except helping others and attended the good and bad events of all. I would be happy when her biography is written but sadness would be there However, I truly admire your passion for me and I would try to follow the suggestion.

Thanks, Pradeep.

From:" (Name Withheld)

On Sat Sep 19, 2015, at 9:20 AM, Good Day Sir Pradeep K. Berry, I am the guy you spoke with earlier over the phone. I decided to send you a message today because I am so worried about your condition and I really wanted to show my deepest sympathy for the death of your wife. I hope that you will be OK soon and be strong. Remember that God has a purpose for all the things happening to our life." I know for certain that we never lose the people we love, even to death. They continue to participate in every act, thought, and decision we make. Their love leaves an indelible imprint in our memories. We find comfort in knowing that our lives have been enriched by having shared their love."

Leo Buscaglia
Return to Alumni Farewells Comments

September 2015 at Mona Berry I have no words to describe her personality. As much I knew her she was a wonderful person, full of life, who wanted to explore the whole world, was a dedicated wife. Her farsightedness, and her way to judge, no one can be like her. We all are missing you Connie aunty. We have lost a gem of our family. Add a comment Your Name

*Return to Alumni Farewells Recent Comments Constance (Fuller) Berry I have no words to describe her personality. As much I knew her she was…

Hi Pradeep,

Again, I am very sorry for your loss, and I am happy to do everything I can make this process easier for you. For security purposes, please attach a scanned copy of the death certificate. This will give us the authorization we need to access their account. Once I have this, I will be happy to look into your request. Thank you for your patience, and again, my sincerest sympathies during this difficult time.

Regards,
Supervisor Customer Support (Name Withheld)

Thanks for your kind words and phrases and advice about Connie. I would discuss few points more with you when you meet me around 5.30 or whatever is okay with you. I would come home from my doctor appointment tomorrow and can be available around 5.30 six whatever is Good, otherwise you give me the date when you can come. I have few doctor appointments this week and one for physical therapy but I can always adjust the time according to your convenience. Wednesday I should be home by Six, Thursday I can be home by 5.30 or six, Friday I can be home by 6.30. Nothing is happening on Saturday and Sunday. MONDAY 12 IS OK. You see your schedule and decide and I would go with your convenience. Hope you find (Name Withheld) Thanks for your help. Pradeep You are not to feel guilty for your dedication to Connie's memories, nor to continue grieving, Pradeep. It's such a tribute to Connie that your love continues.

(Name Withheld)

Thanks for your kind words and support. I would say once a week and if it is not too much for you, you can come over and I can show you. Also, I want you to see the collage pictures and other things, I have put together. I love them and I would like you to see the beginning of our 43 years of marriage pictures and some in between. I would like to put more later on. That gives happiness and sadness. I, therefore, live in two worlds—happy and sad. I can't take Connie out of my mind nor do I want to believe, she is no longer with me. Please let me know if the plants etc. Are too much due to your health. I want you to be frank as your health is first. My flight so far is on the 20th. If you want any other magazine, please let me know too. I would like you to see those pictures and a very rare thing THANKA which Connie bought 35 years ago from India and that was one of her favorite paintings but she wanted to frame and find a place to hang. I got the framework done over here and asked someone to hang it along with other pictures. You could suggest to me too if I should try to hang TANKA somewhere else as Connie would not have allowed me to hang in the living room. So whenever, you have time, come over. Please take care of your health and fitness.

Regards.
Pradeep

Thank you for all your trouble, Pradeep. It's the small things that make some people happy.

(Name Withheld)
Hope your trip arrangements are going smoothly.

Hello Pradeep—
What a lovely idea. I think it will be a wonderful, and therapeutic, thing for you to write about your cherished life with dear Connie. Such a dynamic, well-rounded, thoughtful, and humane person SHOULD be memorialized in writing. And you, who knew her best of all, is the perfect person to put her into words. I'm so sorry for your pain. And I miss Connie, as I'm sure several of us in the building do. Her intelligent, benevolent presence leaves a great void. Pradeep, but I hope this is of at least a little aid. Please take care of yourself.

(Name Withheld)

Dear (Name Withheld)

It was in my mind for sometimes that I talk to you. I am writing a biography about Connie and bringing out our love destiny, true love and just love, quotes from the world's scholars-' going back 520 BC, painful end, my suffering, her education, reading, love for world travel, house was her life, best restaurants and food, our experience of travel, some true episode, some of her best things she always remember, her role as a wife, best friend, sister and a mother with evidence of this written in the Indian century ago books with proof, message from Gandhi, Dr. Nelson Mandela, Dr. Martin Luther King, Jr., our bad relationship with her family and nephews and nieces though she was the best aunt of their and how spoiled they are due to their rich and greedy mother. Some of other experience of all the Broadway shows, Las Vegas show, Mozart and Vienna and her character, her charity and believed only in ethics, honest living, no lies, her contributions in exposing USA culture 43 years ago and so many things under different headings etc. I was wondering if you know someone who can proof read and edit the and just a second eye. I have great respect for you and Connie was Crazy for your intelligence and personality and being a team player. So frankly let me know. Hope you are doing well. It is 7 a.m. morning. People are going to work and I am going to sleep. How life has changed for me without Connie who meant a world for me and I am truly living in pain and the trauma and, in my opinion, Medical malpractice and conspiracy which killed her. I am not going to rest until I find someone to fight as many attorneys has refused to take the case and I would keep trying. I have informed the FBI and Senator. I have recorded 32 minutes of videos and 6 minutes and five minutes videos showing negligence while she was alive and how much I fought with these doctors and I was like a great tiger. God gave me the strength and again second time when they did something behind my back when I was just gone for one hour otherwise I was in the hospital from 20 to 28 had lived on 3—4 hours' sleep. I don't know how I was able to do all that? More later.

Thanks.
Pradeep.

(Name Withheld)

Trust you and your family are doing well. I also hope your knee is better and better and better. I am doing well with my family and family to the market and just to pass time. I do go to the gym for one hour, as there is no indoor swimming pool. I am also getting pain in my kegs which started on May 22 and when I came from India on July 23, I saw few doctors and went for physical therapy. How are everything in the building and our apartment? Connie always remains in my heart and soul all the time and can't believe that she is not more with me. I would never-never able to forget Connie who was my world and precious Diamond. I am writing a biography but has been slow but I am going to spend four-five hours daily. I was writing the whole day sometimes till 6 a.m. in the US. I have to proof reading and editing again and again. Please be in touch.

Pradeep Dear

Trust you are doing well. My name is Pradeep Berry and I am the husband of my darling wife and best friend Constance Berry(Constance Fuller before marriage), a graduate of Carleton College in Minnesota and University of

Michigan, in 1960-61. Constance and I were married for over 40 years. We were two bodies and one soul. We had been getting emails from the University of Michigan for 40 plus years and have taken many trips with the University of Michigan Alumni. To name some, Crotona and Tuscany in Italy, Ireland, Budapest to Amsterdam and Ryan... Later, we cruised with Vantage to Norwegian, and Europe, etc. It breaks my heart and soul to inform you and the university that, Connie—my world expires unexpectedly, in my opinion, due to the negligence of the Doctors in North share health care in Evanston, Illinois on 28th of February 2015. It was Mayo Clinic in Rochester, on November 2, 2014 detected her case as palliative care for, my precious gold. Later, after many painful episodes and series of traumatic things She and later myself went through, I think every movement of my day., I lost my battle and saw my wife taking her last four breath and I could not do anything. I have lost my life and don't think, I would do anything including travel, dining, symphony, Broadway Shows, Oscar winning movies to name some. Finally, I would like to be connected with the University of Michigan. She left money for Carleton and University of Michigan. I would like to continue sending some small donations. I had left very high powered senior management position in 2006 for any darling and never looked back. Connie wanted to enjoy and travel more and more. We truly enjoyed whatever Connie wanted. Having said all that, we had been working and traveling to the USA, India, and Europe, Alaskan cruise and Caribbean Cruise and other countries before also. In our 40 years of marriage, we were both extremely happy. I wrote long as a part of a tribute to Connie.

Thanks.
Pradeep Berry.

Thank you Mr. Berry for the email and information. I have made progress on reviewing the records and expect to be finished by the end of the week and will reach out to you then. Please feel free to provide me any additional information in the interim. Thanks again. I miss all but would not go and remember that with pain as Connie is not with me physically. I would put all in her biography including the following... Seven trips to India and then our 10,000 years civilization, Lord Krishna, Chanukah in 520 BC, Egypt, mummies, many world scholars, Nelson Mandela, Gandhi, Dr.

Martin Luther King, Jr., Mayo Clinic, her favorite music, our happiness—two bodies and one soul. Her clothing, her shoes, her walker, oxygen, her house, I want spotless. I am going to have a cleaning girl for here hours weekly for cleaning, I want to do things which used to make Connie happy, but happy, her plants, her commentary I go every week or twice Mr.: I want to apologize for writing again. I forgot few things; perhaps you have already read and listened through the voice mail. Please think like a Judge or Defense Lawyer. The doctor who ruined Constance's case and handed over on November 25, at 6:30 when he left the message on our voice mail. I still have the same message saying he has been discussing the case with M C and I am going to give the case to Breast cancer and specialist Dr. in the same building, why he was trying to see if would like to talk to me and why he was there in the intensive care with 4 days before when the other doctors assured me that they would be extremely helpful to Constance with her in Palliative care and Constance Berry would be fine and after we have stabilized for 2 I day's and she would be fine and later they all joined hands with B who ruined Constance's case and finally took her tubes in my absence and I without my permission, and my wife died the most same night. Please seriously think over this point.

Regards,
Pradeep Berry

(Name withheld)

Thanks for your kind words of wisdom and prompt response. The reason I wrote on the 27th was, Krishna's birthday is on the 26th and she was keen, however, Mona decided that they can have a party on the 10th and she has no problem if I leave on the 12th. I have confirmed seats on the 12th and can change them for the 27th. I am not worried about Christmas and I would not mind being alone. After all, I have to come either 12th or 27th as regardless, I miss Connie's empty room and her cemetery and my home. I am not doing a whole lot and even if I am busy with kids and in the market etc. Still, I am not in a mood. I didn't want to go to two days function of my half-brother. Connie had told me that I should not go for that marriage, as my half-brother cheated me and my brother. I would never ever go again Connie darling's wishes. Some family is upset about it that I didn't go. But I don't care, Connie Darling' words I can't compromise. That is an extremely powerful hurting too Connie, if I did that. Weather, I would have to bear on the 12 or 27th. Again, I would not feel lonely during holidays. I am lonely to some extent here too. I am writing biography, and I have to find a proof reader and to do the edit work. I would be happy, if you desire to do. I don't want to hurt you, but I definitely would like to pay for that. I mean that extremely strong about it. Please don't get me wrong nor please feel hurt for that. I think I might have 200 pages. I have to edit and proof read me and then I would have to get a second person. Maybe one or two months. I didn't get a whole lot chance to do here due to the other things"''' like going out with my brother and talking with my family and kids. After all they want me to spend time with them. Thanks for your kind words and phrases and time.

Regards.
Pradeep

(Name withheld).

It is 6 AM and I was busy so I would be brief. Mary, if I come on the 27 December rather 12th December. Would there be any problem. Although, I sometimes don't think, I can stay longer than 12th.

(Name withheld).
Today at 9:07 a.m.

Thanks for your kind words of wisdom and prompt response. The reason I wrote for 27th was, Krishna's birthday is on the 26th and she was keen, however, Mona decided that they can have a party. Your coming home on the 27th doesn't affect me. The weather here turned snowy and very cold these last two days. It's supposed to warm up for Thanksgiving. Perhaps you should research what the weather will be like in this area for the winter. At the same time, you will be able to get an idea of what the weather would be like when your plane arrives here. It's such a shock to leave warm weather and walk off the plane into drifts of snow! For no other reason, you can escape bad weather for those two extra weeks. Winter is long and depressing here.

(Name withheld).

p.s. I just realized, Pradeep, Christmas here will be very lonely for you. Even if you are not in the mood for Christmas, if you are here alone, you will feel all the gaiety and joy around you of other families and on the TV shows blasting Christmas music. I never tell people what to do, Pradeep, so it's surprising I'm going to say this: You should return on the 27th and remain there for the holidays. Oh, I just realized, perhaps a trip will be difficult to plan if people are coming and going on flights for Christmas the 25th and then again for New Year's Day. That's a hectic time for travel. You need to research this also.

(Name withheld).

It is 6 a.m. and I was busy so I would be brief, if I come on the 27th December rather 12th December. Would there be any problem. Although, I sometimes don't think, I can stay longer than 12th as I miss Connie and house and everything. But still, I thought if you have any questions or suggestions. In a way 27th looks long compared to the 12th December and I may stick the 12th. However hope you are doing well and good luck with your own home and family and your health. Thanks. Pradeep Enjoy the remainder of your stay, Pradeep. I assume you don't have any holiday in India on our Thanksgiving Day (11/26) which pertains to a part of the history of America. It must be difficult having "a foot in two countries." Thanks for your reply and its contents. Regarding Thanksgiving, you are absolutely right, India never celebrates nor much people know about it. Thanksgiving was extremely important part of my 43 years of marriage with Connie. It was so great. Connie and I always celebrated every year. It was great—but great. Practically, every year Connie used to have Thanksgiving and Easter each year with great style, silver plates, cranberry sauce, mashed potatoes, broccoli, rice, snacks of many kinds, turkey filling on the barbeque, drinks, three kind of desserts,—Banana Cream Pie, Pumpkin pie and nutmeg pie (special only on Thanksgiving). Connie used to make everything from the scratch and just a perfect and absolutely selective. There used to be over 20 so evil but evil. Connie took loan from the bank and we were paying the mortgages. In 2002, Connie got cancer and I am sure those evils put the evil eye on Connie. After that, we used to go to people, including her parents and her brother's family, and his in-laws. That was, I would say were golden days, I used to help Connie and the whole table set up, wine, whiskey, snacks food-you name, it was there. The same at Easter. It all was when we were on the fourth floor—two bedrooms—where Cindy and Tara live. I know we were happy when we moved to our current unit in 2001, we were overjoyed and Connie did an excellent job in renovating and furniture. I told Connie, bluntly, that when her brother and sister-in-law came to see the house—(Connie invited them and the family). Mary, I immediately told Connie, that her brother and sister in law were jealous, and I stated hope these devils have not put bad eye as they were so evil., They thought, how can we afford a bigger unit, and Connie's mother must have given her money. Those evil people were at her brother's house for Christmas and only two times for thanksgiving. Later, we started going out to Prairie Grass in Northbrook, and three-four times we took Sylvia. Prairie Grass has an excellent thanksgiving special—a little expensive. We were only invited for Christmas when it was a gift time and in summer for two days in their Green Lake big house. In January 2011, we bought the garage from Barbara White's brother, after she died, as he was poor and immediately agreed to sell. He had bad relations with Barbara but, somehow, he took the power of attorney of Barbara White from Barbara's father and put his name too. It was alright for us and we were happy to have a garage and especially for Connie. I had promised Connie, I would definitely make sure you have a garage and we were looking for different houses to move from 1310 to have a garage. But my words came true, and we got the garage. After coming back from Sanibel in 2012 and in August 2012, we bought a new car and a garage was there, Connie's Toyota Camry, I started renting from Phyllis. After buying the car, we went to her niece's house in Wauconda near Libertyville and the jealousy and greed they showed. I was mad and told Connie these evils were begging we should give our first new Lexus—first time (we bought in 43 years) as we preferred to travel. Her brother has so many Lexus and whatnot, but these rascals could not stand that, we bought a garage, now Lexus, and right after, Connie started going down. Connie drove Lexus for fifteen minutes when we went to Lake Geneva to try Lexus. That upset and upset me like hell as these rascals, Dracula's, evil souls put a bad eye on my Connie. They never came to see us and when Connie's mother was sick, Connie went through hell and I quit my high-paid position in 2005 to be with Connie and look after her and her mother out of town. Her siblings and family were not on talking terms, and I avoided them and encouraged Connie, I would do anything to make her happy. After Connie's mother died in August 2006, Connie and I arranged all the last rights and Connie paid each and every dime. Her sibling and family did not spend a dime nor do any of them speak at the time of her chapel of peace, except myself and Connie was very happy that I gave wonderful tributes to her mother. But for years, she lived in pain that these siblings had nothing to say about their mother and grandmother who did so much, loved and loved them more than Connie's mother loved us. Her siblings, kids, spouses, grandkids were like a wooden statue. Connie was in pain and pain for years. I bet, it was nothing but great and Connie and I used to work day and nights and weeks to do a perfect job. I am missing Connie, Thanksgiving, and now Christmas regardless of where I am, and would live in pain when I think of these two holidays. I would enjoy myself in my house alone with her pictures and candles and go to the cemetery. Mona gave that advice to me today. Mary, I must say that on Thanksgiving and Christmas I was always with Connie. Last Thanksgiving, I made a good dinner for her at home. Christmas, I bought some nice things and cakes etc. No matter what it was, but being with Connie every moment in her room, movie watching reading and just being with her—just next to her—next to her in the car, next to sit in the kitchen, taking her to the hospital, carrying her on the wheelchair, taking her wheelchair to the bathroom in the hospital, giving a shower to Connie, taking her to her room, filling her water in the morning, afternoon, and at night, her green glass on kitchen table; you can see water there and in her room, in the bedroom which I am still doing and would keep on doing and praying her three-four times, sleeping with her pictures in my home in India in my bedroom, full of her pictures everywhere and going anywhere with her pictures in my pocket, her ashes still in our house in urns, (Though, according to Hindu religion, ashes have to be disbursed but I still took from Liz at the funeral home and got two beautiful urns and they are in our house. I pray to them. I feel closer but live in pain but pain. I am writing all the family episodes, hospitals, our love, our education, her qualities, her love for cooking, dining, traveling, books, magazines, charity, Sanibel, all week. I have cut down going out, not traveling, not spending on clothes, Anything, Connie wanted I would do that but would live very simply. Now Connie is gone, and that is how I am going to go through my life. The most difficult period and painful part of my life—My Connie. Thanks for your nice compliments about our marriage and most importantly, Connie darling. I truly can't describe Connie's beauties along with all the great qualities, knowledge, responsible in every aspect. I can't find any fault whatsoever. "People, who think, they knew Connie, did not know Connie. People, who knew, can't describe Connie. This quote would be in my book. Thanksgiving and Christmas was extremely important in our lives and so were Easter and many other things. Now, I would not enjoy any of these things, regardless, what anyone tells me. Marriage is never going to happen and no way, I can think of that. Connie was Connie. I would marry any day if, God gives me my Connie Darling and I would be more than a king. It would end all my sorrows. But I can't have that unless, God personally make it happen. I know I am dreaming but sometimes dreams and God's blessing seeing the devotion, it can happen. It may not be Connie Darling as a wife, sister, mother, and father. I would accept her in any form, as long as her face and voice and qualities what she had. I think my mind is that I want to be there on Christmas and would put flowers on her cemetery as I did before one day before going to India and it was pitch dark at 6.30 p.m. but I managed with darkness and cell phone battery—Flesh—You can download free from Google and you would like it. They are great. Later, I brought the car and turn on the lights. Peace of mind and sad and that is what I get, but I still like to go for my happiness. Connie's brother and his whole family of sixteen people have never ever visited Connie's parents' cemetery, which is next to Connie Darling. Pradeep Berry is the only person Connie can expect to visit and I would like to do with great pleasure and happiness. I become upset if I don't go there once or twice a week. You do give me great advice about how to get over this most painful thing of my life but I may not be able to treat the problem soon.

Sincerely,
Pradeep

Thanks for your nice compliments about our marriage and most importantly, Connie Darling. I truly can't describe Connie' beauties along with all the great qualities, knowledge, responsible in every aspect.

I can't find any fault whatsoever. "People, who think, they knew Connie, did not know Connie. People, who knew, can't describe Connie". This quote would be in my book. Thanksgiving and Christmas was extremely important in our lives and so were Easter and many other things. Now, I would not enjoy any of these things, regardless, Mary anyone tell me. Marriage is never going to happen and no way, I can think of that. Connie was Connie. I would Mary any day if, God gives me my Connie Darling and I would be more than a king. It would end all my sorrows. But, I can't have that unless, God personally make it happen. I know I am dreaming but sometimes dreams and God's blessing seeing the devotion, it can happen. It may not be Connie Darling as a wife, sister, mother, and father. I would accept her in any form, as long as Her Face and voice and qualities what she had. I think my mind is that I want to be there on Christmas and would put flowers on her cemetery as I did before one day before going to India and it was pitch dark at 6.30 but I managed with darkness and cell phone battery—Flesh—You can download free from Google and you would like it. They are great. Later, I brought the car and turn on the lights. Peace of mind and sad and that is what I get, but I still like to go for my happiness. Connie's brother and his whole family of 16 people have never ever visited Connie's parents' cemetery, which is next to Connie Darling. Pradeep Berry is the only person Connie can expect to visit and I would like to do with great pleasure and happiness. I become upset if I don't go there once or twice a week. You do give me great advice about how to get over this most painful thing of my life but it may not be able to treat the problem soon. I showed your email to. Sincerely, Pradeep, Pradeep. Very few people have those type memories. So many couples struggle with their partner and marriage. You were both so blessed, Pradeep. Such a wonderful life.

(Name Withheld)

What an awful story about Connie's family. She would tell me parts of the conflict, but I never heard the stories of what happened when they had her mother move out and all the rest. No, I don't believe in the evil eye causing harm to Pradeep, but you are entitled to believe whatever you or your spiritual beliefs teach. When I was little, my grandmother and father (both from Calabria, Italy) used to talk about the evil eye and stories from

Italy. The stories would scare me because I was so little and my mother would tell my father to stop scaring the children. We didn't have TV, so his occasional story telling would be our entertainment. However, it would be before bedtime and we would have bad dreams. I envy Connie her skills. I was never a great cook or hostess, although when the kids were being raised and my husband was alive, I did have family over. It was a struggle for me—even to this day. I burn things and am a bundle of nerves. You were blessed to have Connie create such a beautiful ambiance for those times. Please don't feel bad that you gave me much of the story at length—it is so healthy to vent and let things out, Pradeep. You painted a beautiful picture of all Connie created in your lives. Keep hope within you that when your grief lifts, good things may come to you. Don't say no because I have seen it in my own personal family's lives. I will say good night, Pradeep.

Pradeep

Thanks again for calling last week and it was great to hear from you. I'm so happy that you and Connie are doing well and in particular that you're now engaged with teaching and writing. And happy belated 70th birthday last July 29! I'll be happy to share with you my thoughts and observations regarding yourself and Connie as you requested; please also let me know more specifically what might be helpful. What I've largely observed is that you've been an exceptionally devoted and close couple. This is all the more remarkable with you being from India and not having your immediate family here, your heavy job-related travel commitments and Connie's health issues in more recent years. But you've managed to maintain a close and enduring bond through it all for 30+ years. Altogether, your closeness as a couple is what I aspire to for myself. I've been most recently busy working as a Credit and Portfolio Manager in Commercial Lending at a $700 million NY based thrift headquartered in the Bronx. The bank, historically as a thrift bank, has been principally engaged in residential and commercial mortgages, but was recently expanded into commercial lending, including ABL and SBA loans. I've been pleased to continue to work in banking and advance my career here in NY, especially since I turn 60 in January and it gets harder as one gets older. And as I've said, as much as I miss seeing people such as yourself in Chicago to whom I was close,

I've benefited on balance being where I have better opportunities. The biggest event in my life is meeting and marrying on Saturday, November 26th, in Great Neck, NY, a special woman, Karen Ferrare. Karen is an attorney who was born in Brooklyn and grew up in Long Island. Karen is previously married with no children. This will be my third and final wedding in life and the final shot at complete happiness. We've been together for over a year and have shared an apartment on Manhattan's UES since early June. You and Connie are cordially invited and please give me your address for an invitation. Please also feel free to visit us at any time. As you know, there's always so much in do and see in the Big Apple. I plan on coming back to Chicago next spring but have too much otherwise going on till then. In the meantime, let's be sure to continue to stay in touch and I hope to see you in November for my wedding.

Ed Muller—Senior VP Banking New York

Dear Ed,

I am very great full to you for your sincere compliments and I know you mean this. I have known you since 1993 and we have been very close friends. The time we spent at ABL consulting was the one the imaging times. Connie is Connie, I truly mean that. I have never ever seen another person like Connie nor do I would ever. I am writing this from the core of my heart. My Connie is absolutely special. You recall going with Connie and me to Monticello, Indiana for the (name withheld) company in my white Toyota car in 1995 or 1994. A small town and I recall you going to the library there. How much love was developed with Victoria and how much fun was that and the time you came to Sanibel and we took you to Captiva and had grouper fish, lemon-fresh pie, and the beautiful drive and our two-bedroom Condominium. We asked you to stay with us but you had to go to work on Monday. Those memories are good and bad, but the reality is there. People avoid good or bad past, but I think it is nice to remember to share with those people. I am going to thank you again and Connie is very appreciative of what we are doing. Thanks for the nice letter. Best wishes to you and Karen. I am sure you would find yourself in the world of joy with Karen. Best wishes For whomsoever this note is for. I have had the great good fortune to have maintained a close and valued friendship with Pradeep for over twenty years. During this time, he has been a loyal and devoted friend for whom anyone could wish. I can honestly say and truthfully assert that I have never known as close and devoted a couple as Pradeep and Connie. Their abiding love and complete dedication have been abundantly evident. This is particularly noteworthy, given Connie's health issues in recent years. If I even come close to attaining this level of dedication that one can have as a couple in my own impending marriage, I'll be completely happy.

Ed Muller.
Vice President—Banking

In memory of Connie, I am giving my tributes to great piano teacher,

Mildred Honor:

"I am a former elementary school music teacher from Des Moines, Iowa. This is a true story and a beautiful and touching story of love and perseverance. Well worth reading. At the prodding of my friends, I am writing this story. My name is Mildred Honor, and I am a former elementary school music teacher from Des Moines, Iowa. I have always supplemented my income by teaching piano lessons—something I have done for over 30 years. During those years, I found that children have many levels of musical ability, and even though I have never had the pleasure of having a prodigy, I have taught some very talented students. However, I have also had my share of what I call 'musically challenged' pupils, one such pupil being Robby. Robby was 11 years old when his mother (a single mom) dropped him off for his first piano lesson. I prefer that students (especially boys) begin at an earlier age, which I explained to Robby. But Robby said that it had always been his mother's dream to hear him play the piano, so I took him as a student. Well, Robby began his piano lessons and from the beginning, I thought it was a hopeless endeavor. As much as Robby tried, he lacked the sense of tone and basic rhythm needed to excel. But he dutifully reviewed his scales and some elementary piano pieces that I require all my students to learn. Over the months, he tried and tried while I listened and cringed and tried to encourage him. At the end of each weekly lesson, he would always say, 'My mom's going to hear me play someday.' But to me, it seemed hopeless; he just did not have any in born ability. I only knew his mother from a distance as she dropped Robby off or waited in her aged car to pick him up. She always waved and smiled, but never dropped in. Then one day Robby stopped coming for his lessons. I thought about calling him, but assumed that because of his lack of ability, he had decided to pursue something else. I was also glad that he had stopped coming—he was a bad advertisement for my teaching! Several weeks later I mailed a flyer recital to the students' homes. To my surprise, Robby (who had received a flyer) asked me if he could be in the recital. I told him that the recital was for current pupils and that because he had dropped out, he really did not qualify. He told me that his mother had been sick and unable to take him to his piano lessons, but that he had been practicing. 'Please Miss Honor, I've just got to play he insisted. I don't know what led me to allow him to play in the recital—perhaps it was his insistence or maybe something inside of me saying that it would be all right. The night of the recital came and the high school gymnasium was packed with parents, relatives, and friends. I put Robby last in the program, just before I was to come up and thank all the students and play a finishing piece. I thought that any damage he might do would come at the end of the program and I could always salvage his poor performance through my 'curtain closer'. Well, the recital went off without a hitch, the students had been practicing and it showed. Then Robby came up on the stage. His clothes were wrinkled and his hair looked as though he had run an egg beater through it. 'Why wasn't he dressed up like the other students?' I thought. 'Why didn't his mother at least make him comb his hair for this special night?' Robby pulled out the piano bench, and I was surprised when he announced that he had chosen to play Mozart's Concerto No. 21 in C Major. I was not prepared for what I heard next. His fingers were light on the keys; they even danced nimbly on the ivories. He went from pianissimo to fortissimo, from allegro to virtuoso; his speeded chords that Mozart demands were magnificent! Never had I heard Mozart played so well by anyone his age. After six and a half minutes, he ended in a grand crescendo, and everyone was on their feet in wild applause! Overcome and in tears, I ran up on stage and put my arms around Robby in joy. "I have never heard you play like that Robby, how did you do it?" Through the microphone Robby explained: "Well, Miss Honor, remember I told you that my mom was sick? Well, she actually had cancer and passed away this morning. And well… she was born deaf, so tonight was the first time she had ever heard me play, and I wanted to make it special." There wasn't a dry eye in the house that evening. As the people from Social Services led Robby from the stage to be placed in foster care, I noticed that even their eyes were red and puffy. I thought to myself then how much richer my life had been for taking Robby as my pupil. No, I have never had a prodigy, but that night I became a prodigy of Robby. He was the teacher and I was the pupil, for he had taught me the meaning of perseverance and love and believing in yourself, and maybe even taking a chance on someone, and you didn't know why. Robby was killed years later in the senseless bombing of the Alfred P. Murray Federal Building in Oklahoma City in April 1995. Connie was right. Now I am facing my choice of isolated life as I am going through the pain of Connie. But with her watching over me, going to her cemetery regularly gives me a big boost but also pain. I ask at the cemetery, "Connie, please give me the strength so that I can get us justice for the medical negligence you suffered." My Connie would never have requested a DNR order, and wanted full code and she told me this by body language after her cardiac arrest. The delay before she got CPR was the worst thing I saw, and later on the afternoon of the 27th of February, when I made the sin of leaving her room for one hour, the medical staff did what they wanted to save themselves from their negligence. I pray that I get justice, otherwise in the court of the Lord the Supreme Power of this world God; they will be punished millions of times over until they pay their dues. It will happen. Connie's last wishes and her soul and my destroyed life and the curses from the core of my heart will never forgive them. That is how we feel. Many people have been very cruel. A story of a writer who wanted respect and recognition of his work but later realized that he is a candle that will have to burn giving light to others. This writer, director, and producer was Guru Dutt in Indian history. Constance Anne Berry BEST FRIEND & MOST PRECIOUS DARLING WIFE OF 40 YEARS OF PRADEEP BERRY I was thinking and thinking and moved around and saw several other stones which had the same color and design as other people's family and they had a beloved son of XYZ—beloved wife and father or husband of XYZ. I was thinking of a song by Cliff Richard, who was born in Lucknow, UP state in India. He used to come to India around the time that I had finished high school and was sixteen years old. My brother and our very close friends who liked music used to listen to his concerts and saw the hit movies, "Bachelor Boy" and "Summer Holiday." These were hit movies in 1963 and 1964. I was a good singer, and my brother and I used to sing these songs on the stage. Here are the lyrics of those two songs:

Bachelor Boy
Performed by Cliff Richard

When I was young, my father said, "Son, I've got
something to say." And what he told me I'll never forget
until my dying day.

[Chorus 1:]
He said, "Son, you'll be a bachelor boy And that's the
way to stay.
Son, you'll be a bachelor boy until your dying day."
When I was sixteen, I fell in love With a girl as sweet
as can be.
But I remembered just in time what my daddy said
to me.

[Chorus 1]
As time goes by, I probably will meet a girl and fall
in love.
Then, I'll get married, have A-wife and A-child
And they'll be my turtle dove.

[Chorus 2:]
But until then, I'll be a bachelor boy and that's the
way I'll stay-yay-yay,
Happy to be a bachelor boy until my dying day.
Yeah, I'll be a bachelor boy
and that's the way I'll stay-yay-yay,
Happy to be a bachelor boy until my dying day.

Connie always followed the great message of Gandhi, father of the nation of India, that we should be humble and contribute either money or time to teach and give free education to the unprivileged or the weaker section of the community. Connie always wanted to see the weaker section progress and devoted time for teaching and giving her research papers to students all over to read and gain knowledge to advance their careers. Her habit of reading and writing during work and after teaching and coming home to be a great housewife kept her busy most of the time. She was extremely productive every minute of her time for most of our marriage. Yes she loved going out to social events, traveling, attending functions, marriages, birthdays, and dancing, and she was full of joy and fun. We enjoyed a few light drinks. I was a scotch lover and she joined me to keep me company to have two drinks more or less daily with me and when I quit drinking twenty-six years ago, it was her happiness that we could enjoy our dinner around 6 p.m.. and have the whole evening to work and study books, journals, and papers or watch award-winning films and intellectual shows. She chose the movies we would watch in theaters and on Netflix. I cannot even think of that anymore. All of those shows, whether on Broadway or TV, is a thing of the past for me since February 28, 2015. I now watch the news and a few programs like 20/20 or Jimmy Fallon and Seth Meyers, but that, too, is just to occupy my mind. I turn on the TV, but these programs take me back to Connie and I am watching but in truth, I am remembering Connie and then I doze off in her memories and suddenly realize that if I was watching Connie's life with me. It is a daily routine. My mind, no matter what I am doing, is half on my work and half on Connie. Today, June 7, it is 2:15 and I am writing but 90% of my mind is on Connie and I feel I want to write non-stop for forty-eight hours; however, I think of my sleep and health and I have to force myself to stop writing and sleep. I wish God would give me twenty-eight hours to a day instead of twenty-four.

In memory of Connie, I want to share a true episode that happened over 5,000 years back in India during the time of Lord Rama, who was an incarnation of Lord Vishnu. Rama, his wife Sita, and younger brother Laxman were exiled to the jungles for fourteen years on the order of their stepmother who wanted her own son to take the throne. However, after their exile, her son Bharat also went into exile with Rama. His younger brother Shatrugan-ji handled the kingdom without sitting on Rama's throne or wearing his crown for fourteen years, when Rama returned. This is celebrated in the greatest festival of Diwali, Deppawali, in memory of the return of Lord Rama. During that time, Lord Rama had to fight with one of the greatest scholars in Indian history, King Ravana, who had devoted his life to praying to Lord Shiva and was extremely powerful and wise, with the intelligence of ten human beings. King Ravana was destroyed and was granted that he can only be killed by an arrow in his stomach, as his wife had made him drink amrit (an antidote) in his sleep, so he did not know if he could ever be killed by anyone. Ravana's wife was scared that if Ravana found out he had amrit in his stomach he would destroy the world. Only his wife and one of his brothers, Vibushan, knew this. His family begged Ravana not to fight with Lord Rama, and not to abduct Sita. He abducted Sita to see the true power of Rama. When Ravana disregarded their pleas, his brother Vibushan, a secret follower of Rama, told Rama how Ravana could be killed. During the battle between Lord Rama and Ravana, Lord Rama shot an arrow into Ravana's stomach to bleed the amrit out of his body and he died. Lord Rama asked his brother Laxman to go to the dying Ravana and request that he share his knowledge before dying. Laxman-ji went to Ravana and asked him to share his knowledge, but Ravana refused because Laxman had approached his head rather than his feet. Finally, Lord Rama went to Ravana's feet and asked, "Oh King Ravana, please do not take all of your knowledge away. Please share some knowledge before you die. You were my enemy before, but now I have killed you, you are not my enemy. Please consider me your disciple and share your knowledge." Ravana said, "I wish I was your teacher and had not kidnapped your wife. I wish instead I would have acted as your teacher." He further narrated that humans have a tendency to do bad things first and good things later. Please do not postpone good things, postpone bad things. We should withhold our ego and act to help humanity. Immediately after that, King Ravana died. Even to this day, many people in India worship King Ravana or Shanni Maharajah on each Saturday, and people put coins and other things to the devotees and some beggars come with mustard oil in a big pot and ask people to see their shadow.

This is very important in my life, and especially when Connie was sick and was a victim of the conspiracy by her doctors. I prayed and prayed to both Rama and King Ravana to save Connie from her cardiac arrest and that someone should appear in the form of Lord Rama or King Ravana to save my Connie, and I was sure the same episode of amrit in the form of oxygen or anything would save Connie. But the conspiracy of the doctors was so strong that my prayers and amrit became dangerous, and Connie was gone. I was praying to both the lords, all the prayers of our ancestors, praying along with our friend's wife, and nothing happened. Connie took her last breath while I was touching her hands and feet; she died in my presence. I have a video and during her cremation, I can be seen touching her feet and asking for forgiveness and kissing her forehead while she was dying, feet and head, feet and head. But I lost my battle like Ravana, as the conspiracy was much stronger with three doctors and staff. I wish I had not gone that sixty minutes and only had to face one doctor than the ten medical staff I faced. No one can win ten against one. That is what I saw and faced. I wish I had called many of my friends to be with me, but I was totally absorbed and my mind was blocked. Now I think I wish I had called certain extremely close friends, but my innocent bad karmas were stronger than my good karmas. One dirty fish spoils the whole pool. I am paying that as long as I am alive as Connie has gone and I cannot ask anyone to bring her back. There must have been some lack of devotion some years ago which I cannot believe that the sixty minutes was my biggest mistake and that sixty minutes would become the biggest loss of my life and death by losing Connie and I would haunt me each and every second of my life even if I am busy with work. Sixty minutes absence and sixty Minutes was my favorite program from 6 p.m to 7 p.m on Sundays, which was a result of my bad karmas and I will regret it as long as I live. People think, and friends and strangers alike tell me, that I should concentrate on the good times of our forty years of marriage and love, but I cannot accept that. Never ever. I keep thinking and will continue thinking as long as I live: why did I leave her with good faith on the assertion of the hospital staff that I could be gone for an hour. That absence of sixty minutes will never go away from my life I should never have gone. Never. That sixty-minute absence will haunt me throughout my life. Her death took away all the knowledge. I am hoping that *My Connie* will be with me in our next life. That hope will continue to keep me positive and will keep me doing humanitarian deeds. Thanks, Connie, for all you did for me and I have no words to thank and thank you. You are the one who made my career and my success in the US. Please, I pray your soul rest in peace. Loving left alone husband, Pradeep Berry A few more great messages in memory of My Connie.

These messages are from Chankya Neeti (Chankya's Philosophy).

1. "A wise person will come to grief if he does the unwise acts of giving advice to a foolish pupil, looking after a woman of loose character and keeping company of a sad one who has lost his fortune" quote 4, page 8
2. "It is living death to stay in a house where there is an evil natured, badmouthing woman of low morals. Or a cunning and deceitful friend, or an impolite talkative servant, or possibility of the presence of a snake" quote 5, page 9
3. "If you were to choose between evil person and a snake to keep company with, opt for the snake. Because a snake will bite only in self-defense, but an evil person can put a bite for any reason and any time or always" page 31

4. "Skill is man's friend in a foreign land. A good-natured wife is the man's friend. Medicine is a sick man's friend, and charitable deeds are one's only friend after death" quote 15 page 63

In my opinion, quote number three is absolutely true. Quote three represents the wife of Connie's brother, and that was the major factor between Connie and her brothers' artificial love inside an evil that is controlling power in the whole family of their four grown up kids, their spouses and children and grandchildren. I already mentioned that Connie's one real brother never came for Connie's sickness, her death, her cremation and ashes services, memorial and till today, August 4, 2016. Neither have their grown-up children and their children. Not even a telephone call or even a card—nothing. Connie was a lovely aunt and she left some money for her one nephew and three nieces. What a shame, the forty-two years of relations we had are over. They are ruined because of one evil, per Chankya. Quote four is 100% true for Connie who lived honestly, did good deeds, was self-made and was the best wife I can think of her and her deeds even after death are helping many charities, students, cancer patients, blind school and her greatness to still leave a big chunk for her nephew and nieces. If they those nephew and nieces and parents and evil wife have any god in their heart and theses church going people who are wealthy, arrogant, always treated Connie and Pradeep they are above and in our lifetime of fortytwo years never ever wanted to go for trip—to Australia, Europe, Alaska and practically one trip to different parts of the world, in spite of personally asking that we too are travelers and sometimes go. His answer actually came from his sweet wife for him but who was devious inside. He said. "Pradeep, we are busy for the next ten years," twenty-six years ago. In 1992, He told me at the restaurant when asked to join us for a trip. He said, "Pradeep, we are busy for the next 25 years." It was the most hurtful thing one can say to his biological sister's husband. That was the day Connie and I took the oath. I would never ask him or any of them to join us. We were only a token of the family during gifts time, Christmas and Thanksgiving. I strongly recommend and suggest "My readers never depend upon anyone." Children and brothers change once they have their own family. That childhood love is practically over and then if there is an inheritance from the parents, family ties may become a war or may be a civil war in the family. That what is I saw in my Berry family, which was painful. However, Connie's loss has made me very bitter as I had forgotten until now, I am happy not to even ask for my inheritance. Once again, the moment Connie and Pradeep met, my childhood tragedy vanished and I no longer cared. The worst and the most devastating thing I saw was CONNIE's

Sickness and her death was I smashed and lost everything. I still feel it today, August 4, 2016, flying back to Evanston from Delhi after spending five weeks. I know Connie and her house and her cemetery are very lonely, and I am lonely without Connie and her house. However, I get maximum happiness when I go back or stay in our home in Nirvana. Her Commentary visit is a peace of mind but full hidden pain in every vain of my body in all my body till today and forever. Everything on earth lives according to the law of nature, and from that law emerges the glory and joy of liberty; but man is denied this fortune because he set for the Godgiven soul a limited and earthly law of his own. Man built a narrow and painful prison in which he secluded his affections and desires.

(Khalil Gibran)

My sincere, loving and heartfelt tribute to my world, "My Connie." God—or the doctors—have taken My Connie and only God can give me back My Connie in this life or in the next life. Sometimes I think that the blame is not on God but on the doctors who have taken my wife from me. Those doctors do not have the power to return her to me, only God can do this. So who will return My Connie to me? Only God. Always loving husband and our true love for My Connie
Forever—till the next life

Pradeep Kumar Berry
August 16, 2016

50

In my Opinion: The following are Very Strong Points

1. Connie got four extra chemotherapy sessions from Dr. Brockstine, head and neck oncologist, in the middle of March until April 17, 2013. After a little scar in the PET scan in December 2012, he started giving chemotherapy. PET scan in March 2013 showed that she was fine and that the cancer was not there.
2. He insisted on four extra chemotherapy sessions that resulted in neuropathy, which he said would go away. But it did not, and physical therapy was given. Later her oxygen was low, and physical therapy had to be stopped.
3. An X-ray showed water in her lungs, and biopsy indicated breast cancer cells from 2002. He should have given the case to a breast cancer oncologist, as I told him but he said no. He suggested thoracentesis, and I was taking her twice a week for that starting July 2013. On January 14, 2014, we went to Florida, and the doctor at the Florida Cancer Center suggested an injection of Faslodex, which was not suggested by Brockstine. When I called him, he said he did not think of it and it is a good idea. The Florida doctor and Brockstine agreed that when we got back on March 1, 2014, it should be continued. In early January 2013, Connie also saw Dr. Winslow, a pulmonologist at North Shore, who suggested oxygen support and thought Florida's climate and humidity would do better. We flew with oxygen concentration, but Connie bought portable too for the thoracenteses and the injection in Florida.

4. After we came back from Florida, thoracentesis was still going, and water was getting lower.
5. Winslow prescribed a Dulera inhaler, which is actually for asthma. Connie took it accordingly. It ruined her condition, which, too, has been stated in the Mayo Clinic Report.
6. Connie went for thoracentesis in July 2014. Thoracentesis showed 37 mm of water, and North Shore said that it is too little to take out. That water, as shown in the Mayo Clinic Reports, thickens as a flame, heavily blocking her airways. The Mayo Clinic also said that Dulera worsened her breathing. Mayo also mentioned in the report that no bronchoscopy was done in July 2014, and Mayo did all that. That is how they figured out her case was spoiled, and metastasis was in her lung airways. That is how Mayo Clinic put in the report and referred palliative care, which was a shock to us.
7. After coming back from the Mayo Clinic, I called Brockstine several times, but to no avail. 8. Connie was highly educated and intellectual and said that Brockstine ruined her life and is now taking her life. "He must be chomping and worried that a lawsuit is coming."
9. I called the ex-chairman of North Shore at his home, who is a renewed oncologist, too. He was shocked and promised that someone would call. But we waited in vain. After a few days, the chairman called me and asked if I heard from someone. I said, "No." He said he would get involved and find some treatment. Dr. Brockstine called on the 25th of November and left a message as Connie was unable to pick up the phone due to her weakness, and I had gone to get the food. I have that message saved, which said, "Mr. and Mrs. Berry, I could not call as I was reading all the reports of the Mayo Clinic and was discussing. I would hand over this case to Dr. Merkel, a breast cancer oncologist who cured Connie of breast cancer in 2002."
10. Dr. Merkel was angry when we saw him in his office in a locked room. He asked, "Who was on the team?"
11. We said, "Brockstine and Winslow." He asked why they did not consult him as he has been doing this for over 30 years. He was just mad as Brockstine and Winslow ruined Connie's case in December 2014 and one in January 2015. February 20, 2015, was not done as Connie fell down and was taken to the hospital and was to be released on February 21-22. I saw DNR and Mrs. Berry told Dr. Woods and Dr. Fish on call

at North Shore to change to DR, and they assured us, but when Connie had a heart attack, the doctors waited eight to nine minutes before they did CPR. I was a tiger and a lion and blasted them that Dr. Woods and Dr. Fish assured me in the presence of a nurse that it was changed to DR or if I was not a ferocious tiger, they would not have done CPR and Connie would have been dead on February 21, 2015.

12. Why did Dr. Brockstine hand over the case to Dr. Merkel in November 2014? He was hanging over; he keeps coming to see me and leaving a note to talk to me, which I refused. Why was he there as a chief with six other palliative care and nurses to decide to take Connie's tubes on March 27, 2015, vs. March 2, 2015, as it was promised to me in 2014 by the nurses and the cardiac unit? That too when I was just gone for an hour? Also, the palliative care doctor and Brockstine, without my permission and Connie's too took the telephone number from the internet and called her brother on his Florida vacation home using face time, and he said he cannot come. Connie never wanted to see them nor wanted to do anything with them as they had been behaving badly since they inherited lots of money and snobs. Connie's sister-in-law is jealous of why her children and grandchildren like Connie and Pradeep. These doctors went against my wife Connie's wishes. *Shame on all of them.*

They are rich and have no love or passion for her sister except for her four children, spouses, and seven grandchildren. These relatives of Connie and I would say mine, too, have never given me condolences. Only the aunt who left money for them did. Her brother, too, lives in Wisconsin and from January to May. He and his wife go to Sanibel for fun. Children, spouses, and grandkids who have never even called me as they all live in Wisconsin never came to Connie's cremation until today. I am very much bothered about it and do not know what and how I would behave.

1. In my opinion, my darling wife, Mrs. Constance Berry, died due to the absolute negligence of two doctors at the North Shore Health Care System (North) in Evanston. One, Dr. Brockstine, is a specialist in head and neck oncology and head of the department, too. Another one is a pulmonologist, Dr. Winslow, and he too is supposed to be the head of the department.

2. Connie, who was going for her checkup and mammograms at North regularly, was diagnosed with breast cancer in August 2002. She had

surgery by S. Saner, and some nodes were healing, but no breasts were removed. She was given chemotherapy and radiation, suggested by Dr. Merkel—Breast Cancer Oncologist at North.

3. In December 2004, she had some ear infection and went to see her internal medicine doctor at St. Stephens's hospital in Evanston. He suggested a biopsy, as there was some small lump on her right cheek, parotid gland. She was given two weeks of antibiotics, and she took another for two weeks, and her doctor had said that if she does not feel better, she should go and see Dr. Merkel. She did not get better and went to Dr. Merkel in January or February 2005. He said he has no concerns but advised to see an ENT specialist if it does not get better. Her intuition was telling her that her lip movements were bothering her, and she went to an ENT specialist in North. He immediately took a biopsy, and results showed parotid gland cancer, a new one.

4. In a hurry, Dr. Stephen Senor at North did a six-hour surgery on March 31, 2005, and could not save one facial nerve and stated, she would have some problems which only, she and I, could notice when she moves her lips and may have to drink more and more water to eat to make saliva.

5. She was referred to Dr. Bruce Brockstine, head and neck specialist, and he gave her radiation and asked to have a PET scan every six months, etc. She did that.

6. In mid-2006, Brockstine spotted a small scar in the PET scan and treated it with chemotherapy and regular PET scan and MRI. Connie showed him some cancer herbals, which save the cancer cells and helps to tolerate chemotherapy, and gives strength to the body. He said, "Go and take it," while going for the regular PET scan.

7. She was fine until the middle of November in 2011, and Brockstine saw a spot on her node in her lungs after the PET scan and gave her chemotherapy, and she was fine.

8. In September 2012, another spot was detected, and Brockstine said to have another PET scan in December 2013 to be sure. He confirmed and decided to give different chemotherapy, and she can finish that in Sanibel as we wanted to go there. After her chemotherapy on March 18, her cancer was gone, but he decided to give four extra chemotherapy sessions. We were not happy, but we listened to him. Connie had four chemotherapy sessions and was done on April 17, 2013. After that, she developed neuropathy, and in June 2013, they found water in her lungs,

which was detected by x-ray. They were cancer cells from the 2002 breast cancer. He suggested taking water out once every week from one lung and the following day from the second lung. In November 2013, we saw pulmonary Dr. Winslow at the North who suggested oxygen, and Connie was sleeping the whole night with the oxygen concentration. Her condition was not getting better.

9. We flew to Florida with oxygen concentration, and Dr. Winslow and Brockstine also thought that the Florida climate in January until March would do wonders due to hot and humid weather. But she was not finding any improvements at all in Florida. We went to Florida Cancer Center, and the doctor there suggested an injection to dry up the water every month. When we called Brockstine, he said, "It is not a bad idea," and I asked, "Why did you not suggest it?" He said that it was in his mind but was not sure. I told him that it's time we see lung or breast cancer, but he said no. After three injections in Florida, water was reduced pretty fast and got dried up due to the injection. When we came home in February, the doctor in Florida had said to continue the injection, and Brockstine, too, took his suggestion and gave us an affirmation to continue the injection. But her condition was getting worse. Dr. Winslow at North suggested an inhaler, Dulera, used for asthma, which caused more problems. We were very angry with these two doctors at North and told them we were going to Mayo Clinic. They asked, "What would Mayo do that we are not doing? Mayo is a name that has marketing gimmicks only and nothing else."

10. It was Mayo Clinic Dr. Keo who stated that she and Mayo do not believe in PET scan and inhaler and that the small amount of water 17 mm, should have been removed at North. At North, they knew that there was 17 mm water but stated it is not worth taking out. Drake at Mayo ordered many tests, bronchoscopy, air test, water 17 mm to be taken out, cardiac test, etc., in four days.

11. On the fifth day, Dr. Keo said, "Mr. and Mrs. Berry, North did not do the right treatment and ruined your case. They should have done Bronco spy, 37 mm water should have been taken out, and the inhaler Dulera has worsened Connie's case."

12. Dr. Keo said the water became like a big thick flame and blocked the lung airways. The cancer had spread in the lung airways as PET scan

only showed new spots but not the spreading of the cancer. They made four mistakes.

13. In a way, if not directly, but indirectly, it is mentioned in the Mayo Clinic Report. If all that report, which is not very lengthy, a judge, a common doctor, an attorney can make out it was negligence by Brockstine and Winslow and North Shore. What and how more clear one needs? It is a picture worth a thousand words. This report, if given full emphasis, is evidence by itself. We do not need a testimony, a witness, or a murderer being caught red-handed. If it is not a malpractice or negligence per the report, then what is malpractice? Then there is no difference between a free democratic country like the USA and South Africa or Haiti and other poor countries. Malpractice law should then be abolished, and democracy should not be called.

14. North relied on the PET scan, this is not fool-proof and does not show any spreading of the cancer, except the occurrence of new spots. Bronchoscopy should have been done in 2013, which was not done except at Mayo on November 4 or 5, 2015, which showed the spreading of the cancer.

15. Thirty-seven mm water should have been taken out, and that has become like a thick flame or ice, blocking the airways.

16. Sixteen inhalers do not go with the oxygen. It is only for asthma and has worsened the breathing of Mrs. Constance Berry.

17. Air test at North was not done properly, and there was no indication up to where Mrs. Berry could breathe, and the technician was not the right person to be on that job as he was yelling at her to take deep breaths, making her and me nervous. Any normal person would be under stress.

18. They should have fully checked why the air test was not properly recorded and up to what number, from one to fifty, has gone. The technician must be useless, which we know. He was just shouting and making both of us nervous about his style of air test.

19. Dr. Keo at Mayo said, "Had both your doctors at North told you or had given you the permission to come to Mayo or anywhere, Mrs. Berry would have not been in such a serious condition. Now, due to their ego, Connie Berry has no choice but palliative care." It was the most devastating news we ever got. After coming from Mayo, I called Brockstine 10 times, but he did not call back. Connie told me he must be nervous as a malpractice lawsuit must be coming. I called the ex-chairman at North, who is also

a known oncologist at the North. He was shocked and said someone would call but in vain. He called me back after two days and enquired if someone called, and I said no. He said someone would have to call as he was going to step in. On November 22, 2014, Brockstine at North called and left a message on our answering machine saying he was discussing with Mayo and has been reading the reports, etc. Now he is not going to take this case and is transferring it to a breast cancer specialist Dr. Merkel at North (His office is on the same building) would take over. I have saved that message on my answering machine.

Dr. Merkel treated Connie's breast cancer in 2002. When Dr. Merkel came to see us in a locked room around the end of November 2014, he asked, "Who was on the team?" We gave him the names of Dr. Brockstine and Dr. Winslow at North. He said, "Why did they not consult me as this is my area of expertise, and I have been seeing patients and curing them for the last 30 years." He was furious.

The purpose of writing this episode is to enlighten people, a humanity cause, which might save the lives of some. Please don't trust your doctor blindly, and if needed, get a second opinion. Mayo Clinic diagnosed Connie's condition in four days, with different tests, which should have been conducted at her hospital North Shore (HH). We both were still optimistic that Connie would be alive and with me for a long time. In my opinion, her two doctors at the HH ruined her case in the last two years, and now she is dead. What difference does it make to them? They are still working and did not follow the noble cause of being a doctor. We all trust them next to God when sickness occurs.

Do they know this or ever thought of this? Perhaps, in my opinion, they should have been open to tell us to go for the second opinion, but their ego and overconfidence were in place, even with my request. We both were convinced in our opinion that they ruined her life and finally her demise. After visiting Mayo, Connie told me many times, "These two doctors at the HH earlier ruined my life, and now they are taking my life." She said the same thing many times, which was the most painful thing for her and me and would remain the same for me, till I am alive. She was right, and we still thought that she would be alive for a long time as the other specialist (doctor), at HH, agreed to take the case, though he ordered different tests and started different chemotherapy for three months. A test would follow to see if chemotherapy was working; otherwise, he would try different ones. We were very happy. Connie had two chemotherapies in December 2014 and in January 2015. For her third one on February 20, 2015, she fell down at home on February 19, 2015, and an ambulance took her to the hospital for a checkup. She was ready to be discharged on February 21, 2015, and was ready to come home on February 22, 2015. I must mention, I saw the nurse on February 20, 2015, with a checkup machine, and I noticed DNR. I told Connie, who too asked the two doctors on call to change to DR, and both assured us they have changed to DR. She didn't want to eat anything on February 21, 2015, but had a little salad, and in five minutes, she felt short of breath, and that was a cardiac arrest. Nurses came, and doctors refused to perform CPR, as the code DNR to DR was not changed, and they saw DNR. I lost my temper and blasted them. They better perform CPR. Otherwise, I would go to the highest law, as I had two witnesses when doctors stated the DR code has been changed. It still took them seven to eight minutes before they performed CPR; because the DNR code was not changed. I believe this eight-minute delay caused her death. Otherwise, Connie would have been alive and would be with me. She was on the ventilator and tubes from her mouth were to be taken on March 2, 2015, and I had to decide the next step. But doctors went behind me; when I went for short family work. The caretaker was there assuring me Connie is better and I can be away for a short time. Three to six doctors and two nurses took advantage of that and told me that Constance told them to take the tubes out. There is no way Connie was even talking. We were communicating with body language and, I was showing my written notes and she was telling me by her body language, "I should decide whatever I want to do for her." Again, I became furious and blasted six doctors and two nurses. Eight versus one was my first loss and all the palliative care procedures that they promised me were not performed, in spite of my aggressive act and a hundred phone calls. However, I still was positive that she would live. A great message came to my mind. "Never deprive someone from the hope that may be the only thing they may have." "Miracles happen every day." These messages were great tools for us to be happy. I also started thinking about God, to make Connie normal by your miracles, as when Jesus did to Lazarus, be brought back to life, that prayer was heard, so why can't I do it for my lovely wife? At the same time, I thought of a century-old story of Savitri, Satyavan, and the God of Death. It can be read on the internet where Savitri's devotion made God grant her husband's life back. These two incidents made me stronger. I was ready to fight anything. It was a struggle for Connie to go to the doctor's appointments and too much walking in the house, as she had to use the walker and later oxygen. It was not pleasant for us, but her presence and seeing each other's faces were still giving us happiness. Ultimately, I saw my darling's last four breaths and death in my presence. Two nurses and a close couple were with me. That death which I could never have imagined, the way HH killed her is one of the most painful, shocking things that I have ever witnessed. My mind totally went blank. Her face and body, if she was still alive, was another thing I had to witness, and have no words to express the pain in each and every part of my body. Is it true that I would never be able to see her, talk to her, live with her, can go no longer with her? I am left alone. How and when would I get back? Is it possible that God may reward her or me a half-hour to one hour or the next day that she is alive? All these thoughts were running in my mind. Even now on August 20, 2015, and since her death day, every day, these questions keep coming to mind of the most painful scenes I've witnessed every day. How difficult it is for me as her husband to release her body for the cremation at the funeral home. It gives me panic attacks; most of the time comes to my mind. I had stayed with her body another five hours until it was taken. I would never ever forget this trauma. I am suffering from that pain and withdrawal syndromes, which are incorporated in my mind and heart. Later, her two days of cremation and putting ashes in her plot, next to her parents, absolutely broke my heart.

51

April 14, 2016,
Pradeep Kumar Berry

MY CONNIE, MY LIGHT AND MY WORLD and the most precious wife of 40 year.s

- *My Connie,* when you were being neglected by the doctors and staff of the hospital to save your life on February 22, 2015, you had specifically asked the two doctors on call who came in your room, in front of me, the nurses, and your caretaker Florida Harris, to change the DNR Code to full code. They both came to your room in front of the nurses and Florida, stating, *"We have changed it to full code."* We were very relaxed and were waiting to go home on February 23, 2015, from 11 to 11.30 after spending two nights from your fall at home on the morning of February 20, 2015. The paramedics took you to the emergency room for a preventative check. You were fine except for some urinary tract infection, and you were to be released on February 21, then February 22, 2015, due to a lack of paperwork. They decided to let you go home on Monday, February 23, 2015. That day did not come in our lives due to the absolute negligence and malpractice of the doctors. I was there. After having a little salad at 6:15 p.m. on February 22, 2015, you fell short of breath and the staff was unable to see what was happening. The time went by to give you some water or jerk on your back, etc., to make you comfortable. But they did not know what to do until I shouted and repeatedly called for the staff. It was a sign of cardiac arrest and they realized it later. It was their moral duty to perform CPR immediately, but they waited and were confused, while I was yelling and screaming. I wish I had known to perform CPR, which I am going to learn in the near future. My screaming and yelling brought the blue team in front of me, watching that my wife needs CPR; they argued with me that they would not do CPR as the DNR code was not changed. I became furious and told them that I would turn them to the police and FBI and what not if my wife died. They got worried and performed the CPR. There were 10 to 15 people consisting of nurses, assistants, doctors and were watching along with Florida Harris and me—I can still recognize those people if I'm given the chance. All this delay of nine minutes on February 22, 2015, was one of the most important beginning of my wife's death on February 28 in the hospital in conjunction with conspiracy. In my strong opinion, Dr. Brockstine and his team came to the cardiac ICI unit.

- I want to let you know that I was there 24/7 from February 20-28, 2015, except around 12.30 to 1.45 on February 27, 2015. During my absence, Dr. Brockstine, who was no longer her previous doctor from the end of October 2014, along with Dr. Winslow, a Pulmonologist at Evanston Hospital, had ruined my darling wife's case. I took my wife to Mayo Clinic on November 2 through November 7, 2014, and they detected with various tests and reported that palliative care was required. The Mayo doctor verbally told us Brockstine or Winslow should have done bronchoscopy, and 37 mm water in her lungs should have been removed, which now had become like a flame-ice in her lung's airways. By depending upon PET scan only and not by doing a bronchoscopy, they did not realize that her cancer was spreading in her lung airways, blocking her breathing in her throat. Also, Winslow prescribed Dulera inhaler, which had caused a more severe breathing problem, and now Constance Berry's case had been ruined by these two doctors. Now, the only palliative care had been suggested along with some chemotherapy at Mayo or Evanston Hospital.

When we came back on November 7, 2014, I called Dr. Brockstine 10, 15 times, but he did not return my call. I called the ex-chairman and oncologist of Evanston Hospital Dr. Kanedkar at his home, and he was surprised and stated someone would call, but no one called. After two days, Dr. Kanedkar called me at our house and asked if anyone called. I said no. He stated he would get involved, and someone would call. Only after a seven-ten days of waiting, Dr. Brockstine called on our landline on November 26, which I have saved. "Mr. and Mrs. Berry, this is Dr. Brockstine, and I was busy discussing the next course of action. I am going to give this case to Dr. Merkel in the same hospital, who is a breast cancer expert. Please make an appointment to see him."

Constance was highly educated, and she told me on the 9th and 10—14 1-15—16—20 24 November, "Pradeep, earlier Dr. Brockstine ruined my life and made me sick and now he is taking my life and I should not have trusted him and should not have listened to his nonsense that he is on top of his field and that I am not that serious, knowing I was made sick and have to use a walker and portable oxygen since the end of December." In January, she bought portable oxygen and later another better portable oxygen and was not able to do anything without her new walker and new oxygen portable machine. These two things are sitting in her room, and I pray and touch and ask for her blessings from her walker and oxygen, and I would never give it away to anyone as it is a big memory and painful thing in my isolated life. Her pictures are covered on her walker and oxygen, and these are like a church for me. We went there all the time but was gone for an hour. On the same day, she was put on the ventilator for two weeks, and her tubes were to be taken out on March 2, 2015, and I had the power of attorney of her health care. I can furnish that power of attorney if you so desire. I had to make the decision as per the doctors and nurses. What I want to do on March 2 when tubes were to be removed, whether to keep her in the palliative care unit for few days and take her home with the palliative care people? Do the tracheostomy and be with her at the Holy Hospital for two weeks and further two-three weeks in the rehabilitation center as that could have been a second choice for her to live longer and I told them that I want to save her no matter what. I have to stay there and with my body language—as she was not able to speak due to heavy tubes and hands tied with all the vials—decide and desire, if that would increase her chances to survive and later come home and then die at home, that was her desire. She had asked me to promise her that she would die at home in her own bedroom watching TV and watching her beautiful home. It was her absolute great desire, and she had told me this years and years ago. Also, while going to the emergency room, and while on the ventilator by nodding and nodding and reading my notes and confirming that she wants to go home to die watching at her house peacefully with dignity.

- She never ever trusted her one sibling Michael Fuller who, along with his large family of four grown-up kids and grandchildren, has never come for her cremation or her ashes ceremony. Neither did they call, except once. None of them have visited until now, March 29, 2016. She last met them in January 2014 in Florida for a few hours as we also used to go there to the rented cottage. Her family never otherwise came to see her, before knowing she was not well. This point is important as doctors had falsified their records by mentioning Michael Fuller in the medical records which have been furnished and must be read very carefully. It has been falsified. It must be noted that Dr. Bruce Brockstine, who was no longer her doctor since October 2014, came on February 27, 2015, around 12 noon. That was when I just left the hospital for an hour to she was put in conjunction with along with the doctor Bruce Brockstine who was no longer her doctor since October 2014 in front of me as I was there 24 hours with my wife.

- Somebody must have been spying on me as there was social director, Ruth. She used to give out orders, dictating me that I must leave home as my health would be bad if I stay all the time. She was after my blood all the time to see that I do not stay after 8:30 p.m., whereas the other nurses and staff wanted me to be there. I never wanted to leave my wife, and I wasn't even thinking of coming home. Do you think a loving husband whose wife is in the hospital can come peacefully to his home? Absolutely no. It can be inquired and asked in all the hospitals, from all the nurses and other doctors. Since September 31, 2005, I had never allowed her to go to any doctor's appointment without me. I left my high-powered job in September 2005 to be with her, and since then up to now, I have not worked as it's the greatest happiness I had. Anyone is free to inquire, investigate this statement of mine.

Please read carefully below all the events starting from September 2012. (AFTER READING OUR RIGHTS AS USA CITIZENS) AS A USA CITIZEN, I HAVE A MORAL DUTY, AND FOR MY USA BORN WIFE CONSTANCE FULLER (BERRY AFTER OUR MARRIAGE) 40 YEARS AGO. WHY DOES THE LAW DOES NOT PROTECT INDIVIDUAL USA CITIZENS FROM THE MEDICAL NEGLIGENCE STATING THAT IT IS AN INDIVIDUAL CASE AND NOT A FEDERAL OR CIVIL LAWSUIT? The BIGGEST VIOLATION OF USA RIGHT IS WHEN A MEDICAL NEGLIGENCE CAUSED A DEATH IN THE HOSPITAL. LAW IS SILENT ON THAT GIVING ENCOURAGEMENT TO MEDICAL PROFESSION TO DO WHATEVER THEY WANT TO DO,

EVEN DEATH FROM THE MALPRACTICE AND NEGLIGENCE. THE MOST THE HORRIBLE THING IS WHEN THE HOSPITAL FALSIFIES THE MEDICAL RECORDS. The DESTRUCTION OF THE MEDICAL RECORDS AND MAKING IT LOOK LIKE THE THE PATIENT WANTED TO DIE. YES, THAT IS THE CASE WITH MY PRECIOUS WORLD—MY LIFE AND MY DEAREST PART OF MY LIFE–MY WIFE OF OVER 40 YEARS A USA BORN CITIZEN—HIGHLY EDUCATED FROM UNIVERSITY OF CARLTON COLLEGE, UNIVERSITY OF MICHIGAN AND ANOTHER MASTERS IN SPANISH AND TEACHER FOR 34 YEARS. LATER, SHE STARTED TEACHING FREE AND THEN GIVING HER TIME TO THE LIBRARY FOR CHILDREN'S EDUCATION AND TEACHING. WHERE IS HER PROTECTION? AND MY PROTECTION AS USA CITIZEN? WE BOTH CONTRIBUTED TO THE USA. PAID OUR TAXES, LIVED HONESTLY, DID HUMANITY WORK, GAVE DONATIONS TO ALL CHARITIES, CARED FOR THE USA LAW, GAVE DONATIONS TO THE RIGHT DESERVING CANDIDATE FOR USA PRESIDENT AND ATTORNEY GENERAL OF THE ILLINOIS AND CONGRESSMAN.

SHE HAD THE SAME RIGHT TO BE PROTECTED FROM ANY MEDICAL NEGLIGENCE AND FROM THE HANDS OF WELL PROTECTED MEDICAL DOCTORS WHO COMMIT MISTAKES BUT IMPORTANTLY, IN MY OPINION, KNOWS HOW TO ELIMINATE THAT PATIENT WHOSE LIFE THEY RUINED BY NOT GIVING THE RIGHT TREATMENT. THEY MADE MISTAKES AND FALSIFIED HER MEDICAL RECORDS TO LET HER GO TO HEAVEN WHILE SAVING THEIR LIFE. THEY WERE MORE CONCERNED WITH THEIR EGO, JOB, POSITION, REPUTATION AS ONE OF THE BEST DOCTORS IN THE MEDICAL BOOKS AND HOSPITAL PUBLICITY, ETC. WHY ATTORNEY GENERAL OFFICE DO NOT PROSECUTE THEM? THEY SHOULD TAKE MY PRECIOUS WIFE'S DEATH AS A SERIOUS CRIMINAL ACT BY THE SO-CALLED MEDICAL DOCTORS. HER LIFE CANNOT BE RECOVERED COMPARED TO THE CONSUMER FRAUD OR WHERE IT'S A MATERIAL WHICH CAN BE COMPENSATED, AND THE PERSON OR THE CORPORATION—DEFENDANT AND PLAINTIFF ARE STILL ALIVE. IN THE CASE OF MONEY LOSSES, BANKRUPTCY, FRAUD AND OTHER CRIMES, AT LEAST THE PERSON IS ALIVE AND SUFFER FOR SOMETIME WITH HIS FAMILY.

WHAT IF A PATIENT DIED AND HER LOVING HUSBAND AND HIS WORLD OF OVER 40 YEARS IS GONE FROM HIS LIFE? DEATH CAN NEVER BE REPLACED, WHICH IS MUCH MORE THAN LOSING MILLIONS AND MILLIONS OF DOLLARS. MONEY, HOUSE, CAR, AND OTHER DAMAGES CAN BE RECOVERED. HOWEVER, DEATH CANNOT BE BOUGHT BACK WITH ANY WEALTH OR ANY AMOUNT. I THINK. IT'S EXTREMELY IMPORTANT THAT COOK COUNTY ATTORNEY GENERAL, COURT OF LAW MAKE CHANGES FROM FEDERAL CRIME—CIVIL SUIT TO ONLY MEDICAL NEGLIGENCE WHERE ATTORNEYS DO NOT WANT TO TAKE THE CASE AS IT'S EXPENSIVE. REWARDS ARE A GAMBLE AND THE SMALL AMOUNT IF THE CASE IS WON IS NOT SUFFICIENT UNLESS IT IS IN MILLIONS OF DOLLARS. I WORKED IN THE CORPORATE FOR 40 YEARS AND INTERACTED WITH MANY ATTORNEYS. OUR HUGE COMPANY HIRED A TOP LAW FIRM WHEN WE WERE VERY BUSY. NOW I WOULD APPRECIATE IF YOUR OFFICE CAREFULLY EXAMINES AND SERIOUSLY LOOKs AT THE RIGHTS OF THE USA CITIZENS. IT SAYS BY ATTORNEY GENERAL OFFICE THAT IF OUR COMPLAINT SUPPORTS A PATTERN OF DECEPTIVE PRACTICES, IT MAY BE INCLUDED IN FUTURE INVESTIGATIONS OR LITIGATIONS. ONE OF THE MOST VALUABLE WAYS WE CAN LEARN OF PROBLEMS EXISTING IN THE MARKETPLACE IS BY RECEIVING COMPLAINTS FROM CONCERNED CITIZENS. HOSPITALS ARE ALSO LIKE MARKETPLACES. PATIENTS GO TO THE HOSPITALS, GIVE DONATIONS, PAY FOR PARKING, INSURANCE PREMIUM, REAL ESTATE DUTY TO FUND SCHOOLS, COLLEGES, AND MEDICAL HOSPITALS, MEDICARE, AND OTHER DONATIONS FOR MEDICAL RESEARCH. CHILDREN HOSPITAL SALVATION ARMY NTS THESE ARE ALL MARKETPLACES. I WOULD SAY BIGGER THAN ANY DISPUTE FOR TELEPHONE MAIL-INTERNET-TRADE SHOW CONVENTION CENTER. THEIR LOSSES OR FRAUD CAN BE COMPENSATED BY THE LAW BY SETTLEMENT OF MONEY NO MATTER BIG OR SMALL. WHAT ABOUT THE DEATH OF THE EDUCATED PERSON WHO CONTRIBUTED A LOT AND HIS HUSBAND OF OVER 40 YEARS WHO HAS EVERYTHING, BUT HIS LOVELY WIFE WHO HE WOULD NEVER SEE AND NO AMOUNT OF MONEY CAN BRING HIS WIFE BACK? THERE IS NOT ENOUGH MONEY ON THE PLANET WHO CAN GIVE MY CONNIE. WHERE IS THE LAW FOR THAT? OUR RESPECTED ATTORNEY GENERAL MUST

LOOK INTO THIS HIDDEN PLACE, WHERE MANY LIVES ARE RUINED AND USA CITIZENS ARE SUFFERING FOR A LIFETIME. I HAVE THE HOPE THAT OUR RESPECTED ATTORNEY GENERAL LISA MADIGAN LOOKS AT THIS. SHE HAS THE POWER TO CHANGE THE LAW AND PERHAPS WITH THE SUPPORT OF USA CITIZENS CAN CHANGE THE USA CONSTITUTION.

YES. CRIME IS A CRIME. NEGLIGENCE IS NEGLIGENCE. DEATH IS DEATH REGARDLESS OF WHERE IT HAPPENS—OUTSIDE ON THE ROAD OR MALL, GROCERY STORE OR THE PARKING LOT. PROTECTS VICTIMS WHO WERE ROBBED IN STORES, CONSUMER CITIZENS FOR MONEY, ID, FRAUD, $1,000 OR $100,000 DOLLARS WHICH CAN BE RECOVERED. VICTIM CAN BE JAILED AND PUT ON BOND. SHOPS CAN BE CLOSED. DRIVERS CAN KILL ON THE ROAD, ANY OTHER CONSUMER FRAUD, AND MANY OTHER FRAUDS CONSIDER. TAKING IT… THAT WHAT HAD HAPPENED TO MY WIFE AND IT HAS AFFECTED MY LIFE DUE TO THE MALPRACTICE, MISTAKES AND NOT LETTING US OR HER TO GO FOR THE SECOND OPINION UNTIL I TOLD HIM BLUNTLY THAT I AM TAKING MY WIFE TO MAYO CLINIC ON NOVEMBER 2, 2014. HER DOCTORS TOLD WHAT MAYO WOULD DO AND WHAT WE CAN NOT DO. MAYO IS A MARKETING GIMMICK AND WE ARE MUCH BETTER HERE. MURDER CAN BE TRACED. FBI CAN BE INVOLVED IN EVERY CASE AS LONG AS IT IS IN A PUBLIC PLACE, STREETS, GANGS OUTSIDE THE STORE, DOWN IN THE TRAIN, ANYWHERE BUT NOT IN THE HOSPITAL WHERE AN INNOCENT SICK PERSON IS MADE TO DIE SO THAT THE DOCTORS CANNOT BE SUED. WHICH LAW IS PROTECTING SUCH DOCTORS? WHY DO OUR COOK COUNTY ATTORNEY GENERAL, SENATOR ACT FOR ANY CRIME OUTSIDE THE HOSPITAL? WHY NOT APPLY THE SAME LAW TO ALL THE USA CITIZENS LIKE PRADEEP AND HIS BELOVED WIFE CONSTANCE HIGHLY EDUCATED CONTRIBUTED IN THE USA; WHO PAID TAXES, WHO ARE GOOD CITIZENS AND HAVE NOT CHEATED ANYONE, WITH EXCELLENT CREDIT RATION, TAUGHT 34 YEARS IN MORTON GROVE, CALIFORNIA, AND GERMAN TO US MILITARY CHILDREN WENT TO THE UNIVERSITY OF MICHIGAN CARLTON COLLEGE.

CPR was performed after nine minutes, and then medical records I collected two or three times did not have that record. However, by my persistent calling and visiting, I was successful in getting it in papers. I have that record now. You were on the ventilator from February 22 until March 2, and I had the power of attorney. I was thinking of palliative care or Tracheostomy with rehabilitation. However, doctors did not give that chance too.

On February 27, 2015, Florida Harris and Katie were there, and they told me that Constance is okay, and I can take a break for an hour outside. That would remain the most suspenseful and painful day in my life.

Dr. Brockstine, who was no longer your doctor, had no business to come along with other palliative care and must have conspired with the nurse Katie to join hands. When I reached there, they all came and told me, "Mr. Berry, I do not have any more power, and Constance's wishes have to be fulfilled. She wants her tubes out, and we've facilitated that."

They all told me that they called her brother Michael Fuller in Sanibel, Florida, on the face time, and they both waved their hands, and Michel said, "I love you." I was mad that Constance had told me that she does not want Michael and his children and grandchildren to visit them or call them as they had never bothered calling in the last two years nor they ever came to see us. She was extremely hurt by their behavior.

They removed her tubes around 1:30 or so, and Constance was able to speak with me for an hour, and I told her she would be fine, and we would go home with palliative care when they tell us after a day or two. She was happy and was asking if I wanted to go to the bank for selling our Camry car as we had to vacate the rented garage by March. I said, "Wait till we go home," and then she said, "Alright with me as we have till the end of the month to sell." However, she was desperate that she would feel happier to come home and be in her room and her own bed. She said, "If palliative care nurses, doctors come, I would be fine." I said absolutely, and she asked if I had brought her clothes, walker, and oxygen, which she knew was there but asked if it is in the rooms that she should get going in the morning. I said yes. I was very happy that now slowly she would start eating and be improving in the home atmosphere listening to primetime night shows, movies, eating her favorite food like salmon, shrimps, Indian tea, some stuff from Benson Bakery, etc., and slowly, I would take her out for some change. Slowly, she would recover and she can have her treatment in March from Dr. Merkel who was sure that Constance can live for another five to 10 or more but she is not going to die soon as his treatment is reducing her pain and improving her breathing. Even after the tubes were taken out, the palliative care doctors and nurses were happy that we would keep her in the palliative care for two to three days till she is stabilized. We would let her go home and then the nurses and doctors would be in touch to see her condition, but her prognosis looks good Mr. Berry. Your devotion has worked. They told me on the night of the 26th and 27th in the morning and that made me leave the hospital for an hour to go out on some work. being Friday, knowing I cannot go anywhere once she is home and I have to be with her 24 hours with eight hours with Florida Harris, to do the laundry, cleaning, and getting food and I stay in her room with my books, newspapers and serve her food three times a day. How on Earth would I know my happiness would go after nine hours due to not do what they told me and there was no staff as Friday at 4:30 all left for the weekend? Later I saw by 4 p.m. no one was coming and Constance's condition of breathing was getting worse. I started calling the nurses and doctors from the hospital room next to her and I am sure Florida Harris or some nurse made a 32-minute video which I have to prove that I am next to Constance and calling from my cell phone and hospital room. They're using the hospital room and I am shouting and shouting as the hospital phone was ringing. They asked, "What can we do?" I said, "Send the nurse. I am sick and calling for a long time. Over a half-hour has passed and no one is coming. This is medical negligence, and you do not care for my wife. Please send someone."

No one came. Nurses are running around outside to other patients, and it can be easily seen in that video. I have another six minutes of video where after making lots of calls, hospice girl Katherine came and was talking to me and asking Constance if she needs anything. She did not do anything to save her as it was not even in her mind. In my opinion, she could have made attempts to save her or make her give more oxygen, mask, or injection to get her breathing better or called emergency numbers or ER or anything. She did not do that. I am sure she was part of the conspiracy to let Constance Berry die so that this so-called Dr. Brockstine wanted Constance to die. In my opinion, he is the one who had ruined Constance's case and was paranoid when we came from the Mayo Clinic from November 2 to November 8, 2014. Constance was declared on palliative care. Mayo had to put Constance was very sick in the report but did not write why she got so sick and that she had only a palliative care option. If she was not affiliated with Evanston Hospital, she may or may not have written "She was made sick by four things: (1) Giving too much chemo in April 2013. No bronchoscopy after she got water in her lungs in June 2013, Left off the water of 37 mm, which was not taken out at Evanston Hospital and 4) later became a thick flame in November 2014, when bronchoscopy was done in Mayo on November 3, 2014." Dr. Brockstine's PET scan showed in March 2013 that Connie is cancer-free. Had he ordered the bronchoscopy, he would have found that some cells may be spreading, but he was not worried as PET scan showed she is cancer-free. Who made her sick? Dr. Brockstine? These so-called doctors know how to cure and how to kill and protect each other for their own reputation and lawsuit. This is the first time I have realized this thing in my forty-two years in the US. I could have never ever thought it can happen in the world's best country-the US. My life is shattered, devastated, ruined. I no longer have the desire to do anything except to get justice for Constance I promised at her death in front of the doctor who came to certify, in the cremation, at the time her ashes were put in her plot, and all the time when I go to her cemetery in Skokie, I say, "Connie please bless me, I should be able to get justice." I repeat this with my faith and ask God to help me to have a miracle. Some attorneys think I should not take this case where they have to spend time and fight this easy case. Maybe they think they do not have enough chance of making millions of dollars. Also, they read the medical reports and they do not know that many things are falsified in the medical records from February 20 to 28, 2015. Also, Dr. Brockstine, after reading the report in November 2014 from Mayo Clinic, totally ignored our phone calls and after I left 20 messages, he did not call back. I called the ex-chairman of the Evanston Hospital, Dr. Janardan Kanedkar in his house and he was shocked and told me he would make sure someone would call but no one did. Dr. Kanedkar called me after two days and enquired if someone had called. I said no. He said someone would call, and he is going to get involved. He also would ask Brockstine to call. Janardan Kanedkar, in my opinion, had hired Brockstine.

On November 26 at 6:30, Brockstine left a message on our landline, as I had gone to get food, and Constance was in her room and was unable to get to the phone right away. Brockstine left a message saying, "Mrs. And Mr. Berry, this is Dr. Brockstine. I am sorry I could not call back as I was discussing the next course of action for Mrs. Berry. Now, I am going to give this case to Dr. Merkel." I have saved that message, and it can be a great testimony in the court, attorney general office, or wherever, plus 32 minutes of video was made in the hospital in Constance Berry's room. Plus the falsifying report and one page where these so-called doctors wrote, "Mrs. Berry said-nodded-said-nodded-said-after we asked her if she wants her tube out? She nodded as she was unable to talk due to the tubes all over her mouth and neck."

Crime always leaves some traces to solve. What is the crime? This is, in my opinion. She said yes, when they asked her if she can die. She is not able to talk yet they claimed she said, "Yes. I want to die. I want to die right now. Do you want to go home?" Constance said, "No, I want to die in the hospital." "Constance, do you want your husband to make a decision?" Constance said, "No." "Do you want your brother to make a decision?" Constance said, "Yes." Constance could never ever have uttered these words as Michael never wanted to be in the picture and never ever came to see her for years, until now—March 21, 2016. Constance Berry, my wife, died on February 28. Michael and his large family of grown-up kids and grandchildren have not even come nor called. They did not even come for her cremation, ashes—plot, stone—or to see me. No one bothered. Michael called me on the 29th and asked if I knew about her finances. I said no. He said, "You must know." I said, "No." He said, "You better hire an attorney to find out." He again called at a later time for money. They wanted to know how much money my darling wife had and how much she left for them as they were wealthy. They offered to send their forty-year-old daughter to help me find the papers where her money was? I said, "I do not want anyone to come." God has given me the power to find everything. She has left some for four kids as far as I know. Our 42 years relation has gone to the dogs in one day. Would anyone believe that Constance wanted her greedy brother to make a decision? I am grateful to God that I was alive to do my darling wife's best cremation, ashes in her plot, getting the best stone engraved. Otherwise, Michel would have said, "I do not have money. Let the hospital consider her charity case or whatsoever. These are the other human beings, only one real brother. I can tell more and more about what they did to his own mother, father, and later to sister. Why did Dr. Brockstine come in my absence? Why did he not come when I was there 24/7 for eight days? Why did he come when he was not Constance's doctor? Constance had told the nurses and staff when she got admitted that she did not want to see Brockstine and Winslow as they wanted to talk to us for something. Constance said no. Why did he come to the cardiac ICI unit when Constance was there? Dr. Brockstine was no longer her doctor. He is not an expert in cardiac treatment. He is a Head and Neck Cancer expert. In my true opinion, he came well planned to take Constance's life; to let her die to save himself from his fear of a lawsuit from Constance if she survives. He did not know that her loving husband Pradeep Berry is a very strong and dedicated husband who had left his high-powered job in 2005 to be with Constance all the time, every single appointment, any treatment, MRI, CAT scan, PET scan, visit with Constance at each appointment. Pradeep used to tell him, let us go for the second opinion and ask millions of questions that doctor you gave four extra chemotherapy sessions in March 2013 and you did not want us to go in 2013 to see other doctors after her lungs got bad by side effects of chemo in July 2013. I used to take Constance weekly for taking the water out in the intervention radiology water out from her lungs. He never bothered to take much pain.

It was Dr. Dunbar in Florida who prescribed Faslodex injection and not Dr. Brockstine. They did not mention that it was Dr. Dunbar who gave or prescribed and that Dr. Brockstine took his advice. If Dunbar did not prescribe Faslodex. God knows Constance would have had a much more handicapped situation. In two years, my Connie would become incapacitated, and Dr. Brockstine and Dr. Winslow did not care. If I am the prosecutor, I would make him sweat or have him mention in his own words in the court. The judge and the jury would see how these two doctors would try to run or hide or leave the country or whatnot. They have done a blunder. They are free birds, enjoying and thanks to our law, which is not protecting the real individuals but people who lost some money from phone, consumer, and store. He may not get a job, but at least he is free to do any work, or get Medicare or go on the food stamps. He is still alive. Someone may make a movie on his life. He may write a book and people would buy in millions. Should the law be more to go after them or should it be much stronger for people like me whose life has vanished due to other people's mistakes? In my opinion, we worship so-called medical doctors like God. They are not. Medical records from Florida Cancer Center in Fort Meyers can be proof that it was oncologist Dr. Dunbar who was able to help her water dry up. We had been going to Sanibel for the last 14 years, and that is why we went there as part of Constance's treatment for eight weeks, every winter to escape the cold. Where is the paper that states, "We prepared the documents and Mrs. Constance Berry signed it by giving her consent." Where is that document? Where is that? I have called risk management multiple times. They sent me an email claiming that they do not have that document.

Dr. Merkel said I am surprised and angry as to why Brockstine and Winslow did not consult him with his over 30 years of practice and experience. Why Brockstine came to the cardiac unit and wrote whatever when I was absent. Why did he not come when I was there to take my permission? What would I do if it wasn't for my wife as I had the power of her heath care attorney and they all knew that I was the one who had to release her body, do the cremation, get all the legal documents, and what not? Her brother had no power whatsoever. Why did Brockstine and other doctors get called in my absence? I would have never ever allowed them to inform Michael according to my wife's wishes as she never even wanted to see them or wanted me to even let them know. She was very upset that Michael had given a very bad time to his own father, mother and now to her younger sister with the 'Why did he not report this in the medical records? Why did he not come in the cardiac unit when Pradeep Berry, her husband was there?'

Why did he come when he knew I have the power of attorney for Connie's health? Why did he come in my absence, why? It's proof by itself? He had a well-thought-out plan to do damage to eliminate the witness, thereby avoiding a lawsuit against him. That is why he ignored us for 22 days after we came from Mayo Clinic on November 7, 2014, and then he changed the doctor to Dr. Merkel. His intention was if she survived, then good, but knowing that a cardiac arrest could still save her for some time, he plotted to come in my absence and not in my presence. If he had come in my presence, which I doubt he would have, I would have refused him to enter the room. Further, if he had argued, I would have called the police. Yes, if I think about it, I was under maximum stress. I would have called the police and told them along with the caretaker, Florida Harris, that they have come to let her die. Respected Lisa Madigan-Please take this case seriously and save me from suffering. I would donate the money if there is compensation given to me. I would throw that on Brockstine's and Winslow's faces in front of you and tell them to take their money. In my opinion, they may be getting some cuts from the pharmaceutical companies. If I had the power, I would ask FBI to see their records of money, vacation homes or bank accounts, or another way of making or getting kickbacks.

Why had he called his brother a scapegoat? Where was Michael hiding for 13 months? Why did he not come? Why did Michael ask me to not file a lawsuit? If I file, his and his wife's name should not be part of that. Why can't the FBI trace these calls?

DOCTORS CALLED MICHAEL FULLER ON FACE TIME ON MARCH 28, 2015 MICHAEL FULLER CALLED PRADEEP ASKING WHERE CONNIE IS. PRADEEP REPLIED THAT CONNIE DIED LAST NIGHT AT 1:10 AM. HE SAID, "SORRY," AND HE IMMEDIATELY ASKED, PRADEEP IF HE KNEW ABOUT HER FINANCES. PRADEEP SAID, "NO, MIKE. WHY DO YOU ASK? IS THAT WHAT YOU HAVE LEARNED FROM YOUR WIFE AND WHY?" HE STATED HE BETTER HIRE AN ATTORNEY. OTHERWISE, CONNIE'S MONEY WOULD GO INTO THE PROBATE, AND IF PRADEEP WISHES, HE COULD SEND CARE—HIS YOUNGEST 37-YEAR-OLD DAUGHTER TO SPIT OUT THE PAPERS. PRADEEP DECLINED HIS OFFER KNOWING THAT THEY WANT CONNIE'S MONEY BUT CANNOT COME FOR CONNIE'S CREMATION. SHAMELESS CHURCH GOING FAMILY, ESPECIALLY HIS EVIL SNAKE WIFE. SHAMELESS CHURCH GOING FAMILY, ESPECIALLY HIS EVIL SNAKE WIFE, MRS. FULLER. AN ANIMAL IS BETTER THAN THE FULLERS–THEY HAD NEVER ATTEMPTED TO CONTACT CONNIE UNTIL JANUARY 28, 2020 NOR DOES PRADEEP BERRY WANT TO SEE THEM AS HE BELIEVED THAT THEY WOULD BE AWARDED THE JUSTICE OR PUNISHMENT BY THE SUPREME LORD.

52

My Connie the Life and After My Connie

A CREATIVE MIND, A PRODUCTIVE BRAIN, AND IMPORTANTLY, the silent soul is the greatest in your body. It's been difficult to find a great transcript and the title of a second book on my own personal injury and struggle in life after the death of my darling wife Mrs. Constance A. Berry. I was married to her for 44 years, until her unexpected demise on the sad day of February 28, 2015, at 1:10 a.m. It was a big earthquake in my life, when I was watching her dying through the monitor going down from 60 seconds to 10 then to zero. I was trying to do something to bring her breathing back, shaking her body and feet, her beautiful face, forehead, mouth and lips and the one-way crying kisses on her mouth and chicks and each of her ears, hair, different parts of her body which in reality had a great right on her body as her husband. It was the same body which we both shared on the first night of our honeymoon and after that for 44 years until, two years before as she was sick but at least she was alive in all sickness. She was incapacitated, but that was too accepted by her husband and Connie apologized for not being able to offer herself to her husband. That was the most hurtful thing to remember about how a wife surrenders herself to her husband for him to be physically satisfied, how much a wife has to sacrifice for her husband. That is why Chanakya in 521 BC stated that a wife is a good friend, sister, mother, and acts as a wife for physical therapy. Now, it was the same body but no breathing and life and the other functions that what is called demise or death.

Nature and human beings, including the following crimes against humanity and selfish work with no charities to the needy people who are suffering from a variety of reasons. The uneven distribution of wealth in the world under the applicable law of

God is a crime in the eyes of God. When the sun and moon and the stars on the sky are nature and the act of God are under the hands of the Lord, we may have as much technology and research? Innovation, but our technology can't stop the rain, the tsunami, the snow, the act of nature, the storms, the natural disaster on Earth, and the families. The animals, human beings, buildings, bridges? The water destroyed by the act of God. The only thing that we have in our control? We humans don't even own our bodies. Our body and breathing and air and water are given to us by nature? After our birth by our parents and nourished by food? The body has to be destroyed. It was also stated by the Great Mahatma Buddha, Siddhartha, the King who left his kingdom and his wife and a son to find enlightenment. King Siddhartha saw the tragedies on the way to his own chariot—an old lady suffering from a variety of sicknesses, a dying person, a dead body, and a skeleton of a human being. He was extremely young and his ministers explained to him what he saw was a reality. I'm not sure lots of people might know.

Someone not aware of this message is welcomed by the author Pradeep Berry wrote a wonderful book with knowledge, experience, wisdom of the life, death message to the masses. THE BOOK TITLED MY CONNIE BY PRADEEP BERRY IS AVAILABLE ON AMAZON.COM AND BARNES AND NOBLE. INTERNET ACCESS IN THE WORLD. MY CONNIE IS ABSOLUTELY AMAZING AND BEAUTIFUL WRITTEN BY HER HUSBAND PRADEEP BERRY PRINTED IN THE USA IS A WONDERFUL BOOK OF BIOGRAPHY OF CONNIE DARLING AND PRADEEP BERRY WERE MEANT TO BE ONE SOUL AND TWO BODIES FOR 44 YEARS UNTIL, CONNIE DARLING DEMISED ON FEBRUARY 28, 2015. IN MY OPINION BY MEDICAL NEGLIGENCE INCLUDING HER OWN BIOLOGICAL SIBLINGS PLAYED A VITAL ROLE IN THE LAST-MINUTE BETRAYAL TO HIS OWN BIOLOGICAL SISTER MY CONNIE DARLING WIFE OF 44 YEARS WHEN I WAS ONE HOUR AWAY FROM MY CONNIE IN THE HOSPITAL ON FEBRUARY 27, 2015 AROUND 1 OR 2 PM. AT 1:10 AM MY WIFE AND MY LIFE AND BEST FRIEND CONNIE BERRY DIED UNEXPECTEDLY THIS BOOK IS IN MY LIFE AND HEART AND SOUL AND GOD KNOWS THAT MY CONNIE HAS EXCELLENT HISTORICAL DATA AND MESSAGES FROM THE GREAT SCHOLARS OF THE WORLD INCLUDING GANDHI, DR. NELSON MANDELA, BUDDHA, CHANAKYA NITI IN 521 BC, MUMMIES IN THE ANCIENT CIVILIZATION, THE LORD JESUS AND KRISHNA. THE RAVANA THE GREAT SCHOLAR OF SHRI LANKA. HE WAS KILLED BY THE LORD RAM A GREAT IN CREATION OF LORD

VISHNU. LORD RAM FINALLY KILLED RAVANA. AFTER HIS DYING POSITION, LORD RAMA ASKED HIS BROTHER LAXMAN TO ASK HIM FOR SOME KNOWLEDGE. RAVANA REFUSED TO GIVE. LORD RAMA TOLD HIM THAT HE SHOULD GO TO HIS FEET. THAT TIME LORD RAMA ASKED HIM, "OH KING OF SRI LANKA, PLEASE DON'T TAKE AWAY THE KNOWLEDGE, PLEASE GIVE THIS KNOWLEDGE TO US." RAVANA SAID, "PLEASE DO NOT MISS THE GOOD. I WISH, I WAS YOUR TEACHER RATHER THAN KIDNAP HER." HE STATED ALWAYS TO DO A JOB WHICH VARIES DEPENDING UPON THE CENTER. HE GAVE LORD RAMA 10 ADVISES.

My consolation for losing my Connie was the most terrible thing that happened to me in my 44 years of prime age. In my life, the death of Connie was a great shocking thing I saw in my life, which I would never ever be able to get out of my mind. This haunts me every second of my life. The impact of this demise of my Connie would be alive till I meet and get her again.

Please note that my late wife was a victim of medical negligence, in my opinion, and per the medical records and videos taken when she was alive in the hospital in Illinois USA. But these so-called medical doctors are well covered in the hospital and by their medical colleagues and system. This is the USA, and justice was not done on her death after getting a report from the best hospital in the USA, Stating that medical negligence was there and her reports. I have all the medical records of my darling and precious wife. The only book was written by her husband and after her death in February 2015.

Knowing that two years trying to get the latest opinion was a mental struggle. Request if someone would come to help. Refused to go to the world best. Please note that my late wife was a victim of medical negligence, in my opinion, and per the medical records and videos taken when she was alive in the hospital in Illinois US. But these so-called medical doctors are well covered in the hospital and by their medical colleagues and system. This is the USA, and justice was not done on her death after getting a report from the best planet hospital in the USA, Stating that medical negligence was there and her reports. I have all the medical records of my darling and precious and precious wife. KNOWING THAT TWO YEARS TRYING TO GET THE THE LATEST OPINION WAS MIND STRUGGLE. REQUEST IF SOMEONE WOULD COME TO HELP. REFUSED TO GO TO THE WORLD'S BEST. Please note that my late wife was a victim of medical negligence, in my opinion, and per the medical records and videos taken when she was alive in the hospital in Illinois, USA. But these so-called medical doctors are well covered in the hospital and by their medical colleagues and system. This is the US, and justice was not done on her death after getting a report from the best planet hospital in the US, Stating that medical negligence was there and her reports. I have all the medical records of my darling and precious and precious wife.

I request sixty minutes on Channel 2 on Saturday at 6 p.m. invite me to expose the medical records being, in my opinion, were falsified to save the medical doctors in Illinois. Please contact me if you want to do the great work God wants us to do. Pradeep Berry thanks Mr. Choudhary or Mac Sahib. I have written an excellent book available on Amazon and Barnes and Noble. God bless my wife of 44 years, who was a pioneer in making my life success to success. It was a great love, not too many people can have. I owe my life to her. Connie was born in Glenview, Illinois, a rich suburb of Chicago or Illinois with one elder brother, Michael Fuller. Miss. Constance Ann Fuller met me with her student in an Indian restaurant at 1543 North Wells Chicago. Right across Second City. MY CONNIE by Pradeep Berry. Interview with Good Morning America and Europe F Times, Washington Post. US GENERAL. CHANNEL IN ATLANTA AND MIAMI BOOK FAIR ON NOVEMBER 17 TO 19. THIS BOOK HAS BEEN A POPULAR FOR A LONG TIME NOW. CAME IN THE MARKET END OF JUNE. THANKS. CONNIE LEFT CHARITIES TO 12 DIFFERENT UNIVERSITIES AND HOSPITALS AND POOR PEOPLE WHO ARE GOING TO SCHOOL AND COLLEGE. I MISS MY CONNIE THE LIFE OF MY OWN.

53

My Connie Her Death—My New Experiences

Many days of the years from February 28, 2015, were spent in crying and power to get my life in order until December 14, 2017, and going on. It was February 20, 2015. My darling wife Connie Berry, as my life and power to get to go to the hospital in the US for her third chemotherapy to get better after Mayo Clinic November 6, 2014, stated that she stated that she is a palliative care patient. But that was not in our biography of *My Connie,* the first book. Thanks for your nice work to try to return the wallet. I am a great follower of honesty and good deeds. *My Connie,* the best book on the USA network by Pradeep Berry from Evanston, IL, USA, was a wealth of information on life and noble cause caring for my life and power.

MY CONNIE BY PRADEEP BERRY FROM EVANSTON, IL USA, WAS WRITTEN BY PRADEEP BERRY IN MEMORY OF HIS DARLING WIFE CONNIE BERRY FROM EVANSTON, IL, USA. IT IS A WEALTH OF INFORMATION ON LIFE AND NOBLE CAUSE CARING FOR THE HUMANITIES AND SOCIAL WORK. MY CONNIE BY PRADEEP BERRY FROM EVANSTON, IL, USA, ON AMAZON AND GOOGLE AND BARNES AND NOBLE IS THE BEST BOOK.

My Connie was a graduate of the University of Michigan in Ann Arbor and University of Carleton College in Northfield Minnesota University and Ph.D. from the University of Spain international in Mexico and South America and Central America and university and Philippines to teach the students and military personnel in this USA and world. MY CONNIE BY PRADEEP BERRY. Thanks for your help. Thanks for your nice WORK TO try to return the wallet. I am a great follower of honesty and good deeds.

MY CONNIE THE BEST BOOK ON THE USA NETWORK BY PRADEEP BERRY FROM EVANSTON, IL, USA, WAS A WEALTH OF INFORMATION ON LIFE AND NOBLE CAUSE CARING FOR MY LIFE AND POWER. MY CONNIE BY PRADEEP BERRY FROM EVANSTON, IL, USA, WAS WRITTEN BY ME, PRADEEP BERRY, IN MEMORY OF MY DARLING WIFE CONNIE BERRY FROM EVANSTON, IL, USA, IS A WEALTH OF INFORMATION ON LIFE AND NOBLE CAUSE CARING FOR THE HUMANITIES AND SOCIAL WORK. MY CONNIE BY PRADEEP BERRY FROM EVANSTON, IL, USA, ON AMAZON AND GOOGLE AND BARNES AND NOBLE THE BEST BOOK. MY CONNIE WIFE WAS A GRADUATE OF THE UNIVERSITY OF MICHIGAN IN AN ARBOR AND UNIVERSITY OF CARLTON COLLEGE IN NORTHFIELD MINNESOTA AND UNIVERSITY AND Ph.D. FROM UNIVERSITY OF SPAIN INTERNATIONAL IN MEXICO AND SOUTH AMERICA AND CENTRAL AMERICA AND UNIVERSITY AND PHILIPPINES TO TEACH THANKS FOR YOUR HELP YAHOO MAIL ON ANDROID. ONLY ONE THING. MY CONNIE DARLING WIFE OF 44 YEARS IN THE USA AND INDIA.

THE BOOK MY CONNIE BY PRADEEP BERRY IS AVAILABLE ON MORE THAN A MILLION WORTH AMAZON AND BARNES AND NOBLE. THIS BOOK IS ABSOLUTELY AMAZING AND BEAUTIFUL WRITTEN BY HER HUSBAND PRADEEP BERRY PRINTED IN THE USA. THE BOOK MY CONNIE BY PRADEEP BERRY IS A WONDERFUL STORY CUM BIOGRAPHY OF CONNIE DARLING AND PRADEEP BERRY, WHO WERE MEANT TO BE ONE SOUL, BUT TWO BODIES. CONNIE DARLING WAS CONNIE DARLING AND PRADEEP BERRY WENT THROUGH THE LIFE AND HEART AND SOUL AND HAPPINESS. WHEN SHE WAS ALIVE UNTIL FEBRUARY 28, 2015 WITH SOME HOPE THAT SHE IS NOT GOING TO DIE BUT THE UNHAPPINESS WAS ALREADY WAS INSTRUMENTAL IN OUR LIVES SINCE JUNE 2013 WHEN THE ONCOLOGIST TREATING HER HAD RUINED HER CANCER TREATMENT OF THE PAROTID GLAND. SO MANY THINGS HAD HAPPENED DURING THIS TIME. HOWEVER, THE WORST WAS ON NOVEMBER 7, 2014 WHEN MAYO CLINIC DETECTED THE MEDICAL NEGLIGENCE IN MY OPINION AND MEDICAL RECORDS STATED THAT SHE WAS A PALLIATIVE CARE AND HAVE A SHORT TIME TO LIVE IN OUR LIVES. PRADEEP BERRY AND CONSTANCE A. BERRY AFTER COMING BACK FROM The Mayo Clinic stated, Pradeep, earlier Dr. BB ruined her life and now he is taking her life. This sentence would be in my life, and heart and soul would remain a painful message as Connie darling's demise on February 28, 2015. The book *My Connie* was not given the opportunity to write the facts of the medical negligence in my opinion, and the negative side of her family that her biological brother and henpecked husband of his wife and four adult children and their children totaling 17 members never ever came to visit Connie darling and shameless family wanted money gifts and each of these children and adults are puppets in their mother who is the most important part of their 17 family members. Shameless family. Connie Darling was very important in my life, and heart had told me that her brother's wife and children can't come due to the influence of Connie's sister-in-law and a smooth transition woman. She would pay for the evil things she has been doing in the last 20 years unless you are her yes person like her friend Sandy.

CONSPIRACY

MORE THAN A MILLION-WORTH IS A TRAGIC story of loss, redeemed by the courage of one-man seeking justice above all else. Late one February night, 2015, Constance Ann Berry asked her doctor and medical staff to change the Do Not Resuscitate code to full code. The sign was noticed by her husband, Pradeep Berry. She and her husband, Pradeep Berry, had been together in Evanston Hospital since the early hours of February 20. Constance had fallen faint that morning; Pradeep remembers her collapsing to the floor, helpless. The paramedics came, rushing in to take her to the hospital. "She'll be fine, sir," they'd said. "Preventative check." Two days later, with all signs looking clear, Constance looked like she would be okay to be discharged on the 23rd. The doctor and medical staff had long taken care of Connie's request, telling the quiet couple that the DNR code had been changed. They were both relieved; it seemed they were in good hands. Constance Fuller was born a United States citizen. A beautiful, bright girl who entered the world, hungry for knowledge, and was soon studying at some of the country's finest institutions. Her goal? To one day, give back everything she had learned. To become a teacher.

For 34 years, teaching was her passion, and her students loved her dearly for it. Later in life, she would begin teaching without salary-giving up her spare time to go to the library and further the education of children and students in her area. She paid her taxes, donated to charities she believed in, and supported her fellow countrymen and women in times of war and peace alike. For all of this, her husband Pradeep Berry-author of the eye-opening book, *More Than a Million-worth* has one question: Didn't she deserve her medical staff's full attention and care? It was around 6:30 pm on a calm February evening: a moment Pradeep Berry could never forget. They were together; Constance just eating a salad; Pradeep, beside her, talking. Suddenly, Connie began to feel short of breath. This was never a good sign-Pradeep had learned this a long time ago. Since quitting his high-profile position in the financial world to be with his sick wife, he had learned a thing or two about her condition. He informed Constance's caretaker and the nursing staff immediately.

This wasn't normal, though. Pradeep could see that it wasn't helping, and he wanted someone to do something about it. He asked them what was wrong, but they couldn't tell him. They only waited, watching her as if from some great distance, unable to act. Pradeep began to call out for help. He shouted until the medical staff arrived. They knew exactly what was happening—it was an early sign of cardiac arrest. 'She needs CPR,' they told him, but they didn't do anything. They just stood there, hesitating. Pradeep couldn't understand, 'Can't you do something, then!' 'I'm sorry, sir. We can't do anything while that DNR sign is hanging out front…'Pradeep Berry believes that those nine minutes of hesitation had sealed his poor Connie's fate. He had shouted at them to do something. 'What do you mean you can't do anything? She's dying!' He was furious, raging 'like a ferocious tiger', as the Indian-born author would later describe himself. It's a good thing he had. Without his insistence, he believes the staff would not have acted at all.

Following the attack, Constance Berry was put on a ventilator for two weeks. Pradeep sat by her side all the way through, fretting over his wife's condition and doing whatever he could to assist with her recovery.

In early March, Pradeep Berry would need to make a decision. With the full power of attorney over Connie's bodily care, he would need to decide what the next step would be to keep her in palliative care or to take her home and make efforts at recovery there. Fortunately, the decision would not be so difficult. His Connie had already thought of everything.

Many years earlier, Constance Berry had told Pradeep that she didn't want to die in a hospital. 'I want to die in our beautiful home,' she'd said. 'In my bedroom. If I must go, I want to do it peacefully, in a place that I love and with dignity.' Pradeep wanted to be sure that he'd remembered her words correctly: He read them to her in the hospital. By that stage, Connie couldn't respond verbally. Reduced to body language by those awful tubes and wires, she looked to her husband and smiled. She nodded her consent. She wanted to die in her beautiful home, not in this cold hospital.

Sadly, her wish would not be granted. Connie had never gotten along with her family. She didn't trust her sibling, Michael, either. It was no surprise to Pradeep when they didn't come to visit her at the hospital; they hadn't seen each other in over a year.

He was sad, however, when they didn't make the effort to attend any of the services since that final day… Not the cremation, not even to say their last goodbyes; only a phone call, inquiring about the status of Constance's finances, and clearing their names from the the script should any lawsuit be filed on Mr. Berry's behalf. They had known that their dear Constance wasn't well, but still, they didn't visit. Perhaps, Pradeep couldn't even blame them for this-it was tough enough for him to see his angel in her condition. It must be difficult for them, too, he thought. No, the real problem would only show itself later: when Michael's the name appeared in the medical records.

Why was Dr. Brockstine calling Michael on the other side of the country, when Pradeep himself was only a moment away? Knowing full and well that Mr. Berry was in charge of Constance's well-being, that he was her adoring husband and had important information regarding the care of Constance Berry, why was he bypassed on such an important decision? And why would her absent brother Michael's name appear in the medical record when he had never set foot in that hospital?

These were some questions that plagued Pradeep for weeks, months, and they have inspired him to tell his fascinating story. A tale of falsified documents, medical negligence, and a quest for justice.

When the social director, Ruth, told Pradeep that he needed to go home, he thought she was just looking out for him. She said it would be bad for his health to spend so many hours by Connie's side—that he should take a break and get out of the hospital. It soon became clear there was more to it than that. Suddenly, Ruth was insisting that he leave the hospital at 8:30 pm when visiting hours close. None of the other staff had told him that he needed to leave. They seemed to appreciate his presence there, and besides, they knew that he had no other choice. He wouldn't leave his Connie's side if they had to drag him kicking and screaming. Just imagine it: going home to an empty house, knowing that your wife lies sick and dying in hospital. Alone, cold, afraid, and if she were to wake up at any moment without you by her side, what if that were the difference? That if you were away for just a moment, you may never have a chance to speak with her again? No… going home was the last thing on Pradeep's mind. Thank you very much, Ruth. But he would rather stay.

Here, the tale takes a turn for the worse, as Pradeep Berry goes on to explain how medical negligence served a crucial role in his wife's passing. He is convinced that if it weren't for a few key actors, she might have been given a second lease on life. When Dr. Brockstine wouldn't return his calls, Pradeep knew something was off. He'd left 20 messages without receiving a callback. He even called the ex-chairman of the hospital, hoping that he might intervene. The ex-chairman, Dr. Kanedkar, seemed like a nice fellow. He said that he was shocked. "I'll speak with Dr. Brockstine right away." Two days went by without a word, and Dr. Kanedkar called again to ask if Pradeep had heard anything.

"Nothing."

"Oh my. I will take care of this. Don't worry, Mr. Berry." When nothing followed those phone calls, Pradeep Berry became very concerned. In light of all the facts, he is now convinced that the medical records have been deliberately falsified. Along with video records and evidence of false inclusions to the report, he is committed to finding the truth—to giving his Connie the justice she deserves. Most alarmingly, Pradeep found one full page transcript in the report which simply never happened:

- "We asked her if she wants her tubes out. She nodded."
- She said, "Yes, I want to die."
- "Do you want to go home?" Constance replied, "No, I want to die in the hospital."
- "Do you want your husband to make a decision?" Constance replied, "No."
- "Do you want your brother to make a decision?" Constance replied, "Yes," nodding.

Pradeep Berry will never forgive himself for leaving the hospital. After days on end, he had finally given in to Ruth's request and went home to run some errands and make sure their family home was in order. In those hours, he is sure that the medical staff took their opportunity. "If I'd only been there," he laments, "They could never get away with this."

That being said, he still believes that it is an open and shut case. Pradeep Berry is sure that any attorney of law would be walking into the easiest victory of their career. The land is already laid; the plot is set. Pradeep has the falsified documents, he has video footage implicating the medical staff of Evanston Hospital, and he is prepared to do whatever it takes to see the case through. Beyond a call for help, though, this book is a story of one man's undying love for his wife. It is a tale of justice, of standing up against the wrongs of the world and fighting until it is set right. Whatever the cost.

The book leaves us with one final image to remember: "I go to her grave and touch the stone," narrates Pradeep. He puts his head to the ground, holding the grass and soil, and he asks, "Connie, please bless me so that I will reach justice. Speak with God and grant me this miracle so that you can truly rest in peace. It is all that I ask."

Complement this sad but inspiring tale with author Pradeep Berry's first book, *My Connie,* is an uplifting insight into the lasting love that sustained over 40 years of dedicated marriage. *More Than a Million-worth* is available for purchase on

Amazon. com. For a tragic look inside the workings of our current medical system and an inspiring message of love, justice, and fortitude, Pradeep Berry's courageous tale is a must-read for anyone curious about the power of love and the lengths to which it can take us.

The author would almost change his mind and fly back home during a stopover at the Frankfurt airport in Germany, But the the seven-dollar worth of bills in his pocket wasn't enough to buy a ticket back, and so his fate was sealed.

Although young Pradeep had misgivings and felt terribly lonely during his first days in Chicago, a miracle did happen.

He met Miss. Constance Ann Fuller, a beautiful and intelligent young woman on the historic North Wells Street in Chicago. It was love at first sight.

Brewed in an Indian restaurant and sealed in a Chicago court days later! Despite there being no family members present, Connie and Berry were delighted to legalize their union on January 29th, 1976.

According to the author, the chemistry was instant during the first meeting. No other meetings were needed to realize that the couple was destined for each other's arms. And true to that, the marriage would last a lifetime!

This book is a moving personal tribute to one man's deep love of his spouse. Ifs a two-part story. In one part, the author shares the story of a love like no other, shared memories and challenges overcame. It shows that true love is possible!

In the second part, the story takes a twist when sadness that is hard to define and understand takes over happiness.

While most of the book is a narrative about the author's love for his love Connie, the book also offers a glimpse of his life in India before meeting his lovely spouse.

It offers details about an unhappy childhood, the loss of a mother, and a painful atmosphere at home. The author describes meeting his wife Connie as something that catapulted his life into the "best destiny".

Before leaving India, Pradeep graduated from the Shri Ram College of Commerce at the University of Delhi. He was also an eagle scout swimming champion and a chartered accountant from the Institute of Chartered Accountants of India.

While in the US, Pradeep had a very successful career in the financial sector. His employer Heller International, a unit of Fuji bank, acquired Walter Heller, a finance company in Chicago, and Pradeep was sponsored to the Kellogg Graduate School of Management at Northwestern University for the MBA program.

CONNIE studied at Glenbrook high school, Carleton College, the University of Michigan, as well as abroad in Spain and Mexico. She would go on to have a very successful academic career with PHO and MBA qualifications from Carleton College, University of Michigan, and Harvard.

Glenbrook High School Carleton College The University of Michigan Connie worked as a Spanish, French, and German teaching professor in the US, Germany, France, and Spain. She became the star of the family!

Yes. This highly educated academic girl met and married Pradeep Berry. Pradeep Berry worked in the country, as well as abroad, while on assignments in Europe. Now a retired banker, Mr. Pradeep Berry, pours out his love for his wife and their incredible journey together!

In a thorough, heartfelt language, the author remembers how Connie was a great reader and how he would soon pick the same habit to his own benefit! She would read anything to nourish her academic appetite and recommend interesting topics to Pradeep.

The author believes that Connie helped reinforce the reading habit in him. He found himself devouring business sections of all newspapers and professional development, articles on different topics, and anything valuable they could both lay their hands on.

This shared reading habit is one of the author's fond memories with his beloved spouse—Constance Berry. In this unique book, Mr. Pradeep also shares Connie's passion for exploring different foods, restaurants, Broadway plays, and symphonies—as a way of unwinding from life's hustle and bustle.

MORE THAN A MILLION WORTH

Pradeep has valuable memories of their travel in the world together.

He remembers how Connie used to plan the best ocean and river cruises! How they had wonderful trips both within the USA and other exclusive destinations in the world, How his exposure to travel would have been limited without dear Connie in the picture, And how they traveled many times to exciting and nostalgic places in his native India—including the "Palace on Wheels".

Mr. Pradeep particularly describes the Palace on Wheels in India as a beautiful destination that he would recommend to everyone. This historical destination was designed for kings during the British Empire in colonial times.

Palace On Wheels

He also remembers and recommends the Taj Mahal—one of India's foremost tourist destination. People write books all the time!

But sometimes, we see a book that stares into our soul and changes our perspective. *My Connie* is one such book! It shows the love immortal—a miracle! And not only that, Mr. Pradeep shares a wealth of information on life and love.

Making this text a priceless read not only for married couples but also for young people! The book highlights the challenges they overcame and how they attained a happy marriage for over 40 years.

Life and Love Mr. Pradeep abruptly lost the love of his life and had to face a new reality. My Connie offers deep insight into the paradox of life. It explores the happy times shared beautifully by a couple that deeply loved each other, and then there are the sad times.

Pradeep reveals the challenges they overcame together when Connie started getting ill. He remembers fondly how he was dedicated to serving her tea and juice in the morning. How life changed when Connie would find it painful walking to the kitchen for breakfast, having to go to her study room with a walker and portable oxygen.

And how during these trying moments, he found his greatest happiness in serving her! Making the best breakfast and dinner for her and helping in every way he could. Mr. Pradeep Berry, through this book, shows that we can find true happiness in the smallest acts of service to those whom we love.

Acts like taking your spouse to the hospital for that doctor's appointment, offering a cup of tea or water and being a source of encouragement during trying moments! Quitting his job just wasn't enough for Pradeep Berry to serve his partner!

He went above and beyond to be there when he was needed most, and derived happiness by being there for his partner during these challenging moments. The author reckons how Connie remained extremely positive through her illness, and how he summoned his own faith for strength, slept only three to four hours per night, and made this struggle his own!

As fate would have, the unbearably sad phase in this rare union would start on February 29, 2015. This was the day when Pradeep Berry lost his dearly beloved wife—CONNIE. He remembers how it all started eight days before this fateful date.

His beloved wife falling on the floor at 4 am, him summoning an ambulance, and taking her to the emergency room!!

How those breath-taking moments seemed to stop time in its very tracks, and how he fought bitterly like a ferocious tiger to have his beloved Connie accorded the most professional medical care that she deserved.

It is the author's opinion that the unfortunate death of Connie on February 29, 2015, was a result of great medical negligence by Dr. Bruce Brockstine.

He wonders why Bruce Brockstine had to call CONNIE's brother Mike Fuller to Sanibel Island, Florida to discuss details of his wife. When he could just wait one hour to let him make the decision to have his darling put on a rehabilitation center.

Pradeep painfully explains how medical records show evidence of foul play, and he feels he was betrayed by family members-even worse denied his constitutional rights! Mr. Pradeep remembers that when Connie had a cardiac arrest while at the hospital, CPR was delayed—and later only performed when he ferociously complained.

He's also astonished that Connie's siblings did not come to her cremation or any service but would be there to take the money she left for her nephews and siblings. When you lose a loved one, the grief can be devastating. We all react differently as we try to cope! Writing this book, *My Connie,* was the author's way of coping with this overwhelming grief, as well as being let down by close family members!

When Connie died at 1:10 on that fateful February night. Pradeep remembers how he stayed up until the body was washed and taken to the cremation. Connie's brother, Mike Fuller, called him the following morning to ask about her. Upon learning that she had died, he said neither he nor his wife Suzanne Fuller would make it to pay the last respect.

They insensitively proceeded to ask questions about Connie's finances, suggesting that the grieving husband should hire an attorney for that purpose. Mike Fuller and his wife even pushed the author not to mention their names in the case he filed a medical negligence lawsuit.

It was unbelievable that all they wanted was money! And Pradeep was taken aback by their greed and callousness! But he took comfort in the fact that he had been an excellent husband and knew that his beloved wife was in peace.

All these revelations make the book such a deep, personal read! Although this book lays bare a devoted husband's struggle with losing a soulmate, it emphasizes Connie's strengths and highlights the couple's incredibly happy marriage! The author writes to cherish priceless memories after losing his soul mate through medical negligence.

In so doing, Pradeep Berry shares the secrets of their successful and happy marriage with the world, which all the same makes this book a valuable read for both the married and those who are yet to be married.

The author quotes many sources to support his feelings about Connie—from renowned Indian thinkers such as Gandhi and Chanakya to Westerners such as Einstein and Ruskin. He lists small items that remind him of Connie, such as articles of clothing, a diary, a make-up kit, and more. Articles of clothing, a diary, a make-up kit, and more…

He snares his reluctance to use some items that so personally remind him of her, and yet he cannot give these things up, or stop the flow of memories that they bring. This personally thorough book offers deep insight into what it feels like to struggle with the loss of a spouse or family member, and Pradeep Berry empties his heart without worrying about the choice of words or grammatical correctness.

MORE THAN A MILLION WORTH

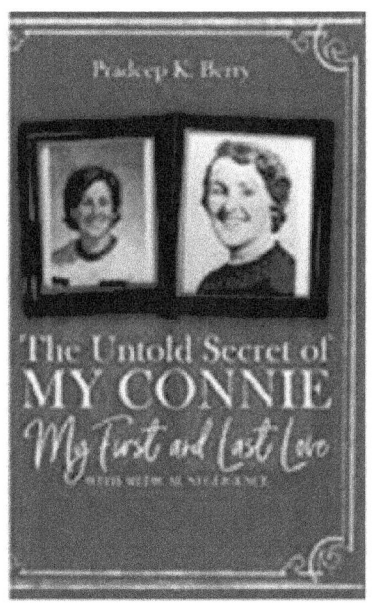

Telling the heartfelt bitter truth! He wrote this book to expose the medical negligence he believes led to the loss of his beloved Connie. He also expresses how Connie's brother, sister-in-law, and their four children never ever came to attend her cremation! In writing these books, the author hopes to let go of the feelings that have so become part of his daily life. On top of that, he hopes to share with the world their unusual love and lessons everyone can learn from it.

And in yet another moving show of the unbreakable bond, Pradeep established MY CONNIE FOUNDATION on her birthday in 2018 to support educational, cancer treatment, and hospice care missions.

MY CONNIE FOUNDATION

Join the author as he shares his story of love, loss, and so much more! Get your copy on amazon.com, authorhouse.com, or Barnes and Noble today!

SYNOPSIS

More Than a Million-worth is a tragic story of loss redeemed by the courage of one man seeking justice above all else. Late night, February 2015, Constance Berry asked her doctor and medical staff to change the "Do Not Resuscitate" code to full code. This sign was noticed by her husband Pradeep Berry. She and her husband, Pradeep Berry, have been together in Evanston Hospital since the early hours of February 20. Constance has fallen faint that morning. Pradeep remembers her collapsing to the floor, helpless. The paramedics came rushing in to take her to the hospital. "She'll be fine, sir," they said, doing a preventative check. Two days later, with all signs looking clear, Constance looks like she'll be ok to be discharged on the 23rd. The doctor and medical staff have long been taking care of Connie's request, telling the quiet couple that the DNR code has been changed. They were both relieved. It seems they were in good hands. Constance Fuller was born a United States citizen, a beautiful, bright girl. She entered the world hungry for knowledge and soon was studying in the country's finest institutions. Her goal was to one day give back everything she's learned to become a teacher. For 34 years, teaching was her passion and her students loved her dearly for it. Later in life, she began teaching without salary, giving her spare time to go to the library and further the education of children and students in her area. She paid her taxes, donated to charity, believed in and supported her fellow countrymen and women in times of war and peace alike. For these, her husband, Pradeep Berry, author of the eye-opening book, *More Than a Million-worth* has one question; didn't she deserve her medical staff's full attention and care? It was around 6:30 pm on a one February evening, a moment Pradeep Berry could never forget. They were together. Constance was just eating a salad, and Pradeep was beside her, talking. Suddenly she began to feel short of breath which was never a good sign. Pradeep has learned this a long time ago. Since quitting his high-profile position in the financial world to be with his sick wife, he had learned about her condition. He informed Constance, her caretaker, and the nursing staff immediately. This wasn't normal though. Pradeep could see that it wasn't helping, and he wanted someone to do something about it. He asked them what was wrong, but they couldn't tell him. They only waited, watching her as if from some great distance unable to act. Pradeep began to call out for help. He shouted until the medical staff arrived. They knew exactly what was happening. It was an early sign of cardiac arrest. They told him she needs CPR but they didn't do anything. They just stood there hesitating. Pradeep couldn't understand. "Can't you do something then?" They only said, "I'm sorry, Sir. We can't do anything while that DNR sign is hanging out front." Pradeep believes that those nine minutes of hesitation have sealed his poor Connie's faith. He had shouted at them to do something. "What do you mean you can't do anything? She is dying." He was furious, raging like a ferocious tiger. As the Indian-born author would later describe himself, it's a good thing he had because, without his insistence, he believes the staff would not have activated it all. Following the attack, Constance Berry was put on a ventilator for two weeks. Pradeep sat by her side all the way through. Threading it over his wife's condition and doing whatever he could to assist her with her recovery. In early March, Pradeep Berry will need to decide with the full power of attorney over his Connie's bodily care; He would need to decide what the next step would be to keep her in palliative care or take her home and make an effort for her recovery there. Fortunately, the decision would not be so difficult. His Connie had already thought of everything. Many years earlier, Constance Berry had told Pradeep that she didn't want to die in a hospital. "I want to die in our beautiful home." She'd said in my bedroom. "If I'd go, I want to do it peacefully in a place that I love and with dignity." Pradeep wanted to be sure that he'd remembered her words correctly. He read them to her in the hospital. By that stage, Connie couldn't respond verbally, reduced to body language by those awful tubes and wires. She looked to her husband and smiled. She nodded her consent. She wanted to die in her beautiful home, not in this cold hospital. Sadly, her wish could not be granted. Connie had never got along with her family. She didn't trust her sibling Michael either. It was no surprise to Pradeep when they didn't come to visit her at the hospital. They had not seen each other for over a year. He was sad however when they didn't make the effort to attend any of the services since that final day, not the cremation, not even to say their last goodbye. Only a phone call inquiring about the status of Constance's finances and clearing their names from the situation should any lawsuit be filed on Mr. Berry's behalf. They had known that their dear Constance wasn't well but still they didn't visit. Perhaps Pradeep couldn't even blame them for this. It was tough enough for him to see his angel on her condition. It must be difficult for them too, he thought. No, the real problem would only show itself later when Michael's name appeared in the medical records. Why was Dr. Brockstine calling Michael on the other side of the country when Pradeep himself was only a moment away knowing full and well that Mr. Berry is in-charge of Constance's well-being? That he was his adoring husband and had important information regarding caring Constance Berry. Why was he bypassed on an important decision and why would her absent brother Michael's name appear on the medical record when he has never in that hospital? These were some questions that would occupy Pradeep for weeks, months, and they had inspired him to tell his fascinating story. A tale of falsified documents, medical negligence, and a quest for justice. When Social Director Ruth told Pradeep that he needed to go home, he thought she was just looking after him. She said it would be bad for his health to spend so many hours by Connie's side. "You should take a break and get out of the hospital." It soon became clear that there's more than do to that. Suddenly, Ruth insisted that he leave the hospital at 8:30 pm when visiting hours close. None of the other staff told him that he needed to leave. They seem to appreciate him being there. Besides, they knew he had no other choice. He wouldn't leave Connie's side if they had to drag him kicking and screaming. Just imagine going home to an empty house knowing that your wife lies sick and dying in the hospital alone, cold and afraid. And if she would wake up at any moment without you by her side, what if they were the difference? That if you were away for just a moment, you might never have the chance to speak to her again. No, going home is the last thing on Pradeep's mind. Thank you very much, Ruth. But he would rather stay. Here, the tale takes a turn for the worst as Pradeep Berry goes on to explain the ways in which medical negligence served a crucial role in his wife's passing. He's convinced that if it weren't for a few key characters, she might have given a second list online. When Dr. Brockstine wouldn't return his call, Pradeep knew something was off. He left 20 messages without receiving a callback. He even called the ex-chairman of the hospital hoping that he might intervene. The ex-chairman seems to be a nice fellow. He said, "I'll speak to Dr. Brockstine right away." Two days went by without a word and the ex-chairman called again to ask if Pradeep had heard anything. Nothing. "Oh my, I will take care of this. Don't worry Mr. Berry." When nothing follows those phone calls, Pradeep Berry became very concerned. In light of all the facts, he is now convinced that the medical records could have been deliberately falsified along with video records and evidence of false inclusions to the report. He is committed to finding the truth to giving Connie the justice she deserves. Most alarmingly, Pradeep found one full-page transcript in the report which simply never happened. We asked her if she wants her tube out, she nodded, she said, "Yes, I want to die." Do you want to go home? Constance replied, "No, I want to die in the hospital." Do you want your husband to make a decision? Constance replied, "No." Do you want your brother to make a decision? Constance replied, "Yes," nodding. Pradeep Berry would never forgive himself for leaving the hospital. After days on end, he finally gave in and went home, ran some errands, and made sure their family home was in order. In those hours, he was sure the medical staff had their opportunity. "If I'd only been there, he laments they could have never gone away with this." That being said, he still believes it's an open-and-check case. Pradeep Berry is sure that any attorney-at-law would be walking into the easiest victory of their career. The land is already laid, the plot is set. Pradeep has the falsified documents. He has video footage, implicating the medical staff of Evanston Hospital, and he is prepared to do whatever it takes to see the case through. The uncalled-for help though is a story of one man undying love for his wife. It's a tale of justice, of standing up the wrongs of the world and fighting until it is set right whatever the cost. The book leaves us with one final image to remember. He goes to her grave and touches the stone as Pradeep narrates. He puts his head to the ground holding the grass and soil and he asks, "Connie, please bless me so that I could reach justice. Speak with God and grant me this miracle so that you can truly rest in peace. It is all that I ask." Complement this said but an inspiring tale with Pradeep Berry's first book *My Connie* and get insights into the lasting love that was sustained over 40 years of dedicated marriage.

MEDICAL REPORTS

Berry, Constance A (MR # 003211828)
Progress Notes by Deamant, Catherine D., MD at 02/27/15 0622 (continued)
- If pt survives the night, recommend hospice enrollment and then transfer to PCU

Thank you for the opportunity to participate in the care of this patient.

Please call with questions or concerns.

Hillarie Joehl, RN, MS, ACNP-BC, ACHPN
Nurse Practitioner
NorthShore University HealthSystem Palliative Care Division
Office: 847-503-4222
Evanston pager: 2747

Total time with patient, husband 4+ hours > 50% spent in education/counseling.

Palliative Medicine Attending Physician Attestation Note:

I have reviewed the medical records, and seen and evaluated this patient, and personally conducted the key elements of the history and exam. I have reviewed and agree with the documentation above, along with the following amendments:

Patient was consistent in her responses through the day while on the ventilator as outlined above with each question posed to her. She shook her head affirmatively that she did not want the ventilator to be continued and with a clear understanding that death could occur shortly after removal of the tube. She also expressed consistently when asked who she trusted to make medical decisions for her if she lost capacity that she selected her brother, Michael C. Fuller. When probed if she thought her husband would be best to make those decisions, she shook her head "no" consistently. When he was present, she still expressed this again. Her husband stated that he did not feel she was able to make decisions and he was informed that she was consistent in her responses and consistent with multiple providers present and on several occasions today and that we will be honoring what the patient is telling us. He expressed that he was upset that her brother had been notified of her condition as he had not called him to let him know that she was in the hospital. He did not believe that she wanted her brother to be able to make decisions for her. We reinforced that it was the patient's request to contact her brother that led us to reach him. Reviewed the patient's conversation with her brother as outlined above. Reviewed that the patient has also been consistent in shaking her head "no" to the question about going home and he was present when she shook her head "yes" to remaining in the hospital until her death. Again, he expressed distress as he felt that she had told him in the past that she wished to be at home. Reinforced that we are listening to the patient's wishes about her care as she is expressing them now and we are guided by the patient's decisions and respecting the choices that she is telling us at this time.

Should the patient survival the night, we will readdress the option of transition to palliative care unit for continued comfort care. Based on the patient's expressed wishes to focus on comfort and allow the natural dying process to occur, I recommend discontinuing medications that do not contribute to her comfort. She has already expressed that she does not want face mask or BiPAP.

Catherine Deamant, MD
Palliative Medicine Physician
NorthShore University HealthSystem
Pager: 8197

Time spent: 9:00-10:30 am; 2:00-3:00 pm; 4:30-6:00 pm

PRADEEP K. BERRY

Berry, Constance A (MR # 003211828)

All Notes (continued)

Progress Notes by Deamant, Catherine D., MD at 02/27/15 0622 (continued)   Version 3 of 3

consistent in her responses and consistent with multiple providers present and on several occasions today and that we will be honoring what the patient is telling us. He expressed that he was upset that her brother had been notified of her condition as he had not called him to let him know that she was in the hospital. He did not believe that she wanted her brother to be able to make decisions for her. We reinforced that it was the patient's request to contact her brother that led us to reach him. Reviewed the patient's conversation with her brother as outlined above. Reviewed that the patient has also been consistent in shaking her head "no" to the question about going home and he was present when she shook her head "yes" to remaining in the hospital until her death. Again, he expressed distress as he felt that she had told him in the past that she wished to be at home. Reinforced that we are listening to the patient's wishes about her care as she is expressing them now and we are guided by the patient's decisions and respecting the choices that she is telling us at this time.

Should the patient survival the night, we will readdress the option of transition to palliative care unit for continued comfort care. Based on the patient's expressed wishes to focus on comfort and allow the natural dying process to occur, I recommend discontinuing medications that do not contribute to her comfort. She has already expressed that she does not want face mask or BiPAP.

Catherine Deamant, MD
Palliative Medicine Physician
NorthShore University HealthSystem
Pager:8197

Time spent: 9:00-10:30 am; 2:00-3:00 pm; 4:30-6:00 pm

Progress Notes by Deamant, Catherine D., MD at 02/27/15 0622   Version 2 of 3

Author: Deamant, Catherine D., MD   Service: Palliative Care   Author Type: Physician
Filed: 02/27/15 2151   Note Time: 02/27/15 0622   Status: Addendum
Editor: Deamant, Catherine D., MD (Physician)
Related Notes: Addendum by Deamant, Catherine D., MD (Physician) filed at 02/27/15 2155
                Original Note by Zzjoehl, Hillarie E., APN-CNP (Advanced Practice Nurse) filed at 02/27/15 2127

NorthShore University HealthSystem Palliative Care Program

Interval History:
Required diltiazem infusion yesterday, now off. Persistent hypocalcemia.

Pt seen with Dr. Deamant, Katie RN, Peggy Lester APN-student. Connie had been off both fentanyl and versed for 1-2 hours. She was awake and alert, communicating clearly and consistently by shaking her head yes and no, also by mouthing words despite ET tube in her mouth. She told us that she was without dyspnea, without pain, without nausea or full feeling.

We asked her if she was comfortable. She said no. We asked her if the ET tube was bothering her. She said yes. We explained to her that she has the ET tube in her mouth/throat, connected to the breathing machine. Explained to her that her lungs have weakened further since her arrest and she has required the support of the breathing machine to continue to breathe. We explained that her pulmonary status has been so weak that if she were to come off the breathing machine, she would likely die within hours or days and would not have a chance of recovery. She understood. We asked her if she wanted to remain on the ventilator to have a chance of recovery AND have tracheostomy and gastrostomy tubes placed for more permanent means of ventilation and nutrition. She said no. We asked her if she wanted the ET tube to come out. She said yes.

Generated on 10/19/2015 8:08 AM   Page 10

MORE THAN A MILLION WORTH

This page perhaps they never wanted to give — until I made many attempts and now they gave me

Berry, Constance A (MR # 003211828)

NORTHSHORE UNIVERSITY HEALTHSYSTEM

Patient Demographics

Name	Patient ID	SSN	Sex	Birth Date
Berry, Constance A	003211828	xxx-xx-8756	Female	02/16/37 (DECEASED)

Address	Phone	EMail	Employer
1310 MAPLE AVE Apt 2B EVANSTON IL 60201	847-328-1355 (H) 312-969-3793 xhusband cell (M)	cfberry@sbcglobal.net	RETIRED

Reg Status	PCP	Date Last Verified	Next Review Date
ELAPSED	Prete, Carole P., MD 847-475-4555	12/04/14	06/02/15

Patient Ethnicity & Race

Ethnic Group	Patient Race
Non-Hispanic	Caucasian

Scan on 2/23/2015 0607 by Fonville-Hibbler, Kimberly A : 2/22/15 arrest (below)

[NorthShore Resuscitation Record form for BERRY, CONSTANCE A, 2/16/1937 Female, Fish, Keith R., MD, CSN: 73701087, Patient ID: 003211828, Date 2/22/15, Time 1834]

This paper was not anywhere in the whole medical report - hiding and had no intention to give it to me

PRADEEP K. BERRY

Berry, Constance A (MR # 003211828)

All Notes (continued)

Progress Notes by Augustin, Catherine, RN at 02/27/15 2338 (continued)   Version 1 of 1
847-475-3002
pgr 6786

Progress Notes by Adegunsoye, Ayodeji O., MD at 02/27/15 2153   Version 1 of 1

Author: Adegunsoye, Ayodeji O., MD	Service: Intensive Care	Author Type: Physician
Filed: 02/27/15 2208	Note Time: 02/27/15 2153	Status: Signed
Editor: Adegunsoye, Ayodeji O., MD (Physician)		

Patient who is currently DNR status noted to be hypotensive with systolic BP in the low 70s. She appears less agitated and calm presently. SpO2 in the 70-80s and supplemental oxygen by nasal cannula increased from 2L to 6L. She has increased oral/airway secretions and appears volume overloaded with anasarca. Husband at bedside and agrees with decision not to give IV fluid boluses given high likelihood of worsening her cardiopulmonary status and increasing airway secretions with respiratory distress. He appears to have come to terms with the patients decision to be terminally extubated. Husband (and family members by phone) offering final prayers. Patients ICU nurse and hospice nurse at bedside throughout above proceedings administering care, comforting the patient and her grieving husband.

[Handwritten: HUSBAND - PRADEEP WAS TOLD and I agreed that TUBES would be TAKEN out on MARCH 2.]

Progress Notes by Deamant, Catherine D., MD at 02/27/15 0622   Version 3 of 3

Author: Deamant, Catherine D., MD	Service: Palliative Care	Author Type: Physician
Filed: 02/27/15 2155	Note Time: 02/27/15 0622	Status: Addendum
Editor: Deamant, Catherine D., MD (Physician)		
Related Notes: Original Note by Deamant, Catherine D., MD (Physician) filed at 02/27/15 2151		

[Handwritten: MJ ABSENT]

NorthShore University HealthSystem Palliative Care Program

[Handwritten: ALL LIES But FRAUD. I was Just went for one hour and Carolakar was there - They look backward of N At]

Interval History:
Required diltiazem infusion yesterday, now off. Persistent hypocalcemia.

Pt seen with Dr. Deamant, Katie RN, Peggy Lester APN-student. Connie had been off both fentanyl and versed for 1-2 hours. She was awake and alert, communicating clearly and consistently by shaking her head yes and no, also by mouthing words despite ET tube in her mouth. She told us that she was without dyspnea, without pain, without nausea or full feeling.

We asked her if she was comfortable. She said no. We asked her if the ET tube was bothering her. She said yes. We explained to her that she has the ET tube in her mouth/throat, connected to the breathing machine. Explained to her that her lungs have weakened further since her arrest and she has required the support of the breathing machine to continue to breathe. We explained that her pulmonary status has been so weak that if she were to come off the breathing machine, she would likely die within hours or days and would not have a chance of recovery. She understood. We asked her if she wanted to remain on the ventilator to have a chance of recovery AND have tracheostomy and gastrostomy tubes placed for more permanent means of ventilation and nutrition. She said no. We asked her if she wanted the ET tube to come out. She said yes. We asked her who she trusts to make medical decisions for her. She said "Mike." We asked if she meant her brother, Michael C. Fuller. She said yes. We asked if she felt Michael was able to make medical decisions for her. She said yes. We asked if she felt comfortable with her husband Pradeep making medical decisions for her. She said no. We asked if she wanted the medical team to let her brother Michael know about the circumstances that brought her to the hospital and update him on her condition. She said yes. We asked her if she wanted to appoint her brother Michael as her health care power of attorney. She said yes. We prepared the document and Connie signed it. We asked Connie if she wanted to die in the hospital. She said yes. We

Generated on 10/19/2015 8:08 AM   Page 6

MORE THAN A MILLION WORTH

Mayo do, that we are not doing" " Mayo is a name and Marketing gimmicks only- but nothing else". We went to Mayo Clinic on November 2, 1014 and came back on November 8th after a most troubling and devastated news From Dr. Katrina Keo- that Connie has to consider Palliative care

11. It was Mayo clinic' Dr. Keo, who stated that she and Mayo do not believe in pat scan, inhaler, and the small amount of water 37MM should have been removed at North. At North, they knew that there was 37MM water but stated" It is not worth taking out" Dr. at Mayo ordered many tests, Bronchoscopy, air test, r 37MM water to be taken out, cardiac test etc. All that took four days.

12. On the fifth day, Dr. Keo said" Mr. and Mrs. Berry, North only relied on Patscan . Broncospy was not done, 37 mm water was not take out at North shore and the Inhaler Dulera has worsened Connie' case.

13. Dr. Keo said "The water become a big thick flame and blocking the lung airways and the cancer has spread in the lung airways as pat scan only shows new spots but not Metastasis of the cancer. As from her words, and medical reports, They made four mistakes.

, If not directly, but indirectly, it is mentioned in the Mayo Clinic Report all these points. If all that report, which is not very lengthy, and any honorable Judge, Attorney can make out it was Negligence by Brockstine and Winslow and North shore. What and how more clear one needs? It is picture worth 1000 words. This report if given full emphasis an evidence itself. We do not need testimony, witness, . If it is not Malpractice- negligence per the report, then what is Malpractice? Then there is no difference in a Free Democratic country USA, or South Africa or Haiti, and other poor countries. Malpractice law then be abolished and democracy should not be called in the USA.

flame and heavy blocking her airways. Mayo also said, Dulera worsened her breathing and in the Mayo clinic reports. Mayo also mentioned in the report, no Bronchoscopy was done in July 2014 and Mayo did all that. That is how they figured out her case was spoiled and Metastasis was in her lungs airways. That is how Mayo Clinic put in the report" and referred Palliative care which was a shock to us..

7.   After coming from Mayo, I called Brockstine several times but he did not call back.

8.   Connie was highly educated and intelecucal and said" Brockstine ruined her life and now taking my Life". "He must be chomping and worried that law suit is coming".

9.   I called the ex-chairman of north shore at his home, who is a renewed oncologist too. He was shocked and promised some would call. But in vain. After few days chairman called me, if I heard from someone. I said no. He said" he would get involved and find some treatment. Dr. Brockstine called on 25th November and left a message as Connie was not able to pick up the phone due to her weakness and I had gone to get the food. I have that message saved" MR and Mrs. Berry" I could not call, as I was reading all the reports of Mayo and was discussing. He said" I would hand over this case to Dr. Merkel a breast cancer oncologist who cured Connie from breast cancer in 2002.

PRADEEP K. BERRY

10. Dr. Merkel was angry when we saw him in his office-- in the locked room. He said" Who was on the team" We said" Brockstine and Winslow" He said" he has been doing this for over thirty years. He was just mad, I am sure he knew Brockstine and Winslow spoiled Connie' case. He suggested one other test and Chemotherapy for three months and after that a test if Chemotherapy is working. Connie had one Chemotherapy In December, 2014, and one in January 2015. She went in February middle but Merkel found shingles, prescribed antibiotics and postponed Chemotherapy till February 20th 2015 was not done as Connie fell on the night of February, 19th, 2015 from her bed and was taken to the hospital and was to be released on February 21-22. I saw DNR and Mrs. Berry Told DR. Woods and Dr. Fish on call at north shore to change to DR and they assured us, but when Connie had heart attack, Doctors waited 8- 9 minutes before they could do CPR. I was a tiger and a Lion and blasted them that Ds. Woods and Dr. Fish assured me in the presence of a nurse that it was changed to DR or . If I was not a ferocious tiger, they would not have done CPR and Connie would have been dead on February 21,2015

11.Why did Dr., Brockstine- who had handed over the case to Dr. Merkel in November,2014, was hanging over keep coming to see me and leaving note to talk to me, which I refused. Why was he there as a chief with other 6 palliative care and nurses to make a decision to take Connie' tubes on March 27, 2015 vs March 2nd, 2015 as it was promised to me by 2015 the nurses and cardiac unit? That too when I was just gone for an hour? Also the Palliative care Dr. and Brockstine, without my permission and Connie's too, took the telephone number from the internet and called her brother in his Florida vacation home-- vacation home from the face time and he said, he cannot come. Connie never wanted to see them nor wanted to do with them as they have been behaving badly with her.These doctors went against my wife- Connie' wishes. Shame to all of them?

 They promised Palliative care after the tubes were taken out at 3 PM and "Connie was talking to me and was saying that she wants to live as she has a beautiful home and she said she did not say anything to doctors as she was not able to speak and was very clear to me she left all the decision to me" and had mentioned -" I want to live and I did not say anything to doctors". I was just furious but no one was listening to me and said" Hospital would put her r in Palliative unit and keep watching and she can go home after few days. Tubes were taken out without her permission and mine, as I was gone for an hour and through the body language and my notes to her, She told in body language- I should decide as she wanted to live. Around 4 and 4.30, assiatnat Physician came and tole me MRs Berry would not survive to night. I was mad and shouting. She came again and said, we do not have any more bed and then No one came. "I was on the phone since then calling all the doctors, Pallative care and Hospice but in vain. I have proof on the Verizon bill as it went way sky as I sed lots of extra minutes. Also I have 32 minutes Video may be nusrse took that How I am yelling at the hospital and one can see that I am on the phone, calling and telling Connie you have to be strong- she was moving her head meaning yes. She was sort of in senses and knew what is going on. Hospital phone is ringing and I was telling " it is abousletrly nonsense, I have been caling nurses and help and no one is coming- This video itself is good Proof how much negligence Northshore hospital did, After my many calls, Cathy a hospice and papptaive care girl came but did not do anything but talking to me and talking to Connie. I have Video. Cathy practically decared Connie is going or die. It was 9PM and I was weeping but two Indian nurses came on duty and I

274

begged them to save my wife, they both did a great job, one putting Oxygen mask and another Morphine Injection, I was happy that God has listened to my prayers and was sure, Connie is going to live. I was holding my blader or bathroom for nine hours and asked the nurses if I can use the bathroom, they said Yes. We are here and she would be okay. I was extremely had a new life. But around 12 40 she took a worse turn and she died in front of me and nurses and I saw her last four breathing. If it is not a negleigence and malpractice, what worse, it can be. My videos are full proof, if these doctors are given warrants, ask for testimony under Oath, I do not know if they would lie or sya truth. FBI can trace all my conversation when I was leaving messeges to Brockstine, Ex chairman of the Northshore, a known Oncologist, his reurn call, Brockstine messge. There are many ways to find Brockstine and Winslow and other Pallative care doctors who also went behind me in helping Brockstine to make the tubes out on Friday, 27th Vs March 2. Brockstine should never had come. Dr. Merkel never ever came till he saw her on the day when he said Shingles and 20th Feburary was the date for Chemotherpay. Till that day, we never ever saw Dr Merkel. In my strong opinion It was a conspiracy. Also, one social worker- head of the team was forcing me to leave hospital by 8 30. as before that when Connie was in her room and in Intensive care, I was there all the time, why suddenly six seven days before Connie death on 27th night- 28th Febuarray, 2015, no one said anything. Rather other staff were offering me to rest in some empty beds at the hospital.   in. it is a case of crimainal trype in my opinion, and some action must be taken. we would lose the humanity, the lord of drkness would paly the role.

1.In my opinion, My Darling wife, Mrs. Constance Berry y of 39/2 half years, in died due to the absolute negligence of two doctors at the North Shore Health Care System (North) in Evanston.   Dr. Brockstine, head and neck oncologist an pulmonary specialist, Dr. Winslow..

2. Connie who was going for regular check up and Mammogram at North regularly was diagnosed with breast cancer in August 2002. She had surgery by S Saner and some nodes were treating, but no breasts were removed. She was given Chemotherapy and radiation suggested by Dr. Merkel –Breasts Cancer Oncologist at North.

3. In December, 2004 she had some ear infection and went to see her Internal medicine Dr. at St Stephens's hospital in Evanston, he suggested biopsy, as there was some small lump on her right chic-parotid gland. She was give two weeks of antibiotics and she took another two weeks and her Dr, had said, if you do not feel better, go and see Dr. Merkel. She did not get better and went to Dr. Merkel in January, or February 2005. He said "he has no concerns: but see ENT specialist, if does not get better. Her intuition was telling her that her lip movements were bothering, and she went to ENT specialist at North. His immediacy took Biopsy and results showed "Parotid Gland Cancer"- a new one.

PRADEEP BERRY

4. In a hurry, .Dr. Stephen Senor at North did six hour surgery on March, 31, 2005 and could not save one facial nerve and stated, she would have some problems which only, she and I, could notice, when she moves her lips and may have to drink more and more water to eat to make saliva

5. She was referred to Dr., Bruce Brockstine, head and neck specialist and he gave her radiation and asked to have pat scan every six months etc. She did that.

6. In mid-2006, Brockstine spotted a small scarf in the pat scan and treated with Chemotherapy and regular pat scan and MRI. Connie showed him some cancer herbals which saves the cancer cells and help to tolerate chemotherapy and gives strength to body. "He said go and take" and while going for regular pat scan

6. She was fine until middle of November in 2011 and Brockstine saw a spot on her node in her lung after Pat scan and gave her chemotherapy and she was fine.

7. In September ,2012 another spot was detected and Brockstine said, have another pat scan in December, 2013 to be sure and he confirmed and decided to give different Chemotherapy and she can finish that in Sanibel as we wanted to go. After her chemotherapy in March 18, her cancer was gone, but he decided to give four extra Chemotherapy We were not happy, but listened to him. Connie had four chemotherapy and was done in April 17, 2013. After that she devolved Neuropathy and in June 2013, they found water in her lungs, which was detected by x-ray and were cancer cells from the 2002 breast cancer. He suggested taking Thoracenteses every weak from one lung and next day from second lung. In November, 2013 we saw pulmonary dr. Winslow at the NORTH, who suggested oxygen and Connie was sleeping who14 . Per Mayo Clinic,North Relied on the pat scan which is not a full proof and does not show any spreading of the cancer, but new spots. Bronchoscopy should have been done in 2013 which was not done except at Mayo on November, 4- or 5th 2015 which showed Metastasis of the cancer in her lung airways.

15. 37 MM water should have been taken out and that has become like a thick flame or ice and blocking the airways.

16 Inhaler does not go with the oxygen. It is only for the Asthma and has worsened the breathing of Mrs. Constance Berry.

17. Air test at North was not done properly and no number up to where MRs. Berry could breathe and the technician was not the right person to be on that job as he was yelling her to take breathing making her and me nervous and any normal person would be under stress.

18. They should have fully seen that why air test was not properly recorded as to up to what number from I to 50 have gone. They did not perform the air test properly and the technician must be useless which we know, he was as he was just shouting and making both of us nervous with his style of air test.

19. Dr. Keo.at Mayo said, Connie Berry has no choice, but Palliative care. It was the most devastated news we ever got. After coming from Mayo, I called Brockstine- Oncologist ten times, but he did not call back. "Connie told me he must be nervous as Malpractice law suit must be coming. I called the ex-chairman at North who is also a known Oncologist at the North .He was shocked and said "someone would call, but in vain. He called me back after two days, if someone called, I said no. He said some would have to call as; I am going to step in. On November 25, 2014, Brockstine at North called and left a message on our answering machine saying "he was discussing with Mayo and has been reading reports etc. Now he is not going to take this case and giving it to Breast cancer specialist Dr. Merkel at North (His office is on the same building) would take over. I have saved that message on my answering machine"

Dr. Merkel treated Connie' breast cancer in 2002. When Dr. Merkel came to see us in the locked room around the end of November. 2014. He said" "Who was on the team" we gave him the names of Dr. Brockstine and Dr. Winslow at North. "He said, I have been seeing patients and curing them for the last 30 years. He was extremely angry"

life and finally her demise. After visiting Mayo, Connie told me many times," These two doctors times, which was the most painful thing for her and for me and would remain the same for me, till I am alive. She was right and we still thought, she would be alive for a long time as, other specialist (doctor), at HH agreed to take the case, though he himself,

'He ordered different tests and started different chemotherapy for three months and a test after, if chemotherapy is working, otherwise, he would try different ones. We were very happy. Connie had two chemotherapies in December, 2014 and in January 2015. For her third one on February 20, 2015 she fell down at home on February, 19, 2015, and ambulance took her to the hospital for checkup, and was ready to discharge her on February 21, 2015 and was ready to come home on, February, 22, 2015. I must mention, I saw the nurse on the 20th February, 2015 with a checkup machine and I noticed DNR. I told Connie who too told the two doctors on call to change to DR. and both assured, they have changed to DR. She didn't want to eat anything on the February, 21,2015
but,
had a little salad and in five minutes, she felt short of breath and that was a cardiac arrest. Nurses came and doctors refused to perform CPR, as the code DNR to DR was not changed and they saw DNR. I lost my temper and was like a ferocious tiger and blasted them, they better perform CPR, otherwise, I would go to the highest law, as, and I had two witnesses, when doctors stated DR code has been changed. It still took them seven to eight minutes before they performed CPR; because of DNR code was not changed. I believe, this eight minutes delay caused her death otherwise, Connie would have been alive and be with me. She was on the ventilator and tubes from her mouth were to be taken on March, 2nd, 2015 and I had to decide the next step. But doctors went behind me; when I went for a short family work. The caretaker was there assuring me Connie is better and I can be away for a short time. Three to six doctors and two nurses took advantage of that and told me that Constance told them to take the tubes out .There is no way, Connie was even talking. We were communicating with body language and, I was showing my written notes and she was telling me by her body language," "I should decide whatever; I want to do for her." Again, I became a ferocious tiger and blasted six doctors and two nurses. Eight vs. one was my first loss and all the palliative care; what they promised me, were not performed, in spite of my aggressive act and 100 phone calls. However, I still was positive that she would live. A great message came to my mind. " Never deprive someone from the hope that may be the only thing they may have"." "Miracles happen every day". These messages were great tools for us to be happy. I also started thinking about God, to make Connie normal by your miracles, as when Jesus that Lazarus, be brought back to life, that prayer was heard, so why can't I do it for my lovely wife? At the same time, I thought of SAVITRI AND SATYAVAN- SATYAVAN AND GOD OF DEATH, in India century ago, and it can be read on the Internet, where Savitr's devotion made God granted her husband" life back. these two incidences made me stronger. I was ready to fight anything. It was a struggle for Connie to go to doctor' appointments and too much walking in the house, as she had to use the walker and later oxygen. It was not pleasant for us, but her presence and being with her was still giving us happiness seeing each other's faces. Ultimately, I saw my Darling" last four breaths and death in my presence. Two nurses and a close couple were with me. That death, which I could never had imagined, the way HH killed her is one of the most painful, shocking, uncalled for things, I have ever witnessed. My mind totally went blank. Her face, body- if she was still alive was another thing I had to witness and have no words of the pain in my each and every part of the body. Is it true, I would never see her, talk to her, live with her, cannot go no longer with her, I am left alone, how would and when would I can get back. Is it possible, that God may reward her or me after half hour to one hour or next day, that she is alive? All

these thoughts were running in my mind and even now on August, 20, 2015 and since her death day, every day, these questions and things keep coming to mind most of the day and night of the most painful seen, and witnessing everyday.. How difficult for me as her husband to release her body for the cremation at the funeral home. It gives me panic attacks; most of the times come in my mind. I had stayed with her body another five hours, till it was taken. I would never ever forget this trauma, till I am alive. I am suffering from that pain and withdrawal syndromes, which are incorporated in my mind and heart. Later, her two days of cremation and putting ashes in her plot, next to her parents was heart breaking and absolutely broken me.

Pradeep Berry

PRADEEP K. BERRY

-------- Original message --------
From: pradeepberry@sbcglobal.net
Date:02/19/2016 12:56 PM (GMT-06:00)
To: "~~~~~~~~~~ (States Attorney)" General Responded ANITA ALVER
Cc: Pradeep Berry
Subject: Fwd: Add.

-------- Original message --------
From: pradeepberry@sbcglobal.net
Date:02/19/2016 12:56 PM (GMT-06:00)
To: "~~~~~~~~~ (States Attorney)" General General MS ANITA ALVERZ
Cc: Pradeep Berry (Attorney General State)
Subject: Fwd: Add.

I can furnish a video taken around 5.30 when Connie was alive. I was calling for help and nurses in the Connie' room were not coming on the 27th evening. I was calling hospital phone and answered, from the desk old we would send the nurse, second time third time the same answer on the phone which can be heard from my 32 minutes video which would be a great evidence of the last medical negligence 9 hours before my wife Constance death. It is the same 27th afternoon when I was just gone for an hour leaving the care taker and team of Doctor and nurses who were on my side on 26th night, in my opinion plotted the plan to do something to my wife who was absolutely not in a position to speak as tubes were in her mouth through the chest and hands were tied with the other tube after she had cardiac arrest on the 22nd and CPR WAS NOT PERFORMED until 8'- 9 minutes after and that too when I blasted the whole team like a frocious lion and a tiger. Otherwise Constance would have died on the same time at 6.27 PM evening. """"This 9 minutes delay was not part of the medical records on four five 1289 pages and CD. .Also, I requested a separate CD of medical records from the 19th February to the 28th February, 2015 when she died. They had hidden this paper of 9 minutes delay from all the CD , I took three four times to send to the doctors or keep myself as a proof in case some doctor or attorney ask. However, I have been telling the attorney all the time. """"" HOWEVER EVEN I DID NOT KNOW THAT THid PAPER OF THE 9 minute delay WAS NOT THERE. NOW, I GOT THE SAME PAPER WHILE RUNNING AROUND THE HOSPITAL AND IT WAS THERE AND NOW THEY GAVE it to ME. I HAVE IT. IT IS EXTREMELY important to note that they said something different to me when I reached on the 27th February's afternoon and I didn't believe them in any case. I ALSO TOLD THESE to the attorney's. . I didn't know on that day what they would write in the medical records. It's only 8 days ago I read which is shocking, though I knew they are not telling me the real story. "I would have taken different approach to save her extremely different and no matter what or whom I had to contact including Police. In my opinion, everything on the the medical report on the 27th February, 2015 the same day after 9 hours Connie died. Now 8 days ago I read two pages----- I am attaching are baseball , falsified , cooked the up and can't ever ever ever ever happen but Dr falsified record to save himself who was her Dr until November .He gae the case to another doctor after Mayo clinic gave Pallative care report. """""" THE important page is still missing or destroyed or was never prepared as Connie' hands were tied up was tube all over her body and were to be taken out on March 2nd. I had to decide what's the best option then to go for Tracheostomy or take her to the palliative unit for few days and bring her home as Connie wanted to be in her home and if she was to die, she had been telling me she would like to die in her own home after seeing her living room, dining room, study room, my study room and our own temple and her bed room and new walking shower. That was her desire. But these doctor and team wrote false, cooked up and absolutely falsifying her desire. It's written that Constance gave us the consent and accordingly they prepared the document and-----CONSTANCE SIGNED"""""".
WHERE IS THAT PAPER" WHERE ARE SIGNATURE, I WANT TO SEE. COURT, HON

3

MORE THAN A MILLION WORTH

[Handwritten annotations surround a medical record document. Handwritten notes include comments such as "This paper has to be destroyed", "Sorry - CPR", "This page perhaps they never wanted to give - unlike I made many efforts and this they gave me", "This paper was not anywhere in the whole medical report - HIDING", "and had no intention to give it to me", "9 minutes delay is the main cause of sudden death - if they did CPR right away and if electric shock - she had been alive", "9 minutes delay IN the Medical report Page 3 also is where the 1st CPR was performed right away - this is the reason they lied to Dr. Joy - I was there with Centre's Core listen Florson Harris...", etc.]

Patient Demographics

Name	Patient ID	SSN	Sex	Birth Date
Berry, Constance A	003211828	xxx-xx-8756	Female	02/16/37 (DECEASED)

Address	Phone	EMail	Employer
1310 MAPLE AVE Apt 2B EVANSTON IL 60201	847-328-1355 (H) 312-969-3793 xhusband cell (M)	cfberry@sbcglobal.net	RETIRED

Reg Status	PCP	Date Last Verified	Next Review Date
ELAPSED	Prete, Carole P., MD 847-475-4555	12/04/14	06/02/15

Patient Ethnicity & Race

Ethnic Group	Patient Race
Non-Hispanic	Caucasian

Scan on 2/23/2015 0607 by Fonville-Hibbler, Kimberly A : 2/22/15 arrest (below)

NorthShore University HealthSystem — RESUSCITATION RECORD

BERRY, CONSTANCE A
2/16/1937 Female
Fish, Keith R., MD
CSN: 73701087
Patient ID: 003211828

Date: 2/22/15 Time: 1834 Location: 555 Name of Code Leader: Zobar
Diagnosis pre-arrest: Breast CA

Top Sheet - Patient's Chart · 2nd Sheet - Dept. of Nursing
MUST USE BALLPOINT PEN

Generated on 2/5/2016 3:46 PM

281

6/7/2016   Fw. Dr Sahib. You can see my beautiful wife

Me & Mrs Berry - I was Busy while Discussing with Mayo Clinic what is the next course of Action. I am no longer going to see you, Please see Dr D. Merkel. Breast & Lung Oncologist in the same location.

CONNIE DARLING

(1) WHY DR BROCKSTONE did not want to see you another Dr for Second Opinion! He knew it was very embarrassing or unpleasant to show he is incapable as he became the Head of the Department Lately after affiliation with University of Chicago.

(2) He did not want to go to US to MAYO — Stating what now they. — Marketing - Gymics and was Reluctant to Send Reports. He had to force him on 10/31/2014

(3) MAYO CLINIC Ruled out in 4 Days the Brockstone and Winston - Gave Wrong Treatment.
① Brockstone — No Bronchoscopy
② 37 Nodes in her Lungs has left over which caused Air Blockage in her Airways along with the Negligence of not doing Bronchoscopy which tells the Malignancy of the Cancer.

(4) Dr Winston gave In her DUCERA — Very strong Dose caused her Oxygen & Breathing worse.

(5) Brockstone did not call for 20 Days after I left & talked to his Secretaries for 15 times. After Pressure he left a Message on

MORE THAN A MILLION WORTH

⑥ Dr Merkel Locked up the Room on Dec 12th. Mr & Mrs Berry who was on the Team to Put your condition into this By coming out from Mayo Clinic the Deleted Palliative care in 4 Days he said Bbockstine - Winslow. Dr Merkel — who else — I said Whitney student physician and other physician Delodal. Merkel: — I have been next Door — why Dr Bbockstine did not tell me all — as he has over 30 years of experience — Do not worry — I how give you Three chemotherapy. Dec 2014, Jan 2015, Feb 2015 and take another test — not PET SCAN — I Do not Believe in pet scan. It will he will some liquid.

Constance had Two chemotherapy on Dec - 14 - Jan 2015 Feb 2015 3rd one — She fell down from her Home Bed Room. I got up & cleaned her Bathroom. lifting was slightly different as I do not know the correct way to left a Person.

⑨ Called Paramedics. and they lifted — her and Sense she was Lying Down Since 4 AM. and I noticed at 6:30 — She was with Oxygen and help and has Weeck. Paramedics look for her Lower B.P. to the emergency Room in 20th/Feb 2015 ⑧

⑩ Dr Fish & Woods Changed the DNR code to Full code in her Absence and especially Gave to her Room that DNR is now Full code.

PRADEEP K. BERRY

Berry, Constance A (MR # 003211828)
NORTHSHORE UNIVERSITY HEALTHSYSTEM

Patient Demographics

Name	Patient ID	SSN	Sex	Birth Date
Berry, Constance A	003211828	xxx-xx-8756	Female	02/16/37 (DECEASED)

Address	Phone	EMail	Employer
1310 MAPLE AVE Apt 2B EVANSTON IL 60201	847-328-1355 (H) 312-969-3793 xhusband cell (M)	cfberry@sbcglobal.net	RETIRED

Reg Status	PCP	Date Last Verified	Next Review Date
ELAPSED	Prete, Carole P., MD 847-475-4555	12/04/14	06/02/15

Patient Ethnicity & Race

Ethnic Group	Patient Race
Non-Hispanic	Caucasian

All Notes

Physician Discharge Summary by Zzhaywood, Audrey E., DO at 03/04/15 1453   Version 1 of 1

Author: Zzhaywood, Audrey E., DO   Service: Internal Medicine   Author Type: Resident
Filed: 03/04/15 1501   Note Time: 03/04/15 1453   Status: Signed
Editor: Zzhaywood, Audrey E., DO (Resident)   Cosigner: Tokarczyk, Arthur J., MD at 03/09/15 0657

Discharge Handoff - NorthShore University HealthSystem

Patient:	Constance A Berry
Date of Birth:	2/16/1937
Admission Date:	2/19/2015
Primary diagnosis:	Sepsis 2/2 UTI
Discharge Diagnosis:	Sepsis, ARDS, aspiration PNA, metastatic breast cancer
Discharge Date:	3/4/2015
Discharge To:	Deceased
Condition at discharge:	Deceased
Admitting MD:	
Discharge MD:	Tokarczyk, Arthur, MD
Brief Summary of hospitalization and incidental findings:	Constance A Berry is a 77 y/O female with history of metastatic breast cancer with malignant pleural effusions s/p frequent thoracentesis (last one was in 5/2014) currently, COPD on home O2 (2.5L), HTN who has been admitted since 2/19/15 for Sepsis secondary to UTI. On 2/22/15 patient went into PEA arrest. She was revived after 2 rounds of CPR/Epinephrine and was placed on hypothermic protocol. Immediately after resuscitation went into atrial fibrillation with rate as high as 180's and amiodarone bolus and gtt were administered, stopped after HR returned toward baseline. Due to increasing

MORE THAN A MILLION WORTH

TO ZAC   FROM PRADEEP BERRY
               PRADEEPBerry@SBCGLOBAL.Net

"In my Opinion: The following are very strong points;"

2. He insisted four extra chemotherapy. That resulted in Neuropathy, which he said, would go away. But it did not, and physical therapy was given. Later her oxygen was low, and Physical therapy had to be stopped.

3. X-ray showed water in her lungs and biopsy indicated breast cancer cells from 2002. He should have given the case to breast cancer oncologist, as I told him. He said no. He suggested Thoracenteses, and I was taking her twice a week for that, from July, 2013, and in January 14, 2014, we went to Florida. Dr. at Florida Cancer center suggested injection Faslodex, which was not suggested by Brockstine. When I called him, he said, he did not think of and it is a good idea. Florida Dr. and Brockstine agreed that when we are back in March, 1,2014, , it should be continued. In early January, 2013, Connie also saw Dr. Winslow a pulmonary Dr. At North shore, who suggested oxygen, and thought Florida climate and humidity would do better. We flew with Oxygen concentration, but Connie bought portable too for going for the Thoracenteses and the injection in Florida.

4. After we came back from Florida, Thoracenteses was still going and water was getting lower.

5. Winslow prescribed Dulera inhaler, which is actually for asthma patients. Connie took accordingly. It ruined her condition- which too has been reported in Mayo Clinic Report.

6. Connie went for Thoracenteses in the second and third week of July, 2014and end of July. Thoracenteses showed 37MM water, and north shore said" it is too little to take out. That water as shown in Mayo clinic reports thickens as a le night with the oxygen concentration. . Her condition was not getting better.

9. WE flew to Florida with Oxygen concentration and Dr. Winslow and Brockstine also thought that Florida climate in January, till March would do wonders due to hot and humid weather. But she was not finding any improvements at all.

10. in Florida. We went to Florida Cancer Center and the Dr.Danbar, over there suggested one injection-Faslodex to dry up the water every month. When we called Brockstine, he said "It is Not a bad Idea" I said, why did you not suggested" He said "it was in his mind but was not sure". I told him that it's time we see the lung or breast cancer, but he said "NO". After three injections in Florida water was reducing pretty fast and got dried up due to the injection , and when we came home in February end, Doctor at Florida had said continue the injection and Brockstine took his suggestion and said, okay to continue the Faslodex injection and Thoracenteses. But her condition was getting bad. Pulmonary Dr. Winslow at North suggested one inhaler, Dulera used for asthma which caused more problems. We were very angry with these two drs. at North and told them, we are going to Mayo Clinic. They said "What would

         Pradeep Berry

PRADEEP K. BERRY

February - 1, 2017

Dear Dr.

Ferdinand Richards 111

Chief Medical Officer.

Dear Dr. Please refer to your letter January, 24, 2017 Medicare HICN 9165 B For Mrs. Constance A Berry – my most precious, priceless Gold and Diamond wife, I was married to her for over 40 t-years. I have ben trying to Rectify, In my opinion, all the medical negligence took place at the Northshore Hospital. We finally went to Mayo Click on November 2, 2014.

Mayo Clinic Detected the findings is four days with various tests and declared My Darling Wife Constance Berry Palliative care.

In your letter, It is absolutely evident in my opinion, that you are just trying to protect Dr, Bruce Brockstine ,a head neck Oncologist only. He is not a breast or lung cancer. Please read my letter very carefully, as you are just trying to hush hush this case and in my opinion going to save these above mentioned doctors. I know very well, that you or any doctor would never ever r go against other doctors. You absolutely played the same role rather being a unbiased Doctors. You never mentioned the most critical point which led to My wife, Death.

1 You tollay ignored to mention about Mayo Clinic in your letter,

2, No mention of Dulera medicine given to Constance Berry by Dr, Winslow which per Mayo Clinic worsened My wife; Condition.

3, You did not care to mention that Mayo Clinic in their medical reports clearly indicated that 37 MM water left in her lings which was not removed from mars berry' Lings became a dangerous point blocking her lings airways. Read Mayo Clinic report.

4. Mayo conducted Broncosppy right away-y by the Pulmonary Doctor Katrina Keo. Dr, Winslow is a pulmonary doctor, why did he not conduct the same. I wrote before, in my opinion, Winslow truly did not do much i=opt take much=h interest in Mrs. berry case.

5.Why did he not conducted Broncosppy and Mayo did. That was big thing.

6. Mayo took out 37 MM water left in her body where as in July 2014 Northshore did not even thought of that. What became ice in Mrs. Berry; . You absolutely omitted that,

7. Why did Brockstine did not wanted us to go to see other doctors. Brockstine did call her

8. Why Dr Winslow said that we are not keen that Constance Berry should go to mayo. He told both of us that what they would do that, WE did go and they took different test

(You mentioned 9 minutes CPR and that is standard? Please don't, compromise on your one standard-time – in 9 minutes as by that time. Have some of your patients stay without Proper dine unit

MORE THAN A MILLION WORTH

(xx) PS: Read where I put BoB

Berry, Constance A (MR # 003211828) *(14)*

All Notes (continued)

Progress Notes by Augustin, Catherine, RN at 02/27/15 2338 (continued) — Version 1 of 1
847-475-3002
pgr 6786

Progress Notes by Adegunsoye, Ayodeji O., MD at 02/27/15 2153 — Version 1 of 1

Author: Adegunsoye, Ayodeji O., MD	Service: Intensive Care	Author Type: Physician
Filed: 02/27/15 2208	Note Time: 02/27/15 2153	Status: Signed
Editor: Adegunsoye, Ayodeji O., MD (Physician)		

Patient who is currently DNR status noted to be hypotensive with systolic BP in the low 70s. She appears less agitated and calm presently. SpO2 in the 70-80s and supplemental oxygen by nasal cannula increased from 2L to 6L. She has increased oral/airway secretions and appears volume overloaded with anasarca. Husband at bedside and agrees with decision not to give IV fluid boluses given high likelihood of worsening her cardiopulmonary status and increasing airway secretions with respiratory distress. He appears to have come to terms with the patients decision to be terminally extubated. Husband (and family members by phone) offering final prayers. Patients ICU nurse and hospice nurse at bedside throughout above proceedings administering care, comforting the patient and her grieving husband.

HUSBAND - PRADEEP WAS TOLD and I agreed that TUBES Would be TAKEN out on MARCH 2n 201.

Progress Notes by Deamant, Catherine D., MD at 02/27/15 0622 — Version 3 of 3

Author: Deamant, Catherine D., MD	Service: Palliative Care	Author Type: Physician
Filed: 02/27/15 2155	Note Time: 02/27/15 0622	Status: Addendum
Editor: Deamant, Catherine D., MD (Physician)		
Related Notes: Original Note by Deamant, Catherine D., MD (Physician) filed at 02/27/15 2151		

In my absence
ALL LIES But FRAUD. I was Just went for one hour and [unreadable] - No there - acknowledge I my AR

NorthShore University HealthSystem Palliative Care Program

Interval History:
Required diltiazem infusion yesterday, now off. ~~Persistent hypocalcemia.~~

Pt seen with Dr. Deamant, Katie RN, Peggy Lester APN-student. Connie had been off both fentanyl and versed for 1-2 hours. She was awake and alert, communicating clearly and consistently by shaking her head yes and no, also by mouthing words despite ET tube in her mouth. She told us that she was without dyspnea, without pain, without nausea or full feeling.

We asked her if she was comfortable. She said no. We asked her if the ET tube was bothering her. She said yes. We explained to her that she has the ET tube in her mouth/throat, connected to the breathing machine. Explained to her that her lungs have weakened further since her arrest and she has required the support of the breathing machine to continue to breathe. We explained that her pulmonary status has been so weak that if she were to come off the breathing machine, she would likely die within hours or days and would not have a chance of recovery. She understood. We asked her if she wanted to remain on the ventilator to have a chance of recovery AND have tracheostomy and gastrostomy tubes placed for more permanent means of ventilation and nutrition. She said no. We asked her if she wanted the ET tube to come out. She said yes. We asked her who she trusts to make medical decisions for her. She said "Mike." We asked if she meant her brother, Michael C. Fuller. She said yes. We asked if she felt Michael was able to make medical decisions for her. She said yes. We asked if she felt comfortable with her husband Pradeep making medical decisions for her. She said no. We asked if she wanted the medical team to let her brother Michael know about the circumstances that brought her to the hospital and update him on her condition. She said yes. We asked her if she wanted to appoint her brother Michael as her health care power of attorney. She said yes. We prepared the document and Connie signed it. We asked Connie if she wanted to die in the hospital. She said yes. We

(xx) ↓ BoB where is that document No where?

I wrote on Feb 23, 2015 at 1:10 PM — Pradeep Berry

DO YOU WANT TO SAY Anything

YOU HAD CARDIAC ARREST AND ON the VENTILATOR

PRAYING TO RECOVER.

DO YOU WANT THAT EVERYTHING SHOULD BE DONE TO SAVE YOU — WITH

If they HAVE To

RIGHT NOW YOU HAVE TUBE IN MOUTH

After Week TUBE CAN GO IN the CHEST WITH A LITTLE INSERTION
AND Feeding TUBE IN STOMACH

Pradeep you Decide
2/23/2015

I WANT TO TRY ALL THAT FOR YOU SO THAT YOU DO NOT DIE.

SHOULD I DO —
SHOULD I DO

(YES) — (NO)

What do you WANT

Gita others she writes yes

32 minutes is inside in my strong opinion video. Doctors planned to let her die to avoid their skin.

Respected ANITA ALVEREZ,

DR Brocksline ruined the C

April 15, 2016

Pradeep Kumar Berry- 847 328 1355, 1310 Maple Avenue Unit 2 B Evanston. pradeepberry@sbcglobal.net

MY CONNIE- MY LIGHT AND MY WORLD AND THE MOST PRECIOUS WIFE OF 40 YEARS.

MY CONNIE, when you were being neglected by the doctors and staff of the hospital to save your life on the 22nd February, 2015, you had specifically asked the two doctors on call who came in your room in front of me, nurses, and your care taker, Florida Harris to change the DNR Code TO FULL CODE. They both came to your room in front of the nurses and Florida stating " WE HAVE CHNAGED THE FULL CODE". WE were very relaxed and were waiting to go home on the 23the, February, 2015 at 11- 11.30, after spending two nights from your fall at home in the morning of the 20th February, 2015 and Paramedics took you to emergency room for a preventive check. You were fine with some urinary track infection, and to be released on 21st, then 22nd, February, 2015 due to lack of paperwork and weekend they decided to let you go home on Monday, 23, February, 2015. That day did not come in our life due to the absolute negligence and malpractice of the doctors, **in my very strong opinion**. After having a little salad at 6.15 PM on the 22nd February, 2015, you felt short of breathing and staff was unable to see what was happening and time went by to give you some water or jerk on your back etc. to make you comfortable. But they did not know what to do until I shouted and called and called the staff. It was a sign of cardiac arrest and they realized it later.., It was their moral duty to immediately perform CPR but they waited and were confused while I was yelling and screaming to perform the CPR. I wish I knew to perform CPR, which I am going to take in the near future. My screaming and yelling brought the blue line team and in front of me watching that my wife needs CPR, they argued with me that they would not as DNR code was changed. I became a furious tiger-hungry lion and told them that" I would turn them to the police and FBI and what not if my wife died. They got worried and performed the CPR. There were 10 to 15

Please do investigate this case - should not happen in world - specially in USA

CRIMINAL ACT CRIME

Here the case - UNDER CRIM FALSE - Medical Neglect & Act

They did most horrible crime on my crippled wife after they did not perform CPR after Cardic Arrest to 9 mini

(X) *I do not imagine she could even pick pen to sign as her hands - were tied well. Vital tubes - and tie with Bed. Mouth too full of tubes.*

① WHY DID They Not perform CPR in 9 minutes - when FULL CODE WAS There. They did not have the paper - Document that CPR was performed after 9 minutes. I went and it was given after I asked many times -

② Where is the Document that MRS Constance Berry signs. This is a CRIME to destroy Medical Records. I WAN to see my wife's signature if she signed.

people of nurses, assistants, doctors and were watching along with me and Florida Harris – her care taker. I can still recognize those people if given me the chance. All this delay of 9 minutes was one of the causes of my wife' death on the 28th February in the hospital in front of me as I was there 24 hours with my wife.

PLEASE READ CAREFULLY BELOW ALL THE EVENTS STARTING FROM SEPTEMBER, 2012. (AFTER READING OUR RIGHTS AS USA CITIZEN)

AS A USA CITIZEN, I HAVE A MORAL DUTY AND FOR MY USA BORN WIFE CONSTANCE FULLER--- (BERRY AFTER OUR MARRIAGE) 40 YEARS AGO. WHY LAWDOES NOT PROTECT INDIVIDAUL USA CITIZENS FROM THE MEDICAL NEGLIGENCE STATING THAT IT A INDIVIUAL CASE AND NOT A FEDERAL OR CIVIL LAW SUIT.

<u>BIGGEST VIOLITATION OF USA RIGHT IS WHEN A MEDICAL NEGLIGENCE CAUSED DEATH IN THE HOSPITAL. LAW IS SILENT ON THAT GIVING ENCOURAGEMENT TO MEDICAL PROFESSION TO DO WHATEVER THEY WANT TO DO- EVEN DEATH FROM THE MALPRACTICE AND NEGLIGENCE AND MOST HORRIBLY WHEN THE HOSPITAL FALSIFY THE MEDICAL RECORDS AND SOME OF THE FACTS ARE WRITTEN ABOULTRLY FALSE, DESTRUCTION OF THE MEDICAL RECORDS AND MAKING IT AS PATIENT HAD TO DIE.</u>

YES, THAT IS THE CASE WITH MY PRECIOUS WORLD- MY LIFE AND MY DEARST PART OF MY LIFE – MY WIFE OF OVER 40 YEARS A USA BORN CITIZEN- HIGHLY EDUCATED FROM UNIVERSITY OF CARLTON COLLEGE, UNIVERSITY OF MICHIGAN AND ANOTHER MASTERS IN SPANISH AND TEACHER FOR 34 YEARS- LATER SHE STARTED TEACHING FREE AND THEN GIVING HER TIME TO THE LIBARARY FOR CHILDEREN EDUCATION AND TEACHING . WHERE IS HER PROTECTION AND MY PROTECTION AS USA CITIZE. WE BOTH CONTRIBUTED IN THE USA- PAID OUR TAXES- LIVED HONESTLY- DID

HUMANITY WORK-GAVE DONATIONS TO ALL CHARITIES- CARED FOR THE USA LAW AND THE GREAT COUNTRY IN THE WORLD. GAVE DONATIONS TO THE RIGHT DESERVING CANDIADTE FOR USA PRESIDENT AND ATTORNEY GENERAL OF THE ILLINOIS AND CONGRESSMAN.

DO A USA CITIZEN, HIGHLY EDUCATED, WENT TO ELITE SCHOOL, TAUGHT STUDENTS FOR 34 YEAR, PAID TAXES, VOTED, LED THE MOST HONES AND ETIHICAL LIFE, COMMUNIT WOEK, VOLUTER WORK, DONATIONS,ALWAYS STOOD FOR USA FOR ANY WAR, SUNAMI, ANY NATURAL DIASSTER AND WHT NOT. SHE HAS THE SAME RIGHT TO BE PROTECTED FRPM ANY MEDICAL NEGLIGENCE AND FROM THE HANDS OF WELL PROTECTED MEDICAL DOCTOTORS WHO COMMIT MISTAKES BUT IMOARTANTLY, IOPININ, KNOWS HOW TO ELIMINATE THAT PATIENT WHOSE LIFE THEY RUIBED BY NOT GICING THE RIGHT MISTAKES AND FALSIFY THE MEDICAL RECORDS TO LET HER GO TO HEAVEN WHILE SAVING THEIR LIFE BUT WORRIED ABOUT EGO, JOB,POSTION, REPUTATION AS ONE OF TE BEST DOCTORS IN THE MEDICAL BOOKS AND HOSPITAL PUBLICITY ETC. WHO ARE PROTECTING THEM. WHAY ATTORNEY GENERAL DO NOT PROSICUTE THEM AS THEY TOOK SOMEONE LIFE WHICH CAN NOT BE RECOVERED COMAPRED TO CONSUMER FRAUD ORWHERE IT'S A MATERAL- MONEY WHICH CAN BE COMPENSTATED AND THE PERSON OR THE CORPORATION- DEFENDAENT AND PLAMTIFF ARE STLL ALIVE. MONET, LOSSES. BANKRUPCY, FRAUD AND OTHER CRIME AT LEAST THHE PERSON IS ALIVE AND SUFFER FOR SOMETIME AND HIS OR FAMILY AND THEY ARE COMPENSATED.

WHAT ABOUT IF A PATIENT IS GONE AND DIED AND HER LOVING HUSBAND AND WORLD OF OVER 40 YEARS AND THE PRECIOS GOLD- KOHINOOR WIFE IS GONE FROM THE HIS

LIFE- DIED CAN NEVER BE REPLACED WGICH IS MUCH MORE THAN LOSING MILIONS AND MILINONS OF DOALLRS. MONET- HOUSE, CAR, AND OTHER DAMAGES CAN BE RECOVERED AND MEDICAID- GOVERNMNET HELP ERTC CAN BE GIVEN AND THE SOLACE ID THE PERSON IS STILL ALIVE. HOWEVER, DEATH CAN NOT BE BOUGHT BACK WITH ANY WEALTHE OR ANY AMOUNT. I THINK. ITS IS EXTREMLY IMPORANT THAT ATTORNRY GENERAL. COOK COUNTY ATTORNRY GENERAL, COURT OF LAW MAKE CHNAGES FROM FEDERAL CRIME- CIVIL SUIT TO ONLY MEDICAL NEGLIGENCE WHERE ATTORNYS DO NOT WASN'T TO TAKE CASE AS ITS EXPENSIVE, REWARDS ARE GAMBLE AND SMALLL AMOUNT IF WIN THE CASE IS NOT SUFFICENT UNLESS IT IS IN MILLIONS OF DOLLARS. FOR ME I WOULD HAVE VERY SIMPLE LIFE NOT WITH TOO

I WORKED IN THE CORPORATE FOR 40 YEARS AND INTEARCTED ALL THE TIMES WITH MANY ATTORNYS AND OUR HUGE COMPANY HIRED TOP LAW FIRM WHEN WE WERE VERY BUSY. NOW I WOULD APPRECIATE IF YOUR OFFICE CAREFULLY EXAMINE AND SERIOUSLY LOOK AT THE RIGHTS OF THE USA CITIZENS.

IT SAYS BY ATTORNRY GENERAL OFFICE" IF OUR COMPALINT SUPPORTS A PATTERN OF DECEPTIVE PRACTICES, IT MAY BE INCLUDED IN FUTURE INVESTIGATIONS ANS OR LITIGATIONS. ONE OF THE MOST VALUABLE WAYS WE CAN LEARN OF PROBLEMS EXISTING IN THE MARKETPLACE IS BY RECIVVING COMAPLAINTS FROM CONCERENED CITIZENS.--------- HOSPITALS ARE ALSO MARKET PLACE WHERE PAITIENTS GO- HOSPITALS ASK OUR DONATIONS- THEYMAKE MONEY FROM PARKING- CITIZEND PAY FOR MEDICAL INSURANCE- PAY FOR MEDICARE- PAY REAL ESTATE FOR THE SCHOOLS WHICH INCLUDES SOMETIMES MEDICAL STUDENTS- THEIR SCHOLASHIPS-WE APY OUR DEDUCATABLE FOR THE HOSPITALS AND INSURANCE COMPANIES- WE PAY FOR MEDICAID THOUGH WE NEVER WANT MEDICAID

HOPEFULLY WE HAVE WORKED HARD TO SAVE FOR OUR
FUTURE AND WEVEN THAEN WE HAVE PAYING
DONATIONS FOR MANY CAUSES- INCLUDING HOSPITALS
AND REDCROSS- CANCER SOCIETY- AMERICAN HERAT
FOUNDATION- SALVATION ARMY- CHILDERNS MEMORIAL
HOSPITALS.

THESE ARE ALL MARKET PLACES- I WOULD SAY BIGGER THAN ANY
DISPUTE FOR TRLEPHONE- MAIL-INTERNET-TRADE SHOW
CONVENTION CENTER- THESES LOSSES OR FRAUD CAN BE
COMPENSATED BY THE LAW BY GIVING OR SETTLEMT OF
MONEY NO MATTER SMALL OR BIG. WHAT ABOUT DEATH
OF THE EDUCATED PERSON WHO CONTRIBUTED A WHOLE
LOT AND HIS HUSBAND OF OVER 40 YEARS WHO HAS
EVERYTHING BUT HIS LOVELY WIFE AND HIS WORLD
WHICH HE WOULD NEVER SEE AND NO AMOUNT OF
MONEY CAN BRING HIS WIFE BACK- I WOULD RATHER
IGNORE PHONE, STORE MAIL INTERNET TARDE SHOW
MONEY WHICH IS NOTHING BUT WHO WOULD GIVE ME
MY LOVELY WIFE? THERE IS NOT ENOUGH MONEY ON THE
PLANET WHO CAN GIVE MY CONNIE. WHERE IS THE ALW
FOR THAT. THE ANSWER IS IMPLE AND THAT OUR
ATTORNRY GENERAL MUST LOOK INTO THIS HIDDEN
PLACE WHERE HOW MANY LIFES ARE RUINED AND USA
CITIZENS ARE SUFFERING FOR LIFE TIME.

*I HAVE THE HOPE THAT OUR RESPECTED ATTORNEY GENERAL ~~USA~~
~~MADIGAN~~ LOOKS AT THIS- SHE HAS THE POWER TO
CHANGE THE LAW AND PERHAPS WITH THE SUPPORT OF
USA CITIZENS CAN CHANGE THE USA CONSTITUTION.*

Respected MS ANITA ALVERZ

YES. CRIME- IS CRIME. NEGLIGENCE IS NEGLIGENCE.DEATH IS DEATH
REAGRDLESS OUTSIDE ON THE ROAD OR MALL, GROCERY
STORE , PARKING LOT OR IMPORTANTLY PROTECTS
VICTIMS WHO WERE ROBBED IN STORES, CONSUMER
CITIZENS FOR MONEY, ID, FAUD, $1000 THOUSNAD
DOLLARS OR $100 THOUSAND DOLLARS. WHICH CAN BE

RECOVERED. VICTIM CAN BE JAILED AND PUT ON BOND. SHOPS CAN BE CLOSED. DRIVERS CAN KILL ON THR ROAD, ANY OTER CONSUMNER FAUD AND MANY OTHE ON LINE FRAUD. COOK COINTY AND ATTORNRY GENERAL TAKES ONLY .

MUCH MONEY BUT HIGH THINKING AND THE WORD GREED IS NOT IN MY BLOOD NOR IT WAS IN MY PRECIOUS DARLING WIFE---- TWO BODIES ONE SOUL? WHERE IS THE LAW FOR THEM? WHY? THEY ARE US CITIZENS AND OUR PASSPORTS SAYS WE WOULD PROTECT OUR US CITIZENS ANYWHERE IN THE WORLD.

WHY CAN'T WE SAVE THEM FROM THE CLUTUCHES FOR MEDICAL PROFESSION, MEDICAL EXPERTS ARE ALL TOGETER AND DO NOT WANT GO AGAINST ANY DOCTOR AND RECIPORCAL. AS A RESULT ATTORNEYS CAN NOT FILE A LAW SUIT FOR THE VICTIM OF THE PERSON WHOSE RELATION RUINED HIS HER LIFE. THEY ARE US CITIZENS. WHY THEY HAVE TO SUFFER.? DOCTOR' JOB IS TO HELP SICK PERSON. IF DOCTOR FAILED TO COPLY WITH THE TREATMENT BY GRED FROM THE PHARAMACUTICALS COMPANIES WHO ARE STILL GIVE THESE DOCTORS SOME FORM OF REWARDS0 EITHER IN CASH, VACATION, SECOND HOME SO THAT THESE SO CALL DOCTORS OF MEDICINE - MD FEEL THEY SPEND LOTS OF MONEY IN SCHOOL RECOVERS MONEY AND SOME WANTS TO LIVE IN STYLE. SOCIETY RESPECT THEM DOCTOR. IF THEY ARE GOD. DR. DR. DR. DR. DR. DR. AND SOCIETRY IS IMPRESSED MY SON IS DOCTOR. MY DAUGHTER OS DAUGHTER. MY SON IN LAW IS DOCTOR. MY DAUGHTER IS GOING TO MARRY DOCTOR. YES, IN ANOTHER CASES, YES MY SON- SON IN LAW IS FROM ELITE WORKING IN THE BANK. MY DAUGHTER- SON OR RELATION WENT TO NORTHWESTEREN – YALE- LOYALA – UNIVERSITY OF ILLINIOIS FOR MBA BUT CANNOT FIEN DJOB . MANY

STUDENTS I KNOW AFTER GRADUTING FROM GOOD SCHOOLS MBA UNDERGRADUATE WORKING IN STARBUCKS TRADERS JOE, WHOLE FOOD, BAKERY- AT AND T SELLING PHONE- DRIVING TAXI.IT IS A CRIME TO PROTECT THESE DOCTORS IF THEY RUIN A CASE. THEY SHOULD ADMIT YES, WE MADE AN ERROR AND HAND OVER THE CASE TO ANOTHER DOCTOR OR SUGGEST THAT I AM NOT TRAINED IN THIS FILED, PLEASE GO TO ANOTHER DOCTOR.

THAT WHAT HAD HAPPENED TO MY WIFE AND IT HAS AFFECTED MY LIFE DUE TO THE MALPRACTICE, MISTAKES AND NOT LETTING US OR HER TO GO FOR THE SECOND OPINION UNTILL I TOLD HIM" BLUNTRLY THAT I AM TAKING MY WIFE TO MAYO CLINIC ON NOVEMBER 2, 2014. **BOTHE HER DOCTORS TOLD"""" WHAT MAYO WOULD DO WHAT WE CAN NOT DO" MAYO IS A MARKETING GYMMICS AND WE ARE MUCH BETTER HERE AS DOCTOR SO THAT WE DO *NOT GO*.**"

MURDER CAN BE TRACED. FBI CAN BE INVOLVE IN EVERY CASE AS LONG IT IS IN THE PUBLIC PLACE, STREETS, GANGS OUUTSIED THE STORE, OUTSIDE ON THE DOWNDOWN. ON THE TRAIN. ANYWHRERE. BUT NOT IN THE HOSPITAL WHERE A INNOCENT SICK PERSON IS MADE TO DIE SO THAT DR. CAN NOT BE SUIED. WHO AND WHICH LAW I SPROTECTING THE DOCTORS./

WHY OUR LAW ATTORNET GENRAEL, ACOOK COUNTY ATTORNRY GENERAL, SENATOR WHY DO THETY ACT FOR ANY CRIME OUTSIDE THE HOSPITAL. WHY NOT THE SAME LAW TO ALL THE USA CITIZENS WLIKE PRADEEP ABD HUIS BELOVED WIFE CONSTANCE HIGHLY EDUCATED CONTRIBUTED IN THE USA. PAID TAXES, GOOD CIITIZEN NOT CHAETED ANY ONE EXCELLENT CREDIT RATIONG TAUGHT 34 YEARS IN MORTON GROVE, CALIFORNIA GERMANT TO US MILITRY CJILDEREN WENT TO UNIVERSITY OF MICHIGAN CARLTON COLLEGE.

1. CPR was performed after 9 minutes and then medical records I collected two- three tines did not had that record. However, by my persistent calling and visiting, was successful in getting. I have that record now.
2. You were on the ventilator from 22nd an till March 2nd and I had the power of attorney as to what have, I have to do is was in my mind and was thinking of Palliative care or Tracheostomy which rehabilitation. However doctors did not gave that chance too.
3. On 27th February, 2015 Florida Harris and Katie were there and they told me that Constance is okay and I can go for one hour and can come back. THAT WOULD REMAIN THE MOST SUSPENSE AND PAINFUL DAY IN MY LIFE.
4. Dr. Brockstine who was no longer your doctor had no business to come along with other palliative care and must have conspired the nurse Katie to join hands. When I reached there they all came and told me" Mr. Berry, I do not have any more power and Constance wishes has to be fulfilled and she wants her tubes out so we would do that and you are nothing now.
5. They all told me that they called her brother Michael fuller in Sanibel, Florida on the face time and they both waved their hands and Michel said " I LOVE YOU". I was mad that Constance had told me that she does not want Michael and his children and grandchildren to visit them or call them as they had never bothered calling in the last two years nor they ever came to see us. She was extremely hurt from their behavior and told me never even answer the home.
6. They removed her tubes around 1.30 or so and Constance was able to speak with me for one hour and I told her she would be fine and we would go home with Palliative care when they tell us after a day or two. She was happy and was saying you want to got to the bank for selling the car as we had to vacate rented garage by March and let' sell our Camry Car. I said wait till we go home and then she said "alright with me as we have end of the month TO SELL.. However, she was desperate that she would feel happier to come home and be in her room and own bed and if Palliative care nurses, Doctors come I would be fine". I said absolutely and she asked if I

had brought her clothes, walker and oxygen which she knew was there but asked if it in the rooms that she should get going in the morning. I said yes. I was very happy that now slowly she would start eating and be improving in the home atmosphere listening to night show, days of lives, movies, food of her taste Salmon, shrimps, Indian tea, some stuff from Benson Bakery, and slowly, I would take her out for some change and slowly- slowly -slowly she would recover and can have her treatment in March from Dr. Merkel who was sure that Constance can live another 5-10 or more or les but she is not going to die soon as his treatment is reducing her pain and improving her breathing and even after the tubes were taken out the palliative care doctors and nurses were happy that we would keep her in the palliative care for two to three days till she is stabilized and we would let her go home and then nurses and doctors would be in touch to see her condition but her prognosis looks good- good – Mr. Berry. Your devotion has worked,.. they told me on the 26th night and 27 the morning and that made me to leave the hospital for an hour to go out on some work being Friday, knowing I cannot go anywhere once she is home and I have to be with her 24 hours with 8 hours with Florida Harris, to do the laundry, cleaning and ergons to get food and I stay in her room with my books, newspapers and serve her food three times a day, HOW THE EARTH I KNEW MY HAPPINESS WOULD GO AFTER 9 HOURS DUE TO NOT DONE WHAT THEY TOLD ME AND THERE WAS NO STAFF AS FRIDAY AT 4.30 ALL LEFT FOR THE WEAK END . Later I saw by 4 PM no one was coming and Constance condition or breathing was getting bad. I started calling the nurses and Doctors from the Hospital room next to her and I am sure Florida Harris or some nurse made a 32 minutes video which I have, to prove that I am next to Constance and calling from my cell phone and hospital room. Their using the hospital room, I am shouting and shouting and hospital phone ringing what can we do? I said send the nurse someone. I am sick and calling for a long time over half hour and no one is coming. I used and can be heard " This is medical negligence and you do not care for my wife and please send s end. No one came. Nurses are running around outside for other patients and its easily can be seen in that video. I have another 6 minutes video where after making lots of calls Hospice girl Katherine came and was talking to me and asking Constance, if she need anything, but only observing that . She did not do anything to save her as it was even in her mind , in my opinion, why bother Constance has to die and no attempt to save her or make her give more oxygen, mask or injection to get her breathing better or calling emergency numbers or ER or anything. She did not do that. I am sure she was part of the conspiracy to Let Constance Berry die so that this so called Dr. Brockstine head and neck oncologist wanted Constance to die, in my opinion, as He is the one who in my 500% opinion, had ruined Constance case and was paranoids when we Came from Mayo Clinic on November 2nd to -8th November, 2014 Constance was declared Palliative care. Mayo had to put Constance was very sick in the report but did not write why she got so sick and that she has only Palliative care option.? If she was not affiliated with Evanston hospital. She may or may not written" she was made sick by four things. (1) Giving too much chemo in April 2013. 2 No Bronchoscopy after she got water in her lungs in June 2013, (3)..Left of water of 37MM which was not take out at Evanston hospital and later became a thick flame in November 2014, when Bronchoscopy was done in Mayo on November 3,2014.

Dr. Brockstine pat scan showed in 2013 March, CONNIE is cancer free. Had he ordered the Bronchoscopy he had found that some cells may be spreading but he was not worried as pat scan showed she is cancer free . Who made her sick? Dr. Brockstine.? These so called humanity doctors knows how to cure and how to kill and protect each other for their own reputation and law suit. This is the first time ,I have realized this thing in my over 42 years in the USA. I could have never ever- ever- ever- ever- ever thought, it can happen on world' best country USA. Dr, Brockstine who is rated one of the best doctors in enology must wanted that his name remain top and that he should be a free bird- no matter, if Constance die and her loving husband Pradeep Berry suffer throughout life without Constance, which I am . My life is shattered, devastated, ruined, has no desire to do anything except to get justice for Constance I promised at her death in front of the doctor who came to certify, , in the cremation, at the time of her ashes put in her plot, at the time of her stone and all the time, I go to her Commentary in Skokie and stay one hour and touch the stone, grass and soil put on my head and says" CONNIE PLEASE BLESS ME, I SHOULD BE ABLE TO GET JUSTICE – I REPAEETA THIS WITH ANGER, BUT WITH MY FAITH AND ASK GOD TO HELP ME TO HAVE A MIRACLE. SOME ATTORNRY- I DO NOT THINK WOULD TAKE THIS CASE WHERE THEY HAVE TO SPEND TIME AND FIGHT THIS EASY CASE.. May be they think they do not have enough chance of making millions

MORE THAN A MILLION WORTH

6/7/2013   Fw: Connie law suit final points september 8, 2015

From: PRADEEP BERRY <pradeepberry@sbcglobal.net>
To: alknorr <alknorr@aol.com>
Subject: Fw: Connie law suit final points september 8, 2015
Date: Tue, Jun 7, 2016 3:11 am

On Thursday, February 11, 2016 5:50 PM, PRADEEP BERRY <pradeepberry@sbcglobal.net> wrote:

Sent from Yahoo Mail on Android

On Tue, Sep 8, 2015 at 3:45 AM, PRADEEP BERRY
<pradeepberry@sbcglobal.net> wrote:

"In my Opinion: The following are very strong points;"

1. Connie got four extra chemotherapy as Dr. Brockstine- head and neck oncologist in the middle of the March till April 17, 2013. After a little scarf in the patscan in December 2012. He started giving Chemotherapy. Pat scan in March, 2013 showed, she was fine and cancer was not there.
2. He insisted four extra chemotherapy. That resulted in Neuropathy, which he said, would go away. But it did not, and physical therapy was given. Later her oxygen was low, and Physical therapy had to be stopped.
3. X-ray showed water in her lungs and biopsy indicated breast cancer cells from 2002. He should have given the case to breast cancer oncologist, as I told him. He said no. He suggested Thoracenteses, and I was taking her twice a week for that, from July, 2013, and in January 14, 2014, we went to Florida. Dr. at Florida Cancer center suggested injection Faslodex, which was not suggested by Brockstine. When I called him, he said, he did not think of and it is a good idea. Florida Dr. and Brockstine agreed that when we are back in March, 1,2014, , it should be continued. In early January, 2013, Connie also saw Dr. Winslow a pulmonary Dr. At North shore, who suggested oxygen, and thought Florida climate and humidity would do better. We flew with Oxygen concentration, but Connie bought portable too for going for the Thoracenteses and the injection in Florida.

4. After we came back from Florida, Thoracenteses was still going and water was getting lower.
5. Winslow prescribed Dulera inhaler, which is actually for asthma patients. Connie took accordingly. It ruined her condition- which too has been reported in Mayo Clinic Report.
6. Connie went for Thoracentesis in the second and third week of July, 2014and end of July. Thoracenteses showed 37MM water, and north shore said" <u>it is too little to take out</u>. That water as shown in Mayo clinic reports thickens as a flame and heavy blocking her airways. Mayo also said, Dulera worsened her breathing and in the Mayo clinic reports. Mayo also mentioned in the report, no Bronchoscopy was done in July 2014 and Mayo did all that. That is how they figured out her case was spoiled and Metastasis was in her lungs airways. That is how Mayo Clinic put in the report" <u>and referred Palliative care which was a shock to us.</u>
7. After coming from Mayo, I called Brockstine several times but he did not call back.
8. Connie was highly educated and intelecutal and said" Brockstine ruined her life and now taking my Life". "He must be chomping and worried that law suit is coming".
9. I called the ex-chairman of north shore at his home, who is a renewed oncologist too. He was shocked and promised some would call. But in vain. After few days chairman called me, if I heard from someone. I said no. <u>He said" he would get involved and find some treatment, Dr. Brockstine called on 25th November and left a message as Connie was not able to pick up the phone due to her weakness</u> and I had gone to get the food. I have that message saved" MR and Mrs. Berry" I could not call, as I was reading all the reports of Mayo and was discussing. He said" I would hand over this case to Dr. Merkel a breast cancer oncologist who cured Connie from breast cancer in 2002.
10. Dr. Merkel was angry when we saw him in his office-- in the locked room. He said" Who was on the team" We said" Brockstine and Winslow" He said" why did they not consult him as he has been doing this for over thirty years. He was just mad as Brockstine and Winslow spoiled Connie' case. In December, 2014, and one in January 2015. February 20th 2015 was not done as Connie fell down and was taken to the hospital and was to be released on February 21-22. I saw DNR and Mrs. Berry Told DR. Woods and Dr. Fish on call at north shore to change to DR and they assured us, but when Connie had heart attack, Doctors waited 8- 9 minutes before they could do CPR. I was a tiger and a Lion and blasted them that Ds. Woods and Dr. Fish assured me in the presence of a nurse that it was changed to DR or . If I was not a ferocious tiger, they would not have done CPR and Connie would have been dead on February 21,2015

11. Why did Dr, Brockstine- who had handed over the case to Dr. Merkel ovein November,2014. He was hanging over keep coming to see me and leaving note to talk to me, which I refused. Why was he there as a chief with other 6 palliative care and nurses to make a decision to take Connie' tubes on March 27, 2015 vs March 2nd, 2015 as it was promised to me by 2014 the nurses and cardiac unit? That too when I was just gone for an hour? Also the Palliative care Dr. and Brockstine, without my permission and Connie's too, took the telephone number from the internet and called her brother in his Florida vacation home from the face time and he said, he cannot come. Connie never wanted to see them nor wanted to do with them as they have been behaving badly with since they inherited lots of money and snobs and Connie' sister in law is jealous why her children and grandchildren like Connie and Pradeep? These doctors went against my wife- Connie' wishes. <u>Shame to all of them?</u>

They are rich and have no love or passion for her sister except for her four 50 to 45 years children, spouses and 7 grandchildren. These relatives of Connie and I would say mine too, have never given me condolence. Only aunt who left money for them. Her brother too lives in Wisconsin and in January to May he and his wife goes to Sanibel for fun. <u>Children, spouses and grand kids who have never even called me nor anyone out of the all as they all live in Wisconsin ever came for</u> Connie' cremation till today.

1.In my opinion, My Darling wife, Mrs. Constance Berry y of 39/2 half years, in died due to the absolute negligence of two doctors at the North Shore Health Care System (North) in Evanston. One Dr. is a specialist in Head and Neck Oncology specialist Dr. Brockstine and head of the department too. Another one is pulmonary specialist, Dr. Winslow and that too supposed to be the head of the department.

2. Connie who was going for regular check up and Mammogram at North regularly was diagnosed with breast cancer in August 2002. She had surgery by S Saner and some nodes were treating, but no breasts were removed. She was given Chemotherapy and radiation suggested by Dr. Merkel -Breasts Cancer Oncologist at North.

3. In December, 2004 she had some ear infection and went to see her Internal medicine Dr. at St Stephens's hospital in Evanston, he suggested biopsy, as there was some small lump on her right chic- parotid gland. She was give two weeks of antibiotics and she took another two weeks and her Dr, had said, if you do not

PRADEEP K. BERRY

Fw: Connie law suit final points september 8, 2015

feel better, go and see Dr. Merkel. She did not get better and went to Dr. Merkel in January, or February 2005. He said "he has no concerns; but see ENT specialist, if does not get better. Her intuition was telling her that her lip movements were bothering, and she went to ENT specialist at North. His immediacy took Biopsy and results showed "Parotid Gland Cancer"- a new one.

4. In a hurry, .Dr. Stephen Senor at North did six hour surgery on March, 31, 2005 and could not save one facial nerve and stated, she would have some problems which only, she and I, could notice, when she moves her lips and may have to drink more and more water to eat to make saliva

5. She was referred to Dr., Bruce Brockstine, head and neck specialist and he gave her radiation on and asked to have pat scan every six months etc. She did that.

6. in mid-2006, Brockstine spotted a small scarf in the pat scan and treated with Chemotherapy and regular pat scan and MRI. Connie showed him some cancer herbals which saves the cancer cells and help to tolerate chemotherapy and gives strength to body. "He said go and take" and while going for regular pat scan

6. She was fine until middle of November in 2011 and Brockstine saw a spot on her node in her lung after Pat scan and gave her chemotherapy and she was fine.

7. In September ,2012 another spot was detected and Brockstine said, have another pat scan in December, 2013 to be sure and he confirmed and decided to give different Chemotherapy and she can finish that in Sanibel as we wanted to go. After her chemotherapy in March 18, her cancer was gone, but he decided to give four extra Chemotherapy We were not happy but listened to him. Connie had four chemotherapy and was done in April 17, 2013. After that she devoloved Neuropathy and in June 2013, they found water in her lungs, which was detected by x-ray and were cancer cells from the 2002 breast cancer. He suggested taking water out every weak from one lung and next day from second lung. In November, 2013 we saw pulmonary dr. 8.Winslow at the NORTH, who suggested oxygen and Connie was sleeping whole night with the oxygen concentration. . Her condition was not getting better.

9. WE flew to Florida with Oxygen concentration and Dr. Winslow and Brockstine also thought that Florida climate in January till March would do wonders due to hot and humid weather. But she was not finding any improvements at all.

10. in Florida. We went to Florida Cancer Center and the Dr. There suggested one injection to dry up the water every month. When we called Brockstine, he said "It is Not a bad Idea" I said, why you not suggested" He said "it was in his mind but was not sure". I told him that it's time we see the lung or breast cancer, but he said "NO". After three injections in Florida water was reducing pretty fast and got dried up due to the injection , and when we came home in February end, Doctor at Florida had said continue the injection and Brockstine too took his suggestion and said, okay to continue the injection and the water out and injection. But her condition was getting bad. Pulmonary Dr. Winslow at North suggested one inhaler, Dulera used for asthma which caused more problems. We were very angry with these two drs. at North and told them, we are going to Mayo Clinic. They said **"What would Mayo do, that we are not doing" " Mayo is a name and Marketing gimmicks only- but nothing else".**

11. It was Mayo clinic' Dr. Keo, who stated that she and Mayo do not believe in pat scan, inhaler, and the small amount of water 17MM should have been removed at North. **At North, they knew that there was 17MM water but stated" It is not worth taking out"** Drake at Mayo ordered many tests, Bronchoscopy, air test, Water 17MM to be taken out, cardiac test etc. in four days.

12. On the fifth day, Dr. Keo said" Mr. and Mrs. Berry, North did not do the right treatment and ruined your case. They should have done Bronco spy, 37 mm water should have been taken out, and the Inhaler Dulera has worsened Connie' case.

13. Dr. Keo said "The water become like a big thick flame and blocking the lung airways and the cancer has spread in the lung airways as pat scan only shows new spots but not spreading of the cancer. They made four mistakes.

In a way, if not directly, but indirectly, it is mentioned in the Mayo Clinic Report. If all that report, which is not very lengthy, Judge, common Dr. Attorney can make out it was Negligence by Brockstine and Winslow and North shore. What and how more clear one needs? It is picture worth 1000 words. This report if given full emphasis an evidence itself. We do not need testimony,witness, murderer was caught red handed. If it is not Malpractice- negligence per the report, then what is Malpractice? Then there is no difference in a Free Democratic country: USA and South Africa or Hiti, and other poor countries. Malpractice law then be abolished and democracy should not be called.

14 .North Relied on the pat scan which is not a full proof and does not show any spreading of the cancer, but new spots. Bronchoscopy should have been done in 2013 which was not done except at Mayo on November, 4- or 5th 2015 which showed spreading of the cancer.

15. 37 MM water should have been taken out and that has become like a thick flame or ice and blocking the airways.

16 Inhaler does not go with the oxygen. It is only for the Asthma and has worsened the breathing of Mrs. Constance Berry.

17. Air test at North was not done properly and no number up to where MRs. Berry could breathe and the technician was not the right person to be on that job as he was yelling her to take breathing making her and me nervous and any normal person would be under stress.

18. They should have fully seen that why air test was not properly recorded as to up to what number from 1 to 50 have gone. They did not perform the air test properly and the technician must be useless which we know, he was as he was just shouting and making both of us nervous with his style of air test.

19. Dr. Keo.at Mayo said, had your both Doctors at North. Told you suggested or given the permission to come to Mayo or anywhere, Mrs. Berry would have been not in such a serious condition. Now, due **to their ego or what, Connie Berry has no choice, but Palliative care. It was the most devastated news we ever got. After coming from Mayo, I called Brockstine Oncologist ten times, but he did not call back. "Connie told me he must be nervous as Malpractice law suit must be coming. I called the ex-chairman at North who is also a known Oncologist at the North .He was shocked and said "someone would call, but in vain. He called me back after two days, if someone called, I said no. He said some would have to call as: I am going to step in. On November 22, 2014, Brockstine - Oncologist at North called and left a message on our answering machine saying "he was discussing with Mayo and has been reading reports etc. Now he is not going to take this case and giving it to Breast cancer specialist Dr. Merkel at North (His office is on the same building) would take over. I have saved that message on my answering machine"**

Dr. Merkel treated Connie' breast cancer in 2002. When Dr. Merkel came to see us in the locked room around the end of November, 2014, He said" "Who was on the team" we gave him the names of Dr. Brockstine and Dr. Winslow at North. "He said, "Why did they not consult me as this is my area, and I have been seeing patients and curing them for the last 30 years. He was extremely angry"

The purpose of writing this episode is for the enlightenment of people, a humanity cause, which might save lives of some. Please "Don't trust your doctor blindly, and if needed, get a second opinion". Mayo Clinic diagnosed Connie' condition in four days, with different tests, which should have been conducted at her hospital North shore (HH). We both were still optimistic that, Connie would be alive and with me for a long time. In my opinion, her two Doctors at the HH ruined her case in the last two years and finally her death. What difference it makes to them, they are still working, did not follow the noble cause of being a doctor. We all trust them next to God, when sickness occurs. Do they know this or ever thought of this? Perhaps, in my opinion, NO they should have been open to tell us to go for the second opinion, but their ego and overconfidence was in place, even with my request. We both are convinced in our

MORE THAN A MILLION WORTH

Berry, Constance A (MR # 003211828)

All Notes (continued)

Progress Notes by Augustin, Catherine, RN at 02/27/15 2338 (continued) — Version 1 of 1
847-475-3002
pgr 6786

Progress Notes by Adegunsoye, Ayodeji O., MD at 02/27/15 2153 — Version 1 of 1
Author: Adegunsoye, Ayodeji O., MD   Service: Intensive Care   Author Type: Physician
Filed: 02/27/15 2208   Note Time: 02/27/15 2153   Status: Signed
Editor: Adegunsoye, Ayodeji O., MD (Physician)

Patient who is currently DNR status noted to be hypotensive with systolic BP in the low 70s. She appears less agitated and calm presently. SpO2 in the 70-80s and supplemental oxygen by nasal cannula increased from 2L to 6L. She has increased oral/airway secretions and appears volume overloaded with anasarca. Husband at bedside and agrees with decision not to give IV fluid boluses given high likelihood of worsening her cardiopulmonary status and increasing airway secretions with respiratory distress. He appears to have come to terms with the patients decision to be terminally extubated. Husband (and family members by phone) offering final prayers. Patients ICU nurse and hospice nurse at bedside throughout above proceedings administering care, comforting the patient and her grieving husband.

[Handwritten annotation: HUSBAND - PRADEEP WAS TOLD and I agreed that TUBES would be TAKEN OUT on MARCH 2n 201.]

Progress Notes by Deamant, Catherine D., MD at 02/27/15 0622 — Version 3 of 3
Author: Deamant, Catherine D., MD   Service: Palliative Care   Author Type: Physician
Filed: 02/27/15 2155   Note Time: 02/27/15 0622   Status: Addendum
Editor: Deamant, Catherine D., MD (Physician)
Related Notes: Original Note by Deamant, Catherine D., MD (Physician) filed at 02/27/15 2151

NorthShore University HealthSystem Palliative Care Program

[Handwritten annotation: My ABsence — ALL LIES But FRAUD. I was Just want for one hour and there careleder — they look acknowledge ? m AR]

Interval History:
Required diltiazem infusion yesterday, now off. Persistent hypocalcemia.

Pt seen with Dr. Deamant, Katie RN, Peggy Lester APN-student. Connie had been off both fentanyl and versed for 1-2 hours. She was awake and alert, communicating clearly and consistently by shaking her head yes and no, also by mouthing words despite ET tube in her mouth. She told us that she was without dyspnea, without pain, without nausea or full feeling.

We asked her if she was comfortable. She said no. We asked her if the ET tube was bothering her. She said yes. We explained to her that she has the ET tube in her mouth/throat, connected to the breathing machine. Explained to her that her lungs have weakened further since her arrest and she has required the support of the breathing machine to continue to breathe. We explained that her pulmonary status has been so weak that if she were to come off the breathing machine, she would likely die within hours or days and would not have a chance of recovery. She understood. We asked her if she wanted to remain on the ventilator to have a chance of recovery AND have tracheostomy and gastrostomy tubes placed for more permanent means of ventilation and nutrition. She said no. We asked her if she wanted the ET tube to come out. She said yes. We asked her who she trusts to make medical decisions for her. She said "Mike." We asked if she meant her brother, Michael C. Fuller. She said yes. We asked if she felt Michael was able to make medical decisions for her. She said yes. We asked if she felt comfortable with her husband Pradeep making medical decisions for her. She said no. We asked if she wanted the medical team to let her brother Michael know about the circumstances that brought her to the hospital and update him on her condition. She said yes. We asked her if she wanted to appoint her brother Michael as her health care power of attorney. She said yes. We prepared the document and Connie signed it. We asked Connie if she wanted to die in the hospital. She said yes. We

PRADEEP K. BERRY

Berry, Constance A (MR # 003211828)
Progress Notes by Deamant, Catherine D., MD at 02/27/15 0622 (continued)

- If pt survives the night, recommend hospice enrollment and then transfer to PCU

Thank you for the opportunity to participate in the care of this patient.

Please call with questions or concerns.

Hillarie Joehl, RN, MS, ACNP-BC, ACHPN
Nurse Practitioner
NorthShore University HealthSystem Palliative Care Division
Office: 847-503-4222
Evanston pager: 2747

Total time with patient, husband 4+ hours > 50% spent in education/counseling.

Palliative Medicine Attending Physician Attestation Note:

I have reviewed the medical records, and seen and evaluated this patient, and personally conducted the key elements of the history and exam. I have reviewed and agree with the documentation above, along with the following amendments:

Patient was consistent in her responses through the day while on the ventilator as outlined above with each question posed to her. She shook her head affirmatively that she did not want the ventilator to be continued and with a clear understanding that death could occur shortly after removal of the tube. She also expressed consistently when asked who she trusted to make medical decisions for her if she lost capacity that she selected her brother, Michael C. Fuller. When probed if she thought her husband would be best to make those decisions, she shook her head "no" consistently. When he was present, she still expressed this again. Her husband stated that he did not feel she was able to make decisions and he was informed that she was consistent in her responses and consistent with multiple providers present and on several occasions today and that we will be honoring what the patient is telling us. He expressed that he was upset that her brother had been notified of her condition as he had not called him to let him know that she was in the hospital. He did not believe that she wanted her brother to be able to make decisions for her. We reinforced that it was the patient's request to contact her brother that led us to reach him. Reviewed the patient's conversation with her brother as outlined above. Reviewed that the patient has also been consistent in shaking her head "no" to the question about going home and he was present when she shook her head "yes" to remaining in the hospital until her death. Again, he expressed distress as he felt that she had told him in the past that she wished to be at home. Reinforced that we are listening to the patient's wishes about her care as she is expressing them now and we are guided by the patient's decisions and respecting the choices that she is telling us at this time.

Should the patient survival the night, we will readdress the option of transition to palliative care unit for continued comfort care. Based on the patient's expressed wishes to focus on comfort and allow the natural dying process to occur, I recommend discontinuing medications that do not contribute to her comfort. She has already expressed that she does not want face mask or BiPAP.

Catherine Deamant, MD
Palliative Medicine Physician
NorthShore University HealthSystem
Pager: 8197

Time spent: 9:00-10:30 am; 2:00-3:00 pm; 4:30-6:00 pm

MORE THAN A MILLION WORTH

 MAYO CLINIC

Patient Copy
Cardiovascular Diseases

7-499-446 13-Nov-2014 14:53
Mrs. Constance Ann Berry

Consult

Generated: 26-Apr-2015 19:48

DEMOGRAPHIC INFORMATION
Clinic Number: ~~7-499-446~~
Patient Name: Mrs. Constance Ann Berry
Age: ▓ Y
Birthdate: 16-Feb-▓▓ Sex: F
Address: Apartment 2B, 1310 Maple Avenue City: Evanston, IL 60201-4375

Service Date/Time: 13-Nov-2014 14:53
Provider: John P. Bois, MD Pager: 127-05632
Service: CV Type/Desc: CON Status: Fnl Revision #: 3

REFERRAL
Karina A. Keogh, MD, Department of Pulmonary Medicine.

CHIEF COMPLAINT/PURPOSE OF VISIT
Mrs. Berry is a very pleasant 77-year-old female with a history of breast cancer status post surgical intervention at an outside institution (2002) and parotid cancer status post surgery and radiation therapy (outside institution, 2005) who has been under the care of Dr. Keogh here at Mayo Clinic for evaluation of recurrent dyspnea and has been found to have findings of metastatic breast cancer involving the lungs, pleural space, and endobronchial mucosa. She is referred to us today for evaluation of dyspnea.

HISTORY OF PRESENT ILLNESS
PRIOR TO CURRENT CONSULTATION
Mrs. Berry's cardiovascular risk factors include age and ongoing malignancy. She has no known smoking history, hypertension, hyperlipidemia, or diabetes mellitus. She has no known prior cardiac events or cardiac interventions. There is no mention of family history or early coronary disease.

Per review of Dr. Keogh's notes, the patient did develop breast cancer in 2002 and had surgery at an outside institution. Three years later (2005) she had surgery and radiation therapy for parotid cancer (it is not mentioned that she had had any radiation therapy for her breast cancer or chemotherapy).

Several years later she developed pulmonary nodules concerning for metastases and most recently developed pleural effusions. These were quite large requiring repeat thoracentesis almost every week. She was initiated on Arimidex therapy followed by Faslodex. Her pleural effusions have decreased in size, but she notes that she has had progressive dyspnea and a 20-pound weight loss.

This decline in functioning status is what initiated the workup here at Mayo Clinic. When seen by Dr. Keogh, the patient had inspiratory and expiratory wheezing. Dr. Keogh was concerned for endobronchial involvement of the patient's malignancy. She sent the patient for a bronchoscopy, and a mucosal lesion has been biopsied and is concerning for malignant involvement. The patient also had a thoracentesis here at Mayo Clinic and noted that there was thick fluid and simple fluid. The simple fluid was able to be removed, and it is also consistent with malignancy. Dr. Keogh has noted that Mrs. Berry's thick fluid in her pleural cavity is not amenable to removal with thoracentesis.

The patient has also undergone an ECG that notes sinus tachycardia with premature atrial contractions. She has had an echocardiogram here at Mayo Clinic that notes a preserved ejection fraction at 61% with grade 1/4 diastolic dysfunction, mild MR, mild to moderate TR, normal RV size and function, with an elevated RVSP of 40 mm Hg. The inferior vena cava size is normal with normal collapse. No strain was performed because of her PACs. CT scan noted increased interstitial thickening throughout the lungs and a question of a lymphangitic carcinomatosis. The right middle lobe is collapsed.

PFTs noted a remarkably low DLCO of 19%, reduced vital capacity of 38%, reduced FEV1 of 37%, and FVC to 30%.

This printout was generated through Patient Online Services and was the most current version as of the date and time generated.

MAYO CLINIC

Patient Copy
Cardiovascular Diseases
Consult

7-499-446 13-Nov-2014 14:53
Mrs. Constance Ann Berry

CURRENT CONSULTATION
A. Clinical.
Patient did not show
B. Testing.
Echocardiogram, ECG, CT chest all noted above. The most recent laboratory tests from November 3, 2014, noted normocytic anemia of 11.0, normal leukocyte count, normal platelet count. Her AST is normal. Her creatinine is 0.4. Her NT-BNP is at 1037.

CURRENT MEDICATIONS
anastrozole 1 mg tablet 1 tablet by mouth one time daily.

calcium citrate capsule 1 capsule by mouth one time daily.

Dulera 200-5 mcg/actuation HFA Aerosol 2 puffs by inhalation two times a day.

fiber tablet 5-6 tablets by mouth two times a day.

Fish Oil 300 mg capsule 1 capsule by mouth one time daily.

herbak- cellutol 300mg* (Free Text Entry) 1 one time daily.

hydrochlorothiazide 12.5 mg capsule 1 capsule by mouth one time daily.

occuvite* (Free Text Entry) 1 one time daily.

potassium chloride 20 mEq tablet sustained release 5 tablets by mouth two times a day.

ProAir HFA 90 mcg/actuation HFA Aerosol 2 by inhalation inhale as needed.
  Indication, Site, and Additional Prescription Instructions:
    2-3 times a day

Synthroid 112 mcg tablet 1 tablet by mouth one time daily.

Vitamin D3 2,000 unit tablet 1 tablet by mouth one time daily.

Xanax 0.25 mg tablet 1 tablet by mouth as needed.
  Indication, Site, and Additional Prescription Instructions:
    unknown

These are the patient's medications as of Thursday, 13-Nov-2014 at 14:53.

ALLERGIES/ADVERSE REACTIONS
  No Known Allergies
  Allergies above current as of Thursday, 13-Nov-2014 at 14:53.

SYSTEMS REVIEW
  Negative other than indicated in the HPI

IMPRESSION/REPORT/PLAN
  Patient did not appear for appointment. Appears it was to have been canceled.

This printout was generated through Patient Online Services and was the most current version as of the date and time generated.

MORE THAN A MILLION WORTH

 MAYO CLINIC

Patient Copy
Cardiovascular Diseases

7-499-446 13-Nov-2014 14:53
Mrs. Constance Ann Berry

Consult

Generated: 26-Apr-2015 19:48

Original: JPB
Electronically Signed: 14-Nov-2014 15:08 by J.P. Bois, MD

PRADEEP K. BERRY

 MAYO CLINIC

Patient Copy
Medical Oncology

7-499-446 17-Nov-2014 09:19
Mrs. Constance Ann Berry

Consult

Generated: 26-Apr-2015 19:40

Page 1 of 3

DEMOGRAPHIC INFORMATION
Clinic Number: ~~7-499-446~~
Patient Name: Mrs. Constance Ann Berry
Age: 77 Y
Birthdate: 16-Feb-~~1937~~ Sex: F
Address: Apartment 2B, 1310 Maple Avenue City: Evanston, IL 60201-4375

Service Date/Time: 17-Nov-2014 09:19
Provider: Prema P. Peethambaram, MD Pager: 4-7865
Service: ONCL Type/Desc: CON Status: Fnl Revision #: 4

REVISION HISTORY
Nov-17-2014 13:09:19 - Modification to PAST MEDICAL / SURGICAL HISTORY

REFERRAL
Dr. Karina A. Keogh, Pulmonary Medicine.

CHIEF COMPLAINT/PURPOSE OF VISIT
This patient was not personally interviewed or examined. The history and examination findings are based on the clinical documentation provided and/or discussion with a physician or provider who had personally interviewed and examined the patient.

1. Metastatic breast carcinoma to the lungs.
2. History of parotid carcinoma.

Are there any other treatment options for the patient?

The patient was not seen by me. Only Mayo records including some scanned-in records were available.

HISTORY OF PRESENT ILLNESS
1. In 2002, diagnosed with Breast carcinoma, treated with lumpectomy, radiation, and adjuvant Adriamycin/Cytoxan chemotherapy. Unclear if any adjuvant endocrine therapy was given at that time. Stage and other details of cancer not available to me.
2. Salivary gland adenocarcinoma diagnosed in 2005, no distant metastasis, at that time, had parotidectomy.
3. Metastasis to the lung presumed from the parotid primary, unknown if these lesions were biopsied at that time. Received carboplatin/etoposide with complete response.
4. Cancer-free until 2011, when she had a spinal metastasis and completed radiation therapy to the thoracic spine in August 2011.
5. Retroperitoneal lymph node metastasis noted in September 2011, which was biopsied and showed poorly differentiated carcinoma. Completed five cycles of carboplatin and etoposide until January 2012.
6. Diffuse lymph node and bone metastases, November 2012. Treated with weekly Taxol from December 2012 until April 25, 2013.
7. Dyspnea on exertion around June or July 2013 due to pleural effusion requiring multiple thoracenteses, and cytology was positive for metastatic breast carcinoma, estrogen/progesterone receptor-positive. Initiated on Arimidex in August 2013 and continued until May 2014. Faslodex was added in early 2014. *By Dr. Don Bark - in Florida*
8. Patient seen in Mayo Pulmonary Department by Dr. Karina Keogh for symptoms of cough and dyspnea. Patient was being treated with several inhalers and had worsening of performance status. She is also using oxygen 2 L at night and 4 L during the day. Patient's last thoracentesis was in April 2014. Patient complained of wheezing and 20-pound weight loss. Examination per Dr. Keogh showed that the patient was comfortable at rest, without any adenopathy in the head and neck region. Diffuse inspiratory/expiratory wheeze with stridor throughout both lung fields and 2-plus edema bilaterally.
9. Bronchoscopy at Mayo Clinic on November 5, 2014, showed hemorrhagic secretions from right upper lobe and

Patient Copy
Medical Oncology
Consult

7-499-446 17-Nov-2014 09:19
Mrs. Constance Ann Berry

hypervascularity in the right upper lobe spur. There was a mucosal defect in the bronchus intermedius and involvement of the distal bronchus intermedius to the middle lobe and lower lobe involvement with malignant process; biopsies were taken. There was also a submucosal process in the superior segment of the left lower lobe. Pathology confirmed metastatic adenocarcinoma, consistent with breast primary. ER was diffusely positive, TTF negative, CDX-2 negative, PAX8 and p63 negative. Cytology from left pleural effusion was negative for malignancy at Mayo Clinic.

10. CT chest done at Mayo Clinic, November 5, 2014, compared with outside PET/CT September 2014 shows interval increase in interstitial thickening and nodularity; particularly, left lower lobe suggestive of a lymphangitic carcinomatosis that is progressive. Complete collapse of the right middle lobe. A few lesions in the liver that were difficult to characterize and diffuse sclerotic and lytic bone metastasis. I have reviewed scans available on QREADS. Echocardiogram at Mayo Clinic showed EF 61% on November 4, 2014, with moderate tricuspid valve regurgitation, mild mitral valve regurgitation. No pericardial or pleural effusion noted. An EKG showed sinus tachycardia with a rate of 114 and premature atrial complexes.

REVIEWED INFORMATION AS NOTED ON THE CURRENT VISIT INFORMATION FORM, DATED 03-Nov-2014 AND ON THE PATIENT FAMILY HISTORY FORM, DATED 03-Nov-2014.

CURRENT MEDICATIONS

anastrozole 1 mg tablet 1 tablet by mouth one time daily.

calcium citrate capsule 1 capsule by mouth one time daily.

Dulera 200-5 mcg/actuation HFA Aerosol 2 puffs by inhalation two times a day.

fiber tablet 5-6 tablets by mouth two times a day.

Fish Oil 300 mg capsule 1 capsule by mouth one time daily.

herbak- cellutol 300mg* (Free Text Entry) 1 one time daily.

hydrochlorothiazide 12.5 mg capsule 1 capsule by mouth one time daily.

occuvite* (Free Text Entry) 1 one time daily.

potassium chloride 20 mEq tablet sustained release 5 tablets by mouth two times a day.

ProAir HFA 90 mcg/actuation HFA Aerosol 2 by inhalation inhale as needed.
  Indication, Site, and Additional Prescription Instructions:
    2-3 times a day

Synthroid 112 mcg tablet 1 tablet by mouth one time daily.

Vitamin D3 2,000 unit tablet 1 tablet by mouth one time daily.

Xanax 0.25 mg tablet 1 tablet by mouth as needed.
  Indication, Site, and Additional Prescription Instructions:
    unknown

These are the patient's medications as of Monday, 17-Nov-2014 at 10:42.

PAST MEDICAL/SURGICAL HISTORY
Hypothyroidism.

This printout was generated through Patient Online Services and was the most current version as of the date and time generated.

Patient Copy
Medical Oncology
Consult

7-499-446 17-Nov-2014 09:19
Mrs. Constance Ann Berry

Osteoarthritis.
Colon polyps.
Essential hypertension.
Peripheral neuropathy from chemotherapy.
History of shingles.
Squamous cell carcinoma of the skin.
Melanoma in situ, left forearm.
History of polio with transient right lower extremity weakness as a child.
History of cataracts.
Dacryocystitis.
History of breast cancer, 2002.
COPD.
History of hypokalemia.

IMPRESSION/REPORT/PLAN
LABORATORY
Laboratory tests reviewed. Hemoglobin 11 with a slightly increased RDW. Normal white count, platelet count. Slight decrease in lymphocytes. Creatinine low at 0.4. NT-Pro BNP was quite elevated at 1037 pg/mL.

IMPRESSION/REPORT/PLAN
#1 Metastatic breast carcinoma to the lungs, bones, and lymph nodes, ER-positive, HER-2 unknown
#2 History of parotid adenocarcinoma

It appears that patient is failing fulvestrant and anastrozole therapy, given the progression noted in the lungs between the September PET/CT scan and the November CT scan of the chest. This could account for her increasing respiratory symptoms.

At this juncture, I would favor using palliative chemotherapy if patient is so inclined to consider. Options include eribulin day 1/day 8 out of a 21-day cycle, if tolerated. Yet another combination therapy that could be considered would be gemcitabine and cisplatin. Navelbine or oral Xeloda could be other options.

I have requested that immunostaining be performed on the biopsy done from the bronchoscopy at Mayo Clinic. If indeed HER-2 is overexpressed, then she could benefit from HER-2-directed therapy in combination with chemotherapy.

Although the option of Aromasin and everolimus is available, the response rate would be about 17% and would add only little meaningful clinical benefit to the patient at this juncture.

She could have all of these treatments closer to home, and I do not see any additional benefit in patient returning to Mayo Clinic for a face-to-face consultation at this time. If patient's performance status is really poor, chemo could pose more risks than benefits and supportive and symptomatic care alone may also be a reasonable option.
Thank you for this eConsult. Please call me at 4-7865 if you have any further questions.

DIAGNOSES
#1 Metastatic breast carcinoma to the lungs, bones, and lymph nodes, ER-positive, HER-2 unknown
#2 History of parotid adenocarcinoma

Original: PPP:cah by slr
Electronically Signed: 18-Nov-2014 17:52 by P.P. Peethambaram, MD

This printout was generated through Patient Online Services and was the most current version as of the date and time generated.

 **MAYO CLINIC**

Patient Copy

Pulmonary and Critical Care Medicine

Multi-system Evaluation

7-499-446 03-Nov-2014 10:04
Mrs. Constance Ann Berry

Generated: 26-Apr-2015 20:07

calcium citrate capsule 1 capsule by mouth one time daily.

Dulera 200-5 mcg/actuation HFA Aerosol 2 puffs by inhalation two times a day.

fiber tablet 5-6 tablets by mouth two times a day.

Fish Oil 300 mg capsule 1 capsule by mouth one time daily.

herbak- cellutol 300mg* (Free Text Entry) 1 one time daily.

hydrochlorothiazide 12.5 mg capsule 1 capsule by mouth one time daily.

occuvite* (Free Text Entry) 1 one time daily.

potassium chloride 20 mEq tablet sustained release 5 tablets by mouth two times a day.

ProAir HFA 90 mcg/actuation HFA Aerosol 2 by inhalation inhale as needed.
  Indication, Site, and Additional Prescription Instructions:
    2-3 times a day

Synthroid 112 mcg tablet 1 tablet by mouth one time daily.

Vitamin D3 2,000 unit tablet 1 tablet by mouth one time daily.

Xanax 0.25 mg tablet 1 tablet by mouth as needed.
  Indication, Site, and Additional Prescription Instructions:
    unknown

These are the patient's medications as of Monday, 03-Nov-2014 at 11:51.

ALLERGIES/ADVERSE REACTIONS
No Known Allergies
Allergies above current as of Monday, 03-Nov-2014 at 10:04.

SYSTEMS REVIEW
PAIN SCALE
Patient's pain was reported using the numeric pain scale. Patient/caregiver rates pain at 0/10.

VITAL SIGNS
Height: 149.7 cm. Weight: 52.6 kg. BSA(G): 1.4615 M2. BMI: 23.47 KG/M2. Temperature: 36.1 degrees C, tympanic. (03-Nov-2014 10:02)

Blood Pressure: 108/67 mmHg, single reading, right arm sitting. Pulse Rate: 110/minute, regular. (03-Nov-2014 10:02)

SpO2: 92%. Oxygen Amount: 1 lpm. (03-Nov-2014 10:02)

PHYSICAL EXAMINATION
General: Patient comfortable in no distress.
Eyes: Conjunctivae normal.
ENT: Mildly boggy nasal mucosa.

This printout was generated through Patient Online Services and was the most current version as of the date and time generated.

PRADEEP K. BERRY

 **MAYO CLINIC**

Patient Copy

Pulmonary and Critical Care Medicine

Multi-system Evaluation

7-499-446 03-Nov-2014 10:04
Mrs. Constance Ann Berry

Generated: 26-Apr-2015 20:07   Page 1 of 3

DEMOGRAPHIC INFORMATION
Clinic Number: 7-499-446
Patient Name: Mrs. Constance Ann Berry
Age: 77 Y
Birthdate: 16-Feb- Sex: F
Address: Apartment 2B, 1310 Maple Avenue City: Evanston, IL 60201-4375

Service Date/Time: 03-Nov-2014 10:04
Provider: Karina A. Keogh, MD Pager: 4-6893
Service: PULM Type/Desc: ME Status: Fnl Revision #: 4

REFERRAL
Bruce E. Brockstein, M.D. (847-570-2515)
NorthShore University Health System
2650 Ridge Avenue
Evanston, IL 60201

CHIEF COMPLAINT/PURPOSE OF VISIT
Cough and dyspnea in the setting of known metastatic breast cancer.

HISTORY OF PRESENT ILLNESS
This is a very pleasant 77-year-old, never smoker, no history of prior lung disease, who developed breast cancer in 2002. This was treated surgically. Then in 2005 she developed parotid cancer. This was treated with surgery and radiation. She developed some pulmonary nodules several years later, and there was a concern this was metastatic parotid disease I believe. She then in 2013 developed pleural effusions. Cytology was consistent with breast cancer. She was started on Arimidex. In January 2014, she was started on Faslodex instead. Up until January she was requiring very frequent thoracenteses, up to once a week. That all got much better after she was put on the Faslodex. However, Mrs. Berry feels that she progressively has not been doing as well as previously, and is wondering what the cause of this is, and what can be done about it. She has lost about 20 pounds over the last year. For the last three to four months she has been following with a pulmonologist locally in Illinois and has been tried on several inhalers including Dulera and albuterol, which she is not sure are helping. The Dulera seems to exacerbate the dryness in her mouth, presumably this is primarily related to her previous radiation therapy. She has been using a walker since 2013, but she feels that even with this, she is progressively able to do less. She is going around the clinic in a wheelchair. Since January of this year, she has been using oxygen at night. She typically goes to Florida and that trip earlier this year precipitated starting on oxygen during the day for the flight, which she has continued on. She is using oxygen 2 L at night and 4 L during the day. She has followed up locally with her oncologists. She has had serial PET scans. The pulmonary nodules appear to have improved. She does have uptake in the lymph nodes in the pelvis. She did have a biopsy of one of these several months ago which was apparently benign. She does have persistent uptake around her pleural effusion. Probably some of this is pleural thickening. When they last attempted to do a thoracentesis in June, they felt there was not much fluid there and did not proceed. Her last thoracentesis was in April. When these started in 2013, they were removing close to a liter at time. This then diminished to about 700 cc, 500 cc, and the last few thoracenteses last spring only removed 200 to 300 cc.

Mrs. Berry and her husband are noticing a wheeze that is not always present but is there most of the time. She has no history of asthma as a child. Other than her breathing and her weight loss, she is feeling reasonably well. She does also have known metastatic disease in her bones.

REVIEWED INFORMATION WITH PATIENT AS NOTED ON THE CURRENT VISIT INFORMATION FORM, DATED 03-Nov-2014 AND ON THE PATIENT FAMILY HISTORY FORM, DATED 03-Nov-2014.

CURRENT MEDICATIONS
anastrozole 1 mg tablet 1 tablet by mouth one time daily.

This printout was generated through Patient Online Services and was the most current version as of the date and time generated.

MORE THAN A MILLION WORTH

 MAYO CLINIC

Patient Copy
Pulmonary and Critical Care Medicine
Multi-system Evaluation

7-499-446 03-Nov-2014 10:04
Mrs. Constance Ann Berry

Generated: 26-Apr-2015 20:07

Lymph: No cervical or supraclavicular lymphadenopathy.
Heart: Normal S1, S2. No added sounds. No murmurs appreciated.
Lungs: Diffuse inspiratory and expiratory wheeze/stridor heard throughout the lung fields.
Extremities: Peripheries--2+ edema bilaterally.
Gait: Mildly antalgic.

IMPRESSION/REPORT/PLAN
#1 Dyspnea

I think this most likely is secondary to her history of metastatic disease with lung involvement. Given her physical exam, with the inspiratory wheeze as well as expiratory, I would be concerned for potential endobronchial involvement from the tumor versus scarring from her previous surgeries and radiations affecting her large airways. I think it would probably be reasonable to do a bronchoscopy. I would like to start with a CT scan of her chest. I will see her back after that and then tentatively plan to proceed with bronchoscopy. I will also get pulmonary function tests.

I think it would be helpful for her to visit with Oncology. I am calling for the cytology from the pleural fluid from earlier this year. I have scanned some of her records denoting her oncologic history into the electronic medical record. We did discuss the risks and benefits of bronchoscopy. Mrs. Berry would like to proceed. Given her increased peripheral edema which has been present for quite awhile but has been progressively slowly worsening, I think it is reasonable to get an echocardiogram and a BNP with other routine lab work.

Mrs. Berry is comfortable with this plan.

ADVANCE DIRECTIVES
Patient does not have an Advance Directive at Mayo Clinic in Rochester, MN and is not interested in more information.

DIAGNOSES
#1 Dyspnea

Original: KAK:slk by kak
Electronically Signed: 07-Nov-2014 10:47 by K.A. Keogh, MD

This printout was generated through Patient Online Services and was the most current version as of the date and time generated.

Procedure and Sedation Assessment — Anesthesiology

Patient: Berry, Constance Ann (Mrs.) — 7-499-446
Apartment 28, 1310 Maple Avenue, Evanston IL 60201-4375
Age: 77 Y, Sex: F, Birth date: 16-Feb-1937

Provider: Gillespie, Shane M, DO
Service Date/Time: 05-Nov-2014 11:39

Identification
☒ ID band present and validated as correct

- Patient Identified by: Shane M. Gillespie, DO
- Procedure Verified by: Shane M. Gillespie, DO
- Site Verified by:

☐ Procedure Cancelled
☐ OB – IV Start Only
☐ Local Only
☐ Surgical Date Unknown / > 30 days

☐ Procedural pause conducted to verify: correct patient identity, procedure to be performed and as applicable, correct side and site, correct patient position, and availability of implants, special equipment or special requirements.

Procedure Information

- **Proceduralist:** E S EDELL
- **Procedure Date:** 05 Nov 2014
- **Procedure Time:**
- **Primary Service:**
- **Referring Physician:**
- **Phone / Pager:**
- **Pre-Procedure Indication:** RML COLLAPSE, METASTATIC BREAST CANCER
- **Procedure Planned:** 1. FLEXIBLE BRONCHOSCOPY: AIRWAY INSPECTION, BIOPSY VISIBLE LESIONS (IF NO VISIBLE AIRWAY LESION, TRANSBRONCHIAL BX).
- **Pre-Medications:**

Height (cm)	Weight (kg)	BMI (kg/m2)	Temperature (C)	Blood Pressure (mmHg)	Pulse Rate (/min)	SpO2%	NPO Verified
149.7	52.6	23.5					

Patient Belongings: ☐ Dentures ☐ Glasses ☐ Hearing Aids ☐ Blankets ☐ Jewelry ☐ Toys

Current / Past Medical And Surgical History
☐ Within Normal Limits Unless Otherwise Specified

Respiratory / Pulmonary
never smoker
Dyspnea
2013 developed pleural effusions.
lost about 20 pounds over the last year.
Mrs. Berry and her husband are noticing a wheeze that is not always present but is there most of the time. She has no history of asthma as a child. Other than her breathing and her weight loss, she is feeling reasonably well. She does also have known metastatic disease in her bones.

Endocrine
developed breast cancer in 2002

ENT
2005 she developed parotid cancer.

Allergy / Adverse Reactions
☐ Allergy band present and validated as correct
No Known Allergies
Allergies above current as of Wednesday, 05-Nov-2014 at 11:40.

Current Medications
anastrozole 1 mg tablet 1 tablet by mouth one time daily.

calcium citrate capsule 1 capsule by mouth one time daily.

Dulera 200-5 mcg/actuation HFA Aerosol 2 puffs by inhalation two times a day.

fiber tablet 5-6 tablets by mouth two times a day.

Fish Oil 300 mg capsule 1 capsule by mouth one time daily.

herbak- cellutol 300mg* (Free Text Entry) 1 one time daily.

hydrochlorothiazide 12.5 mg capsule 1 capsule by mouth one time daily.

occuvite* (Free Text Entry) 1 one time daily.

potassium chloride 20 mEq tablet sustained release 5 tablets by mouth two times a day.

ProAir HFA 90 mcg/actuation HFA Aerosol 2 by inhalation inhale as needed.
Indication, Site, and Additional Prescription Instructions:
2-3 times a day

Synthroid 112 mcg tablet 1 tablet by mouth one time daily.

Vitamin D3 2,000 unit tablet 1 tablet by mouth one time daily.

Xanax 0.25 mg tablet 1 tablet by mouth as needed.
Indication, Site, and Additional Prescription Instructions:
unknown

These are the patient's medications as of Wednesday, November 5, 2014 at 11:40 AM.

Initial Assessment and Vital Signs

MORE THAN A MILLION WORTH

Procedure and Sedation Assessment — Anesthesiology

7-499-446
Berry, Constance Ann (Mrs.)
Apartment 2B
1310 Maple Avenue
Evanston IL, 60201-4375
Age: 77 Y, Sex: F   Birth date: 16-Feb-1937

Provider: Gillespie, Shane M, DO
Service Date/Time: 05-Nov-2014 11:39

Height (cm)	Weight (kg)	BMI (kg/m2)	Temperature (C)	Blood Pressure (mmHg)	Pulse Rate (/min)	SpO2%	NPO Verified
149.7	52.6	23.5					

Physical Assessment

General / Constitutional: Cachectic;
Airway (HEENT): Mallampati scores I–II; Thyromental Distance Adequate; Neck ROM Adequate; Jaw Opening Adequate;
Thyroid:
Lymphatic:
Cardiovascular: Regular Rate and Rhythm;
Pulmonary: Clear to auscultation bilaterally;
Abdomen:
Skin:
Musculoskeletal:
Neurologic:
Psychiatric:

Laboratory Tests

Tests	Date	Result	Tests	Date	Result
Basophils	03 Nov 2014	0.02 x10(9)/L	Creatinine (w/eGFR)	03 Nov 2014	0.4 mg/dL *
Eosinophils	03 Nov 2014	0.12 x10(9)/L	Erythrocytes	03 Nov 2014	3.88 x10(12)/L *
Hematocrit	03 Nov 2014	34.0 % *	Hemoglobin	03 Nov 2014	11.0 g/dL *
Leukocytes	03 Nov 2014	8.7 x10(9)/L	Lymphocytes	03 Nov 2014	0.86 x10(9)/L *
MCV	03 Nov 2014	87.6 fL	Monocytes	03 Nov 2014	0.79 x10(9)/L
Neutrophils	03 Nov 2014	6.92 x10(9)/L	Platelet Count	03 Nov 2014	281 x10(9)/L
RBC Distrib Width	03 Nov 2014	16.8 % *			

Labs pulled from MICS 05-Nov-2014

Tests	Date	Result	Tests	Date	Result

Labs pulled from MICS
Other Labs:

Non Invasive Cardiac Test

Stress ECG   Positive   Negative   Other
Lipids Drawn   Yes   No   Nuclear Report Date

EF: 61 %   EF value updated in MICS 04-Nov-2014,   EF pulled from MICS 05-Nov-2014

Reports Summary

Reports pulled from MICS 05-Nov-2014

05-Nov-2014 09:40:00 Exam: CT CHEST wo + 3D Depend WS
Indications: Effusion Pleural;Metastatic Breast Ca Female NOS
ORIGINAL REPORT – 05-Nov-2014 10:54:00 GONDA
EXAM: CT scan of the Chest without IV contrast including 3D maximum intensity projections/volume renderings on a non-independent workstation
COMPARISON: CT chest dated 4/23/2014 and PET/CT dated 9/30/2014.
IMPRESSION:
1. Interval increase in interstitial thickening and nodularity, particularly in the left lower lobe suggesting progression of lymphangitic carcinomatosis. 2. Complete collapse of right middle lobe.
3. Additional similar findings to PET CT from 9/30/2014 consistent with metastatic breast cancer.
FINDINGS: When compared to most recent exam (PET/CT from 9/30/2014), there is interval complete collapse of the right middle lobe which had previously small amount of aeration along the medial aspect. There is also increased septal thickening and studding in the posterior left lower lobe concerning for progression of lymphangitic carcinomatosis. Otherwise CT appears relatively similar with moderate bilateral pleural effusions, loculated, with peripheral pleural nodular thickening. Bilateral septal and axial interstitial thickening with narrowing of the central airways with near occlusion of the central right middle lobe airways and occlusion of the left basilar rhonchi. Multiple scattered peripheral nodules are present such as the right lower lobe image 188 of series 2, 3 mm nodule.
Right IJ Port-A-Cath with tip in the upper SVC. Status post left mastectomy with postoperative changes to include left axillary dissection clips. Poor definition of mediastinal fat planes without visualized lymphadenopathy. There is a patulous appearance of the esophagus with small hiatal hernia and mid esophageal air-fluid level. Aortic atherosclerotic calcifications present. Left calcified hilar lymph node is and bilateral calcified granulomas in the lungs. Punctate calcifications within the spleen and liver. Few poorly defined low-attenuation subcentimeter foci in the liver are too small to definitively characterize. Right lateral chest wall nodule on image 208 of series 2 measures 8 x 7 mm, similar to prior PET/CT. Diffuse sclerotic and lytic bony metastases present.
Thank you for this consultation.
Electronically signed by:
C. Cox MD 8-9549 05-Nov-2014 10:54

Date: 04-Nov-2014 13:53, Service Description: Echo - Transthoracic, Author: GURA, GEORGE M.
This report is a PDF document which can be viewed in Synthesis or MICS Lastword.

04Nov2014 11:17
VENTRICULAR RATE 114
Sinus tachycardia
Premature atrial complexes
with paired Premature atrial complexes
Rightward axis
No previous ECGs available

7-499-446	MAYO CLINIC	**Procedure and Sedation Assessment**	Page 3 of 3
Berry, Constance Ann (Mrs.) Apartment 2B 1310 Maple Avenue Evanston IL, 60201-4375 Age: 77 Y, Sex: F Birth date: 16-Feb-1937		Anesthesiology Provider: Gillespie, Shane M, DO	Service Date/Time: 05-Nov-2014 11:39

Reports Summary (continued)
47507^EVANS JR MD^TITUS

Anesthetic / Sedation Plan

Date of History and Physical exam: 03-Nov-2014

Select one of the following:
- ☐ General Anesthesia
- ☐ Combined General / Regional Anesthesia
- ☐ Regional Anesthesia
- ☒ Monitored Anesthesia Care
- ☐ Sedation Care – RN

History and Physical Update:
Assessment of patient history, patient exam, medications, allergies, and previous anesthetic history reviewed on: 05-Nov-2014
- ☒ Patient seen, evaluated and approved for anesthesia / sedation

Select one of the following:
- ☒ Discussed risks / benefits / alternatives of anesthesia / sedation and obtained informed consent
- ☐ Emergency exception: consent implied due to medical emergency and inability to obtain timely consent from the patient or an alternative decision maker

ASA Physical Status 3

Signature Shane M. Gillespie, DO

Comments / Plan
MAC. Nonmedically directed.

Vital Signs / Parenteral Fluids / Medications

Vital Signs and Medications Graph

(Graph: Time vs mmHG / Pulse, 0–240, Legend: Systolic = V, Diastolic = ^, Pulse Rate = ⊕, Value outside plot range = ✕)

Vital Signs and Medications Data

Parameter	1	2	3	4	5	6	7	8	9	10	11	12
Time												
Blood Pressure												
Pulse Rate												
Pain Score												
Respiration Rate												
SaO2												
RASS												

Parameter	13	14	15	16	17	18	19	20	21	22	23	24
Time												
Blood Pressure												
Pulse Rate												
Pain Score												
Respiration Rate												
SaO2												
RASS												

Parenteral Fluids Administered

Time Start: By Whom	Solutions	Fluids and Time Added	Amount Started	Time Discontinued : By Whom	Total Amount Infused

Contributing Authors
Gillespie, Shane M, DO 3-5249;   Sylvester, Connie J 127-05047

Printed 26-Apr-2015 20:03   Electronically Signed: 05-Nov-2014 15:01 by Shane M Gillespie, DO
Performed at Mayo Clinic in Rochester

MORE THAN A MILLION WORTH

Patient Copy
Pulmonary and Critical Care Medicine
Subsequent Visit

7-499-446 05-Nov-2014 11:43
Mrs. Constance Ann Berry

Generated: 26-Apr-2015 20:00

DEMOGRAPHIC INFORMATION
Clinic Number: 7-499-446
Patient Name: Mrs. Constance Ann Berry
Age: ~~84~~ Y
Birthdate: 16-Feb-~~1921~~ Sex: F
Address: Apartment 2B, 1310 Maple Avenue City: Evanston, IL 60201-4375

Service Date/Time: 05-Nov-2014 11:43
Provider: Karina A. Keogh, MD Pager: 4-6893
Service: PULM Type/Desc: SV Status: Fnl Revision #: 2

IMPRESSION/REPORT/PLAN
#1 Dyspnea in the setting of known metastatic breast carcinoma
Mrs. Berry returns today after a CT scan of her chest. I have reviewed the images with her. She has persistent right middle lobe collapse. This may be why I am hearing wheeze on auscultation. I would be concerned with regard to a possible endobronchial tumor versus mucus plugging. The plan will be for a bronchoscopy today.

NOTE TO BRONCHOSCOPIST
I will ask the bronchoscopist to inspect the airways and biopsy any visible lesions. If there are no visible lesions, I think it would be reasonable to obtain transbronchoscopic biopsies. Her CT scan is suggestive of lymphangitic carcinomatosis. Mrs. Berry is not on any anticoagulants. She has bleeding diathesis. She is on chronic oxygen therapy.

I did discuss the risks and benefits including bleeding and pneumothorax. She wishes to proceed.

Mrs. Berry also has a persistent probable fluid collection around both lungs (left greater than right). At home when they last looked at this several months ago, they felt it was not free flowing and did not perform a thoracentesis. I think it is reasonable to reassess this also while she is here, and that tentatively is going to be scheduled for tomorrow.

DIAGNOSES
#1 Dyspnea in the setting of known metastatic breast carcinoma

Original: KAK by kds
Electronically Signed: 07-Nov-2014 11:21 by K.A. Keogh, MD

This printout was generated through Patient Online Services and was the most current version as of the date and time generated.

PRADEEP K. BERRY

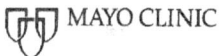 **MAYO CLINIC**

Patient Copy
Pulmonary and Critical Care Medicine
Miscellaneous

7-499-446 07-Nov-2014 10:38
Mrs. Constance Ann Berry

Generated: 26-Apr-2015 19:53   Page 1 of 1

DEMOGRAPHIC INFORMATION
Clinic Number: ~~7-499-446~~
Patient Name: Mrs. Constance Ann Berry
Age: 77 Y
Birthdate: 16-Feb-1937 Sex: F
Address: Apartment 2B, 1310 Maple Avenue City: Evanston, IL 60201-4375

Service Date/Time: 07-Nov-2014 10:38
Provider: Karina A. Keogh, MD Pager: 4-6893
Service: PULM Type/Desc: MIS Status: Fnl Revision #: 2

CHIEF COMPLAINT/PURPOSE OF VISIT
Summary note. Mrs. Berry was not able to attend her subsequent visit appointment today.

IMPRESSION/REPORT/PLAN
Since I last saw her, she did undergo a bronchoscopy. I did speak to the bronchoscopist. Her findings were very consistent visually with some mucosal metastatic disease and likely breast cancer. This obviously fits with her clinical history as well. The samples from the bronchoscopy are suggestive of malignancy. We did also receive her outside cytology from her pleural fluid analysis in 2013 confirming malignancy. We did also obtain a thoracentesis here. There was only a small amount of fluid that could be aspirated (37 cc.) Given all of the findings, Mrs. Berry's symptoms are consistent with metastatic breast cancer. She has severe abnormalities on PFTs with a mild restriction based on a reduced TLC with a severe reduction in the forced vital capacity. She also has a severely reduced diffusing capacity. Unfortunately, there are no further bronchoscopic management options for her airway disease. The pleural effusions seen on the CT scan is complex and not amenable to removal by thoracentesis. From a pulmonary standpoint, we do not have good options for improving her dyspnea. We had referred to her to Oncology here. They have not had any availability to see her. I did call this morning, and there were no openings. She likely will followup with her oncologist at home.

DIAGNOSES
#1 *Metastatic breast cancer*
#2 *Dyspnea secondary to No. 1*

Original: KAK by kds
Electronically Signed: 10-Nov-2014 14:31 by K.A. Keogh, MD

MORE THAN A MILLION WORTH

7-499-446
Berry, Constance Ann (Mrs.)
Apartment 2B
1310 Maple Avenue
Evanston IL, 60201-4375
Age: 77 Y; Sex: F Birth date: 18-Feb-1937

MAYO CLINIC — Diagnostic Radiology Assessment
US Radiology

Provider: Monfre, Julia M, RN

Service Date/Time: 06-Nov-2014 11:29

Page 1 of 2

Patient Information

Actual Height (cm)	Actual Weight (kg)	BMI (kg/m2)	Reported Height (in)	Reported Height (cm)	Reported Weight (lbs)	Reported Weight (kg)	BMI (kg/m2)
					114.20	51.80	

Non-English Language   Interpreter   ☐ Verified patient using two identifiers

Nothing by mouth (NPO) since

Allergy / Adverse Reactions   ☐ ID band/Allergy band present and validated as correct

No Known Allergies
Allergies above current as of Thursday, 06-Nov-2014 at 11:30.

Current Medications   ☐ Medication list obtained / reviewed

Completed assessment of patient's allergies and medications on the inpatient medication profile in the context of radiology care prior to medication administration.

Learning Needs Assessment

A learning needs assessment was completed with the patient. The potential barriers to learning that were assessed included cultural, religious/spiritual, motivational, physical/cognitive, language, and emotional areas. The patient does not have barriers to learning.

Procedure / Monitoring

☑ Patient states they are staying within 30 miles tonight   Patient here for: Thoracentesis

Informed Consent   Date: 06-Nov-2014

☐ Procedural pause conducted to verify: correct patient identity, procedure to be performed and as applicable, correct side and site, correct patient position, and availability of implants, special equipment or special requirements.

Does patient have advance directive? ☐ Yes ☐ No   Location

☐ Patient discussed with physician   ☐ Social Work contacted per patient request   ☐ Patient < 18 years old
☐ Patient did not discuss with physician; physician notified   ☐ Patient not interested

Comments

Procedure-Related Labs

Lab Tests	Date	Result	Lab Tests	Date	Result
Basophils	03 Nov 2014	0.02 x10(9)/L	Eosinophils	03 Nov 2014	0.12 x10(9)/L
Erythrocytes	03 Nov 2014	3.88 x10(12)/L *	Hematocrit	03 Nov 2014	34.0 % *
Hemoglobin	03 Nov 2014	11.0 g/dL *	Leukocytes	03 Nov 2014	8.7 x10(9)/L
Lymphocytes	03 Nov 2014	0.86 x10(9)/L *	MCV	03 Nov 2014	87.6 fL
Monocytes	03 Nov 2014	0.79 x10(9)/L	Neutrophils	03 Nov 2014	6.92 x10(9)/L
Platelet Count	03 Nov 2014	281 x10(9)/L	RBC Distrib Width	03 Nov 2014	16.8 % *

Labs pulled from MICS 06-Nov-2014 11:30:25 AM

Vital Signs and Medications Data

Parameter	1	2	3	4	5	6	7	8	9	10	11	12
Time	1140	1155										
Blood Pressure	131/71	134/67										
Pulse Rate	95	89										

Pain Score
Respiratory Rate 14
SaO2
RASS

Progress Notes / Post Procedure Comments

11:43 Procedural Pause/Procedure Start
11:47 Patient tolerated Lido injection with minimal discomfort
11:52 Normal Yueh attempted for aspiration from L lung and no fluid able to be aspirated
11:55 Radiologist attempting again with 8.0F Yueh Catheter to see if fluid can be aspirated with larger gauge catheter
12:02 37cc of Fluid drained with 8.0F catheter and sent to lab. Patient reports no pain or discomfort post-procedure

Fluid volume removed (cc): 37   Specimen labeling process completed by (initials): jmm sa   Specimen was: sent to lab

☑ Patient tolerated the procedure and is stable   ☐ Patient sent to chest x-ray   Patient discharged to: Hospital room

Impression / Report / Plan

Allergies/Adverse Reactions: No Known Allergies
Allergies above current as of Thursday, 06-Nov-2014 at 11:30.

HEMARAJ@ARTOURSINC.COM
773 764 4544

7-499-446		Diagnostic Radiology Assessment	Page 2 of 2
Berry, Constance Ann (Mrs.)	MAYO CLINIC	US Radiology	
Apartment 2B 1310 Maple Avenue Evanston IL, 60201-4375 Age: 77 Y, Sex: F Birth date: 16-Feb-1937		Provider: Monfre, Julia M, RN	Service Date/Time: 06-Nov-2014 11:29

Contributing Authors

Monfre, Julia M, RN M044607

Printed 26-Apr-2015 19:57 Electronically Signed: 06-Nov-2014 12:08 by Julia Marie Monfre, RN
Performed at Mayo Clinic in Rochester

MAYO CLINIC

Patient Copy
Pulmonary and Critical Care Medicine
Subsequent Visit

7-499-446 05-Nov-2014 11:43
Mrs. Constance Ann Berry

Generated: 26-Apr-2015 20:00   Page 1 of 1

DEMOGRAPHIC INFORMATION
Clinic Number: 7-499-446
Patient Name: Mrs. Constance Ann Berry
Age: 77 Y
Birthdate: 16-Feb-1937 Sex: F
Address: Apartment 2B, 1310 Maple Avenue City: Evanston, IL 60201-4375

Service Date/Time: 05-Nov-2014 11:43
Provider: Karina A. Keogh, MD Pager: 4-6893
Service: PULM Type/Desc: SV Status: Fnl Revision #: 2

IMPRESSION/REPORT/PLAN
#1 Dyspnea in the setting of known metastatic breast carcinoma
Mrs. Berry returns today after a CT scan of her chest. I have reviewed the images with her. She has persistent right middle lobe collapse. This may be why I am hearing wheeze on auscultation. I would be concerned with regard to a possible endobronchial tumor versus mucus plugging. The plan will be for a bronchoscopy today.

NOTE TO BRONCHOSCOPIST
I will ask the bronchoscopist to inspect the airways and biopsy any visible lesions. If there are no visible lesions, I think it would be reasonable to obtain transbronchoscopic biopsies. Her CT scan is suggestive of lymphangitic carcinomatosis. Mrs. Berry is not on any anticoagulants. She has bleeding diathesis. She is on chronic oxygen therapy.

I did discuss the risks and benefits including bleeding and pneumothorax. She wishes to proceed.

Mrs. Berry also has a persistent probable fluid collection around both lungs (left greater than right). At home when they last looked at this several months ago, they felt it was not free flowing and did not perform a thoracentesis. I think it is reasonable to reassess this also while she is here, and that tentatively is going to be scheduled for tomorrow.

DIAGNOSES
#1 Dyspnea in the setting of known metastatic breast carcinoma

Original: KAK by kds
Electronically Signed: 07-Nov-2014 11:21 by K.A. Keogh, MD

PRADEEP K. BERRY

Berry, Constance A (MR # 003211828)

NORTHSHORE UNIVERSITY HEALTHSYSTEM

Patient Demographics

Name	Patient ID	SSN	Sex	Birth Date
Berry, Constance A	003211828	xxx-xx-8756	Female	02/16/37 (DECEASED)

Address	Phone	EMail	Employer
1310 MAPLE AVE Apt 2B EVANSTON IL 60201	847-328-1355 (H) 312-969-3793 xhusband cell (M)	cfberry@sbcglobal.net	RETIRED

Reg Status	PCP	Date Last Verified	Next Review Date
ELAPSED	Prete, Carole P., MD 847-475-4555	12/04/14	06/02/15

Important to Note

Patient Ethnicity & Race

Ethnic Group	Patient Race
Non-Hispanic	Caucasian

I HAVE found the Paper Saying 9 minutes Delay - they DID not give Perk to the Medical Report

All Notes

Physician Discharge Summary by Zzhaywood, Audrey E., DO at 03/04/15 1453 — Version 1 of 1

Author: Zzhaywood, Audrey E., DO Service: Internal Medicine Author Type: Resident
Filed: 03/04/15 1501 Note Time: 03/04/15 1453 Status: Signed
Editor: Zzhaywood, Audrey E., DO (Resident) Cosigner: Tokarczyk, Arthur J., MD at 03/09/15 0657

Discharge Handoff - NorthShore University HealthSystem

Patient:	Constance A Berry
Date of Birth:	2/16/1937
Admission Date:	2/19/2015
Primary diagnosis:	Sepsis 2/2 UTI
Discharge Diagnosis:	Sepsis, ARDS, aspiration PNA, metastatic breast cancer
Discharge Date:	3/4/2015
Discharge To:	Deceased
Condition at discharge:	Deceased
Admitting MD:	
Discharge MD:	Tokarczyk, Arthur, MD
Brief Summary of hospitalization and incidental findings:	Constance A Berry is a 78YO female with history of metastatic breast cancer with malignant pleural effusions s/p frequent thoracentesis (last one was in 5/2014) currently, COPD on home O2 (2.5L), HTN who has been admitted since 2/19/15 for Sepsis secondary to UTI. On 2/22/15 patient went into PEA arrest. She was revived after 2 rounds of CPR/Epinephrine and was placed on hypothermic protocol. Immediately after resuscitation went into atrial fibrillation with rate as high as 180's and amiodarone bolus and gtt were administered, stopped after HR returned toward baseline. Due to increasing

Say my Opinion

They DID not CPR for 9 minutes as the Doctors failed to change the DNR and I han they Should should and DID the CPR

they DID not Say "No" they BLASTED Mom and just caused More of less Mess

ALL FALSE as they DID not only Performed after a minute were Hasted a minute or other

Generated on 10/19/2015 8:08 AM

MORE THAN A MILLION WORTH

Angie Juarez

From:	pradeepberry@sbcglobal.net
Sent:	Wednesday, February 24, 2016 6:35 AM
To:	Citizens for Lisa Madigan
Cc:	Pradeep Berry
Subject:	Re: Extremely important new evidence

Thanks. I have sent three emails with attachments now. Please please please please please please please please please please send by hook or crook to her office as Hilda told me that one she has the letter. , Lisa would meet me face to face. Please help me no matter what you have to do .it's not a big deal to send by email or print and send by mail. Time is running out due to the limitations of the law. Please show humanity as we are all going to support Lisa for the next election and even when she stands for the governor. We did lots of Indian Community help and Lisa like Indian federation of Chicago and all the Indian American vote for her. Lisa would be happy to see me. We all are democrats. Thanks. Pradeep Berry. 847 328 1355. Please please please please please please please please please do this.

Sent from my Verizon Wireless 4G LTE smartphone

-------- Original message --------
From: Citizens for Lisa Madigan
Date:02/22/2016 9:35 AM (GMT-06:00)
To: pradeepberry@sbcglobal.net
Subject: Re: Extremely important new evidence

Thank you for your message.

Please note that this is a campaign email account. You should contact
the Office of the Illinois Attorney General (312-814-3000) during normal business hours for assistance.

Regards,

Citizens for Lisa Madigan

On Mon, Feb 22, 2016 at 5:52 AM, pradeepberry@sbcglobal.net <pradeepberry@sbcglobal.net> wrote:
Respected our Attorney General.
Never deprive someone from the hope that must be the only thing they may have. My darling wife Constance Berry of 40 years and an American born in Glenview went to Carlton college, university of Michigan and other degrees in Spanish and french was absolutely, in my opinion was a victim of the medical negligence. Doctors were against going to the Mayo clinic knowing that they are confused and didn't want to be exposed stopped us by going to the Mayo Clinic on the second November, 2014 and after finding out that they have ruined her life and close to her not getting better and may demise in the near future. They played such a inhuman, criminal act by dumping the case to another in November and he was no longer her doctor. I have his saved voice message on our house and would not delete as an evidence. Another Dr in the same hospital was angry why he didn't give me this case after getting Pallative care report from Mayo clinic by different tests which her doctors didn't know or thought. OTHER Dr knew what should have been done at her hospital in where we live in Evanston. My Wife Constance Berry"""" Fuller before marriage and was my world, my life 24/ 7 love for 40 years and true example of love in millions and millions took two treatment in Evanston from other Dr. On the 20th February, 2025 she fell down from the bed and was fine but Ambulance took for safety to get it checked. She

PRADEEP K. BERRY

was coming home on 21 st February 2015 and finally on the 23 the February but had a cardiac arrest on the 22nd February 2015 and CPR WAS REFUSED TO BE performed until her tiger and lion husband---------I Praddeep Berry blasted and yelled at them to perform as I had two witnesses who were there when Constance told doctors on call Save me if I get any problems and keep me alive as long you can as i want to enjoy my house and new walking shower, my reading and so much more. But they didn't for 9 minutes which was serious and ventilation was put in for her breathing. Tube were to be taken on the March 2nd and I being her power of attorney they told me you decide hoe to handle two choices. I fought the whole battle my self .Her one brother only and his family are cold blood but good actor. They never ever ever came for years and now not even now. It is important to mention this point as doctor who ruined the case and no longer her doctor was snicking at the iCi uni and came wit the nurses and doctors who were nice to me till 26th night but in the afternoon they all joined his hands and did most inhuman thing to let her die and falsify medical records and tw extreme important papers were not in the medical records but I fought and got one showing 8- 9 minutes delay and second 9 days ago found out that is missing or destroyed or5nv on the medical records . It's still not there. I can furnished and it's missing. I can furnish. Thanks. Pradeep Berry 847 328 1355 cell 312 969 3793

Sent from my Verizon Wireless 4G LTE smartphone

 -------- Original message -------- From: pradeepberry@sbcglobal.net Date:02/22/2016 3:20 AM (GMT-06:00) To: "DONALD PECHOUS (States Attorney)" <donald.pechous@cookcountyil.gov> Cc: PRADEEP BERRY <Pradeepberry@sbcglobal.net> Subject: Extremely important new evidence

---------- Forwarded message ----------
From: "pradeepberry@sbcglobal.net" <pradeepberry@sbcglobal.net>
To: "DONALD PECHOUS (States Attorney)" <donald.pechous@cookcountyil.gov>
Cc: PRADEEP BERRY <Pradeepberry@sbcglobal.net>
Date: Mon, 22 Feb 2016 03:20:35 -0600
Subject: Extremely important new evidence
This must be read very carefully. This in my opinion, would be like retrial or opening the case again as In the last 9 days, i was able to get the three papers which were not given with the medical records. It's a criminal act, falony, perjury, one paper luckily not destroyed and another one------the most critical paper on the 27th February, 2015 which might have been prepared at the noon when, I was not there and was told me differently. In the last 9 days, I found out is written falsifying the record and it's strong backup--------- extremely important can't be found after three days search in every part of the medical records and risk management. It's a sign of destruction of the evidence. Furthermore the Video, I made after three hours for 32 minutes and six minutes in the hospital, when Mrs Constance Berry was alive before her demise with me and can be furnished which is absolutely different from what they prepared. It's a criminal act, crime, perjury, in my opinion, destroyed to avoid malpractice negligence and dr who ruined the case gave the case to another Dr on November, 26th, February, 2014 ----------- why did he showed up in my absence with power of attorney was me----- her 40 years husband.

Sent from my Verizon Wireless 4G LTE smartphone

MORE THAN A MILLION WORTH

JUDGE, PROSECUTOR Jury wants to see that. But there is no such paper. It's a absolutely criminal and and federal perjury and very serious crime in my opinion like a murder to avoid any law suit. However, like a murderer leave a crime scene with some trace ---- weapons, paper, shoe, blood, cloth, cigarette etc., they left this trace of not having her consent in writing.

Please consider this case as a well planned conspiracy to get the witness eliminated he ruined her health and was worried after we came fr5 the Mayo clinc in November 2 to 7 the 2014. He did not think about my wife" life and her husband------ me, what is my life and happiness. I am living in the most isolated life and absolutely ruined my happiness, no desire to do anything and suffering..Your office by not getting involved is a big bonus for the doctor and the medical professional to keep taking human life. Killing in the hospital with full protection and killing on the road neans culprit have to be investigated and give justice to the victims and their families. At least they get some consolation but where is my justice? . Law or your office has to come when police can't solve , FBI and COMES WHEN POLICE IN CERTAIN CASES CAN NOT solve SECRET SERVICE. . It is the same thing in my wife " case. I am a victim of losing my 40 years of wife and my life and I have to suffer. I have not slept for more than 3 hours and fighting for the justice while they made a falsifying the medical reports. I would request you to look it seriously and with a different view to get me the justice. My hope lies with you and your office and I request you to do this for me. I am a us citizen and deserve to get justice in my own cook county. American government goes out of the way to protect American citizens in the foreign countries. I am talking in the USA and that too where I reside and vote. Thanks for your time and hope you would not let me down. Pradeep Berry

Sent from my Verizon Wireless 4G LTE smartphone

 -------- Original message -------- From: pradeepberry@sbcglobal.net Date:02/19/2016 11:34 AM (GMT-06:00) To: Pradeep Berry <Pradeepberry@sbcglobal.net> Subject: Add.

---------- Forwarded message ----------
From: "pradeepberry@sbcglobal.net" <pradeepberry@sbcglobal.net>
To: Pradeep Berry <Pradeepberry@sbcglobal.net>
Cc:
Date: Fri, 19 Feb 2016 11:34:23 -0600
Subject: Add.

Under Oath, I, Pradeep Berry husband of Constance Berry, I state""after I arrived around 1.30 PM , all the team of doctors and nurses who were category told me a night before, ""Mr Berry, I am coming in the morning and I would be here looking after your wife like my mother and nothing would happen till March, 2nd when tubes have to be taken out and you have four days to decide what you want us to do. Do the hole in her throat and feeding tube of course as its now. Your wife would be much comfortable with the small hole as she can talk to you and it's much lighter tube and she may recover and after that she would be transferred to the rehabilitation center and that's in the Holy family hospital near mount prospect Illinois, but you would be inconvenient by driving there and staying--- don't know if they have enough big room but they would do something so that you can be with your wife as I know you can't leave her for a minute. I wish, I can have someone loving me like you. I would take care of your wife trust me as I have seen a rare but rare husband like you and we would make sure you have to decide by March 2nd. OTHER choice is to take her home after tubes be taken out to take her home with the pallative care . her Name is Kattie. However, when these pallative care doctors came who told me the same. I was struggling to decide what to do but my mind was to save Connie no matter what. But Kattie was a totally different and joined the team and told me that Mr Berry you don't have any power and the same with the other doctors who promised me the same thing. One point that was the first time <u>Dr Bruce Brockstin</u> was there and I hated why he was there as he handed over the case to Dr Merkel and I was very angry with all of you and what business it was to come when I was not there as i have to do the best for her as i have her power of attorney for the health. But they said now that power is gone as Mrs Wanted that she wanted her tube out. Tha is. They did not tell me that she said she does not want me to make the decision

REVIEWS

The succeeding pages encompass all of the professional book reviews for my books—My Connie and The Medical Conspiracy Behind My Wife's Demise.

Pacific Book Review

When a loved one dies, the grief can be overwhelming. For some survivors, this grief manifests in all different manners of behaviors in an effort to keep the memory of that lost loved one alive. For Mr. Berry, in the aftermath of the death of his beloved wife of 41 years, it manifested in him writing this loving tribute, My Connie. While most of this narrative details his love for Constance "Connie," we are also provided a glimpse into Mr. Berry's life in India before him meeting his adored spouse. We learn about his unhappy childhood, the loss of his mother and stepmother, and the painful atmosphere in his home life. He left his homeland, as a young man with only seven dollars in his pocket, with mixed feelings about living in America. Once in the U.S., he did, however, spend time creating friendships with other immigrants from his homeland. And then he met Connie, which catapulted his life into what he calls his "best destiny." She was his wife, friend, sister, mother, and soul mate, all rolled up into one lovely person. He says about her, "When the girl in your heart, when the girl in your soul's arm, then you have everything of the world." Factor in that this smart, respectful, hardworking, attractive woman also adored her husband and it's not hard to understand the depth of Mr. Berry's sorrow. It's palpable in his writing. He says, "I want to write my heart out for this book because Connie was my world."

His heartache is evident in every chapter that highlights Connie and their life together. Mr. Berry details her passion for reading, music, and arts, her enthusiasm for travel and great cuisine, and her devotion to their home and home life, and her fierce protection of her spouse from unnecessary distractions. Their bond, unshakable and indefatigable, was the key to their successful, long-term marriage. This is perhaps why the struggle for Mr. Berry to find meaning in his life after her death is so difficult. There are moments in this narrative, with truly his grief-stricken soul laid bare, that are almost too painful to read. "The death of one half becomes the living death for the other half," he laments.

Mr. Berry's writing about his shared life with Connie is very thorough. He provides details which help the reader really know who they were and why their marriage was so happy. He also intersperses a smattering of wisdom from those like Nelson Mandela, Mahatma Gandhi and various Indian spiritual leaders, attempting to find a way forward after his tragic loss. The ups of Mr. Berry's life with Connie always outweighed the downs, until that fateful day of her death when his whole world came to an abrupt end. The strength of this book is not about her death, but about her life seen through the eyes of one devoted husband. It's a tribute well-worth reading.

The US Review of Books

My Connie
by *Pradeep K. Berry*
AuthorHouse
reviewed by *Barbara Bamberger Scott*

"We immediately knew on our first meeting that we were in love, and there was no need to have a second meeting."

Author and finance consultant Berry lost his wife, Connie, to cancer in 2015. As a young man, he turned his back on professional opportunities in his native India to travel to the US seeking better prospects. But as soon as he arrived, he began to have misgivings, feeling unbearably lonely. Fortuitously, he found employment almost immediately, met Constance Ann Fuller, fell in love, and married her soon after. They were a faithful, happy couple for 42 years. In 2002, she was diagnosed with cancer; in 2005, he left his employment to spend more time with her. Ten years later, he was with her when she passed away. Though he expresses bitterness toward family members who offered no help or care, and toward doctors who, he believes, didn't do all they could have for his beloved wife, his book is in the main a praise-filled, sorrowful recollection of his life with Connie.

Though the author disavows any special writing ability, his book, though at times repetitive, shows caring and courage. He is obviously a man profoundly bereaved who has so far been unable to rebuild a life alone. He quotes from many sources to support his feelings about Connie: Indian thinkers Gandhi and Chanayka and Westerners Einstein and Ruskin. He lists small items that still remind him of Connie such as her clothing, diary, and make-up kit. He speaks of reluctance to use the shower they had made for her when she became an invalid. Yet he can't give these things up, or stop the flow of memories they evoke. Some readers may see his story as obsessively morbid, while others might wonder how they would react in similar circumstances. A paean to lost love, Berry's book invites a sequel, which the author has hinted at, and perhaps to be written when some healing has taken place.

Blueink Review

My Connie
Pradeep K. Berry
AuthorHouse, 253 pages, (paperback) $20.99, 9781524695101
(Reviewed: July, 2018)

In 2015, author Pradeep Berry lost his wife of 41 years. His new memoir, however, isn't an account of moving through grief to healing; rather, it's a repository of his pain. Like a personal journal, its entries reflect his roller-coaster emotional state, recurrent thoughts about his wife's death and grief-stricken lamentations.

Berry clearly intended this tribute for publication. However, it is written in a rambling style that jumps around in time and is often repetitive and confusing. The result is a deeply personal project likely to distance readers.

Following accountancy training in his native India, Berry moved to Chicago to further his career, planning to return home shortly—until he met and married Connie. Berry writes that she was his destiny: "We were two bodies with one soul." Settling in Evanston, Ill., they had no children.

Berry began his book soon after his wife suffered a fatal heart attack in a hospital. Berry had taken her in following a fall and eight days later witnessed her final breaths. "I relive that painful episode, and it gives me panic attacks." Berry revisits this scene many times throughout the book.

Bereavement and rancor are some of Berry's themes. "The main problem with me is that Connie did not die of natural causes—her life was snatched away by these doctors." He frequently mentions "medical negligence" without specifics. His bitterness extends to family members and friends who he believes failed him and Connie in various ways. He also ponders love, immortality and God, cites spiritual texts and names Connie's many virtues.

No doubt loving and well-meant, the book is profoundly personal: "Please note that this writing is from my heart without forethought," he notes. "I am pouring my heart on this book, typing whatever my heart is telling me to write." The approach was perhaps cathartic for him, but unfortunately too personal for a wider readership.

Also available in **hardcover** and **ebook**.

Clarion Review

My Connie
Pradeep K. Berry
AuthorHouse (Jun 9, 2017)
Softcover $20.99 (298pp)
978-1-5246-9510-1

Berry's book mirrors the stages of grief, including personal examples of bargaining with God, anger, and depression.

Pradeep Berry's grief-steeped memoir My Connie is a tribute to the author's late wife as well as a search for closure.

Berry meets Connie shortly after immigrating to the United States from India. They fall deeply in love and soon marry. After forty-two years of marriage, Connie passes away in the hospital, leaving Berry bereft.

The book jumps back and forth in time, repeatedly returning to the trauma of discovering that Connie has passed away and the sadness of her cremation. In between these scenes, Berry elaborates on Connie's excellent qualities and his memories of her, most notably their mutual international travels.

As much as it is a biography of Connie, the book is most focused on describing Berry's grieving process. Descriptions of Connie are specific in some ways—for example, listing all of the things she kept clean in their home—but overly general in others, repeatedly noting that she was a wonderful teacher without providing details from her teaching life. The book acknowledges its own tendency toward repetition, but the text reads as unpolished because of it nonetheless.

Generalizations about other people's grieving processes, experiences of love, and lack of empathy for Berry lead to contradictory and unclear moments in the text. His frustration with former friends becomes a focal point, and his anger at his in-laws and other family members is apparent.

The preface reveals that Berry's book is very much an exercise in relieving his pain, but such relief is not showcased by the end. Because of its inward focus, the project is not generally accessible.

The close, first-person narration ably conveys Berry's acute pain and grief. Vague word choices hold audiences at a distance, and Connie herself never seems fully developed. The book is organized in a stream-of-consciousness way; a section about the couple's vacations may easily circle back to Berry's anger and grief, forgoing conclusions to most accounts. Curiosity about Connie is prompted but not satisfied.

Wisdom literature, including various Indian spiritual texts, is quoted throughout; it adds depth to Berry's mourning process but is interjected without substantial or contextualizing introductions. In focusing on authenticity, the book mirrors the stages of grief, including personal examples of bargaining with God, anger, and depression; it rings emotionally true but is often frustrating to navigate.

My Connie is a heartfelt, if repetitive, account of a husband's grief.

LAURA LEAVITT (July 16, 2018)

Kirkus Review

TITLE INFORMATION
MY CONNIE
Pradeep K. Berry
AuthorHouse (298 pp.)
$31.99 hardcover, $20.99 paperback, $7.99 e-book
ISBN: 978-1-5246-9511-8; June 9, 2017

BOOK REVIEW

A debut author pays tribute to his deceased wife in this memoir.

Berry's spouse of 41 years, Constance "Connie" Berry (née Fuller), died of cancer in February 2015. Soon afterward, he began writing this book to chronicle the love that they shared: "I can say with great pride that we were truly two bodies with one soul. Our love was a special gift granted by the supreme Lord." The author met Connie shortly after he immigrated to Chicago from Delhi, India, 42 years ago. She was first diagnosed with cancer in 2002, but she initially recovered, and Pradeep strongly believed that she'd outlive him. Her final illness was brief and surprising, and her passing was devastating to the author. Over the course of nearly 300 pages, Pradeep works through his pain, reflecting on his life with his wife, musing on the natures of death and love, telling stories from Indian religion and history, seeking inspiration from the lives of great world leaders, and railing against those whom he thinks weren't responsive enough to his wife during her sickness. The prose style is sometimes stilted and other times histrionic. However, it occasionally achieves moments of quiet lyricism, as when the author tells of a moment shortly after his wife's death: "I could not do anything but look at her lovely face with no breath and her shining body.... What is missing? Breaths. Death means sleeping with no breaths." There are many books available about grief, but this one is unusual in that it's very clear that its author is still in the process of grieving. His anger at relatives on both sides of the family is quite strong, and the memoir's tone is hagiographic. As a result, it doesn't have much to teach readers about how to get over a loss. Rather, it's a raw document of the middle of grief and all the emotions that come with it. An emotional elegy that's somewhat undisciplined in style.

MORE THAN A MILLION WORTH

Kirkus Indie, Kirkus Media LLC, 6411 Burleson Rd., Austin, TX 78744
indie@kirkusreviews.com

Hollywood Book Reviews

Title: The Medical Conspiracy Behind My Wife's Demise
Author: Pradeep K. Berry
Publisher: Notion Press ISBN: 978-1647607975
Pages: 332
Genre: Biographies & Memoirs
Reviewed by: Anthony Avina

Grief is one of the most powerful things in the universe. As Henry David Thoreau once said, "Every man casts a shadow; not his body only, but his imperfectly mingled spirit. This is his grief. Let him turn which way he will, it falls opposite to the sun; short at noon, long at eve. Did you never see it?"

In author Pradeep K. Berry's The Medical Conspiracy Behind My Wife's Demise, the author channels his grief over the loss of his wife. After his wife Connie passes suddenly from an unforeseeable medical illness, the author explores the life they shared and the love they have for one another throughout their lives and into the next in order to cope with his grief. The author takes readers through their life together, from moving to America and meeting her, to introducing her into his family and building a life together. He also investigates the suspicious circumstances around her passing, which came all too suddenly.

This book is an emotional, heartfelt and engaging read. The author brings a true sense of loss and grief to his writing, and showcases how grief is powerful due to the love and depth of connection shared between the grieved and the person in grief. The writing is strong and conveys a sense of the author's struggling emotions during his loss. Getting both sides of the story, readers are able to see the emotional relationship formed between the author and his late wife, and the more practical side that dives deeply into the malpractice and manipulation of a group of medical professionals which led to a death that could possibly have been prevented.

This is a read for anyone who connects with emotionally driven memoirs, who have felt the injustice of medical malpractice and need to identify with others who feel the same way, and those who enjoy true love stories that showcase the dedication between two people to the love they share. Readers will be moved by the various points the author shares of his relationship with his late wife, both good and bad. The interesting thing is when the author showcases how various aspects of their lives tied their romance together even more tightly; including religion and a shared love of travel.

A powerful and evenly-paced read, this is a tragic yet must-read book. The author captures the raw emotion of loss eloquently and gives readers a chance to see what love shared and grown together over the course of decades looks like, and how it changes the people involved forever. Truly one of a kind, author Pradeep K. Berry's The Medical Conspiracy Behind My Wife's Demise is a well written read that everyone should read for themselves.